RETAIL AND COMMERCIAL PLANNING

CROOM HELM SERIES IN GEOGRAPHY AND ENVIRONMENT
Edited by Alan Wilson, Nigel Thrift, Michael Bradford and Edward W. Soja

Retail and Commercial Planning

Ross L. Davies

CROOM HELM
London & Sydney

ST. MARTIN'S PRESS
New York

© 1984 R. Davies
Croom Helm Ltd, Provident House, Burrell Row,
Beckenham, Kent, BR3 1AT

Croom Helm Australia Pty Ltd,
GPO Box 5097, Sydney,
NSW 2001, Australia

710 2137825

British Library Cataloguing in Publication Data

Davies, Ross
  Retail and commercial planning. – (Croom Helm series
  in geography and environment)
  1. Retail trade – Great Britain – Planning
  I. Title
  381'.0941   HF5429.6.E7
  ISBN 0-85664-566-4

Library of Congress Cataloging in Publication Data

Davies, R.L.
  Retail and commercial planning.

  Includes index.
  1. Store location–Planning. 2. Retail trade–Planning.
  I. Title.
HF5429.275.D37   1984   307'.333   83-51435
ISBN 0-312-67798-7

Typeset by Columns of Reading
Printed and bound in Great Britain

CONTENTS

FIGURES

TABLES

ACKNOWLEDGEMENTS

To my parents
 for all the Rowntree's fruit gums

This book has been written over several years and hence the help and services of a number of people have been drawn upon. I hope that members of the clerical and technical staff of the Department of Geography at the University of New England, Armidale, will recognise their inputs, as should those from the Department of Geography at the University of Newcastle upon Tyne. My most recent thanks go to Kim Thompson, Yvonne Lambord, Susan Clothier, Judith Vickers, Deborah Edyvean and Mary Davies for their assistance with the final manuscript. I am also grateful to several professional colleagues and various agencies for permission to use material from their own publications; and the specific sources for these are cited under the appropriate tables and diagrams within the book. Any omissions, mistakes or unintentional misrepresentations of fact are, of course, my responsibility.

PREFACE

One would like to introduce the subject of a textbook by first outlining the historical roots to its evolution, the way in which the subject has changed in recent years because of new problems and methods of tackling them, and discussing different viewpoints within academic and professional circles as to how the subject is best defined and interpreted. This is not possible in the case of retail and commercial planning, at least not in a systematic or coherent way, because the subject has never really been treated before as a formal area of inquiry with distinctive disciplinary bounds. This is not to suggest that it is an infant subject, finally outgrowing its nurture within the parent body of town and country planning, for it has often commanded specialist interest in the past. Rather it is a subject that has been dealt with in a piecemeal fashion, sometimes commanding particular attention when a controversial innovation is made, but more often being treated as an appendage to the general field of land use studies.

The lack of clear identity is perhaps best illustrated by thumbing through some of the more established and weightier textbooks on town and country planning. There rarely appears an individual chapter on retailing and commercial matters and most commentary and information is limited to a few paragraphs. These then tend to focus on one or two particularly contentious issues, such as the impact created by new superstore developments, the problems confronting small shops or the effectiveness of alternative modelling techniques, which have been the topics most heavily researched. Where specific books on the retailing and commercial theme have appeared, these have largely been confined to a specialised account of what has been happening within the distributive trades themselves.

What explains this apparent neglect of an important subject matter in planning? Part of the answer lies in its relationship to other land use studies, that compared to issues in employment, housing, transport and the welfare services it commands a relatively low priority in terms of problems to be addressed by local authorities. Most planning departments, hard pressed to deal with more urgent and politically sensitive matters, simply cannot find the time or allocate sufficient resources

1

to pursue this area of inquiry in a comprehensive way. Linked to this practical state of affairs is the fact that many planners do not really see a need to become widely involved with the distributive trades because they constitute one of the most efficient sectors of the economy and have their own special responsibility to serving the public at large. There is much less sense of a spatial disparity in the distribution of retail and commercial activities and much less criticism of the quality of the shopping environment accorded consumers than occurs in other aspects of life.

This rather complacent attitude towards the distributive trades, however, needs to be looked at against the background of what types of planning interventions have actually occurred. Generally speaking, retail and commercial planning policies to date have been almost solely concerned with guiding the implementation of development controls. The chief question addressed by central government has been whether to continue concentrating new large investments in existing places or to encourage a more dispersed pattern of resources particularly into suburban localities. The preoccupations of local authorities have been with determining the precise sites for new developments, improving the physical conditions of outworn facilities and estimating the overall amount of floorspace devoted to retailing and commercial uses which any urban area can support. While these central considerations have often been dealt with through a distinctive research programme, typically concerned with an assessment of the existing health of the retail and commercial stock within an area, the point of emphasis in the planning approach has been on establishing a set of land use controls rather than formulating some wider socio-economic goals.

There are two particular limitations that derive from this approach. Firstly, current planning policies tend to be rather negative in their stance because they are constituted as a response to new pressures for change that come from the retailing and commercial community. Planning policies seldom seek to lead or meet in a positive way what might be the aspirations of the public as a body of consumers. The typical situation that develops in most planning departments is that a restrictive attitude is taken towards new proposals and permissions for change are only granted if strong evidence can be shown that there will not be too much disruption of the existing *status quo*. This inbuilt cautionary and sometimes reactionary role then tends to antagonise certain entrepreneurs and a mood of mistrust emerges to the detriment of all concerned. Secondly, the situation is not helped by the simplistic way in which retail and commercial activities are defined and categorised for development control purposes. The distributive trades are never viewed as a collective, integrated system of activities, there being a separate policy formulated for retailing or shopping issues with wholesaling and warehousing usually treated in the context of industrial land uses, and services (of a business and leisure kind) either ignored altogether or submerged into the policies directed towards office and recreational functions. The massive changes which have occurred in recent years in vertical channels of distribution are given virtually no recognition whatsoever inside these separate types of policies.

The aim of this book is to try to compensate for these deficiencies by outlining a broader framework for the field of retail and commercial planning. It does not seek to establish a theoretical or methodological basis for the subject as an academic area of inquiry. Most of the concepts that underlie the management of retail and commercial activities in space have been discussed elsewhere. The emphasis here is on reporting the wider responsibilities of planning as a profession with most focus being given to the problems that should be faced and how they might best be overcome. The book is therefore about the formulation of practical policies and the way in which the retail and commercial environment, writ large, might be improved.

The chapters that follow are organised into three distinctive sections. Part I deals with the rudimentary considerations involved in retail and commercial planning. A description is given of the basic features of the distribution system and how these are changing, together with an outline of the main types of plans within which retail and commercial matters are treated. The first section ends with a chapter that seeks to redefine the scope of these plans, distinguishing on the one hand between a series of general management plans and on the other between a set of more specific plans oriented to more specific problems. Part II deals with the content of the general management plans in more detail. Examples are given of the past nature of strategic (structure) plans and local (district) plans and recommendations follow as to how the two-tier planning process might be improved in the future. Two further chapters also distinguish between the responsibilities of the upper and lower tiers of local government in accommodating new forms of development and managing the renewal of the major concentrations of retail and commercial activity, namely the central areas of the largest towns and cities. Part III is devoted to an examination of four kinds of problems for which special-purpose plans should ideally be prepared. These comprise the impact of new shopping schemes, the difficulties faced by small shops and related small activities, a variety of problems linked to transport and accessibility, and problems that appear to be highly localised to particular parts of the urban area.

Throughout all of the chapters, an attempt has been made to discuss the background to the issues presented as well as dealing with them from a planning perspective. In this way, it is hoped the book will serve as a useful reference source for the subject material of retail and commercial planning, whether the reader agrees with the type of planning approach adopted or not. It is also hoped the book will stir some professional interest in what has been a sadly neglected field of planning endeavour.

Part I

THE BASIS TO RETAIL AND
COMMERCIAL PLANNING

1 THE SYSTEM TO BE PLANNED

It was stated in the Preface to this book that professional planners have rarely treated the distribution system in an holistic way in the past, preferring instead to formulate separate plans for retailing and shopping activities, to link the intermediary functions of wholesaling and warehousing to broader industrial and employment concerns and to deal with services in the context of office and recreational provisions. We have to acknowledge that there are certain sound reasons for this approach: retailing and shopping activities constitute the largest and most distinctive theatre of events and thereby lend themselves to special attention; wholesaling and warehousing, by comparison, create fewer problems and pressures in spatial management terms; services comprise such a heterogeneous group of endeavours that it is difficult to define them in a collective sense and easier to allocate them to other land use categories. Against this, there is the fundamental fact that all three different forms of trade are highly interactive with one another, with each contributing but one part to the general process of distribution. They are essentially complementary elements of the same system of activity, often displaying similar growth characteristics and making similar locational demands. Any major planning interventions in one sector of trade can have considerable consequences for the others, not only in terms of the conduct of their business operations but also for the opportunities they eventually afford consumers. Some recognition of the integrated nature of the distributive trades must therefore be brought into the public policy-making field, if only to provide a broad co-ordinating framework within which three varying types of plans will then be prepared.

This chapter considers what this framework should be. It begins with a broad description of the process of distribution and the ways in which the process is changing. It then examines the composition of each element of the distributive trades giving stress to those most important trading activities to which planning ought to be addressed. Finally, it looks at the main locational characteristics of the distribution system as a whole, both at the national and local levels, and shows how past forms of unco-ordinated planning interventions have led to markedly different patterns of development.

The Process of Distribution

The term 'distribution', in the sense employed here, refers to the transfer of goods and services from a body of producers to a set of consumers. The producers are usually manufacturers of commodities ultimately used in the home but include certain agricultural practices such as horticulture and dairying and office activities concerned with the generation of technical advice, monetary transactions and new fashions or ideas. The consumers are mainly the population at large, particularly those people concentrated in family groups, but also include the various institutions engaged in distribution since these require their own specialist products and information services to help conduct their businesses.

The process of distribution refers to the steps or stages through which goods and services are directed in their movement from producers to consumers. Since this involves some form of organisational structure, such stages are commonly referred to as channels of distribution.[1] Traditionally, there have been four dominant types of channels of distribution recognised: one-stage channels, meaning the direct selling and shipment of goods and services from producers to consumers; two-stage channels, meaning trade between producers and retailers and subsequently retailers and consumers; three-stage channels, involving relationships between producers and wholesalers, wholesalers and retailers, and retailers and consumers; four-stage channels, where two different kinds of wholesalers are brought in or other agencies such as import brokers if goods and services are being transferred from abroad.

These basic types of channels of distribution, whilst still recognisable within the modern world, have become extremely complicated in three main respects. Firstly, because of widespread technological change it is not always possible to differentiate clearly between the principal actors involved. The business of production is now sometimes carried through into the distribution process itself, so that certain prefabricated goods may be assembled or further refined at warehouses or other trans-shipment points on their way to consumers. The functions of wholesaling and retailing have become blurred to the point where many wholesalers now engage in direct selling to the public and retailers act as their own stockists and terms such as retail warehouse, discount retailer and discount retail warehouse are common-place. Consumers themselves have become much more the assemblers of kits, the users of professional agencies and advice bureaux, and even in some cases, particularly in North America, have formed their own buying groups.

A second factor at work in altering the traditional relationships involved in distribution has been the changing pattern of controls and management exerted over the system. Most conspicuous in this respect is the increased power conveyed by the larger retailing groups who have established their own networks for the supply of goods and services.[2] These networks have displaced the need for wholesaling intermediaries and enabled some firms to dictate the types and quality of products made available to them. The classic cases of where retailer power has extended into the production sector are the impact made by Marks and Spencer and Sainsbury; but the increasing use of 'self-branding' techniques reflects on a general trend amongst multiples to impose their own standards on the products they sell. Producers too, however, have expanded their direct channels of distribution to retailers so that the independent wholesalers have really been squeezed out from two ends. As long ago as 1970 nearly three-quarters of all manufacturers' sales in the northern region were derived from direct shipments to shops with particularly high rates being recorded in the confectionery, tobacco, clothing and electrical trades.[3] Within these trades, it is of course the small firms that continue to rely most heavily on the traditional methods of distribution.

The third factor which is bound up with these considerations is the general growth in scale economies of operation and the introduction of bulk merchandising practices. The production of goods and services has become concentrated in fewer, larger firms and consumption (as reflected in shopping habits) has become geared to purchasing much greater quantities of items on more infrequent occasions. Retailers and wholesalers alike have responded to these changes by amalgamating and building increasingly larger facilities which in turn have meant the further development of integrated channels of distribution. The recent increased costs in transportation, the effects of inflation on wage levels and the earlier abolition of resale price maintenance have all enhanced the advantages of dealing in bulk transactions. Perhaps the most striking single outcome of these developments has been the formation of the voluntary trading groups or symbol chains amongst the small, independent wholesalers and retailers.[4] Initiated mainly from within the wholesaling sector, these groups (most notably Spar,

Mace and VG) provide common sources of goods and services via their own vertically co-ordinated channels of distribution to vast numbers of affiliated shops. The spectacular growth of cash and carry depots through the late 1960s also reflects on the small, independent traders' attempts at achieving economies of scale, although in this case preserving the rudimentary structure of separate channels of distribution.

The enormous changes which have occurred within the process of distribution in recent years make it difficult to identify a clear-cut set of activities, especially one that would be relevant to different sectors of trade. The most pervading trend has been the decline of wholesaling as a specialised pursuit and its replacement by networks of warehouses and trans-shipment centres. Indeed, except in reference to cash and carry depots, green markets and a few traditional wholesaling establishments, the term wholesaling itself has become almost anachronistic and the function it once served has been supplanted by what might be more appropriately called bulk transference. The new intermediary facilities which have been built, usually either by manufacturing or retailing firms, are essentially designed to ease the business of dispatch and have little or nothing to do with the actual selling of goods or services. This emphasis on transference has also led to the growth of specialised transport consortia, some acting as direct hauliers for particular firms but others acting as parcel carriers for a diversity of trades drawing on a multiplicity of domestic and import suppliers.[5] Some again specialise in long-distance transfer; others operate a more localised set of deliveries to the 'high street' from trans-shipment centres that may be collectively owned or rented by specialist retailers (such as in the clothing trade). These transport developments are particularly significant for local authority planners from the standpoint also of the locational requirements of new terminal facilities and through the pressure created on existing roads and service areas, especially within town and city centres.

The distribution system in its fullest sense, however, involves not only the movement of physical commodities from producers to consumers but also the conveyance of information, money, professional advice and the sharing of risks. Collectively we might refer to these as business services and distinguish them from other services that involve more tangible products, such as the catering and leisure services and the personal services of dry cleaning, hairdressing, health improvement and the like. Within any of these service categories there exists a similar set of organisational relationships between the sources of supply and points of demand to that which exists within the field of physical distribution. Money derived from the Bank of England, channelled through the clearing banks and merchant banks, manifests itself in the high street banks and building societies before reaching the hands of the population. Cafés, petrol stations and public houses deal with commodities distributed in much the same way as conventional shops, either through direct shipments or via redistribution points; dry cleaners, hairdressers and the like are similarly controlled and organised on parallel lines to the retail trade. One specific point of difference is the stronger entrenchment of franchising operations, especially within the motor trade and 'fast-food' chains, although there are certain resemblances here to the voluntary trading associations between wholesalers and small shops. More generally, but particularly with respect to business services, there may be a greater number and more complicated array of interactions with other agencies, such as government bodies, at all stages in the distribution process. These external linkages and the utilisation of professional services, however, have also been growing rapidly in recent years in all sectors of the distributive trades.

Specific Elements for Control

Those parts of the distribution system which come under the direct control of retail and commercial planning, at least in terms of their spatial pattern of development, include: the intermediary functions of wholesaling, warehousing and those more direct forms of shipment which we have summarised as bulk transference activities; retailing; and service provisions. As we have indicated, the complex interactions within and between these broad categories of trade pose special problems for defining their constituent members or individual types of business. Some comprehensive list or classification of all the variable types of business to be found is important, however, for without an agreed set of terms it is virtually impossible for planners to discharge their responsibilities in an efficient and equitable way.

There have historically been two main sources of documentation guiding the classification of the distributive trades for planning purposes in Britain. First is the general Use Classes Order[6] that provides the statutory framework for the implementation of land use development controls throughout urban and rural areas. The major headings employed in this are listed in Table 1.1. Of the 28 different classes recognised, perhaps six (numbers I, II, X, XI, XVII and XVIII) are of

Table 1.1: Town and Country Planning Use Classes Order, 1972

Class I: Shop use
(includes retail services as well as pure shops, such as hairdressers, travel agencies and post offices, but excludes launderettes, petrol stations, restaurants and banks)
In strict terms defined as 'Use as a shop for any purpose except as:
a. a shop for the sale of hot food
b. a tripe shop
c. a shop for the sale of pet animals or birds
d. a catmeat shop
e. a shop for the sale of motor vehicles'
Class II: Office use
(includes estate agents, employment agencies and building societies as well as banks, but not betting shops which are probably not covered in any class)
Class III-IX: Industrial uses
(these classes encompass three groups of light, general and special industrial uses, the latter of which is further subdivided into five classes)
Class X: Storage use
'Use as a wholesale warehouse or repository for any purpose'
Class XI: Hotel etc. use
'Use as a boarding or guest house, or an hotel providing sleeping accommodation'
Class XII: School use
Class XIII: Religious use
Class XIV, XV: Health and welfare uses
(split between those that have a residential function, like hospitals, and those that don't)
Class XVI-XVIII: Public and community uses
XVI: use as an art gallery, museum or other public facility
XVII: primarily entertainment facilities, such as cinemas, theatres and concert halls
XVIII: mainly sports facilities, e.g. skating rinks, swimming baths and dance halls

---

direct significance here. The scheme is not an exhaustive one, however, for it omits important commercial activities such as builders' yards, transport depots and driving schools and a wide variety of bulk transference activities that may involve more than simply the storage of goods. It also contains the anachronistic references to tripe shops and cat meat shops while failing to give special attention to the newer, more controversial, developments in retailing such as discount retail warehouses, superstores and hypermarkets. On services, there is the suggestion of strict moral undertones, stemming from a pre-war era, for many modern twilight activities are not really referred to in the scheme.

While one does not wish to see a detailed classification dictating the implementation of development controls, the Use Classes Order seems to be in need of some repair. Certainly, it has little to offer the wider management functions of retail and commercial planning as, for example, in dealing with the problems of either small or very large businesses.

Table 1.2: Relevant Sections of the Standard Industrial Classification

---

Order XXIII: The distributive trades

This is disaggregated into the following minimum list headings

810	Wholesale distribution of food and drink
811	Wholesale distribution of petroleum products
812	Other wholesale distribution
820	Retail distribution of food and drink
821	Other retail distribution
831	Dealing in coal, oil, builders' materials, and agricultural supplies
832	Dealing in other industrial materials and machinery

Other orders of relevance include:

Order XXII: Transport and communications

(which contains a heading on miscellaneous transport services and storage)

Order XXIV: Insurance, banking, finance and business services

(which includes headings for banking, property-owning institutions and other business services)

Order XXVI: Miscellaneous services

This has the following minimum list headings of significance

881	Cinemas, theatres, etc.
883	Betting and gambling
884	Hotels and other residential establishments
885	Restaurants, cafés and snack bars
886	Public houses
887	Clubs
889	Hairdressing and manicure
893	Dry cleaning
894	Motor repairers, distributors, garages and filling stations
895	Repair of boots and shoes

The second source for distinguishing the component parts of the distributive trades has traditionally been the Census of Distribution,[7] itself derived from certain sections of the Standard Industrial Classification (relevant extracts of which are shown in Table 1.2). Like other censuses in Britain, this, when first introduced in the 1930s, was intended to provide a comprehensive body of statistical information at regular intervals in time; but the principle was abandoned in the mid-1970s and no Census of Distribution was undertaken in 1981.

However, the three decennial inventories of 1950, 1961 and 1971 provide an instructive record on post-war developments in the distributive trades, although wide changes occurred in the type and range of data presented. The most significant changes were the exclusion of statistics on wholesaling in the 1961 and 1971 censuses and the concomitant expansion of retail information, particularly for smaller places. The data furnished on services have mainly been limited to certain personal services, namely those under the minimum list headings of the SIC, numbers 889, 893 and 895. While it is again easy to criticise the Census of Distribution for its inconsistencies in coverage and narrow perspective on the distributive trades, it nevertheless provides an improvement over the Use Classes for the policy-making aspects of planning and is used here as a starting-point for our own attempts at classification.

Wholesaling, Warehousing and Bulk Transference Activities

The distinctions drawn between different types of wholesaling and warehousing activities in the Census of Distribution for 1950, although now much outdated, provide a more detailed and satisfactory insight into this sphere of trade than any subsequent central government report. Statistics were given for both kinds of businesses found and their method of trading. A total of 22 kinds of business were defined ranging from wholesalers engaged in agricultural products to dealers in coal, builders' materials, clothing, paper, second-hand goods and including a separate category of warehousing. There were ten main groupings for methods of trading: wholesale merchants, export merchants, import merchants, invoicing agents (including manufacturers' agents and auctioneers), non-invoicing agents, government departments, marketing boards, purchasing branches of overseas firms, wholesaler producers and a separate category on warehousing again. This tabulation by method of trading is particularly significant for it gives major recognition to the role of a number of agencies not always identified with wholesaling and warehousing because they are not necessarily located in the same physical premises as the actual distributors. It is important that planners appreciate the wider organisational linkages in the field so that their work is not wholly focused on the bricks and mortar of large distribution plants. Subsequent surveys by the Board of Trade[8] in 1961 and 1968 and the Department of Trade and Industry[9] in 1974 have unfortunately reported their findings only in terms of business type, although making a threefold distinction between dealers, distributors and marketing boards.

Table 1.3: A Planning Framework for Classifying Intermediary Activities

	Disposition	Role types Storage	Transformation
Trade links			
Retail	Traditional whole- salers	Small stockists	Redistribution centres
	Self-service operators	Retail ware- houses	Packing plants
Industry	Agents and brokers	Transport services	Bulk terminals
	Manufacturers' sales	Industrial warehouses	Refineries
Agriculture	Marketing boards	Machinery suppliers	Product assemblers
	Markets and auctions	Grain storage	Dairies/ Abattoirs

Note: This is a revised scheme to that originally proposed by the author in 'A Conceptual Framework for Commercial Planning Policies', *Town Planning Review*, vol. 48 (1977), 42-58.

While the 1950 Census of Distribution provides a useful indication of the wide boundaries of the intermediary trades, however, it predates many of the radical changes in forms of distribution that have taken place in recent years, particularly the development of cash and carry operations, the formation of voluntary trading groups and the growth in transport services between producers and retailers. A revised classification is required that will not only be relevant to modern trading practices but can also be used as the basis for the collection of future statistics by various independent bodies. Ideally, this should also reflect on contemporary and developing planning problems and perhaps be supportive of an updated Use Classes Order. One approach is suggested in Table 1.3 which distinguishes between the major functions that can now be perceived and cross-tabulates these against those special linkages which occur with other elements of the distributive trades. The scheme is not intended to be fully comprehensive, for only generalised examples of each different category of activity are shown; but additional businesses can be readily accommodated within the basic framework and these disaggregated if necessary according to size, ownership, volume of turnover, etc.

While we cannot claim that each major functional component has its own discrete types of planning problems, there are nevertheless recurring themes that permit some generalisation. Broadly speaking, the dispositional activities, those engaged in marketing transactions where there is buying or selling of goods and materials, have experienced or created for themselves a series of operational difficulties that require special attention. Examples include: the conflict of interest that has arisen when cash and carry wholesalers have sought to deal not only with retailers but also with the public at large; the demise of the traditional delivery merchants, whose problems are bound up with the wider ones of small business decline; the need for many agents, brokers and manufacturers' sales representatives to communicate more regularly through trade fairs and trade centres, and the relative lack of these facilities in Britain when comparisons are made with other European countries; the congestion that hampers efficient trading practices in those wholesale green markets that are still sited in the middle of town or city centres. In contrast, the problems associated with storage activities, that group of functions concerned much more with just the physical retention or transport of goods and materials, are mainly the result of pressures for new locations brought about by the growth in new forms of warehousing. Examples here include: the need for small stock units in close proximity to independent retailers who, by their use, would be able to reduce their own in-store stocking space and expand upon their sales areas; the need for more accessible sites in variable positions throughout the urban area for retail as distinct from industrial warehouses; greater provision of lorry parks and associated rest facilities for the workforce engaged in haulage; careful assessment of those agriculturally-related storage activities that might need to penetrate green belt areas or historic market towns. Finally, the problems that emanate from the transformation activities, those functions where some further processing of the goods and materials received is undertaken before they are passed on, are most commonly bound up with environmental matters. The large size of the facilities needed here, the smells and pollution associated with chemical refineries, the unsavoury image associated with livestock slaughtering and trans-shipment, all combine to make these activities potential nuisances to other land users, particularly residential communities.

Retailing Activities

The Census of Distribution became, in its last two publications, effectively a census of the retail trades. These contain a wealth of data which, despite their outdatedness, are still extensively employed today by both government departments and private companies. Since 1976, a new series of retailing statistics has been published, known as the Retail Inquiries.[10] These are based on annual surveys of approximately 10 per cent of all those retail businesses filing VAT returns; hence there is considerable under-reporting of very small shops. The Retail Inquiries are further limited as an information source for they provide statistics only for Great Britain as a whole and there is no spatial disaggregation of the data to either regions or individual towns. At one time, plans were made to compensate for this deficiency with the publication of a special Shops Register in 1981; but following a pilot survey in 1977, these too have been abandoned.[11] What remains significant about the Retail Inquiries, nevertheless, is that such data as have been presented are organised along broadly similar lines to those contained in the past censuses (except for the most recent volume).

As in the case of the intermediary trades, this organisational framework has mainly involved distinguishing retailing activities by their kinds of business and their methods of trading. Both the Census of Distribution and the Retail Inquiries refer to seven broad categories of kinds of business which (until 1980) have comprised: grocers and provision dealers; other food retailers; confectioners, tobacconists and newsagents; clothing and footwear; household goods; other non-food retailers; and, in the case of the census, general stores (that incorporate department stores, variety stores and mail order houses), but which are redefined as mixed retail outlets in the Retail Inquiries (and include certain kinds of superstores and discount retail warehouses). These categories were further subdivided into a total of 23 different groups in the census and 26 in the Retail Inquiries (with the difference mainly accounted for by new types of development). The principal distinctions drawn on methods of trading have been between independent businesses, multiples and co-operatives. Independents were identified in the census as businesses which have less than ten outlets, but the Retail Inquiries differentiate between single outlet retailers and other small businesses which they designate as small multiples. Both sources, however, provide a finer breakdown of businesses by numbers of outlets that are owned.

The main information conveyed within these categories relates to numbers of shops, outlets or establishments found, to turnover and to employment. In the case of the 1971 Census of Distribution, statistics were also furnished on floorspace. The 1971 census was most noteworthy, however, for its comprehensive presentation of

Table 1.4: Definitions of Modern Types of Retailing Operations

---

Supermarkets: self-service operations providing mainly foodstuffs with at least 4,000 square feet (372 m²) of selling area floorspace. Earlier studies have adopted a threshold size of 2,000 square feet (186 m²) but the trend to larger shop sizes now makes this unrealistic and smaller units are more properly MINI-MARKETS or SUPERETTES. Mini-markets may be independently owned, part of voluntary trading groups or the smaller branches of multiple grocers

Superstores: self-service operations emphasising either foodstuffs or household goods, usually with the cheaper lines of clothing, hardware and domestic appliances. Sizes range from 25,000 to 50,000 square feet (2,323-4,647 m²) and they are usually integrated into town centres or outlying district centres. Examples include Asda, Woolco and Co-op superstores

Hypermarkets: the largest self-service operations, emphasising mainly foodstuffs but with a wide range of general merchandise. They sometimes incorporate separate units of cafeterias, tobacconists, chemists, etc. Sizes range from 50,000 to over 100,000 square feet (4,647-9,294 m²) and they are most typically located in free-standing positions on the outskirts of a town. Few real hypermarkets have been built in Britain but examples include Carrefour, Savacentre and Tesco hypermarkets

Discount retail warehouses: self-service operations resembling superstores but where there is minimum attention to merchandise display and goods are often retained in their original packing for customers to sort through. There is much specialisation in limited lines of electricals, domestic appliances, carpets, furniture and other household goods. They are sometimes housed in former industrial buildings but increasingly occupy purpose-built facilities in a variety of mainly off-centre locations. Examples include Comet, Status, Kingsway stores

Catalogue showrooms: these are a relatively new development, on an old trading theme, where customers can choose items from catalogues or a showroom and these are then sold in a pre-packed form. Most emphasis is placed on either household goods or clothing and textiles. The stores are usually integrated into existing shopping centres. Examples include Argos and Brent

Limited food discounters: these are smaller versions of discount retail warehouses, focusing on food goods only and with an accent on cut-prices achieved by minimal attention to the attractions and decor of the stores. Many smaller branches of the multiple food retailers have been converted to these forms. They occupy a variety of neighbourhood settings, often competing with supermarkets. Examples include Price-rite, Kwik-Save and Shoppers Paradise (Fine Fare)

Modern convenience stores: these are modern counterparts to corner stores,
but larger in size (usually about 2,000 square feet (186 m²) and with an
emphasis on grocery goods, magazine and liquor sales. Their opening hours
are longer than other stores and in Britain they are most commonly located
near to transport terminals or other nodal points. The main trading chain is
the 7-Eleven group

---

data in a spatial form. Detailed information about retailing activities
was provided for all towns over 20,000 in population size and for
certain larger places there were separate statistics for their central areas.

In considering the census and the subsequent Retail Inquiries as a
basis for the classification of retailing activities for planning purposes,
the chief drawback again lies with their lack of special recognition of
the more modern types of operation. Although the modifications
brought into the Retail Inquiries permit some identification of new
types of development, it remains impossible to distinguish accurately
between such stores as supermarkets, superstores, hypermarkets or
discount retail warehouses. Such stores must be incorporated into a
planning-oriented classification since, as we have indicated with modern
wholesaling practices, they will continue to provide the main pressures
for further development in the immediate future and to be the main
source of those planning problems that will need to be addressed. A
fuller list of those stores that warrant particular attention is given in
Table 1.4. The definitions given do not relate to any nationally agreed
set of criteria but are informally, in trade journals and market research
surveys, widely adhered to.[12]

Our own suggestions for a classification go back once more to the
basic functional differences that can be perceived within the wide
spectrum of the retail trades, in this case to the different kinds of interaction that occur between retailers and their customers (Table 1.5). The
idea for the scheme comes from Nelson[13] who several years ago dis-
criminated between stores that are generative, comparative (or supportive) or suscipient to the trade drawn within any shopping area.
Generative stores are essentially those magnet or attractor stores that
draw most potential customers to a high street or shopping centre.
Comparative or attractor stores are those which associate themselves
with the magnet stores and both contribute to and share in a further
accumulation of trade that results from the agglomeration. Suscipient
stores are those which tend to provide little drawing power by themselves but obtain their own trade by locating in close proximity to the
other major types of stores. These three main functional components

Table 1.5: A Planning Framework for Classifying Retailing Activities

| | | Role types | |
	Generative	Comparative	Suscipient
Trade forms			
Bulk provisions	Superstores Discount warehouses	Supermarkets Limited-line discounters	Mini-markets Self-service stores
Specialisms	Fashion stores Furnishing stores	Boutiques Large durable shops	Small food shops Small durable shops
Assorted goods	Department stores Variety stores	Small variety stores Catalogue stores	Convenience stores Newsagents

are then cross-tabulated against the three most distinct forms of store operation today: the mass-merchandisers or bulk providers, the specialists and those engaged in assorted goods or scrambled merchandising practices. The scheme can again be expanded or disaggregated within the basic framework provided, to accommodate either further business types or to discriminate between stores in terms of sizes, ownership, volume of turnover, etc.

Two of the main uses to which retail classifications have been put in the past include an assessment of the retail conditions to be found in an urban area, as a basis for determining the amount of future development that can be absorbed, and an assessment of the general structure of shopping trips by consumers, in order to guide the allocation of new resources within some spatial organisational strategy. Thus syntheses of census data have been made in terms of the amount of floorspace devoted to convenience-goods, durable-goods and comparison-goods activities, and sales or expenditure incurred on daily, weekly or occasional shopping needs.[14] The census categories employed for the amalgamations, however, are rather unsatisfactory and it is questionable whether the distinctions drawn in shop types and shopping trips are really appropriate to the modern age. The present underlying system of activity appears to be one of simply food, non-food and mixed provisions with separate purchases being made of a casual, regular or special kind; but this becomes complicated by the different sizes and operating characteristics of stores and their variable use for different trip purposes by consumers. The main need in taking stock of an urban area's resources is surely to discriminate between the most important trade generators to be found, those of intermediate or supporting status and those with only a small contribution to make; likewise, in inferring about the structure of shopping trips, it seems important to distinguish between those which focus on large-scale facilities, those relating to more medium-sized stores and those which are still linked to the smallest outlets. The above scheme is intended to allow for assessments to be made in these ways.

A number of more specific problems can be raised with respect to the locational requirements of the three main functional sets of activities, however. Broadly speaking, new branches of the generative stores require a range of special sites to which careful planning evaluation has to be given. The mass-merchandising operations will usually seek sites with extensive car parking provision and good accessibility and, because of their attunement to the more modern forms of shopping, can be made the basis to new growth centres either within the suburbs or within the inner city. The more conventional fashion, department and variety stores have displayed increasing competition for the prime sites along the high street or within new covered shopping centres and this raises the question as to how much duplication of these conditions can or should be made. The comparative or supportive stores must be recognised as a set of activities which are just what their term implies, that in themselves they are too weak to provide the nucleus to new shopping centre developments but, given the installation of larger, attractor stores, they will readily add to the resource base needed in new schemes. Finally, the suscipient or 'convenience' stores encompass such a variety of business forms, some with poor records of trading performance but others surprisingly strong, that much closer attention must be given to their individual needs than has hitherto been the case.

Service Activities

The Census of Distribution has always been inadequate in its coverage of service activities, reporting only on the personal services of shoe repairers, hairdressers and laundering facilities. A similar criticism can be made of the new Retail Inquiries which omit services altogether. In seeking to classify this sector of the distributive trades, we are also hampered by the lack of alternative government sources or independent surveys on the subject, at least in the rather discrete way in which we are treating it. The problem stems from the fact that most services which contribute to the overall distribution system also have strong affiliations with other systems of activity and tend to be included within these whenever data collection exercises are mounted or planning policies formulated. Thus business services tend to be grouped in with office activities; many of the personal services that are government controlled (such as the citizen advice bureaux and information centres) are linked up with social provisions; vehicle-oriented services become part of the transport sector; and entertainments and leisure facilities form part of the general area of recreational interests. This overlap of the sector with other major systems of activity is further complicated by the overlaps which occur within distribution itself. Thus many of the services we would now like to separate out for special attention form part of the realm of the intermediary trades, which we have already discussed — namely the agencies involved in importing and exporting, manufacturers' sales agents, auctioneers and the like.

Table 1.6: A Planning Framework for Classifying Service Activities

	Information	Role types Commodities	Reparation
Trade sectors			
Business	Employment agencies (Estate agents)	Banks Post offices	Rent offices (Betting shops)
Leisure	Travel agents	Catering facilities	Clubs
	Booking agents	Public houses	Hotels
Personal	Citizen advice bureaus	Chemists	Dry cleaners
	Consumer group offices	Opticians	Hairdressers
Vehicle-oriented	AA offices	Service stations	Garage repairs
	(Information centres)	(Car dealers)	Car body shops

Those services which are most readily recognised and amenable to systematic classification are those with particularly strong retail links, either because of their interactions with the retailing community itself or because of their preference for similar locations to shops, derived from a mutual interest in the trade potential of large crowds of people. These may be sub-divided into three main functional groups on the basis of the prevailing types of trade they engage in (Table 1.6). First is a set of services concerned with disseminating, and usually selling, information to both other businesses and the public at large; second, there are services involved in dispensing physical commodities, such as money, refreshments, health aids, etc.; third, there are services providing repair work for damaged articles and improvements to the comfort and well-being of individual persons. This last group includes such facilities as hotels and social clubs as well as dry cleaners and garages for these are broadly concerned with the welfare of people. Collectively, we can regard these services as being engaged in reparation (for want of a better term). The extreme variability in activities within this and the other main groups can be highlighted, however, when they are cross-tabulated against those broad affiliations to other sectors of trade which we described in the previous paragraph: namely the designation of business, leisure, personal and vehicle-oriented services. As with our other schemes, only some of the more prominent examples of activities which fall into each category are shown and various statistical criteria can be superimposed to distinguish between the relative importance of constituent establishments.

Most of the present and potential planning problems that relate to the scheme derive from the competition for sites between services and retailing activities. These problems are most acute where there has been rapid growth within certain service categories in recent years as, for example, in the business and leisure-oriented activities engaged in selling commodities.[15] Banks and building societies in particular have sought to expand along the high street and other major shopping streets to be closer to their increased shopping clientele; the 'fast-food' chains have sought both to penetrate traditional shopping streets and to locate alongside major traffic arteries leading out of the city centre. The former trend is seen to be undesirable on the grounds that business services create 'dead' frontages and detract from the retail attractions of a street; the latter causes concern from the point of view of congestion, especially where large facilities may face on to busy roads. Other problems of a locational kind, however, pertain to the diminishing number of sites available for many vehicle-oriented services, particularly sites within those most accessible parts of the city and where there is most consumer demand. Within the commodity group of services, too, there are trading problems linked to the declining resource-base of chemists and post offices, especially within rural areas. The information group of services is a relatively small one that has so far proved rather uncontroversial in its demands; the heterogeneous reparation group is one where many small problems involving environmental or land use incompatibility have been found, as in the case of advertising signs that might accompany entertainment activities located within a conservation zone or the proliferation of so-called twilight activities in older residential areas of the city.

Spatial Patterns of Activity

Much of the emphasis we have given in our discussion of the main elements of the distributive trades has referred to the locational needs or problems of different types of business activities. In considering the distribution system as a whole, however, we ought now to examine the way in which these variable locational characteristics interact to form broad patterns of business concentration over wide areas. The patterns we can discern, nevertheless, have changed quite dramatically over time, partly in response to the radical innovations within distribution itself and partly because of a compounding effect of increasing planning controls (at least until the last few years). There are at least three separate features to the underlying spatial structure of activity that can be perceived: the legacy of the pre-war system of distribution that was largely unfettered by planning controls; the early post-war developments that showed much similarity in functional character to previous business conformities but which were much more organised in terms of layout and design; and the more recent, larger-scale facilities that show marked departures both in function and form but whose locations have still been even more tightly controlled. Paradoxically, in fact, while the operational characteristics of the distributive trades have tended to become more complicated and blurred during the last few decades, their spatial manifestation has seemed to become much simplified — with a much greater areal segregation occurring between the intermediary trades and retailing and services, when previously they were more physically jumbled together and confined to a few, common locations.

The National and Regional Pattern

Since most forms of distribution take place within urban areas, the spatial pattern of retail and commercial activities at the national and regional scales has usually been described in the context of the size relationships between towns and cities — in what is termed the hierarchy of settlements, where different size orders of towns and cities are recognised according to their degree of importance as central places providing a wide range of goods and services to a surrounding hinterland.[16] The hierarchy concept has supported a number of geographical studies in the past, some aimed at comparing the mix of retail and commercial activities,[17] others focusing more specifically on just one facet of distribution.[18] While this has been an appropriate framework historically, however, it essentially rests on the notion that activities are highly constrained to certain localities only, mainly the central areas of towns and cities, and an interpretation of the contemporary pattern of distribution in this way would conceal the important changes that have been taking place internally in urban areas through the decentralisation process. The concept has varying degrees of relevance for different sets of activities, nevertheless; hence we shall consider it further in a separate discussion of the main elements of the distributive trades.

Wholesaling, Warehousing and Bulk Transference. There has recently been some debate in the geographical literature about the particular relevance of the hierarchy concept for describing national or regional patterns of wholesaling.[19] Vance[20] has suggested that wholesaling became concentrated in towns and cities, at least in America, not so much through a response to the needs of locally surrounding areas but through programmes of investment initiated from elsewhere. In an historical context, wholesaling grew up in conjunction with the exploitation of trade and resources in newly emerging settlements rather than those which were already well established. It therefore became a rather specialised function of certain settlements only, especially those along river routes, which subsequently grew in further importance through the forces of agglomeration. In older countries, such as Britain, however, wholesaling may have grown up more gradually over a longer period of time and, induced more from internal than from external sources, became more widely distributed as a basic function of most towns and cities. Certainly, Carter[21] found in the late 1950s that wholesaling was a particularly sensitive measure of the general centrality of towns and cities in his studies of the hierarchy of settlements in Wales.

The recent decline in wholesaling as a distinctive function, however, and the marked decentralisation that has accompanied its associated activities of warehousing and bulk transference suggest that the hierarchy concept is an outmoded framework even for describing aggregate patterns in Britain. Thorpe's[22] careful studies of the development of cash and carry depots, for example, show little relationship between either the spread of these or their subsequent density and a traditional ranking of towns and cities by central place importance. Cash and carry depots, at least in the formative period of their growth, became far more densely concentrated in the West Midlands and North West than in the South East, particularly around London; and modern ware-houses, redistribution centres and trans-shipment centres have shown a marked gravitation towards smaller communities, particularly new towns, or those close to motorway interchanges, albeit that these may be close to the major metropolitan areas.

Where the hierarchy concept retains some significance, however, has less to do with the sizes and locations of settlements than with the organisational structures imposed by firms on their physical distri-bution networks. Increasingly, both manufacturers and large retailers utilise two or three distinctive types of centre for the storage and trans-shipment of their goods and services. These may include a limited number of large, central warehouses for stockpiling purposes, a greater number of smaller, dispersed warehouses for regular dispatches to local-ised areas (where these may include the shared facilities of redistribu-tion centres), and perhaps further special-purpose warehouses close to their largest selling outlets used for holding limited inventories. Two recent case studies reported upon illustrate the point. The Boots Company[23] directs 80 per cent of its transactions initially through three central warehouses, at Nottingham, Aldershot and Heywood, which send out trunk lorries on a weekly basis to 19 redistribution centres which then act solely as despatching agents, sending out daily deliveries to the 1,462 retail branches. Certain of the largest stores, however, such as those in Newcastle and Manchester, then have access to their own local warehouses used for storing both the company's and other suppliers' goods. In contrast, Woolworths[24] operates a system geared towards more direct supply from manufacturers to branch outlets, revolving around four major trans-shipment centres at Bristol, Radlett, Warrington and Cumbernauld. These are supplemented by a series of smaller warehouses closer to the main centres of population for storing goods for local needs.

Retailing.   The fact that most retailing activities in Britain remain concentrated in town and city centres means that the hierarchy con-cept, utilised in the context of the national urban system, still has continuing relevance for describing the general pattern of this sector of trade. The latest exercise in a large number of geographical studies is a ranking of towns and cities produced by Schiller[25] from central

Figure 1.1: Schiller's Hierarchy of Shopping Centres in Great Britain, 1971

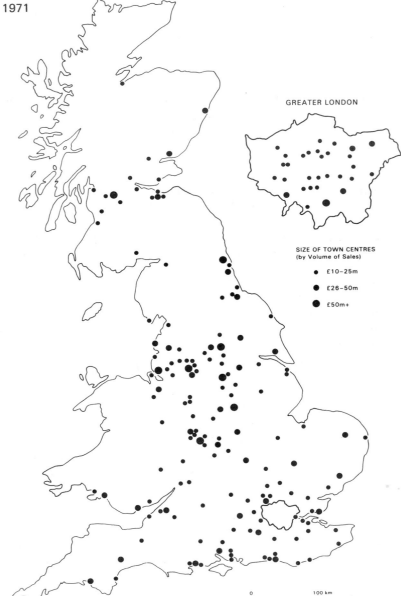

Source: Hillier, Parker, *Map of Major Shopping Centres in Great Britain* (London).

area sales figures reported in the last Census of Distribution. The three largest size orders of centres are shown in Figure 1.1. Ten centres in Britain were grouped at the top of the hierarchy, namely London, Glasgow, Manchester, Liverpool, Birmingham, Leeds, Nottingham, Sheffield, Newcastle and Croydon. Thirty-seven centres were classified as secondary regional shopping centres, including places like Leicester, Derby and Chester. One hundred and thirty-six centres formed minor or sub-regional shopping centres and included such places as Stockton, Lincoln and Carlisle. Comparison of the individual rank placements of these largest centres with earlier studies based on data for 1961 suggests there has been considerable stability in the upper levels of the hierarchy, a fact confirmed over a longer time period by Smith[26] using additional information on services. At the lower levels of the hierarchy, however, there have been considerable changes mainly associated with the decline in shopping status of industrial towns and a concomitant growth in market centres and suburban areas brought about by the decentralisation of convenience activities.

The changes taking place in the national hierarchy, however, need to be considered against the background of new developments in retailing, particularly the introduction of new covered shopping centres into central areas and the spread of superstores and hypermarkets. Along with the general reduction in small, independent shops, these have led to significant alterations to the composition of retailing at all levels in the hierarchy. Of most interest is the fact that these developments, like the cash and carry depots and other modern forms of wholesaling, first penetrated and became more strongly entrenched in the northern rather than southern parts of the country. This means that there has sometimes been a substantial improvement to the retail stock of industrial centres otherwise in decline and conversely the perpetuation of a more traditional structure in commuter settlements experiencing growth. In the case of large towns and cities, a general picture of sluggish retail growth conceals important shifts in trade from traditional shopping streets to both new central area facilities and those created on the periphery.[27]

The reasons why new retail developments were adopted earlier in the North than in the South have partly to do with the greater receptiveness of planning departments to their introduction in industrial areas and partly to the foresight of certain firms who were themselves more active in these parts. Many northern local authorities saw both covered shopping centres and superstores as real opportunities to modernise their shopping resources especially if this could be achieved at little cost to the ratepayers. Most southern authorities, in contrast, particularly those with important historical legacies to protect, were more fearful of the adverse trading effects that might ensue and the environmental intrusions created by the schemes themselves. Two of the major pioneers of both forms of development were also Yorkshire-based: the Town and Cities Property Development Company in Bradford that promoted the Arndale chain of covered centres; and Asda (part of Associated Dairies Ltd.) in Leeds that initiated a chain of superstores under that name.

Recent evidence, however, suggests that the South is now catching up on other areas in its proportion of new central area retail floor-space and that by the mid-1980s there will be relatively little regional disparity in numbers of covered shopping centres.[28] A degree of saturation of these developments has begun to set in and the trend is towards building smaller schemes in smaller places in the hierarchy. A marked exception is the case of London which, like other capital cities in the world, has experienced relatively little redevelopment in its central area, mainly as a result of the high development costs involved. The emerging picture for superstores and hypermarkets is less clear, however, for while there has been some spread of these developments into the South, the outer ring of London in particular still looks to be greatly underprovided and there are few signs of a relaxation in the planning constraints now operating against them.

Services. The national pattern of services seems to accord very strongly with that for retailing, although the diverse nature of activities in this sector makes it difficult to generalise with confidence. The lack of comprehensive statistics has meant that few studies have been undertaken by geographers except in the use of certain service criteria for indexing the centrality of places and delimiting hierarchies of so-called service centres.[29] In this respect, the business and personal services have been most useful, for their distribution is closely allied to shops, although banks, building societies and insurance companies have had strong regional concentrations in the past. One suspects that, through the effects of mergers and the growth of this set of activities in relation to the growth of incomes, there has been considerable dispersion of these former enclaves in recent years. The really unknown quantities in the service sector, however, are the developments in leisure facilities, particularly hotels, which must have become spatially biased in their national pattern both towards new tourist centres and those places with a special transport nodality.

Figure 1.2: A Classification of the Urban Retail System in Stockport

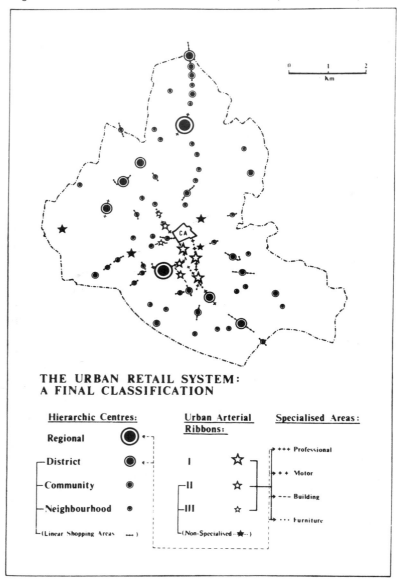

Source: Potter, R.B., *The Urban Retailing System: Location, Cognition and Behaviour* (Gower Press and RPA, Aldershot, 1982).

The Urban Pattern

The spatial distribution of retail and commercial activities inside towns and cities has traditionally been described in terms of the physical configurations which they form. Three distinctive types of configuration have been recognised, referred to in the parlance of American geographers as nucleations, ribbons and specialised functional areas.[30] An example of such a classification is shown in Figure 1.2. Nucleations are essentially the more compact shopping centres widely dispersed throughout an urban area that comprise shops primarily catering for the domestic shopping requirements of a surrounding population; ribbons are those beaded clusters of activities strung out alongside major roads particularly in the inner parts of an urban area that may contain a large number of shops but also contain a high incidence of services and sometimes a mixture of small wholesaling and manu- facturing establishments; specialised functional areas are those quarters or districts, mainly to be found in and around the central area, that contain a high concentration of particular activities, such as: retail and wholesale markets, entertainment districts, wholesaling and ware- housing districts, areas of high-quality shops and the like. The central area itself of course is also a distinctive physical entity, although in its various component parts it constitutes a microcosm of the pattern of trade found throughout the rest of the town or city, by virtue of its comprising compact shopping facilities, ribbons extending through its boundary frame as well as the specialised functional areas referred to above.[31]

Within the category of nucleated shopping centres, geographers and also planners have discerned a clear hierarchy structure that reflects once more on their sizes or levels of business importance. In large cities, a five-tier structure can be recognised, comprising: local centres (small parades), neighbourhood centres, district centres, sub-regional centres (usually town centres absorbed into a metropolitan area) and the city centre, although in smaller places only the first three levels may be represented. The typical characteristics for each of these, in terms of numbers of shops and functional composition, are given in Table 1.7. A distinction is made here, however, between those characteristics surviving from the inter-war and early post-war years and those found in more recent, purpose-built developments. The chief difference lies in the number of shops that can now be supported at any level in the hierarchy because of the trends to larger sizes of stores and bulk pur- chasing in shopping trips. What one finds in reality in any urban area today are the remnants of the earlier 'unplanned' form of the hierarchy,

Table 1.7: Characteristics of the Urban Hierarchy of Shopping Centres

	Legacies of older developments	Contemporary planning norms
Central Area	No definitive size characteristics but evolved around the high street and other major shopping streets	Concentration of multiples within the high street (often pedestrianised) and new purpose-built schemes
Regional centres/ sub-regional centres	Typically found in conurbations where they constitute former town centres that have become absorbed into a wider urban area (e.g. Gateshead in the Tyneside conurbation)	Purpose-built regional shopping centres have mainly been built within the central area. They comprise at least 250,000 sq ft and up to 100 shops. Sub-regional centres are often the new town centres of new towns
District centres	These relate to a catchment area of about 30,000 people and comprise about 100 shops (of small unit size)	Catchment areas vary from 20,000 to 100,000 people. Mainly based around a superstore and 15-20 other stores
Neighbourhood centres	These relate to catchment areas of 5,000-10,000 people with 15-35 shops	Catchment areas of 10,000 people can support a large supermarket and about 6 other shops but, below this threshold, neighbourhood centres are no longer tenable
Local centres/ isolated stores	Traditionally a mixture of corner stores and small parades of shops serving catchment areas of 500 to 2,500 people	The modern equivalent would be a single modern convenience store or mini-market integrated with a petrol station

largely remaining in the inner city; a more organised version of this with emphasis on neighbourhood centres, mainly concentrated within the middle parts of the city; and a more rationalised system of centres, particularly accentuating the role of district centres, emerging in outlying areas.

Although there has been much debate again about the continuing relevance of the hierarchy concept as a framework for controlling the spatial evolution of shopping centres within urban areas,[32] it remains the basic organisational principle adhered to in virtually all the local authority Structure and District Plans which have appeared in recent years. The reason for this seems to lie in its direct relationship to housing policies: where different sizes of centre can be equated with different sizes of trade areas and these in turn approximated by different groupings of residential accommodation or estates. The presumption is made that each discrete neighbourhood or community should be provided with an adequate range of shops to suit its size so that there will be an equitable provision of retailing throughout the urban area.

It is precisely because many of the latest retail innovations, namely the superstores, hypermarkets and discount retail warehouses, command larger trade areas or draw from a wider mix of consumers than those concentrated within the organised housing areas that their introduction into towns and cities was for long so strongly resisted. Local authorities saw them (and many still do) as depleting the trade of existing centres, suiting only those households with a car, creating monopoly positions in areas of weak competition, overloading local roads with traffic, and creating visual intrusions out of proportion with the scale of other, mainly residential, land uses.[33] Where they have been allowed in it has usually been to specific localities only: superstores serving as the basis to new district centres for very large housing tracts or helping to revitalise a town or city centre; hypermarkets being integrated into the new town centres of new towns; discount retail warehouses being guided to sites in the frame of the central area or into industrial trading estates.

A restrictive planning approach has also been adopted with respect to the ribbon developments of urban areas where both new types of development and growth within existing facilities have been severely curtailed. The basis to this policy appears to be a concern over the physical problems they cause, mainly the common occurrence of blight and decay and traffic hazards for pedestrians. There has been much clearance and redevelopment of the older ribbons, which grew up originally in most towns and cities in response to the tram networks, and suffocation of the newer ones, through car parking limitations and constraints on changes of use. The result is that, compared to most other countries, ribbon developments in Britain are relatively weak features of the spatial pattern of activity, surviving largely as vestiges of a bygone age but occasionally interrupted by new garages, car dealers, public houses and the like.[34] It is not possible to describe a comprehensive range of different types of ribbons as is the case in North America.[35]

The traditional locations of wholesaling and warehousing have also been markedly affected by recent planning policies although many of the changes which have ensued here, as we have indicated, have been the result of market forces. The principal feature has been the exodus of large numbers of firms from the central area and inner city to the outlying trading estates. The process of decentralisation has been exaggerated of course by a 'birth and death' process, particularly the replacement of former delivery merchants by cash and carry operations and other bulk transference activities.[36] Much of the vacant property left in the central area fringe has simply been renovated to form new specialised functional areas as, for example, in the conversion of warehouses into cinemas, bingo halls and discos to form an entertainments quarter. But there are large tracts in the outer parts of many city centres, in what is often referred to as the 'twilight zone', which are now in a derelict and abandoned state.

The core parts of the central area in most towns and cities provide a mixture of traditional patterns of activity with modern developments superimposed upon them.[37] The main thrust of planning policies here has been to segregate the predominant land uses of retailing and offices and to remove the conflict between pedestrians and vehicular traffic by promoting pedestrianised or precinct schemes. There has generally been a contraction of the areal extent of the shopping core as many former attenuating streets have been truncated at their margins by new ring roads or major arterials, although the most important locus of shopping activity has often been expanded by the construction of new shopping centres. Some of the older, historic quarters of the business core have been designated as conservation zones but much peripheral office development has taken place which, in its 'high-rise' building form, has often compromised the aesthetic character of the traditional townscape. While much progress has been achieved in improving safety in movement within the central area, congestion remains a serious problem, an inevitable consequence perhaps of retail and commercial policies that seek to keep the bulk of shopping and office activities concentrated within town and city centres.

Conclusion

This chapter has been concerned with describing the subject material of retail and commercial planning. We have taken the view that the field of study should be an expansive one, dealing with the distribution system as a whole rather than simply the business of shopping and those activities most closely allied to it. It is recognised, however, that in the day-to-day affairs of most planning departments, proportionately much more attention will be given to retailing than to the intermediary or service trades, because of the greater range of problems with which it is associated and its greater interaction with other land uses and the public at large. A similar emphasis on retailing will in fact be given in the subsequent chapters of this book. We have elaborated at some length on each of the major elements of the distributive trades, nevertheless, for at some stage in the plan-making process there will be the need to take stock of the distribution system in its entirety, to examine strengths and weaknesses in each of its constituent parts and to formulate comprehensive policies to meet those variable pressures for change which are likely to emerge in the future. The inadequacies of our existing classifications and data sources to do this effectively have been pointed to and some alternative suggestions made as to what might be more suitable frameworks to adopt. Lastly, because so much of the management function involved in retail and commercial planning is concerned with the implementation of development controls over the spatial evolution of the distributive trades, a general description has been given of the main patterns of activity to be found, both nationally and inside urban areas. This has shown that the cumulative effects of rather stringent development controls during the last two decades have led to marked departures from the types of patterns produced in earlier years as well as strong contrasts with those patterns found in other advanced Western economies.

References

1   Guirdham, M., *Marketing: The Management of Distribution Channels* (Pergamon, Oxford, 1972); Stern, L.W. and El-Ansary, A.I., *Marketing*

Channels: Structure, Strategy and Management (Prentice-Hall, Herts, 1982).

2   Christopher, M., Walters, D. and Gattorna, J., *Distribution Planning and Control: A Corporate Approach* (Gower Press, Farnborough, 1977).

3   Thorpe, D., Kirby, D.A. and Thompson, C.H., *Channels and Costs of Grocery Distribution* (Manchester Business School, Retail Outlets Research Unit, 1973).

4   McFadyen, E., *Voluntary Group Trading: Six Case Studies* (HMSO, London, 1971).

5   See, for example, McKinnon, A.C., *The Historical Development of Food Manufacturers' Distribution Systems* (University of Leicester, Department of Geography, Occasional Paper no. 7, 1981).

6   Ministry of Housing and Local Government, *Use Classes Order*, Statutory Instrument no. 709 (HMSO, London, 1963).

7   Business Statistics Office, *Censuses of Distribution*, Business Monitor SD23 (HMSO, London, 1950, 1961 and 1971).

8   Board of Trade, 'Inquiry into the Distributive and Service Trades for 1959. The Wholesale Trades in 1959', *Board of Trade Journal*, 7 April 1961, pp. 799-804; Board of Trade, 'Inquiry into Wholesaling and Dealing for 1965. Wholesale Trades in 1965', *Board of Trade Journal*, 26 July 1968, pp. 238-49.

9   Department of Trade and Industry, 'Inquiry into Wholesaling and Dealing for 1974', *Trade and Industry*, 28 October 1977.

10 Business Statistics Office, *Business Monitor SDA25: Retailing* (HMSO, London, annual publication).

11 Business Statistics Office, *Business Monitor SDA27: Retail Shops Inquiry for 1977* (HMSO, London, 1979).

12 One of the most widely used definitions for superstores and hypermarkets is that given by the Unit for Retail Planning Information in *List of Superstores and Hypermarkets* (Reading, 1982). However, this definition precludes large non-food stores and restricts itself to stores selling food or a combination of food and non-food goods.

13 Nelson, R.L. *The Selection of Retail Locations* (Dodge, New York, 1958).

14 See, for example, the distinctions made in: National Economic Development Office, Distributive Trades EDC, *The Future Pattern of Shopping* (HMSO, London, 1971).

15 Fernie, J. and Carrick, R.J., 'Planning for Quasi Retail Uses', *Town and Country Planning*, vol. 51, no. 2 (1982), pp. 14-15.

16 The hierarchy concept and its role in geographical and planning studies is discussed in Davies, R.L., *Marketing Geography – with Special Reference to Retailing* (Methuen, London, 1977).

17 For example, Carruthers, W.I., 'Major Shopping Centres in England and Wales, 1961', *Regional Studies*, vol. 1 (1967), pp. 65-81.

18 For example, Thorpe, D., 'The Main Shopping Centres of Great Britain in 1961; their Locational and Structural Characteristics', *Urban Studies*, vol. 5 (1968), pp. 165-206.

19 Vance, J.E., 'On Freedom of Evolution in the Geography of Wholesaling – Comments on a Florida Hierarchical Case Study', *Tijdschrift Voor Economische En Sociale Geografie*, vol. 64 (1973), pp. 231-6; Rabiege, W.E., and Lamoureux, L.F., 'Wholesaling Hierarchies, A Florida Case Study', *Tijdschrift Voor Economische En Sociale Geografie*, vol. 64 (1973), pp. 226-30.

20 Vance, J.E., *The Merchant's World: The Geography of Wholesaling* (Prentice-Hall, New Jersey, 1970).

21 Carter, H., *The Towns of Wales* (University of Wales Press, Cardiff, 1965).

22. Thorpe, D. and Kirby, D.A., *The Density of Cash and Carry Wholesaling* (Manchester Business School, Retail Outlets Research Unit, 1972); Thorpe, D. and Thorpe, S., *The Density of Cash and Carry Wholesaling: An Industry Reaching Maturity?* (Manchester Business School, Retail Outlets Research Unit, 1976).
23. 'Boots Speed Turnaround – A Case Study', *Freight Management*, November 1976, pp. 26, 28, 30.
24. 'Woolworth's New Trans-shipment Centres', *Freight Management*, February 1978, pp. 44, 46.
25. The study was summarised in a map produced by Hillier, Parker, 'Major shopping Centres of Great Britain' (Hillier, Parker, London, undated).
26. Smith, R.D.P., 'The Changing Urban Hierarchy', *Regional Studies*, vol. 2 (1968), pp. 1-19.
27. Bennison, D.J. and Davies, R.L., 'The Impact of Town Centre Shopping Schemes in Britain: Their Impact on Traditional Retail Environments', *Progress in Planning*, vol. 14, part 1 (1980), pp. 1-104.
28. Hillier, Parker, *British Shopping Developments* (London, 1979, 1980 and 1981).
29. For example, Carruthers, W.I., 'A Classification of Service Centres in England and Wales', *The Geographical Journal*, vol. 123 (1957), pp. 371-85.
30. Potter, R.B., *The Urban Retailing System: Location, Cognition and Behaviour* (Gower and Retailing and Planning Associates, Aldershot and Corbridge, 1982).
31. Davies, R.L., 'Structural Models of Retail Distribution: Analogies with Settlement and Urban Land Use Theories', *Transactions, Institute of British Geographers*, vol. 57 (1972), pp. 59-82.
32. See, for example, Dawson, J.A., *The Marketing Environment – An Introduction to Marketing Geography* (Croom Helm, London, 1979).
33. Sumner, J. and Davies, K., 'Hypermarkets and Superstores: What do the Planning Authorities Really Think?', *Retail and Distribution Management,* vol. 6, no. 4 (1978), pp. 8-15; Shaw, G. and Williams, A., 'Structure Plans and Retail Planning', *Retail and Distribution Management*, vol. 8, no. 1, pp. 43-7.
34. Davies, R.L., 'Nucleated and Ribbon Components of the Urban Retail System in Britain', *Town Planning Review*, vol. 45 (1974), pp. 91-111.
35. Berry, B.J.L., *Commercial Structure and Commercial Blight* (University of Chicago, Development of Geography, Research Paper no. 85, 1963).
36. Watts, D., 'The Impact of Warehouse Growth', *The Planner*, vol. 63, no. 4 (1977), pp. 105-8.
37. Davies, R.L., 'A Framework for Commercial Planning Policies', *Town Planning Review*, vol. 48, no. 1 (1977), pp. 42-58.

2 PRESSURES FOR CHANGE

We have stressed that the distribution system is extremely dynamic and the changes which have occurred in the last 10 to 15 years have probably been greater than in any comparable period in the past. These changes, however, while manifest in the form of new retail and commercial developments, are not only the result of innovations from within business itself but reflect on adaptations and responses to new pressures from the consumer population. Most consumers, taking a broad perspective on the last two decades, have continued to become increasingly more affluent, more mobile, more knowledgeable and more independent, displaying an ever-burgeoning range of tastes and demands. Whether the distribution system actually progresses mainly because of these external forces or through its own internal initiatives is a question that is often posed. The answer is that it moves forward largely on the interactions between both, that there is a complex mixture of cause and effect.

Planning has also become an increasingly significant factor in the evolution of the distributive trades not only in terms of its spatial constraints on new retail and commercial developments but through its wider effects on housing provision, employment and transport policies and the general regulation of the economy. A startling contrast is found at the international level between distribution systems in the highly planned economies of Eastern Europe and the relatively free economies of North America.[1] In Britain's celebrated 'mixed economy' the interventions of various forms of planning have led to a slower rate of distributional change than in many other Western economies in recent years but they have also protected the nation against excessive adverse side-effects that have accompanied more rapid growth elsewhere. One can see in a global context in fact a marked lag since about 1965 between the introduction of new innovations into distribution in North America and Western Europe and their subsequent adoption in Britain.

Such international comparisons are instructive for keeping a balanced perspective on the amount and consequences of change taking place in this country and will be developed further at various stages in this chapter. Our primary concern, however, is with identifying in more detail the principal factors at work in the process of change. We begin with a discussion of the forces involved on the demand side, contrasting the prevailing influences on consumer behaviour in the recent past with what can be expected to assume more importance in the future. We then proceed to an account of the more significant developments that have occurred to date in the system of supply and again examine the question of what new types of trading conditions are likely to emerge in the 1980s and 1990s.

The Background to Behavioural Change

The late 1970s may well prove to be a watershed in modern history for two fundamental changes that occurred in the social and economic conditions of Britain and many other countries of the Western world. Firstly, because of a reduction in the birth rate, there was a virtual stabilisation of population growth and, in the middle part of the decade, an actual net decline in numbers of people for the first time during peacetime this century. Secondly, because of the compounding effect of inflation on primary goods, energy constraints and a diminution of the manufacturing base, large sections of society experienced a lowering of their living standards with little prospect of improvement. The extent to which these new circumstances will remain relatively permanent or long term is, as yet, difficult to say; but it seems certain that in the future they will be recorded as more than minor aberrations to the general post-war trends. The implication for those involved in the distributive trades is that the outlook for further business growth, at least in the next few years, is much more circumspect than it has been in the past.

Although there appear to be severe limitations on the further expansion of the distribution system as a whole, however, the demand for goods and services in certain sectors of trade remains quite high. This is because a majority of the population has remained relatively affluent and there has not been a complete reversal or check to the earlier pattern of behavioural change. In the short term we shall continue to see the development of what we might call 'the modern forms of shopping': with increased reliance on the use of cars, more single-purpose trips for convenience and durable goods, longer, more infrequent journeys to shopping centres, more bulk purchasing of commodities, and greater discrimination in types of stores patronised.

The primary contributors to this to date have been the broad mass of middle-class people living in the outer and middle parts of the city, and particularly family groups where the wife goes to work. The corollary picture of traditional shopping habits, with regular trips to local corner stores for small quantities of goods, remains most conspicuous in the inner city where there are, of course, greater concentrations of the poor, elderly and minority groups.

The Determinants of Modern Forms of Shopping

The development of modern shopping is highly correlated with the introduction of supermarkets, superstores and purpose-built shopping centres, but has at its roots a more fundamental relationship to the loosening of traditional values and dependencies in society. While there is a complex interplay of social and economic considerations involved in this, we shall limit our attention here to those more clear-cut influences that have been at work. These include the changes which have occurred in people's residential locations, their jobs, levels of purchasing power and mobility, and changes in their attitudes and expectations occasioned by new fashions and opportunities made available.

Changes in Residential Location. The widespread suburbanisation of the population during the last two decades, and the concomitant reduction in numbers of people living in the inner city, has perhaps been the single most important background consideration for retail planners in recent years. Although there are a few signs of new pockets of growth within the inner city at the present time, related either to immigrant groups or the gentrification process, the broad picture remains one of continuing shifts to outlying locations. The trends have been most vividly portrayed in two studies conducted at the London School of Economics [2] and the University of Newcastle which have compared changes in population growth from 1951 to 1981 between commuting areas and major employment centres (urban cores). A summary of the results is given in Table 2.1 which also defines some special terms used to denote different parts of the urban region.

The table shows that during the period 1951-61 there was only relatively little growth in the outer suburbs of Britain for the population living in urban cores increased by 486,000 people. Between 1961 and 1971, however, the urban cores lost a total of 729,000 people, with the commuting areas (the metropolitan rings and outer metropolitan rings combined) gaining a massive 3,298,000 people. This represented a loss of 2.8 per cent of the population in inner

Table 2.1: The Population of Urban Zones in Britain, 1951-1981

	1951 Absolute (000s)	%	1961 Absolute (000s)	%	1971 Absolute (000s)	%	1981* Absolute (000s)	%
Urban cores	25,767	52.7	26,253	51.2	25,524	47.4	24,058	44.4
Metropolitan rings	12,914	26.4	14,635	28.5	17,147	31.9	18,355	33.9
SMLAs	36,681	79.2	40,887	79.7	42,671	79.3	42,413	78.4
Outer metro rings	7,808	16.0	8,053	15.7	8,838	16.4	9,165	16.9
MELAs	46,489	95.2	48,940	95.4	51,509	95.7	51,578	95.3
Unclassified areas	2,366	4.8	2,344	4.6	2,312	4.3	2,540	4.7
Britain	48,855	100.0	51,284	100.0	53,821	100.0	54,118	100.0

Definitions:
Cores are contiguous local authority areas with employment densities greater
than 5 per acre, or a total employment of over 20,000.
    A metropolitan ring comprises local authority areas having more than 15% of
the economically active population commuting to the core.
    An outer metropolitan ring comprises all other contiguous local authorities
having more economically active population commuting to a particular core
than to any other core.
    The core and metropolitan ring define the Standard Metropolitan Labour
Area (SMLA) and the SMLA and outer metropolitan ring define the Metropoli-
tan Economic Labour Area (MELA).
 * The definition of the zones changed slightly between 1971 and 1981
Source: Drewett, R. *et al., British Cities: Urban Population and Employment
Trends, 1951-71* (HMSO, London, 1976); and unpublished statistics, Centre for
Urban and Regional Development Studies, University of Newcastle upon Tyne.

areas and a gain of 27 per cent in outer areas. Since the urban cores
effectively correspond to the traditional administrative boundaries of
towns and cities, the average percentage loss in inner areas in fact
conceals substantially greater reductions for certain parts of these
areas, particularly those close to the town or city centre. Some of the
inner, former boroughs of London, for example, lost up to one third
of their population, partly through 'natural' out-migration but also
through an enforced migration caused by redevelopment.[3] Between
1971 and 1981, there was a further reduction by 4.2 per cent of the
population of the inner areas as a whole and an increase by 19.2 per
cent of that within the outer areas. For the first time, there was also an
increase in population in rural (unclassified) areas and by as much as
8.8 per cent.
    The experiences of the United States provide an even more dramatic

case of changing patterns of population concentration for here the suburbanisation process has proceeded at a more rapid pace involving a larger scale of movement over a longer time period than in Britain or other West European countries. The 1970s were particularly noteworthy, however, since for the first time in America there was a relative decline in the growth of metropolitan areas as a whole as more and more people sought to reside in outlying satellite communities. Although the traditional suburbs of cities continued to grow at an average annual rate of 1,084,000 people between 1970 and 1975, the average annual exodus of people from central city locations reached 1,403,600 persons, four times the average annual exodus between 1961 and 1971.[4] The overall out-migration focused partly on small, rural communities in adjacent areas but also on new urban centres in the so-called 'sunshine belt' of the southern and south-western states. The metropolitan areas with the greatest amount of decline were primarily concentrated in the north-eastern and east-central states and, since the out-migrants were almost entirely white sections of the population, the concentration of blacks in the inner parts of the cities became intensified.

Such massive shifts in residential location within the United States have been accompanied, of course, by enormous changes in the spatial pattern of retailing, involving a phenomenal growth of new suburban and outlying shopping centres and a commensurate decline of inner city, particularly city centre, provisions. It is estimated that in 1982 there were 23,300 new developments comprising 3.2 billion square feet (297 million m^2) of floorspace (gross leasable area) and capturing 43 per cent of total retail sales.[5] In Britain, by contrast, the decentralisation process has been much more restrained and mainly associated only with an outward expansion of the convenience trades. The great majority of new shopping centres that provide a parallel to the developments in North America (particularly the new 'covered' shopping centres) have been built in town or city centre locations. The strongest growth in outlying shopping facilities in Britain is found in the traditional market towns, particularly those bordering the conurbations, and in the new town centres of the New Towns.

The main impact on consumer behaviour that has resulted from the retail decentralisation process and changes in residential location is to be seen in the greater orderedness of shopping trips for those people living in the suburbs compared to those in the inner city. Essentially, this involves the division of all trips into two distinct journey purposes: with those trips concerned primarily with the acquisition of convenience (mainly food) goods being undertaken locally, and those trips involving more specialised purchases being focused, in the case of Britain, on town or city centres and which hence incur longer journeys and are thereby concentrated on Saturdays.[6] The importance of weekend shopping in Britain is also explained by a number of other factors, however, not least the growth in female employment.

The Growth of Female Employment. Women have always been the principal body of shoppers in Britain and hence any change which affects their domestic circumstances will have a crucial bearing on consumer behaviour. From April 1957 to March 1977, the total number of females in all forms of employment (full- and part-time) in Great Britain rose from 7,851,000 to 8,945,000, while the total number of working males declined from 16,145,000 to 12,976,000.[7] While there has been a significant reduction in both sets of later figures in the last few years, due to high levels of unemployment, the fact remains that women now account for a much higher proportion of the total workforce than they did 20 years ago.

The growth of female employment has had two main implications for consumer behaviour: firstly, through the increased purchasing power created by additional incomes going into households and the greater freedom of control exercised on household spending by women; secondly, through the time constraints imposed on shopping, particularly for women engaged in full-time work. There has been more money to spend but effectively less time to spend it in. The general result has been an increase in bulk buying (especially for food) and a reduction in the number or frequency of shopping trips.

Bulk buying of grocery goods has, of course, been facilitated by other factors including the increase in refrigerator and freezer ownership which is in turn partly the outcome of improved household incomes. The number of households in Britain with a refrigerator grew from 72 per cent in 1971 to 95 per cent in 1980; for freezers, the figures were 6 per cent and 42 per cent.[8] Most food shopping now takes place on a single day in the week, Friday being the most popular, although increasing numbers of working women take advantage of later evening trading hours, particularly on a Thursday. There has been a strong upsurge in lunchtime shopping which is most conspicuous within town and city centres and includes shopping for durable goods and fashion items as well as food. One quarter of working women in Britain are now estimated to undertake their major shopping trips from their workplaces rather than from the home.

The shift in place of origin (and also the termination) of shopping trips has had a small but nevertheless significant influence on the locational pattern of many retail trades. Supermarkets, superstores and discount retail warehouses often seek sites in industrial areas. not only because of the building facilities and space to be found, but also because of the market potential that may exist within the local workforce. Banks, building societies and other business services have been competing more strongly for central positions along traditional high streets because of the greater use of these services by working women and their incorporation into the function of shopping. Many specialist food and catering trades have shown rapid growth in recent years, particularly in town and city centres, taking advantage of the overall increase in lunchtime shopping in these areas; and, in a few cases, new shopping centres with an emphasis on the convenience trades have been located directly in association with new office complexes or other areas of high employment concentration.

The Increase in Purchasing Power. The variable growth in different sectors of retail trade, however, has more to do with the overall increase in household incomes than with the specific contributions of working women. Until the mid-1970s there had been a progressive increase in purchasing power for virtually all sections of the population, despite minor fluctuations from one year to the next. Coupled with the growth in population numbers this led to a marked improvement in general consumption and supported the expansion in particular of the durable-goods and comparison-goods trade sectors.

With the decline in the birth rate and the effects of hyper-inflation during the middle part of the decade, nevertheless, spending in all sectors of retailing became severely depressed. There was a reduction in average *per capita* expenditure, measured in real terms, that amounted to about 5 per cent over a four-year period for the industry as a whole (Table 2.2). Subsequently, spending picked up during the end of the decade although it has again receded in the early years of the 1980s due to the increase in unemployment, sharp rises in VAT and the general state of the national economy. The present downturn has been softened somewhat, however, by falling interest rates and the lowering of inflation.

These cyclical trends need qualification of course in terms of how they have affected particular types of businesses. In both the food and non-food trades, the bigger companies were much more able during the 1970s to contain the effects of inflation on prices than their smaller counterparts due to the scale economies achieved in new, large stores that were opened. Table 2.2 shows that the so-called mixed retail businesses, comprising superstores and discount retail warehouses,

Table 2.2: Average *Per Capita* Expenditures on Retail Businesses
in Great Britain, 1971-1980

	Convenience businesses £	Comparison businesses £	Mixed businesses £	All businesses £
	Expenditure at 1976 prices			
1971	292	166	105	563
1972	291 (−0.3%)	180 (+8.5%)	116 (+10.4%)	587 (+4.4%)
1973	287 (−1.5%)	195 (+8.7%)	128 (+10.3%)	610 (+3.9%)
1974	281 (−2.0%)	191 (−2.0%)	130 (+1.4%)	602 (−1.3%)
1975	266 (−5.3%)	188 (−1.7%)	137 (+5.2%)	591 (−1.8%)
1976	258 (−2.9%)	188 (+0.1%)	143 (+4.9%)	590 (−0.2%)
1977	253 (−2.2%)	184 (−2.2%)	142 (−0.8%)	579 (−1.9%)
1978	253 (+0.1%)	205 (+11.3%)	153 (+7.5%)	611 (+5.5%)
1979	258 (+1.8%)	223 (+8.8%)	156 (+2.2%)	637 (+4.2%)
1980	259 (+0.5%)	225 (+0.8%)	158 (+0.9%)	641 (+0.6%)

Source: Unit for Retail Planning Information, *Information Brief 82/1* (Reading, 1982).

as well as variety stores and department stores, fared much better than those of a more traditional convenience or comparison-goods kind. The relative health of the bigger companies was therefore maintained through an increase in the market share caused principally by a growing disparity in the prices of goods offered at different stores but also assisted by the increasing ability of people to incur the larger expenditure outlays necessary to travel greater distances and to shop in bulk. A National Consumer Council survey undertaken in 1977 showed that 24 per cent of all adults purchased their food in bulk at that time, achieving an average family cost saving of £3.00 per week.[9] Numerous other surveys also reported that the prices of a broad mix of goods found in superstores or hypermarkets were typically 10 to 15 per cent lower than those in conventional supermarkets or small independent shops.[10] To some extent, these differentials have become reduced in recent years through greater competition, but significant differences still exist as between the very largest and very smallest of stores.

The benefits of cheaper shopping, however, can be said to have fallen mainly to the more affluent sections of the population, albeit these are in the majority. There remain large numbers of relatively poor people, particularly the elderly on limited pensions, single-parent householders and the unemployed, who still lack the ability to buy in bulk or to travel to superstores and hypermarkets. Arguably, smaller households could not achieve the same cost savings as larger households because of the differences in shopping needs; but a recent survey in Tyne and Wear has shown that the prices of small quantities of the most standardised items will on average be 5 per cent cheaper in superstores and hypermarkets than in conventional supermarkets.[11] Perhaps little can be done in the immediate future to remove the root problem of low levels of purchasing power. However, some measures could be taken to improve the accessibility of disadvantaged consumers to large store developments, either through the introduction of special transport services or by encouraging more investment in those inner city areas where the poor are particularly concentrated.

The Increase in Mobility.   The growth in car ownership and car usership for shopping purposes has been a further factor involved in the trend to bulk buying and the shift from daily shopping to shopping on just one or two days in the week. The convenience element that the car brings to shopping is quite obvious; and it allows for a greater freedom of choice in centres to visit and the combination of multipurpose activities on any single trip. The fact that the number of driving licences issued to women in Britain has lagged behind that for men has also meant there has been an increase in family participation in shopping in recent years, particularly on Saturdays and during late-night opening hours in the evening.

The general effects of the growth in car ownership on public transport usage are illustrated in Figure 2.1. This graph refers to all types of trips, including journeys to work and recreational travel, however,

Figure 2.1: Comparison of the Differential Usage of Cars and Buses in Great Britain, 1955-1980

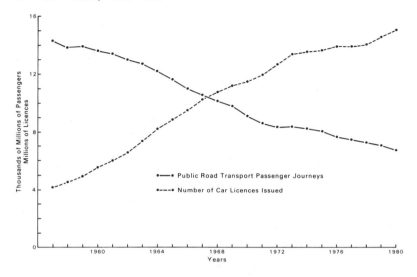

Source: Central Statistics Office, *Annual Abstract of Statistics* (HMSO, London).

and it is not possible to identify the specific decline in bus usage for shopping trips from the national statistics available. Since most shopping trips are also rather localised it is important to bear in mind the spatial variations in car ownership growth that have occurred both between and within different parts of the country. In this respect the National Travel Surveys conducted in 1965 and 1972 are instructive for whilst providing data again about the aggregate of all types of trips they indicate the relative disparities in transport services and individual mobility that have arisen around Britain in recent years.[12] Thus the proportion of all trips undertaken by local bus in rural areas declined from 19 per cent to 10 per cent during the seven-year period; in the case of London from 30 per cent to 19 per cent; for the provincial conurbations, from 47 per cent to 32 per cent; and for smaller urban places (those between 50,000 and 100,000 population size), from 24 per cent to 15 per cent.

The most conspicuous growth in car usage for shopping purposes has occurred in the suburbs, particularly in relation to the development of new district centres, superstores and hypermarkets. Hypermarkets especially cater almost exclusively to car-borne shoppers, surveys of the Carrefour developments at Caerphilly and Chandless Ford having established that more than 90 per cent of customers use their own forms of transport on Saturdays.[13] Even where superstores have located in traditional town centres they seem to command proportionately more car users, further surveys of the Asda superstore in Coatbridge, in an area of relatively low car ownership levels, indicating that more than 50 per cent of customers there had used their own forms of transport (as against 25 per cent travelling by bus).[14] Some evidence also exists to suggest that new town and city centre shopping schemes attract proportionately more car users than traditional shopping streets, partly by virtue of the greater provision for car parking made available within them.

The increased use of cars for shopping purposes, despite spiralling petrol cost rises, has provided the retail planner with a special challenge in recent years because of its direct relationship to the pressure for new types of retail development. Although the majority of households now have an independent means of travel, however, a substantial minority remain tied to public transport services and depend on local shopping facilities to which they can walk. The basic problem is to reconcile the two sets of needs without prejudicing the scope for change or allowing disparities in shopping opportunities to arise.

Changes in Attitudes and Expectations. The increase in independent mobility for large numbers of people in recent years has been one of several conditioning factors that have led to changes not only in patterns of shopping behaviour but also in types of goods and services sought and the budgetry characteristics of household spending. There has been a substantial growth, for example, in car accessory shops, the linking of service stations with superstores, the development of convenience stores within service stations and a whole series of specialised repair establishments connected with different aspects of the motor trade. Advertising and the impact of television programmes have been another influence at work, generating considerable growth within the mail order trade, particularly for textile goods, electricals and more recently books and records, and causing marked changes in eating and drinking habits and thereby in the sales performance of different kinds of catering activities. A number of technical innovations both in selling practices within stores and in the running of people's houses have also led to an increased efficiency in shopping with implications for what stores are patronised and what household goods are bought. Such innovations range from the introduction of credit cards to the scanning operations at check-out points, the increased use of store trolleys, catalogue shopping and the expansion of frozen food products. A further conditioning factor has been the general improvement in many types of retail environment, including precincts, pedestrianised streets and new covered shopping centres, which have often led to marked shifts in the concentration of shopping within town or city centres and the growth of those traditional shopping centres which are perceived to have better accessibility conditions and car parking provisions.

Besides the effects of these mainly physical circumstances surrounding the business of shopping there have been various more subtle changes in society's values which are more difficult to articulate but which have nevertheless had a profound influence on people's attitudes and expectations and hence on various forms of retail response. One general area of change relates to the liberalisation of the traditional sex roles in running the home and the loosening of former moral codes of behaviour. Shopping, especially for bulk grocery goods, is much more a shared experience than it was in the past; younger people have ushered in the concept of unisex facilities, particularly in hair salons, jeans shops and boutiques; the so-called permissive age has led to a proliferation in 'twilight' activities that would not have been countenanced 15 years ago. New fads and fashions have always had a significant part to play in the relative growth or decline of more specialised trades, and in recent years the volatility of changes in ideas has seriously jeopardised the survival rate of new stores. A lasting exception of course has been the development of the boutique which has had a major impact on the strength and character of traditional clothing chain outlets. Accompanying the temporary nature of many new ideas has been a greater fragmentation of accepted or conventional modes of dress and the way homes are furnished. This has led to much greater variety in the product-mix of some stores, particularly those in the apparel and durable-goods sector. In contrast, however, new stereotyped forms of behaviour have emerged with respect to the more routine and convenience aspects of shopping leading to considerable uniformity in goods offered and store designs amongst the larger chain outlets.

There has been little systematic evaluation, however, of people's changing viewpoints towards planned provisions in shopping, especially large shopping centre developments. The increase in public participation exercises conducted by local authorities has led to some gauge of public opinion but mainly in a retrospective way and on broad environmental matters. It is extremely difficult, of course, to obtain rational assessments about the possibilities for future shopping schemes, when the average person has a limited knowledge of the technical problems involved and the wider planning implications that might arise; but much more advice could be sought from experts either involved or simply interested in the distributive trades.

Questions for the Future

The earlier reference to the changing demographic conditions in Britain in the 1970s needs elaboration at this point because of the strong implications they carry for the state of the retail market in the 1980s. The net decline in population between 1974 and 1975 (from 56.0 millions to 55.9 millions) has subsequently been reversed by a gradual increase in the birth rate again[15] but the full benefits of any sustained population growth will not be seen until the end of the present decade. In the intervening period we can expect to see a continued shift in the composition of the population, to proportionately more elderly people and fewer youths, and proportionately more single adults and less married couples. Combined with the decline in retirement ages and the growth in family sizes of immigrant groups this suggests a much more variable set of consumer characteristics than has hitherto been found.

It is difficult to generalise on how this greater segmentation of the market will work itself through to a retail response but one suspects the recent trend to increased specialisation among smaller shops will continue and the desire for more personal service within the larger stores will make itself felt. This carries some threat to the major chain groups, particularly those who have trimmed their labour force and perpetrated a duplicity in functions with competitors. Conflicting with these trends, however, are the uncertainties over income growth and spending power in a climate of economic deline which may suggest some countervailing requirements for yet further reductions in the relative prices of goods which can themselves only come from store economies and increased competition in the same lines of trade. What we may well see as a result of this is a clearer distinction between those stores catering for what we might call occasional needs and those oriented to more regular demands. This is in addition to the traditional differences between convenience or food and durable or comparison-goods shops.

Further encouragement to the development of these two contrasting styles of shopping will likely come in the long term through the introduction of computer facilities within both stores and people's homes. In both cases, we can expect to see the growth of viewdata systems that emphasise a certain range of goods or services available to consumers and which can be purchased either 'on-the-spot' within a store or remotely from the home in what has come to be called tele-shopping or armchair shopping. Already some use is being made of Prestel (British Telecom's viewdata system)[16] to provide information about stocks and shares, packaged holidays and theatre programmes, etc., and a number of projects are underway to enable orders to be placed and financial transactions effected for more routine shopping needs. The major breakthrough in computerised home-based shopping, however, will probably be deferred until there is a fairly extensive network of cable TV and programme channels specialising in retail advertising have become established. American experience is instructive in this respect for several experiments have been conducted there into varying types of home-based shopping services,[17] some of which have been conspicuously unsuccessful. Most success has been achieved with 'informercials' where entire programmes are devoted to displaying selected goods from a retail or manufacturing company and at the end of which consumers place orders through hand-held terminal pads. The goods are then paid for by keying in credit card numbers. Such a service, of course, is really just an extension of the telephone-based, catalogue method of trading where goods are ultimately received through the mail.

The possibility that more revolutionary changes in shopping behaviour might occur in the 1990s, however, should not be ignored. By that time, there will have been significant advances in the automation of goods handling procedures which will make the commercial prospects of developing home-based grocery shopping services that much brighter. This poses a special threat to the local authorities in the sense that, much like the car, the use of personal computers for common shopping purposes might prove to be extremely socially divisive. It would be the better-off sections of society who would initially be able to bear the costs of supporting such services and to whom the benefits of a greater convenience in shopping would first fall. Several other socio-economic implications arise in relation to the rate at which such developments might take place, not least their potential impact on the structure of employment in retailing and the likely creation of a much smaller workforce.[18] Already the introduction of product codes and scanning techniques has reduced the need for labelling in stores and rationalised the process of stock control; once remote ordering and payment for goods comes in on a large scale, fewer workers will be required at check-out points, although some might be diverted to packing and delivering goods.

A further problem for the future concerns the impact which any new international oil crisis might have on petrol costs and availability. Already there has been a marked swing towards the purchase of small cars rather than large ones but as yet there has been no evidence of a marked diminution in the use of cars for shopping purposes, at least in bulk-purchasing trips. The uncertainty of the future, however, and the indications that there will be less growth in the number of two-car households in the next decade, have led some retail firms to seek fewer suburban locations for their outlets than in the past and to focus instead on town centre sites with good public transport connections. Nevertheless, it may be that the development of remote computerised shopping services will again alleviate any constraints imposed on motorised travel for one can visualise women dialling up their needs during the daytime and their husbands (or themselves) collecting the goods on the way home from work. In Britain, too, the effects of energy shortages are likely to be less than in many other Western countries, not simply because of the North Sea reserves, but because of the more concentrated pattern of shopping facilities to be found and their traditional centrality to the surrounding population. The USA and other 'new' countries with a more dispersed pattern of retailing may also suffer heavier penalties in higher distribution costs for supplying stores and through higher service costs associated with maintaining artificial temperatures in more adverse climatic conditions.

At variance with these potential curbs on independent mobility will be the growth in leisure time available for large sections of the population to undertake their shopping and the extended trade times that can be expected to accompany new retail outlets. It is possible that there will be a mismatch between the opportunities available to visit stores and centres and the ability of people to finance the excursions involved. Given that these circumstances may apply in the future to other trips, for recreational, educational and other social purposes, the case for concentrating more public-oriented facilities closer together seems a strong one. Attempts have been made in recent years to combine more service provisions with purpose-built shopping centres in Britain, but the amount of diversification involved has been small and the general outcome of most central area redevelopment schemes has been for an increased segregation rather than integration of land uses to occur. Retail and commercial planners need perhaps to be much more imaginative about how they see the role of large centres in the future, be they suburban district centres or traditional town centres, and to consider how they might return to the advantages of multi-purpose activity that characterised the market place of old.

Changes within the Distributive Trades

The questions that need to be asked about future changes in consumer demand have their parallel on the supply side and focus on what new types of distributional activity, besides the impact of computer technology, can be expected to develop in the 1980s. The last two decades have seen enormous changes in the structure and organisation of distribution and there is little reason to doubt that further innovations will occur, most likely at an accelerating rate. While the 1960s and 1970s saw changes taking place largely as a result of general economic growth, however, the new constraints operating against further development of the market suggest there will be much more variable and perhaps sometimes volatile reactions from within the industry than has hitherto occurred. We are likely to see, for example, much more contraction and operating difficulties arising amongst the larger corporate groups in the field when previously most of the adverse consequences of change fell on the smaller, weaker elements of trade. Prior to examining these and other probable trends in the future, nevertheless, we should take stock of what has happened, in prevailing terms, in the recent past.

The Revolutions of the 1960s and 1970s

Besides the economic background against which changes in the distributive trades have taken place in the last two decades, one needs to be aware of the improving technological capabilities which occurred and the increasing political intervention into the entire system of supply. There is a complex set of considerations here which space limitations prevent full exploration – but suffice to say that on the one hand transport developments, the automation of goods handling procedures and advances in forecasting and marketing methods and, on the other, new forms of taxation (especially the introduction of VAT), wage and price legislation, and the extension of quality control standards over goods sold, all contributed to the way in which new types of activity were fostered and evolved. While these external influences have clearly been important, we shall focus here on the internal expressions of change which took place, concentrating once again on the retail sector as the most dominant theatre of events, but also giving more attention to its close association with the service and intermediary trades than was relevant in the previous section. The most significant features to note are the changes which have occurred in the structure of retailing, the introduction of new types of stores, and development of new types of shopping centres, the rationalisation which has taken place in the intermediary trades and the differential growth of service activities.

Structural Changes in Retailing.   The revolution in the methods and organisation of retailing during the last two decades began with the introduction of self-service techniques on a widespread scale and was further induced by the trend to larger scales of operation, both in the corporate structure of the firms and in the sizes of individual stores. The general outcome was a massive growth in the trading strength of the multiple groups and a concomitant decline in the number of small, independent businesses. While the seeds of the revolution date from the early post-war years and beyond, the first visible impact was seen in the late 1950s when the erstwhile trend of a progressive increase in total numbers of establishments in Britain peaked and subsequently through the 1960s a substantial decline set in. During the intercensal period of the 1960s, there was a reduction in total establishments from 542,301 to 504,781; and between 1971 and 1980 (using a different statistical base), a further reduction to 354,131.[19]

Various interpretations can be given to the growth in the market share of the multiple groups, but if we take the Census of Distribution definitions of these groups (firms with 10 or more outlets and excluding the co-operative societies), their share rose from 29 per cent in 1961 to 44 per cent in 1976 with present estimates suggesting a figure around 50 per cent. Adding smaller, local chain firms and the co-operative societies to the assessment would bring the current figure closer to two-thirds. The experiences of the co-operative societies, however, have been different from those of the other multiple groups, with their proportion of total turnover declining from 11 per cent in 1961 to 7 per cent in 1971, since when there has been a stabilisation of their market share at this lower figure. The principal gains amongst the other chain companies have been in the grocery field, where the larger groups have improved their market share from 27 per cent in 1961 to 44 per cent in 1979.[20]

Within these broad patterns of growth and decline, nevertheless, variable circumstances can be traced in relation to both the more successful multiple groups and the weaker independent trades. Thus much of the achievement in performance terms of the large grocery chains has been at the expense of their own small branch outlets, where the closure rate (proportionally) has sometimes outpaced that of the small business community as a whole. Amongst the independent food traders, the survival rate has been conspicuously much higher for those affiliated to voluntary trading groups than for those remaining unaffiliated. Certain of the more specialised independent traders in the durable-goods and comparison-goods trades also registered considerable growth during the 1960s,[21] although their record since then has been rather disappointing. Other small specialists, however, such as the haberdasher, hatter and traditional outfitter have all but disappeared.

Nor is the picture presented one that is unique to Britain for similar changes have occurred in most advanced Western economies. In North America, the greatest period of decline in small, independent shops occurred in the 1950s (with the total number of establishments in the US falling from 537,000 in 1948 to 319,000 in 1963), during which there was a phenomenal increase in supermarkets (from 2,313 to 14,518 over the same period).[22] In continental Europe, particularly France and Belgium which have stronger traditions of independent ownership especially in the food trade, the decline in numbers of food shops occurred more recently and has been more closely bound up with the development of superstores and hypermarkets. Table 2.3 indicates the record of events that took place throughout the Common Market in the 1960s, although the figures here refer to changes in market share between the principal retail groups. The table, while somewhat dated for deducing contemporary trends, is also instructive for indicating what have been the prevailing structural characteristics of retailing within these countries during the post-war years — the chief differences being the greater strength of the multiples in Britain, the continuing importance of the co-ops in Denmark, the entrenchment of voluntary trading groups in West Germany, and the surviving dominance of small, independent traders in Italy and Luxembourg. It must be remembered, however, that numerically the independent traders remain by far the largest group of retailers in all countries, accounting for more than 80 per cent of all retail establishments even in Britain.

The Introduction of New Stores. The principal feature of change in Western Europe in the 1960s was the extensive development of super-

Table 2.3: Retailer Market Shares within the EEC during the 1960s

	Independents' % of total trade		Multiples' % of total trade		Voluntary chains' % of total trade	
	1962	1971	1962	1971	1962	1971
Belgium	77.6	71.7	4.0	9.9	6.8	7.0
Denmark	69.5	60.1	3.1	6.0	13.5	16.7
France	69.0	55.7	8.6	15.2	11.6	15.6
Germany	42.1	27.8	9.1	14.6	34.5	39.6
Ireland	82.0	65.1	6.0	10.2	5.3	13.2
Italy	93.2	85.6	1.3	3.0	2.0	5.6
Luxembourg	91.0	86.8	—	—	6.5	10.0
Netherlands	55.8	46.2	17.6	20.3	20.0	24.7
UK	47.6	39.7	24.0	29.1	6.9	10.0

	Co-ops' % of total trade		Dept & Variety's % of total trade		Mail orders' % of total trade	
	1962	1971	1962	1971	1962	1971
Belgium	3.0	2.4	8.1	8.2	0.5	0.8
Denmark	10.3	11.4	—	5.6	0.1	0.2
France	2.6	2.9	7.5	9.5	0.7	1.1
Germany	3.1	3.0	7.7	10.3	3.5	4.7
Ireland	—	—	6.5	11.3	—	—
Italy	1.3	1.7	2.1	3.9	0.1	0.2
Luxembourg	—	—	—	—	—	—
Netherlands	1.7	1.6	4.3	6.3	0.6	0.9
UK	10.2	7.1	8.8	10.3	2.5	3.8

Source: National Economic Development Office, Distributive Trades EDC, *The Distributive Trades in the Common Market* (HMSO, London, 1973).

markets. In 1961, there was a total of only 500 supermarkets in the nine countries that make up the present European Community; by 1971, there were 8,200 and estimates for the year 1981 range from 18,000-20,000.[23] Although Britain has some of the largest supermarkets in the Common Market, however, she now ranks sixth in terms of the number or density of supermarkets serving the national population, with only Italy and Ireland having a lower proportion. The overall impact created by supermarkets in Britain might therefore be judged to be less than in other countries, but such an interpretation must be qualified by the fact that supermarkets tended to be adopted earlier here than elsewhere and during the 1970s there was a marked increase in the sizes of stores. In 1969, only 16 per cent of new supermarkets built in Britain were larger than 10,000 square feet (930 m^2) in size; by 1980, 62 per cent of the new openings were more than 15,000 square feet (1,400 m^2) in size.[24] A similar trend had occurred in the US a decade before: the percentage annual increase in new supermarket openings declining from 63 per cent in 1958-9 to 12 per cent in 1966-7, but with the average size of new stores growing from 10,000 to 30,000 square feet (930-2,800 m^2) of gross lettable area.[25]

Table 2.4: Superstores and Hypermarkets in Britain and Continental Europe

	Growth in number of superstores and hypermarkets in Britain[a]		Number of hypermarkets in Europe in 1976[b]
1970	18	Belgium	72
1971	23	Denmark	4
1972	32	France	305
1973	44	Germany	538
1974	58	Italy	8
1975	71	Netherlands	12
1976	92	Switzerland	22
1977	115	Austria	23
1978	150	Finland	11
1979	172	Spain	5
1980	198	Sweden	36
		Britain	4

Sources: a. Unit for Retail Planning Information, *List of Hypermarkets and Superstores* (Reading, 1982).
b. MPC and Associates, *Hypermarket Expansion in Europe, 1973-76* (Worcester, 1976).

The trend to larger sizes in store operations, however, is most spectacularly seen in the development of superstores and hypermarkets, which many observers regard as a second or even third generation of supermarkets. Belgium is credited with having the first superstore, opened in 1962; France with the first hypermarket, opened in 1963.[26]

Although there are differences in the meaning of the terms superstores and hypermarkets (as we have indicated in Chapter 1), these are not universally recognised and indeed many statistical sources in continental Europe do not distinguish between them. Two alternative sets of figures based on different definitions are presented in Table 2.4, one describing the recent number of hypermarkets to be found throughout Western Europe, the other the growth of both superstores and hypermarkets in Britain.

Taking the two sets of figures together, what is most noticeable is the contrast in the amount of development to be found between Britain and most other countries, apart from the Netherlands and Denmark (and taking into account population differences). Britain has appeared to lag behind most other countries, primarily because of the strict planning controls exerted against these ventures in the late 1960s and early 1970s. The nature and effect of these controls will be elaborated upon in the next chapter. For the moment, it is sufficient to note that the lower rate in development of these stores has had two apparently beneficial results: firstly, there have been much less adverse trading repercussions on smaller shops than has occurred elsewhere in Western Europe; secondly, there has been much less radical change in the spatial pattern of retailing. Most of the superstores and hypermarkets developed on the Continent have been established in free-standing locations on the outskirts of towns and cities, thereby acting as major agents of the decentralisation process.

The greatest quantity of superstore and hypermarket development has been built in West Germany although the worst excesses in terms of suburban intrusion are usually associated with France. In 1981, there were 433 superstores and hypermarkets in France accounting for almost one-fifth of food sales and approaching 10 per cent of non-food sales.[27] The rapid expansion of these stores and particularly their burgeoning increase in size (up to 250,000 square feet or 23,250 m^2), however, led to the introduction of restrictive legislation in 1973 of a similar kind to that which had existed in a more informal way in Britain.[28] Belgium followed suit with the introduction of special controls in 1975 and the Netherlands tightened its vetting procedures in 1976. With special disincentives operating against the development of superstores and hypermarkets in Italy, Luxembourg and Eire, West Germany and to a lesser extent Denmark now appear to be the only countries which have not sought positively to discriminate against further development in the early 1980s. Even here, however, general planning laws are being more widely used than formerly to inhibit the locations which new stores can occupy, hence the heyday of large store development throughout Western Europe, but with the important exception of Britain, seems to be over.[29]

While North America has produced its own variant types of super-stores and hypermarkets in the form of junior department stores and giant superstores, a more interesting development in that continent has been the resurgence of the so-called convenience store, a modern equivalent to the old 'ma and pa' corner shop. The difference from the traditional type of establishment is a larger size (up to 5,000 square feet or 465 m^2), a more diversified merchandise mix emphasising liquor, petrol and magazine sales as well as grocery goods, sites either free-standing or adjacent to supermarkets or other large stores where there is ample parking and a trading policy that keeps most of them open 24 hours per day, every day of the week.[30] Since 1967, when the first full census was taken of these new developments, the number of modern convenience stores has grown from 8,000 to 35,000 at the present time.[31] The new stores have apparently flourished because the trend to increasing size and lower density of supermarket building has led to large voids occurring in the mass markets of the suburbs where there is little legacy of small, independent shops and oppor-tunities to 'top-up' on the bulk weekly shopping expedition are rela-tively limited. There has been some penetration of these stores into Western Europe in recent years and one may well expect to find increas-ing development, particularly in those countries which appear to have a surfeit of superstores and hypermarkets.

The Development of New Shopping Centres. The modern, purpose-built shopping centre is another phenomenon widely regarded as having its origins in North America, but the history of development here is more complex with innovations also occurring in Western Europe. As far back as the turn of the century, the first shopping centres in both continents were conceived largely in terms of new integrated con-courses or parades serving new planned communities. Where the Ameri-can influence came to prevail was in the development, mainly after the Second World War, of free-standing, car-oriented shopping centres located in the expanding suburbs. In 1950, there were estimated to be 100 new shopping centres of various sizes in the US; by 1981 the num-ber had grown to 22,750 and they accounted for 42 per cent of total retail sales within the country.[32] Several hundreds of the new shopping centres may be described as regional shopping centres, with sizes extending to one million square feet (100,000 m^2) of floorspace and having two or three department stores as well as a wide range of fashion and durable-goods shops.

Developments in Britain in the early post-war years were largely associated with town or city centre reconstruction schemes and the implementation of the precinct idea, particularly in conjunction with the building of New Towns. The introduction of covered or enclosed shopping malls, however, first seen in the Arndale shopping centre at Crossgates in Leeds in 1962, was very much based on American ideas. Since the mid-1960s, more than 150 similar centres have been built in Britain, the majority of them constituting town centre or 'in-town' schemes but a large number also serving as district shopping centres in outlying residential areas. Over the same period, a slightly larger number of open or partially covered schemes continued to be developed, although these gradually became less prominent during the late 1970s (Figure 2.2). Hillier, Parker[33] have estimated that, by 1981, some 69,847,000 square feet (6,500,000 m²) (gross) floorspace had been provided by all the various types of schemes, but that the annual provision had declined from a peak reached in 1976. Further development can be expected to take place throughout the 1980s but with an emphasis on smaller schemes being constructed in smaller sized places.

A similar record of events is to be found in other West European countries, with the greatest quantity of development again having been realised in West Germany. Here there were estimated to be 500 new shopping centres of all sizes in 1977, of which 57 were classified as being regional centres.[34] A contrast is found with Britain, however, in that several of these centres, as is the case in France and to a limited extent in Belgium, have been built in the American ideal of a 'greenfield' site. Apart from the district shopping centres referred to above, Britain does not have an 'out-of-town' centre in the true sense of this term, although the Brent Cross development and certain of the new centres of the new towns (especially Washington) come close to fulfilling this role. Several attempts have been made to establish 'out-of-town' centres in Britain, nevertheless, as we shall see later, but like most of the applications for hypermarkets and large free-standing superstores, they have not been allowed.

Rationalisation Within the Intermediary Trades. The revolutionary changes which have occurred in the methods and organisation of retailing have been paralleled in the intermediary trades of wholesaling, warehousing and bulk transference activities. The most spectacular manifestations of these changes and those developments creating most

Figure 2.2: The Annual Number of Openings of Town Centre Shopping
Schemes in Britain, 1965-1978

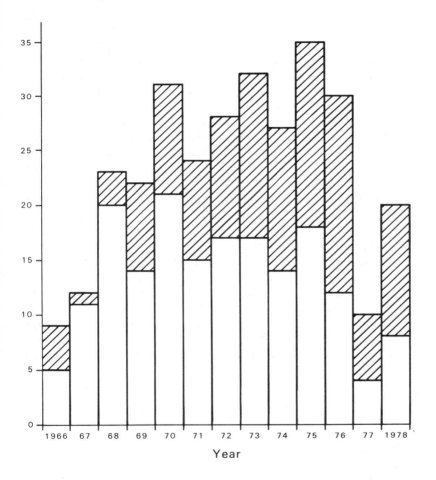

Source: Benninson, D.J. and Davies, R.L., 'The Impact of Town Centre Shopping Schemes in Britain — Their Impact on Traditional Retail Environments',
Progress in Planning, vol. 14, part 1 (1980), pp. 1-104.

pressure on local authorities have been the cash and carry operations and their sister outlets serving the voluntary chain organisations. The record of growth of these innovations closely resembles that for super-markets, so that there was very rapid expansion in the number of new wholesaling facilities in the 1960s but fewer openings, because of the trend to larger sizes, in the 1970s. Thorpe[35] has suggested that a peak number of 658 cash and carry depots was reached in 1971, following which there was a decline to 640 in 1975 but concurrently an increase in average floorspace (sales area) size from 17,101 square feet (1,589 m^2) to 24,464 square feet (2,274 m^2). (Nielsen surveys have provided an alternative estimate, suggesting there was a slight continuation in growth in numbers over the same period from 578 depots to 606.[36]) Whichever figures are correct, both mask the important fact that there remained a strong birth and death process at work in the industry, with 120 new depots opening during the first half of the 1970s (according to Thorpe), most of which were new purpose-built facilities replacing converted warehouses or factory buildings usually found in the inner parts of towns and cities. These new developments contributed an increase in floorspace of 38.7 per cent over that exist-ing in 1971, thus indicating that trade within the industry continued to expand; although in the second half of the 1970s, the signs were that real growth had begun to taper off.

The trend to larger sizes of depots that emerged in the early 1970s was accompanied by extensive rationalisation in the ownership of firms. Nineteen seventy-one marked the end of what Thorpe described as a period of small firm innovations and the beginning of a new period of conglomerate organisation. By 1975, 60 per cent of all cash and carry floorspace was owned or operated by the ten largest firms com-pared to 44 per cent only four years earlier. The most important firms were, and still are, Wheatsheaf, Nurdin and Peacock, Booker McConnell and Alliance. Considerable mergers and consolidations also took place between firms for common promotional activities and often in asso-ciation with the voluntary trade organisations. Thus the trade name of Trademarket represents a common marketing group comprising Wheat-sheaf, HBT and Watson and Phillip. Value Centres operate on behalf of Linfood, Morgan Edwards, James Hall and several others.

The last decade, however, has perhaps been more noteworthy for the expansion of direct manufacturing shipments to shops and retailer controlled distribution practices than the continued development of cash and carry operations. It is difficult to obtain summary statistics on the extent of this change but it goes hand in hand again with the growth of multiple stores and their own trend to larger sizes of units. It has been visibly obvious in the proliferation of various types of warehouses in suburban industrial estates and the emergence of new haulage firms that we have referred to before. So far these developments have been less contentious in a planning context than cash and carry operations (where abuses have sometimes occurred through wholesalers selling directly to the public and unemployment arising from the closure of delivery firms has been more conspicuous) but two much broader issues may need to be addressed in future. The first concerns the fear that the enormous trading strength of the retail multiples in Britain, when compared to other countries, has enabled foreign manufacturing companies to penetrate our market with their goods more easily than our own industrialists selling abroad. The effect of retail multiples buying 'in bulk' has led, and will continue to lead, to major changes in the means of production with all that this implies for employment and profitability in the manufacturing sector. Secondly, bearing in mind the rapid adoption of computers for improving the efficiency of physical distribution systems and the future potential for computerised remote shopping services that have been mentioned before, it is a relatively short step to conceive of a link-up between those terminals placed in the home and central processing units established in warehouses rather than conventional stores. In other words retailers, having entered the warehouse business in a major way in the 1970s, may find themselves seeking to use this as the basis to their selling practices by the end of the 1980s.

Growth and Decline in the Service Sector. Computers are already extensively used in customer transactions in a number of retail-related services, particularly by banks, travel agents and hotels and increasingly by betting shops, fast-food outlets and petrol stations. The service sector as a whole has been growing more rapidly in recent years and has become more technologically sophisticated than retailing itself, although there are of course considerable variations in the progress achieved by different categories of activity. Recent surveys conducted by the Unit for Retail Planning Information suggest that, from 60 shopping centres examined, there has been an average annual compound increase in all services of 2.9 per cent since 1965 while the growth in the number of retail outlets has been more static (an earlier period of actual decline being compensated for by a slight resurgence in the first half of the seventies).[37] The proportion of total establishments in the centres occupied by retailers declined from 80.1 per cent to 76.6 per cent in 1975 while the occupancy rate for services grew from 19.9 per cent to 23.4 per cent. The largest shifts in these proportions also occurred within the largest shopping centres, and the major contributors to this growth were the business and catering services.

While most of this growth, too, is associated with the larger financial institutions, the 1970s saw a considerable increase in the number of central and local government service provisions, ranging from job centres and recruitment outlets for the defence forces to citizens advice bureaux and libraries. Many new sports and recreational centres also sprouted, particularly in the inner areas of cities where government aid for the Inner City Partnership Schemes could be used. Both public and privately sponsored leisure and entertainment activities grew steadily during the decade although there were several casualties related to passing fads and the decline of cinemas continued unabated. Generally speaking, however, most of these new kinds of resources became concentrated in the largest places and the scope in opportunities found in smaller communities, particularly for younger people, was reduced rather than improved.

Those types of services that fared poorly during the decade were primarily the personal services, and particularly chemists, post offices, shoe repairers, photographers and men's hairdressers. Once again, it was the small independent businesses that suffered most decline, the number of chemists falling from 12,202 in 1971 to 10,623 in 1979.[38] The closure of chemists and also post offices causes considerable concern, especially in rural areas and the inner parts of cities, because of their essential social function in the dispensing of health aids, pensions and child allowances. The poor prospects for opening up new premises in suburban areas, because of the low marginal returns from such businesses, also mean that large numbers of households in outlying estates lack convenient accessibility to these facilities. The latest statistics, however, indicate a slight resurgence in the number of registered chemists in Britain.[39]

The category of vehicle-oriented services, including such activities as petrol stations, garages and body-repair shops, has experienced fluctuating fortunes in recent years because of the periodic high increases in petrol costs and its sensitivity to the general conditions of the economy. While there has been an underlying trend to continued growth in the demand for these services, however, the scope in opportunities for new businesses to originate has steadily been diminished. The problem here is less one of the financial risks and rewards involved and relates more to the lack of appropriate sites to be found in those areas where there is more chance of survival. Small businesses in the motor trade typically grow up from slender resources and an inception in semi-derelict property or premises that are extremely cheap to lease or buy. Ideally, these need to be located alongside main roads and in the middle or outer parts of the city, but strict planning policies aimed at the curtailment of ribbon development (as we have indicated in Chapter 1) have reduced the possibilities for such seed-bed conditions emerging. The prospect of a new set of free enterprise zones was seen by some as a means for alleviating these constraints;[40] but the choice of where the zones should be established has been disappointing in the sense that they embrace largely derelict land in inner city areas away from the main sources of consumer demand.

Potential Developments in the 1980s

Although the Conservative government has created a new political climate within which there will be a general loosening of planning constraints, it is unlikely that this will lead to radical departures in the spatial pattern of retail and commercial activity for some years to come. The economic circumstances of the country seem, in the short run at least, to be at odds with any new found freedom of movement. Most retail and commercial planning policies, too, are effected at the local level and remain subject to variable political views and the interpretation of goals and objectives which may have been formulated some time ago. There should be no shortage of ideas in the first half of the 1980s, however, which, once they have been tried and tested, may make a significant spatial impact towards the end of the decade.

A number of trends we have described for the 1960s and 1970s, therefore, can be expected to continue through the coming years, including the further demise of the small, non-specialist shop and the more inefficient branches of the chain companies. Although there will be further increases in the average sizes of most types of stores, nevertheless, there are several indications that fewer very large establishments will be built. Some of the signs pertain to the energy constraints we have noted before, particularly the question of service or maintenance costs, others to the degree of saturation that has set in in suitable sites and the probable decline in sizes of new shopping centres. Much of the growth in new stores in the late 1970s amongst those trades seeking additional economies of scale also took place through limited-line discount outlets, new convenience stores and catalogue showrooms, none of which represented physically large businesses or major occupiers of space.

Among the largest retail companies, too, the trend to diversification in product mix, or 'scrambled merchandising', has made many of their operations appear very similar. There is in some shopping centres now little difference between the assortment of goods offered by a Boots, W.H. Smiths, British Home Stores, Asda or Tesco, beyond the traditional specialisms offered by these groups. As the profit margins on staple commodities have declined, through the trend to bulk-buying and price-cutting campaigns, so more and more firms have sought to expand their selling of the newer, more lucrative lines of trade. The future competition between these firms is likely to become more intense with substantial amalgamations taking place and also some liquidations amongst those with the greatest similarities in functions. Some pundits have forecast that, by the end of the decade, there will be only four national supermarket chains left in Britain and two of the four department store groups.

Within the distinctions that were drawn earlier in the discussion on future consumer behaviour between an emerging category of mass merchandising retailers and a growing set of highly specialised businesses, most radical innovation in merchandising techniques will likely emanate from the latter rather than the former. The big conglomerates in retailing will perpetuate their efficiency and capitalise extensively on computer-based developments, leading ultimately to major changes in shopping habits, but it will be the small-scale entrepreneur at the sharp end of consumer demand who will best recognise new tastes and fads in the coming years. We have not yet seen a positive response to the growing sophistication of the elderly in the population, although there have been clear reactions in the past to the very young (such as from Mothercare), teenagers (the jeans outlets) and immigrant groups (through cafés and restaurants). Nor have we seen much integration of compatible lines of specialised trade, such as sports accessories, health foods and cosmetics into a single type of 'personal care' store, nor 'hobby centres' or those with an educational bias. In the provision of services, however, we have seen the emergence of health centres, recreational centres and entertainment complexes.

Much scope for innovation also exists for the smaller shopping centre developer, prepared to work against the prevailing trend of stereotyped mall developments and arcades. In North America, in recent years, a number of special-purpose centres have been created, some linked to office complexes and emphasising convenience trades, others to high-income suburbs and concentrating on fashion trades still others to a tourist clientele, providing craft products, fancy goods and leisure pursuits. Certain of these last centres have been established in old factories or warehouses, such as the Ghirardelli Center in San Francisco (occupying an old chocolate factory) and the Foundry in Georgetown, Washington, DC (occupying a former ironworks). The nearest parallel in Britain is the conversion of the old Covent Garden market complex to a new centre for small shops and service activities. With the general growth in specialised trades and the diminution of appropriate sites within the core part of the central area at rents that can be afforded, the opportunities for further developments along these lines would seem to be quite large.

The outer parts of the central area have been subject to little commercial redevelopment or renovation in recent years, since most local authorities and private developers have been preoccupied with improving the retail and office attractions of the core. They emerge perhaps as the most challenging parts of the entire city for new planning initiatives in the 1980s and might become increasingly attractive to investors if energy constraints reduce the advantages of suburban locations. Already some retail firms see them as an ideal base for new superstore development, where relatively large tracts of land can be acquired at comparatively low cost to support both extensive store facilities and surrounding car parking. So, too, there has been a 'natural' gravitation to these areas of a wide range of commercial activities including car dealers, builders' supply merchants, discount retailers and small wholesaling stockists. In a period of government cutbacks in expenditure and the liberalisation of planning controls, one cannot envisage this potential growth being accommodated and organised in grandiose schemes. Rather, encouragement should be given to ordered piecemeal development and the evolution of what we might call free-form business complexes to distinguish them from purpose-built facilities. If our former suggestions about the long-term impact of computer technology should come true, particularly in affecting employment levels and the nature of shopping behaviour, the central area frame might well become the future nexus of retailing and distributional activity.

Conclusion

This chapter has taken stock of the major changes which have occurred in consumer behaviour and the distributive trades within recent years and attempted to identify what new types of development can be expected to emerge in the future. It has inevitably been sketchy and focused more on the interactions between shopping demands and retail supply than other aspects of the distribution system. It has also been deliberately slanted to an assessment of those factors contributing to spatial rather than simply structural change. There is a complex mixture of considerations which means adjudicating the effects of market forces against a background of planning interventions, recognising the underlying shifts in political attitudes and socio-economic conditions and balancing the impact of spectacular short-run innovations against the more enduring and prevailing trends at work. A complete inventory of changes taking place, however, is perhaps less important than providing understanding about the basic pressures involved and the directions towards which the distribution system is headed.

There are in summary perhaps three major currents of change occurring within Britain. Firstly, there remains a fundamental metamorphosis of the distribution system from a traditional, fragmented network of activity that evolved in the first half of the century, to a more modern, integrated and technologically-based set of operations. This is most clearly seen in the continuing development of the large multiple chain stores and the extension of what we have called the modern forms of shopping with their emphasis on carborne, bulk-buying trips. Secondly, the new demographic circumstances of the late 1970s, together with a series of economic constraints but a different political outlook, mean that we are entering an age of greater uncertainty than has occurred in the last few decades, with the likely outcome being one of a slowing-down of past prevailing trends but some dramatic changes ensuing in individual elements of trade, not least among the bigger companies. We can also expect less ambitious local authority participation in large-scale developments but a more relaxed approach to the locational needs of new innovations. Thirdly, the most profound changes in the longer term are likely to result from the introduction of computer-based shopping systems and the extension of machine-controlled functions throughout the field of distribution. To date, there has been considerable progress in the application of computers to stock control, costing and checkout procedures but the visible, spatial effects have been small and it will not be until the public is drawn into a more direct interactive role on the ordering and purchasing side that the really dramatic repercussions will unfold.

References

1. See, for example, the case studies in Beaujeu-Garnier, J. and Delobez, A., *The Geography of Marketing* (Longman, London, 1980).
2. Drewett, R. *et al.*, *British Cities: Urban Population and Employment Trends, 1951-71* (HMSO, London, 1976).
3. Kirby, A., *The Inner City — Causes and Effects* (Retailing and Planning Associates, Corbridge, Northumberland, 1978).
4. Berry, B.J.L., *Urbanisation and Counter-Urbanisation* (Sage, New York, 1976).
5. US Department of Commerce and International Council of Shopping Centers, Washington, DC.
6. The organisation and structure of shopping trips in Britain have been described in a number of reports: Daws, L.F. and Bruce, A.J., *Shopping in Watford* (Building Research Establishment, Garston, 1971); Davies, R.L., *Patterns and Profiles of Consumer Behaviour* (University of Newcastle, Department of Geography, Research Series no. 10, 1973); Parker, A.J., *Consumer Behaviour, Motivation and Perception — A Study of Dublin* (University College, Dublin, Department of Geography, Research Report, 1976).
7. Central Statistical Office, *Monthly Digest of Statistics* (HMSO, London, annual).
8. Office of Population Censuses and Surveys, *General Household Survey, 1981* (HMSO, London, 1982).
9. Reported in the International Association of Department Stores, *Retail Newsletter*, no. 223, 1977.
10. Thorpe, D., *Food Prices — A Study of Northern Discount and Superstores* (Manchester Business School, Retail Outlets Research Unit, 1972); Unit for Retail Planning Information, *Hypermarkets and Superstores — Report of a House of Commons Seminar* (Reading, 1976); Wood, D., *Food Prices Near Three Superstores: Carrefour, Eastleigh; Tesco, Northampton; Sainsbury, Cambridge* (Social and Community Planning, London, 1976).
11. Davies, R.L. and Champion, A.G., *Social Inequities in Shopping Opportunities — How the Private Sector Can Respond* (Tesco Stores Limited, Cheshunt, 1980).
12. Department of the Environment, *National Travel Survey 1972/73* (HMSO, London, 1976).
13. Department of the Environment, *The Eastleigh Carrefour — A Hypermarket and its Effects* (HMSO, London, 1976 and 1978); Lee, M., *Caerphilly Hypermarket Study* (Donaldsons, London, 1973, 1975, 1979); Bruce, A.J., 'Shopping Trips to Superstores and Other Centres — Some Comparisons', Unit for Retail Planning Information, *Information Brief 78/6* (1978).
14. Evely, R.W., *The Impact of a Town Centre Superstore: A Study of the Effects of the Asda Store in Coatbridge* (Development Analysts, Croydon, 1977).
15. Office of Population Census and Surveys, *Population Trends*, vols. 21-26 (1980-1) (HMSO, London, 1980).
16. There are numerous trade articles on viewdata systems. See, for example, 'Hey Prestel! And Now We Have . . .', *Computer World*, 1 October 1980; Marti, J.V. and Zeilinger, A.J., 'Videotext in the High Street — the impact to retailer and consumer', *Retail and Distribution Management*, vol. 10, no. 5 (1982), pp. 21-6.

17. Kriss, M., 'Forcasting Likely Developments on the Basis of the US Experience', and Kelly, W., 'The Future of Video Shopping', in *European Congress on Automation in Retailing, EPOS 1982 — Conference proceedings* (London, 1982).

18. National Economic Development Office, Distributive Trades EDC, *Technology: The Issues for Distributive Trades* (NEDO, London, 1982); Union of Shop, Distributive and Allied Workers, *First Report of the Working Party to Review the Implications of New Technology on the Union's Membership* (London, 1980).

19. Business Statistics Office, *Business Monitors: Retailing, 1976 and 1980* (HMSO, London).

20. A.C. Nielsen Company Limited, 'Ten Year Trends in Grocers', *Nielsen Researcher*, no. 3 (1982).

21. Schiller, R., 'What the Census Says About Shops', *Chartered Surveyor*, vol. 109, no. 6 (1977), pp. 190-2.

22. US Bureau of the Census, *Census of Business* (Washington, DC, quinquennially).

23. National Economic Development Office, Distributive Trades EDC, *The Distributive Trades in the Common Market* (HMSO, London, 1973).

24. Institute of Grocery Distribution, *Retail Grocery Trade Review 1981* (Letchmore Heath, Hertfordshire, 1981).

25. Food Marketing Institute, *Facts About New Supermarkets* (Chicago, annual). See also, Padberg, D.I. and Thorpe, D., 'Channels of Grocery Distribution: Changing Stages in Evolution — A Comparison of the USA and UK', *Journal of Agricultural Economics*, vol. 25, no. 1 (1974), pp. 1-19.

26. Commission of the European Communities, The Aspects of Establishment, Planning and Control of Urban Retail Outlets in Europe, Commerce and Distribution Series 4 (Brussels, 1977).

27. Dawson, J.A., *Commercial Distribution in Europe* (Croom Helm, London, 1982).

28. Freis, J., 'Government Intervention in France: How Has it Affected Development?', *Retail and Distribution Management,* vol. 6, no. 2 (1978), pp. 41-5.

29. Davies, R.L. (ed.), *Retail Planning in the European Community* (Saxon House, Farnborough, 1979).

30. Kirby, D.A., 'The Convenience Store Phenomenon', *Retail and Distribution Management*, vol. 4 (1976), pp. 31-3.

31. National Association of Convenience Stores, *Annual Reports* (Falls Church, Virginia).

32. International Council of Shopping Centers and Shopping Center World, Washington, DC.

33. Hillier, Parker, *British Shopping Developments, 1978* and *Annual Supplements* (London).

34. International Association of Department Stores, *Retail Newsletter*, no. 222, 1977.

35. Thorpe, D. and Thorpe, S., *The Density of Cash and Carry Wholesaling, 1976: An Industry Reaching Maturity?* (Manchester Business School, Retail Outlets Research Unit, 1976).

36. A.C. Nielsen Company Limited, 'A Profile of the Cash and Carry Trade, Retail Chemists, Food and Unemployment in 1981', *Nielsen Researcher*, no. 2 (1982).

37. Unit for Retail Planning Information, *Service Outlets in Shopping Centres: Report of an URPI Workshop* (Reading, 1979).

38. A.C. Nielsen Company Limited, 'Pharmacies at the Crossroads?', *Nielsen Researcher*, no. 1 (1980).
39. A.C. Nielsen Company Limited, *Nielsen Researcher*, no. 2 (1982).
40. Banham, R. *et al.,* 'Non-Plan: An Experiment in Freedom', *New Society*, March (1969), pp. 435-43; Jones, P.M., 'The Prospects for Retailing – Enterprise Zones', *Estates Gazette*, vol. 259, no. 6053 (1981), pp. 1037-41.

3   THE CONVENTIONAL PLANNING PROCESS

Retail and commercial planning has been accorded relatively little formal or official status as a distinctive field of activity in Britain. There is no special ministry or government department concerned exclusively with the development of the distributive trades, as is found in industry, housing, transport and agriculture; nor is there a major council or advisory body that commands the influence that exists in the arts, sports and rural affairs. Retail and commercial planning is effected through a number of channels, the most important being the Department of the Environment in England and the Welsh and Scottish Offices, with supporting roles being played by the Department of Trade and Industry and the Department of Prices and Consumer Protection. These, besides providing a national set of guidelines and controls, oversee the implementation of policies conducted by local authorities, the most relevant of which emanate from the Planning, Estates and Consumer Services Departments, except in those cases where corporate planning has become strongly entrenched and where there may be separate committees dealing with retailing and commercial matters. At the local level, reference may be made to a retail and commercial plan but this is nearly always incorporated as a series of policy statements and specific proposals in the broader Development Plans. The Development Plans themselves remain primarily concerned with the exercise of spatial management controls over a wide range of activities; hence retail and commercial planning, in its current conventional form, is mainly oriented to the resolution of physical and land use problems, rather than those of a socio-economic kind.

Although retail and commercial planning is subsumed within a more general process of planning, and mainly Town and Country Planning, however, it offers, particularly in its shopping concerns, a rather discrete area of work within which a distinctive research methodology has emerged. There has been much progress in the development of survey and modelling techniques and, while these have sometimes been controversial in terms of their representativeness and reliability, they have made a significant contribution to the application of a systems approach in planning. The nature of this approach and its relevance to retailing considerations is elaborated upon in the final section of this chapter. We begin with a discussion of the role of central government and the statutory framework with which Development Plans are prepared.

The Role of Central Government

The absence of a separate government department dealing with the interests and problems of the distributive trades can be viewed with mixed feelings. On the one hand, it is arguable that, because distribution is one of the more efficient sectors of the economy, has a good record of labour relations and is accountable to the public at large through the business of shopping, it is well able to look after itself and will act relatively responsibly in the absence of bureaucratic encumbrances. On the other, the fact that excess profits may be earned by certain groups, that spatial inequalities in shopping provisions can arise and shortcomings often occur in the quality of goods sold, suggest that some comprehensive monitoring and regulation are required. During recent years, there has in fact been a progressive increase in legislation directed towards the distributive trades, but because this has emanated from several different governmental quarters, it has tended to lack clear direction and effect. The two main themes that are most apparent concern attempts to extend the scope of consumer protection and to curtail the growth of monopoly powers. Some of the more recent major pieces of legislation to be introduced along these lines are listed in Table 3.1.

There has been considerable revision and modification of the various Acts cited, in part reflecting changing political attitudes but also indicating some shortcomings in the earlier legislation that had been passed. The record regarding the development of consumer protection is better, by and large, than that for the containment of monopoly powers.[1] It has never perhaps been entirely clear as to what the objectives of limiting corporate growth and market dominance should really be. One assumes that, besides an overlap with consumer concerns, an attempt is made to foster fairer competition among the components of the distributive trades, with special regard being given to the well-being of small businesses. Little of the legislation directed to pricing constraints on the larger companies has been of benefit to small businesses, however; and the revocation of resale price maintenance in 1964, together with the imposition of the complex Value

Table 3.1: Legislation on Trading Policies and Consumer Protection

---

Shops Acts, 1950 and 1965
  dealt with opening hours and regulations concerning conditions of employment, particularly among young people.
Consumer Protection Acts, 1961 and 1971
  provided general powers to central government to protect the public from
  risks of death, injury or disease by imposing standards on goods manufactured
  and sold.
Weights and Measures Acts, 1963, 1976 and 1979
  dealt with the regulation of weighing and measuring devices and labelling of
  quantities of goods being sold in prepacked form.
Offices, Shops and Railways Premises Act, 1963
  specified the form of employer obligations for the health, safety and welfare
  of employees.
Resale Prices Act, 1964 and Restrictive Trade Practices Act, 1976
  abolished resale price maintenance although certain retail trades could claim
  exemption provided they were registered (consolidated in the latter Act).
Hire Purchase Acts, 1964 and 1965, and Consumer Credit Act, 1974
  developed protection for hire purchase customers and clarified contractual
  obligations over all moneylending operations.
Trades Description Acts, 1968 and 1972
  originally abandoned the requirement that goods should be marked with
  their origin of manufacture but re-invoked in 1972.
Fair Trading Act, 1973
  establishment of a Director General of Fair Trading to centralise the implementation of consumer protection policies and control monopoly powers.
Supply of Goods (Implied Terms) Act, 1973, and Unfair Contract Terms
Act, 1977
  tightened up on exclusion clauses in contractual agreements between consumers and retailers and finance companies.
Prices Acts, 1974 and 1975
  empowered central government to require that prices of goods be displayed
  in shops and service establishments.
Food and Drugs Act, 1976
  gave power to the courts to close food premises that were unsatisfactory on
  health grounds.
Price Commission Act, 1977 (and Prices and Incomes Board, 1965-71)
  required certain businesses with large turnovers to notify the Board, later
  Commission, of intending price increases; recommendations would then
  be made as to whether central government should intervene to control such
  increases.

Added Tax laws in 1973, have been seen to have worked to their
disadvantage. There has been much ambivalence, therefore, in central
government's attempts to influence the structural and organisational

characteristics of the distributive trades with virtually no positive or co-ordinated policies being applied. A similar criticism may be levelled at central government's approach to the spatial organisation of new and existing forms of distribution, where again it has tended to formulate policies in a reactive, piecemeal way rather than defining comprehensive, forward-looking locational strategies. In this case there is but a single authority involved, namely the Department of the Environment and its counterparts, the Welsh and Scottish Offices.

Responsibilities of the Department of the Environment (and Welsh and Scottish Offices)

The primary obligations of the Secretaries of State for the Environment and the Welsh and Scottish Offices (in so far as town planning matters are concerned) are to supervise the orderly use and development of land according to nationally agreed procedures. These procedures are laid down in the Town and Country Planning Acts of 1968 and 1971 for England and Wales (and 1969 and 1972 for Scotland) and earlier planning legislation, and involve three separate but interrelated kinds of responsibility. Firstly, the Secretaries of State are charged with providing guidance on the evolution of spatial patterns of activity as these take place at the local level. The main way in which this is effected is through the issue of advisory documentation, such as the handbook published on how Development Plans should be prepared[2] and a continuing series of circulars and memoranda about changes or priorities in policies that should be applied to specific problems. Secondly, they have a duty to ensure that there is consistency and continuity between local authorities in their implementation of development controls and their interpretation of the statutory requirements of planning. This is accomplished by vetting the Development Plans which are produced and by acting as arbiters in appeals made against local authority planning decisions. Thirdly, the Secretaries of State are also expected to initiate new ideas in the planning field and assess the practical implications of those constructive suggestions which may be made by others. This area of responsibility is less clear cut but can be seen at work in the special initiatives taken towards the New Towns (over which they have direct control) and inner city problems, the encouragement given a decade ago to the formulation of sub-regional plans, and their financial support for experimental projects in academic research centres.

It is in the first area of responsibility, the direction given to general policy-making, that the central planning authorities have been found most lacking in the retail and commercial field. Part of the reason for this has been the attempt to convey as much flexibility as possible in central–local governmental relations, and allow local authorities considerable power to meet their own special needs. Part refers, too, however, to the rather rigid guidelines suggested in the manual on Development Plans and the negative, restrictive tone of subsequent Development Control Policy Notes issued on the subject of large-scale retailing innovations. The proposals contained in the manual are elaborated upon in the next section of this chapter but they essentially amount to a view of how the distribution system should be analysed and its spatial characteristics controlled that was prevalent in the early 1960s before the widespread revolutionary changes in demand and supply had really taken hold. The Development Control Policy Notes reflect a largely hostile reaction to the revolutionary changes that emerged (at least in their earlier form) and contrast markedly with some of the more positive directives on town centre improvements that were issued shortly after the war.

Since 1969, the Department of the Environment has issued a number of Development Control Policy Notes that have a direct bearing on local authority reactions to new retail and commercial proposals. These are listed and briefly outlined in Table 3.2. The two most significant Notes in terms of the controversy that ensued are Nos. 13 and 14 dealing with out-of-town shops and shopping centres[3] and warehouses.[4] In the first case, local authorities were advised to treat each application for an outlying shopping facility (specifically proposals for new developments outside existing city, town or district centres) on its own merits but to be cautious about the granting of permission. It recommended that consideration be given particularly to whether the proposal might have an adverse effect on the trading conditions of existing shops, whether it might mean an undesirable intrusion into green belt land and whether there might be undesirable traffic implications resulting from the overloading of local roads. In accompanying circulars issued to local authorities, the Department of the Environment (Circular 17/72 and Welsh Office Circular 48/72) asked to be informed of any proposals for new developments over 50,000 square feet (4,600 m²) in gross floorspace (outside existing centres) in order that they could consider whether to 'call in' the applications for their own inspection. In Scotland, the threshold was set at 20,000 square feet (2,000 m²) (Scottish Office Circular 43/71).

These requirements were subsequently revised in 1976 in DOE

Table 3.2: Development Control Policy Notes on Retail and Commercial Matters

No. 3	Industrial and commercial development	

No. 3   Industrial and commercial development
Covers planning decisions dealing with industrial developments in three broad categories: light industrial, special industrial and general industrial. Also deals with offices, shops, betting offices and vending machines.

No. 5   Development in town centres
Calls for systematic planning which will take account of the needs of the town centre as a whole and lays down the framework for its future development and growth.

No. 8   Caravan sites
The main objects of policy are to enable demand for sites to be met in the right places and to allow sites, where permitted, to be established on a permanent or long-term basis. Caravans considered as homes, for holidays and for gypsies.

No. 9   Petrol filling stations and motels
Emphasis on what effects filling stations will have on traffic and road safety; also the design and appearance of filling stations. Similar considerations apply to motels.

No. 11   Amusement centres
Factors to be considered are their effects on amenity and the character of the surroundings and their effects on road safety and traffic flow. Noise, opening hours and kind of amusement are also considered.

No. 12   Hotels
The increase in demand for development of hotel accommodation calls for careful consideration of the surrounding environment, and effects of noise, traffic congestion and car parking.

No. 13   Large new stores
Distribution and retailing are adapting to meet changing economic and social circumstances, e.g. increased mobility of shoppers. Proposed sites will be assessed in terms of floorspace available and contribution made to overall policy objectives.

No. 14   Warehouses: wholesale, cash and carry, etc.
Deals with the problems of definition of warehouses, and emphasises their primary role for storage purposes.

Circular 71/76 (Welsh Office Circular 98/76 and Scottish Office Circular 65/78) to refer to proposals of over 100,000 square feet (10,000 m^2). While these later adjustments represented a relaxation in the vigil kept by central government over new potential developments, the seeds of a restrictive stance towards large suburban shopping schemes had already been well planted in local authority planning departments; and many of the subsequent Structure Plans to be produced contain clear statements that any such proposals will be resisted.[5] During the intervening period between the publication of the two sets of circulars, the Department of the Environment and Welsh Office called in 28 proposals for their own inspection of which only six were granted permission to proceed, a further one was allowed subject to qualifications being met, and the rest were refused.[6] Since then, however, there has been a slight upsurge in the number of outlying developments permitted, particularly on the outskirts of the larger industrial towns.

Development Control Policy Note 14, published in 1974, was designed to remove much of the ambiguity that had arisen over what properly constitute cash and carry wholesaling activities and warehouses for storage purposes as distinct from those engaged in a discount retail function. The problem had been recognised in Note 13, where oblique statements were made that proposals for commercial development that contained a retail selling practice should be treated in the same way as applications for large stores; but many local authorities remained unclear as to what their attitude should be, particularly over ensuring that any intended wholesale use did not subsequently become converted to a retail operation. Note 14 advised local authorities to require that any applications submitted to them include precise descriptions of the trading characteristics envisaged by the firm and that in granting permission for wholesaling or warehousing purposes they could stipulate that no later retailing operations could be performed. The Note also recognised, however, that there are some firms (such as builders' suppliers) that might legitimately be allowed to engage in both wholesaling and retailing activities; in which case it suggested that planning departments should stipulate the proportions of floorspace to be allocated the different functions, provided the application as a whole was deemed to be acceptable. The discrimination the Department of the Environment sought to impose was mainly aimed at those discounting facilities in the grocery and durable-goods trades that were seeking to establish themselves in industrial estates and using an initial cover of being wholesaling establishments to secure their sites.

Neither of the two Development Control Policy Notes have been entirely satisfactory as statements of policy. Note 13 had had the effect of promoting a concentration of new retail facilities within existing town and city centres, but there was no clear indication within this document, nor has one been given elsewhere, that this was the underlying goal in central government thinking. Moreover, the subsequent softer approach to applications for superstores and hypermarkets may be taken as a sign that the Department of the Environment was not itself entirely convinced of the wisdom of the earlier severe restrictions, particularly as many studies had shown that the impact of these developments was not nearly so great as had been feared and the benefits they brought, in terms of cheaper prices, were considerable in a period of excessive inflation. Note 14 can also be questioned as to whether it has penalised the introduction of discounting operations that would have brought significant price reductions to consumers as a by-product of enforcing the distinctions between wholesaling and retailing. But this Note again provides little direct recommendation as to what locational strategy should be adopted by local authorities over discount retail warehouses and if and when they should be restricted from industrial estates and diverted to other, specific kinds of locations. In seeking local authorities to adjudicate appropriate floorspace allocations for those mixed retailing and wholesaling uses, it seems further to be making demands that planning officials are not capable of or qualified to fulfil.

The hidden nature of most central government policies towards retail and commercial matters has led many planners to look for evidence of a prevailing view in the record of appeal decisions made by central government inspectors. In an appeal, an inspector has complete freedom to reverse a local authority decision over a planning application, to modify it according to certain conditions, uphold it or make it dependent on further constraints. While each case is obviously decided according to the specific circumstances surrounding it, a number of general principles are often invoked which tend to reflect a particular government stance. An interesting study has been made by Langton[7] of those types of policies that would seem to have been applied to a range of appeal topics addressed since 1975. Some extracts of his findings for those topics categorised under the heading of Town Centre Appeals are given in Table 3.3. For a more detailed assessment of planning inquiries held in connection with proposals for outlying shopping developments and discount retail warehouses, the reader is referred to some alternative studies by Lee and Kent and Lee and Roberts, and by Gibbs.[8]

The initiatives taken by central government with respect to the New Towns and conditions in the inner city have not generally included special proposals in the retailing or commercial field. By and large, the Development Corporations and planning teams working within the auspices of the Inner Area Partnership Schemes have been free to follow their own ideas, subject of course to the usual approval procedures. A number of the Development Corporations have established impressive New Town centre shopping schemes in recent years,

Table 3.3: Summary of Appeal Decisions on Town Centre Proposals in 1975

1.   Infill schemes in historic towns
      'Local authorities who have refused developments on design grounds, have seen their policies strengthened by the decisions of the DOE, in this area in 1975, where the buildings are within Conservation Areas, and in historic town centres'
2.   Larger-scale mixed redevelopments
      'The era of the ubiquitous indoor shopping mall development appears to be either slowing down, or else relatively few developers go to appeal. There were only two such schemes dealt with by a public inquiry, at Enfield, North London and Hereford. In both cases, the S. of S. directed that the applications be referred to him for decision, and not dealt with by the local authorities concerned'
3.   'Fringe' retail uses
      'The changes of use of a cinema to a shop, and of a public house were both dismissed, as was a group of buildings used for the auction and sale of goods and livestock'
4.   Non-retail shopping uses
      '. . . deals with uses traditionally found in town centres such as banks and estate agents, together with the more recent ones, in particular building society branch offices and employment agencies. These seem to have met with resistance from local authorities, on grounds that they are not proper shops and are "dead frontages" in shopping zones. In most cases, however, this view has not been upheld on appeal'
5.   Moral uses
      'A large number of applications for planning permission are still being refused for uses such as betting shops, prize bingo establishments and amusement centres. Very often the refusal is on flimsy planning grounds and in nearly all these cases the appeal is allowed. We have grouped these cases under "moral uses" because it seems to us that the underlying reason for refusal is an unspoken moral one'

Source: Langton, T. (ed.), *Planning Appeals* (Ambit, Gloucester, undated).

most notably at Runcorn, Washington, Telford and Milton Keynes. Washington provides a good example of where both a hypermarket and superstore have been integrated with a modern, covered shopping centre and how the town centre of a New Town can act not only as the focal point of shopping for the local urban population but as an out-of-town facility for an adjacent conurbation as well. Milton Keynes, despite uncertainty over its future trade area viability, demonstrates a visionary attempt to bring more humanism and architectural flair to a vast new retail complex. The record regarding new schemes in inner city areas is almost the reverse to that in the New Towns, amounting to a sorry saga of failures, both in commercial and environmental terms and ultimately in the social inadequacies found. Two major studies have recently been published[9] which have examined the nature of the deficiencies found, but apart from recommending considerable investment in the inner city, they provide little guidance on how such areas can be improved in a piecemeal or gradualist way. Their main recipe is one we have indicated before, namely to encourage the development of superstores in the inner city, both to act as a stimulus to retail regeneration and to provide a greater range of shopping opportunities at generally cheaper prices for the local population.

The regional development policies fostered through the former Regional Economic Planning Councils and Development Boards in Britain have likewise contained little reference to the part which new retail and commercial activities could play in regenerating employment or upgrading the environment of large areas. Where various regional studies have included research on the retail and commercial theme, it has usually been to project through to the future anticipated floorspace needs and assess the likely consequences on various centres of new developments in particular localities. Two of the best of the early studies were undertaken in Scotland, the Lothians Regional Survey Plan,[10] published in 1966, and the Grangemouth-Falkirk Regional Survey Plan,[11] of 1968, both of which provided comprehensive analyses of existing and required shopping facilities. Scotland retains the advantage over England and Wales in still maintaining regional authorities (nine regions with strategic planning powers having been created in the Local Government Act of 1973) which enables a broader perspective to be taken on retail and commercial matters. To date, the most complete work undertaken by these new authorities has probably come from Strathclyde.[12] Some of the earlier English regional studies are also noteworthy, however, for their incorporation of modelling exercises on the retail system, as can be found in the East Midlands and North West Studies.[13] Much of the theoretical and technical groundwork for these applications was also prepared by the sub-regional studies of the late 1960s and early 1970s, most notably the Leicester and Leicestershire, Notts-Derby and Severnside Studies.[14]

Supporting Bodies and Pressure Groups

Many of the shortcomings we have described with respect to central government's intervention in the distributive trades have to some extent been recognised by the various governmental departments themselves. Partly perhaps because of more pressing commitments in other areas and partly as a result of the need for outside opinion and expertise, the various departments have often solicited advice about what policies they should formulate and have both directly and indirectly established a number of advisory bodies and research groups. In addition, they are clearly conscious of a wide range of lobbyists and independent associations, representing the interests of both traders and consumers, who exert considerable pressure on where and when needed changes in legislation or planning procedures should be made.

Foremost among the more supportive bodies sponsored by central government is the Economic Development Committee for the Distributive Trades of the National Economic Development Office. Its influence was particularly marked during the last decade through three publications: *The Future Pattern of Shopping*,[15] a monograph dealing with trends in retailing through the 1960s and 1970s and indicating likely regional floorspace capacities for the 1980s; *Urban Models in Shopping Studies*,[16] a monograph reviewing various techniques available for forecasting floorspace requirements at the local level and also testing the consequences of alternative locational strategies for new stores and shopping centres; and *The Distributive Trades in the Common Market*,[17] a comparative work on the structure of retailing and wholesaling within member countries of the EEC and which also suggested relative levels of efficiency achieved. Other publications have also dealt with important questions regarding the changing nature of wholesaling; the training qualifications of the workforce engaged in distribution; the problems of retailing in the inner city (referred to earlier); and the likely impact of technological change.[18]

The first of the aforementioned works is especially significant for having made a number of recommendations about the objectives of retail planning and the ways in which the preparation of retail plans might be improved. While many of the conceptual and methodological suggestions have been taken up by local authorities, however, certain of the more general pronouncements seem to have been ignored. There were five particular charges made, in fact, which still appear as relevant today as they did ten years ago: that too much delay exists in the approval or rejection of applications for new development made to local authorities; that there has been too little co-ordination by central government of neighbouring local authorities' planning policies; that many local authorities have pursued extensive redevelopment schemes involving new shopping developments without regard to their repercussions on other centres; and, on the matter of regional policy, two criticisms that ought to be reported in full — '. . . although

the Department[of the Environment] has the responsibility of considering the structure plans of individual planning authorities and of co-
ordinating them, it has made no public statement of national or
regional strategy in respect of shopping provisions'; and '. . . regional
shopping strategy must be adequately developed: from our point of
view it is immaterial whether this function is carried out by regional
planning councils, by provincial councils or by the Department itself,
so long as it is carried out effectively'.[19]

This publication also suggested that a new research centre be established to serve the needs of both planners and retailers particularly
through the provision of updated information about trends and developments in the distributive trades. This the Department of the
Environment responded to and, in conjunction with several firms and
local authorities, founded the Unit for Retail Planning Information in
1975. The Unit itself has now published a wide range of documentation
dealing with such topics as floorspace, turnover, consumer behaviour,
the characteristics of superstores, hypermarkets and discount retail
warehouses, shopping centres, services, retail employment and many
others. In 1980, however, it experienced financial difficulties and
governmental involvement was withdrawn, although the Unit was
subsequently taken into private ownership and continues to operate
on more slender means. Other bodies which have provided a useful
research contribution to central and local government include the
Building Research Establishment (hitherto focusing on behavioural
studies and the development of modelling techniques), the Geography
Departments at Newcastle University (mainly through work on redevelopment schemes) and St David's College, Lampeter (emphasising the
problems of small shops), and the College of Estates Management at
Reading University (specialising in the development process). In the
past, the now defunct Retail Outlets Research Unit of the Manchester
Business School was an important source for detailed case studies on
developments in the distributive trades and held several seminars on
some of the more specific issues confronting local authority planners.

Two of the more active trading associations which take a special
interest in planning issues are the Retail Alliance and British Multiple
Retailers' Association (formerly the Multiple Shops' Federation). These
were particularly vociferous in the early 1970s during the debate over
hypermarkets; and more recently they have argued strongly for an
improvement in such physical provisions as car parking and goods
servicing facilities. A group known as the Planning and Transportation,
Research and Computation Company (PTRC) has conducted a number

of annual seminars about retail planning issues and these have become an important forum for an exchange of views between the public and private sectors. The Institute for Grocery Distribution has published several reports about the development of supermarkets and superstores, although the orientation of these is towards providing facts and figures rather than identifying locational problems and needs. Unlike many continental European countries, Britain has no special research institute concerned with the interests of small shops, the Small Firms Service being preoccupied with the manufacturing sector.

Central government, however, has been responsible for creating special bodies to represent consumer interests and intervene in trading disputes on their behalf, if necessary, as we have indicated. The two principal agencies are the National Consumer Council and the Office of Fair Trading. The National Consumer Council has no statutory powers but acts as a pressure group for the extension of consumer rights over a wide range of areas, such as advertising standards, the law and government information services, and also represents the consumer on a number of government committees and the nationalised industries. The Office of Fair Trading provides the executive function of ensuring that consumer interests are met by informing the public of their entitlements, issuing codes of practice for different traders to abide by and recommending to the Consumer Protection Advisory Committee where court action should be taken over cases of consumer neglect. These powers are supported by the independent and voluntary codes of practice on goods marketed put forward by the British Standards Institution and the Retail Trading Standards Association. Many voluntary organisations also exist amongst consumers themselves, of course, the most important being the Consumers' Association which seeks to influence the standards of goods sold by making comparative analyses of like kinds of products and giving publicity to their strengths and deficiencies – most notably through the magazine *Which?*. This type of information service also extends through to a myriad of local groups, and includes the comparative price surveys undertaken by many local authority Consumer Services Departments. Last, but not least, are the Citizens Advice Bureaux which assist the general public, among other things, to find their way through the tangle of official and unofficial channels of support that can be drawn upon!

Development Plans and Development Control

The new planning system ushered in by the Town and Country Planning Acts of 1968 (England and Wales) and 1969 (Scotland) and later consolidated in 1971 and 1972 attempted to introduce a more flexible and democratic approach to plan-making on the part of local authorities than had hitherto been found. A distinction was drawn between the preparation of a series of Structure Plans and Local Plans, with the former providing essentially strategic guidelines on development and the latter more detailed specifications on where, when and how any development could or should take place. The two types of plans, however, were conceived in advance of the local government administrative reorganisation that took place in 1972 and 1973 (for Scotland) and the original intention was that both plans would be produced by the same authority (in a one-tier system of administrative units throughout the country). The subsequent implementation of a two-tier system of local authorities created a separation of powers in plan-making that has led to a number of practical difficulties (particularly in England and Wales) over the integration of the plans and their compatibility in meeting common underlying objectives.[20] The Scottish circumstances are somewhat different for the 1973 Act here gave a greater degree of independence to the preparation of Local Plans, requiring that these be produced as quickly as possible irrespective of progress achieved on the Structure Plans.

Structure Plans

It is important to note that while the two new sets of plans are collectively referred to as Development Plans, they differ substantially from the development plans produced under the 1947 Town and Country Planning Act. The differences are particularly marked in the case of Structure Plans which, rather than being embodied in a map form, comprise a written statement of policies to be pursued and illustrations of how these may be realised spatially in a series of schematic diagrams. There is no rigid zoning of land use allocations, only a broad indication of what sorts of activities would be preferred in certain locations. Structure Plans are prepared not only for the shire and metropolitan counties but also for county boroughs and other important places, however, and in this respect resemble the scale of planning under the old system, which provided County Maps and Town Maps. The Scottish procedure is again at variance with this, where Structure Plans may be prepared for parts of the new regions and can serve in fact as an alternative to the requirement for Regional Reports.

The general functions of the Structure Plans are specified in the 1970 manual on Development Plans:

1. to interpret national and regional policies appropriate to a county or large town
2. to establish aims, policies and general proposals for a county or large town
3. to provide a framework for the preparation of Local Plans
4. to indicate action areas for intensive treatment or priority in planning
5. to provide guidance for development control effected by Local Plans
6. to provide the basis for co-ordinating decisions between different authorities
7. to bring before the Minister and public the main planning issues and decisions arrived at.

For organisational purposes, these functions need to be pursued in terms of a set of subjects or problem areas which the manual also identifies. Special reference is made to the important topics of employment, housing and transportation, but the distributive trades are disaggregated and specific suggestions made only for the category of shopping. The sorts of concerns that are considered to be relevant here are listed in Table 3.4.

A general procedure for the preparation of a Structure Plan is also indicated in the manual and parts of which are apparent in Table 3.4. A Report of Survey is first required that essentially involves a diagnosis of the existing conditions for any subject or problem area. Thus, for shopping, the diagnosis has typically included an inventory of retail floorspace throughout an area, calculation of the turnover achieved by certain centres and some assessment of the relative accessibility and health of competing facilities. This has been enjoined by estimates of emerging trends in consumer demand and retail supply and forecasts of what future developments will need to be accommodated. Alternative strategies for the allocation of new resources and improvement of existing conditions have then been tested, ultimately leading to the selection of a preferred policy programme or overall plan. It is this final stage that constitutes the Written Statement on decision-making within the Structure Plan. It will have been arrived at through public participation exercises and consultations with relevant, concerned bodies and be subject to continued monitoring and review.

Table 3.4: Example Contents of Shopping Considerations in a Structure Plan

Policies, general proposals and related information[1]	Supporting information[2]

Policies, general proposals and related information[1]

1 General policy to e.g.
   a establish hierarchy of centres
   b foster growth in town centres
   c create new centres
   d develop district centres
   e rely on mobility in rural areas
   f relieve congestion in town centres

2 Quantity floorspace at significant stages

3 Distribution of 2 in
   a main centres
   b whole area

4 Criteria and policies for
   a location of new development in relation to e.g.
      i distribution of population
      ii other centres
      iii public transport
   b local planning and development control in relation to e.g.
      i servicing and storage
      ii other uses
      iii distribution depots and warehousing
      iv car parking
      v principal routes
      vi underused backland
      vii pedestrian safety
   c existing development in relation to e.g.
      i conservation
      ii conversion

5 Priorities and phasing e.g.
   a action areas including nature of treatment
   b linkages; removal of shops from astride traffic route

6 Implementation e.g.
   a promotion and assistance by local authorities
   b assembly of sites by local authorities
   c scope of private development

Supporting information[2]

Survey
A Existing situation analysis of e.g.
   i floorspace by centres
   ii turnover by trade and centres
   iii accessibility of centres
   iv prosperity of centres

B Recent trends affecting shopping provision e.g.
   i retailing methods
   ii mobile shops
   iii customers' habits
   iv changes in transportation

C Commitments e.g.
   i new shopping centres
   ii new pedestrian precincts

Estimates
D Future changes e.g.
   i increases in personal income
   ii increased expenditure per head
   iii changes in retailing methods

E Future needs e.g.
   i more out-of-town centres
   ii fewer shops in main centres
   iii more district centres

F Constraints e.g.
   i lack of adequate access to centre
   ii lack of plots of adequate size for development

G Assumptions (about D, E & F), e.g.
   i future income level
   ii attraction of out-of-town centres

H Alternative policies e.g.
   i strengthening of suburban facilities to enable town centre to function more effectively
   ii provision of additional floorspace in central area

I Conclusions in relation to H and leading to policies and general proposals in the plan

J Programme (10-year)

Notes: 1. Set out in Written Statement.
2. Set out in Report of Survey and summarised in Written Statement.
Source: Department of the Environment and Welsh Office, *Development Plans — A Manual on Form and Content* (HMSO, London, 1970).

The key spatial elements of the preferred policy programme are also summarised in a schematic diagram as we have indicated. Extracts of an example given in the manual for shopping proposals in a county borough are shown in Figure 3.1. The chief features include designation of a hierarchy of centres, indications of where new retail development may be encouraged and redevelopment undertaken, and proposals for curtailing the spread of a commercial area, such as in this case along a main road. A separate diagram or inset (Figure 3.2) may be provided for policies to be applied to the central area or indeed to any action

Figure 3.1: Structure Plan Shopping Proposals for a County Borough

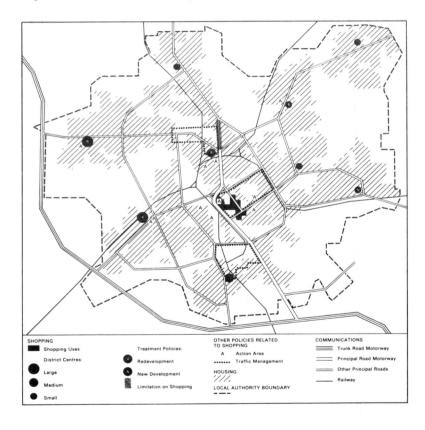

Source: Department of the Environment and Welsh Office, *Development Plans —
A Manual on Form and Content* (HMSO, London, 1970).

Figure 3.2: Structure Plan Shopping Proposals for a Central Area

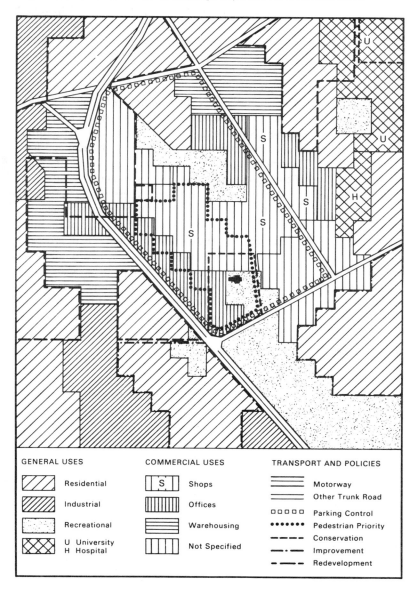

Source: Department of the Environment and Welsh Office, *Development Plans —
A Manual on Form and Content* (HMSO, London, 1970).

area that may have been identified. Policies directed towards the inter-mediary trades will generally have been incorporated in a diagram on industry and/or employment and some services embraced within a diagram on recreational or leisure activities.

The general format of Structure Plans has been described here, rather than individual cases actually produced by local authorities, for by and large the example specifications laid down in the manual for retail and commercial policies have been quite faithfully followed. This means that, in the absence of clear central government directives on strategy, most current retail and commercial policies at the broad scale of urban planning in Britain remain rooted in physical and loca-tional concerns. The emphasis is placed on examining the existing stock of resources and then adjudicating what corrective action needs to be taken to reduce any spatial imbalances found. There is no reference to how the distribution system can be helped to become more efficient or consumers provided with a wider choice and cheaper range of shopping provisions. Nor is there consideration for the employment prospects afforded by new stores or the social problems that may accompany the decline of small shops. This lack of socio-economic perspective is not only disappointing but seems at variance with the wider stated inten-tions for Structure Plans: 'the aims of the plan should be designed to satisfy social and economic aspirations as far as possible' and 'the term structure is used here to mean the social, economic and physical systems of an area'.[21]

Local Plans

Local Plans in England and Wales are intended to elaborate on the proposals of Structure Plans for specific areas. They are prepared by the district authorities and are expected to 'inform the public of the [district] authority's intentions, property owners of how their interests are affected, and intending developers where the opportunities lie as far as these can be foreseen'.[22] They therefore provide a set of mainly land use designations which, because they need to be specified in detail, are shown on a map with an Ordnance Survey base to give clear indica-tions of the scale and extent of any changes to be made. The map for a Local Plan is therefore a much more authoritative document than the diagram in a Structure Plan and serves as the basis for implementing development controls. It differs from the maps produced under the old planning system, however, to the extent that it defines only sites where an alteration to existing uses is proposed and hence is a 'proposals map' rather than a comprehensive 'zoning map' for an entire area. It is accompanied by a Written Statement which describes the problems and potential of specific sites, alternative ways in which change may be effected and how and why the local authority has come to the decisions that it has. Public consultation and participation in the decision-making process are again expected to take place. The system of Local Plan preparation in Scotland is not significantly different from this, although Local Plans are a mandatory requirement of the Minister when they are left to the discretion of local authorities in England and Wales.

The diverse nature of the issues to be confronted at the local level and the need to retain some flexibility in dealing with them has led to three different types of Local Plans being produced. First are the District Plans which are designed to cope with a wide range of inter-related considerations over relatively large areas. They might refer to the development programme envisaged for a particular town, extensive rural tract within a county or the central area of a major city. Second, there are Action Plans that are concerned with areas that are intended to undergo immediate and intensive change as a result of renewal, redevelopment or new development proposals. Examples here would include the improvement of a housing area, commercial revitalisation in a town or city centre, and the design and establishment of a new recreational facility. Third, there are Subject Plans which deal with a more systematic treatment of a particular problem area, either throughout the country as a whole or for large parts of it. The subjects or problem areas are typically conservation, landscaping, mineral extraction and the like. These plans may also define the spatial limits within which special policies apply, such as in conservation zones or areas of outstanding natural beauty, etc.

As far as retail and commercial matters are concerned, the three types of Local Plans offer much scope for addressing a wide variety of issues, as some of the examples have already indicated. Generally speaking, however, relatively little use has been made of the machinery available to provide more than a broad shopping policy within a District Plan, examine the implications of a new centre in an Action Area Plan and calculate additional retail floorspace that can be absorbed throughout a large area in a Subject Plan. Physical considerations have again tended to overshadow those of a more socio-economic kind, although a more favourable balance has been achieved in some of the more recent Local Plans. Such criticism is easy to render, however, and must be measured against the time, resources and expertise available within district authorities for a broader range of problems to be confronted. Too often within a planning department, the identification of significant issues within distribution is left to a single, junior officer and any proposals formulated for a more visionary approach to their treatment become dissipated among a number of other policies ostensibly concerned with more important events.

The guidelines furnished by Structure Plans and the more specific proposals contained in Local Plans do not mean, of course, that any developmental intentions that appear in harmony with these will be automatically allowed. Such applications will be received sympathetically, but the statutory control over development follows a series of regulations that are themselves not manifest in any diagram or map but refer back to the law. The chief instruments employed for the vetting of applications remain the Use Classes Order and the General Development Order which pre-date the introduction of the new planning system. These are intended to define what constitutes development, for it is development rather than simply change that is subject to control. The Use Classes Order was described in Chapter 1 and prescribes categories of land use where, generally speaking, any functional alteration to a property that means a shift from one class to another (as from a retail establishment to a warehouse) becomes development and thereby needs permission; but functional alteration within the same class (as from a grocer's shop to a toy shop) is allowed, subject perhaps to meeting building or structural regulations. The General Development Order exempts certain activities from these constraints, such as particular kinds of local authority developments or the construction of agricultural buildings, and has less relevance to retail and commercial concerns (except that a few restricted retail activities, such as hot food shops, can be converted to other types of shops but not vice versa). In addition to these development controls, there are also other assorted pieces of legislation that affect the workings of the distributive trades, including the Advertisements Regulation Act (revised in 1971), which governs the size and location of display material, the Transport Act (1968), which prohibits the use of roads by vehicles at certain times of the day and can thereby affect delivery schedules, and special purpose enactments, such as the Caravan Sites and Control Development Act (1960), designed to contain the proliferation of new caravan parks to selected areas. In view of the concentration of many business activities within town and city centres, special observance must be given too to the laws on amenity and conservation.

Methodology and Research

Although the preparation of retail and commercial plans, within the framework of Structure and Local Plans, has been weak in terms of goals and objectives and a comprehensive approach to problem-solving, the common emphasis on controlling the spatial pattern of physical change has led to much refinement of the technical aspects of planning. This is particularly seen in the methodology now widely employed for shopping appraisals at the county level where there has been considerable adherence to the procedural suggestions of the manual on Development Plans and also the contemporaneous publications of the National Economic Development Office referred to earlier. There has been growing criticism in recent years of some of the techniques utilised particularly for modelling purposes, but much of this criticism has been directed towards the way in which the techniques have been applied, rather than the inherent value of the techniques themselves. Shopping models have suffered much the reaction that the systems approach to planning in general has experienced, which is bound up with a wider critique of the philosophy rather than methodology of the field.

Our view of what the major methodological elements have been during the last decade of retail (Structure) planning is summarised in Table 3.5. It should be stressed that this is a statement of what has been seen to exist rather than what is desirable in the future. Five main functions have been identified involving a range of both statistical and

Table 3.5: Summary of the Major Methodology Employed in Retail (Structure) Planning

Function	Approach	Subject areas and general procedures	
		Demand	Supply
Description	Survey and analysis	Behavioural patterns (consumer interviews)	Structural characteristics (retail inventories)
Forecasting	Step-by-step approach	Expenditure trends (linear extrapolations)	Sales and floorspace (ratio techniques)
Allocation	Interaction models	Accessibility conditions (gravity models)	Potential development (entropy models)
Evaluation	Public consultation	Needs and preferences (postal questionnaires)	Growth prospects (invited comments)
Organisation	Hierarchical principle	Spatial inequalities (neighbourhood provisions)	New innovations (integrated centres)

more qualitative techniques that are grouped under the headings of studies of demand and supply. The ordering of these functions shows a general progression in plan preparation, but there has been no universal adoption of this and some avenues may in fact have been pursued simultaneously by certain local authorities.

Description

All local authorities, however, have begun with a description of the existing shopping system as a prelude to diagnosing its relative strengths and deficiencies. The scope and depth of these studies has varied but the most ambitious projects have involved countywide consumer surveys and retail inventories.[23] Some authorities incorporated questions on shopping habits and attitudes in their sample (10 per cent) household questionnaire surveys of 1976 to compensate for the cancellation of the Census of Population for that year; others have relied on pavement interviews in the major shopping centres of their areas. In each case, the broad objective has been to collect information on the spatial and socio-economic characteristics of behaviour, to serve as a basis for identifying areal imbalances in shopping provisions and disadvantages that may accrue to particular groups. The retail inventories have typically focused on the number of establishments and floorspace sizes of individual shopping centres throughout an area, intended to give both an overall indication of the existing stock of resources to be found and a further insight into where there is over- or under-endowment in provisions. A few authorities have also attempted to assess the environmental and trading conditions of shops and centres to help discriminate between those with growth prospects or those in decline.[24] Both the consumer surveys and retail inventories conducted may also have been designed in part to collect data to use as inputs in subsequent modelling exercises.

Forecasting

The second concern in the process of plan preparation has usually been one of providing estimates of likely future trends in demand and supply, both to obtain a broad picture of what pressures would materialise and to establish more specifically how much further growth in retailing can or should be accommodated. The key variables here have been the trends expected to occur in expenditure amongst different consumer groups and the sales levels likely to be achieved for different trade categories within shopping centres. Both sets of projections have ultimately been based on extrapolations of national or regional figures which, because the changing social and economic conditions of the 1970s and the insensitivity of global statistics to local circumstances, have led to many erroneous forecasts in recent years. Future amounts and patterns of expenditure have usually been calculated for the trade areas of the largest shopping centres within an urban area, and the urban area as a whole, from relationships between anticipated population growth and extrapolated figures from the annual *Family Expenditure Survey*.[25] These may indicate in themselves where new sources of demand will need to be met in the future but they have also been converted to likely sales levels to be achieved in centres and throughout the urban area as a check against the separate projections made for this variable. Sales forecasts have then been derived from past data contained in the Censuses of Distribution and/or the more recent Retail Inquiries and have usually been split into the categories of convenience and durable-goods (or comparison-goods) trade. These again have been used to suggest where growth or decline will take place; but since the planner's real interest has been in determining what sorts of changes in floorspace will or should occur and how much overall floorspace can be supported in the future, the sales figures have been converted by ratio methods into expected floorspace sizes. These conversions have been made not only for the different categories of trade referred to above but also for broad organisational types of retailing (particularly the split between independents and multiples) to try to compensate for some of the variations in sales to floorspace performance standards between modern and older store operations.[26] Even so, the resulting figures have not been very reliable and have been much criticised for their insensitivity to the variable performance standards between individual firms.[27] Taken together, therefore, the various steps we have outlined in the business of forecasting have doubtful validity and have not been significantly improved (because of data inadequacies) by the application of alternative statistical techniques, particularly regression analysis. Their merit seems to lie in establishing some kind of yardstick against which to monitor actual change. A traditional example of this type of work, described as a 'step-by-step' approach, is summarised in Figure 3.3.

Allocation

An alternative method of projecting the future capacity of the retail system has been to use some form of spatial interaction model. However, since these models, particularly the so-called 'retail potential' model, depend on independent forecasts about expenditure and sales

Figure 3.3: The Traditional Step-by-Step Approach to Retail Forecasting

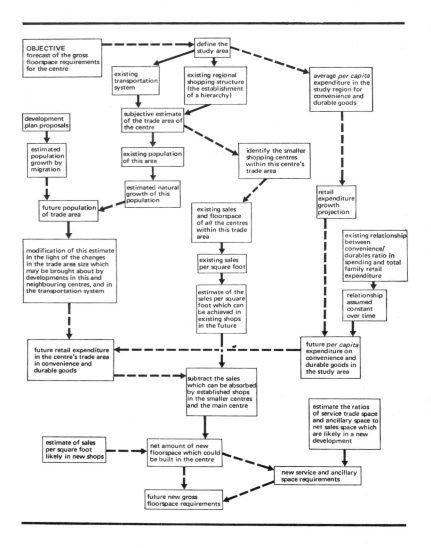

Source: National Economic Development Office, Distributive Trades EDC, *Urban Models in Shopping Studies* (NEDO, London, 1970).

and then serve mainly to redistribute these between areas and centres, it seems preferable to treat them as part of the allocation function and to discuss their role in determining precisely where and in what form any new retail floorspace should be established in the future. There are two ways in which this has been approached in the past. First, some authorities, for example Birmingham Corporation, have used a gravity model to calculate the trade areas around centres (both for a present and future time period) in terms of a series of probability contours. The basic procedure for this was laid down by Huff[28] in 1963 and is described in the first half of Table 3.6. By examining changes in the

Table 3.6: The Basic Forms of Two Types of Spatial Interaction Models

A. The Huff Model

$$Pij(\hat{n}) = \frac{Wj \times Cij^{-\hat{n}}}{\sum\limits_{j=1}^{m} Wj \times Cij^{-\hat{n}}}$$

Where

$Pij(\hat{n})$ is the probability that a resident in zone i would shop in centre j
Wj is a measure of the attractiveness of a centre
Cij is the travel time between i and j
$\hat{n}$ is an independent variable to be estimated
m is the total number of zones within an area

B. Wilson's Entropy-Maximising Model

$$\sum\limits_{i=1}^{m} Sij(\hat{a}, \hat{b}, Ai) = \text{sales in centre j}$$

from
$$Sij(\hat{b}, Ai) = Ei \times Pi \times Wj \times Ai\,(\hat{b}) \times exp.(-\hat{b} \times Cij)$$
and
$$Ai(\hat{b}) = (\sum\limits_{j=1}^{m} Wj \times exp.\,(-\hat{b} \times Cij)\,)^{-1}$$

Where

Sij is the flow of retail expenditure from residential zone i to a centre j
Ei is the mean expenditure per head in zone i
Pi is the population in zone i
$\hat{a}$ and $\hat{b}$ are independent variables to be estimated
Ai is the balancing function
Other notations as above.

Source: Openshaw, S., 'Some Theoretical and Applied Aspects of Spatial Interaction Shopping Models', *CATMOG Series No. 4* (Geo-Abstracts, Norwich, 1975).

probability surfaces over time, a clearer insight can be gained of changing accessibility conditions in different areas and where certain centres appear to gain over others. Corrections to any imbalances found can be made by assigning new centres to designated areas or encouraging redevelopment within existing centres – and the trade area implications arising from this can then be further simulated. The second, more common approach has been to use a 'production constrained' model of the retail potential type to test out the resulting ramifications of alternative strategies about assumed future sizes and locations of centres. The different strategies may involve concentrating most new growth within the dominant city centre, encouraging more strength amongst a series of district shopping centres, allowing certain new, large, free-standing stores to be established (such as hypermarkets, superstores and discount retail warehouses) or promoting some combination of these. The earliest procedure used for this was the Lakshmanan-Hansen model[29] but attention then turned to Wilson's entropy-maximising technique,[30] which is summarised in the lower half of Table 3.6. The main object was to see what impact or competitive effects the enlargement of selected centres or the creation of new ones would have on the rest of the retail system. To this extent the use of spatial interaction models also became part of the evaluation stage in retail plan preparation; and Coelho and Wilson have taken them further into the final design stage with their suggestion of a model for the optimum locations and sizes of shopping centres.[31] Clearly, spatial interaction models can perform a multi-purpose role in retail planning and a wide variety of different types of models are now in use. Their record of success in prediction has not been good, however, and there has been much criticism of their application from poor data sources (when erroneous calibrations can be made).[32] The general requirement is that the models must be calibrated against information on shopping trips, either mean trip lengths or expenditure patterns, rather than the characteristics of centres.

Evaluation

Relatively little attention has been given to the evaluation of alternative shopping strategies for the accommodation of future growth, particularly in the conventional sense of cost-benefit analysis or the use of goals-achievement criteria.[33] This stems back in part to the lack of clear guidance on what the real objectives of any strategy should be. Spatial interaction models have been used in a specific way to measure the trading effects of new centres or large stores, as we have indicated, but this should not be undertaken in isolation from environmental and social considerations. (In a slightly different context, when privately sponsored shopping proposals have gone to appeal, the element of the trading impact has been measured against a wide range of other factors, such as the economic benefits to be realised by consumers, the repercussions on local traffic, the degree of land use compatibility to be found, etc.; and indeed some inspectors have had the experience of being confronted with two sets of conflicting model results, one from a local authority and the other from the applicant.) More generally, the way most local authorities have sought appraisal of their alternative proposals has been through public participation exercises. There has been a statutory duty to provide publicity to the Report of Survey of a Structure Plan and the Written Statement has been subject to an examination in public; but most authorities have also actively drawn on public views at a time when they have narrowed down their own viewpoints to a few choices. Sometimes this has involved an ambitious questionnaire survey with individual households; at other times a more limited campaign conducted through a local newspaper. Retailers, developers and other informed groups have been canvassed for a more definitive, positional view; and in the case of Cheshire County Council, a special panel on shopping (made up of representatives of the general public and concerned bodies) was established in the mid-1970s to advise on appropriate policies to adopt.[34] While much criticism has often been directed at the real effectiveness of these types of exchanges in a number of other areas of planning, in the case of shopping, a subject on which most people are relatively well informed, a significant contribution can and has been made to the final decision-making process by public participation schemes.

Organisation

The final step in the conventional retail planning process has been to specify a spatial organisational framework to guide the control of new development and encourage change. This has probably been the weakest element in the entire methodology of plan preparation for there has been little experimentation with new design concepts and not much departure from those sorts of principles adhered to more than two decades ago. Basically, there have been three types of principle followed. Firstly, large-scale development, particularly new purpose-built shopping schemes, has been channelled into existing commercial areas or established as new integrated district centres in the midst of residential areas. A major by-product of this has been to ensure the continuing dominance of the town or city centre; and few, true 'out-of-town' shopping centres and large stores on greenfield sites have been built as we have indicated in the previous two chapters. Secondly, apparent shortages in local shopping resources within new housing estates have been compensated for by the provision of new neighbourhood shopping centres and sometimes the development of new corner shops. Attempts have also been made to upgrade the retail environment of inner city areas through redevelopment, with a further by-product of this being the eradication of traditional ribbons, as has been mentioned before. Thirdly, the general balance of resources throughout the city or county has been organised according to a hierarchical system, with existing centres designated a local, neighbourhood, district, regional or city centre role and new centres assigned a comparable role to these, usually at the lower levels of the hierarchy. No new strip developments have been envisaged; no new mixed commercial areas (beyond some covered shopping centres incorporating office or recreational activities); no new 'unplanned' centres where incremental growth could take place without some purpose-built scheme. Where variations have occurred in retail planning strategies, and the testing of alternatives through spatial interaction models, therefore, it has mainly been in terms of relatively minor modifications to the basic hierarchical form.

Conclusion

This chapter has taken a rather critical view of the conventional planning process in so far as retail and commercial considerations are involved. Despite the general importance of the distributive trades to the economy as a whole, there has been little formal interest on the part of central government in how the inherent strength of this field of activity can be used to its best effect. While there has been much expansion of the protection afforded consumers, in terms of the goods and services they buy, the environment for these transactions appears to have been badly neglected. The neglect is found not so much in terms of an inadequate machinery of controls (for it can be argued perhaps that these are too strict) but in the lack of clear social and economic objectives of what the implementation of environmental planning policies should achieve. The new Development Plans were designed in part to encourage local authorities to take a wider socio-economic view in their plan preparation but, in the absence of central government guidance on the distribution system, these have effectively been realised as just a further set of blueprints on the management of physical change. Apart from the actual nature of plan preparation, however, a feature that sets the new Development Plans apart from their predecessors, is the emphasis that has been given to the application of modern statistical techniques and modelling procedures for analysing existing patterns of retailing and estimating consumer demands. While the underlying theory and potential capability of these methods has been much advanced, nevertheless, their practical results, particularly in forecasting, have so far been disappointing and often criticised. A final deficiency of the current approach to retail and commercial planning has been the the almost universal preoccupation with shopping matters and their separate treatment from other components of the distributive trades.

References

1. There is considerable literature on the growth of consumer protection in Britain. Two contrasting examples are: Cranston, R., *Consumers and the Law* (Weidenfeld and Nicolson, London, 1978); and Thomas, W.H. (ed.), *Encyclopedia of Consumer Law* (Sweet and Maxwell, London, 1980). For a general discussion of the control of monopoly powers, see: Pass, C.L. and Sparkes, J.R., *Monopoly* (Heinemann, London, 1980); Stanlake, G., *Monopolies and Restrictive Practices* (Ginn, Aylesbury, 1980).
2. Department of the Environment and Welsh Office, *Development Plans — A Manual on Form and Content* (HMSO, London, 1970).
3. Department of the Environment, 'Out of Town Shops and Shopping Centres', *Development Control Policy Note 13* (HMSO, London, 1972); revised as 'Large New Stores' (HMSO, London, 1977).
4. Department of the Environment, 'Warehouses: Wholesale, Cash and Carry, etc.', *Development Control Policy Note 14* (HMSO, London, 1974).
5. See, for example, the review of planning policies in Thorpe, D., *Town Planning for Retailing* (Manchester Business School, Retail Outlets Research Unit, 1975).
6. Department of the Environment, *Department of the Environment Circular 71/76*, and *Welsh Office Circular 98/76* (HMSO, London, 1976).
7. Langton, T. (ed.), *Planning Appeals*, vols. 1, 2 and 3 (Ambit, Gloucester, undated).
8. Lee, M. and Kent, E., *Planning Inquiry Study* (Donaldsons Research Report 1, London, 1976); updated in Lee, M. and Kent, E., *Planning Inquiry Study 2* (Donaldsons Research Report 5, London, 1978) and Lee, M. and Roberts, C., *Planning Inquiry Study 3* (Donaldsons Research Report 8, London, 1981); Gibbs, A., *An Analysis of Retail Warehouse Planning Inquiries* (Unit for Retail Planning Information, Reading, 1981).
9. National Economic Development Office, Distributive Trades EDC, *Retailing in Inner Cities* (NEDO, London, 1981); Unit for Retail Planning Information, *Retailing in Inner Cities: Report of an URPI Workshop* (Reading, 1980).

10. Scottish Development Department, *Lothians Regional Survey and Plan* (HMSO, London, 1966).
11. Scottish Development Department, *Grangemouth-Falkirk Regional Survey and Plan* (HMSO, London, 1968).
12. Wilkinson, M. and Black, R., 'A Report on Shopping within Strathclyde Plans', *Planning for Retailing, Planning Exchange Forum*, no. 8, February 1977 (Planning Exchange, Glasgow, 1977).
13. East Midlands Economic Planning Council, *East Midlands Study* (HMSO, London, 1966); Department of Economic Affairs, *The North West: A Regional Study* (HMSO, London, 1965).
14. Leicester City Council and Leicestershire County Council, *Leicester and Leicestershire Sub-Regional Planning Study* (1969); Nottinghamshire County Council, Derbyshire County Council, Nottingham City Council and Derby County Borough Council, *Nottinghamshire and Derbyshire Sub-Regional Study* (1969); Central Unit for Environmental Planning, *Severnside: A Feasibility Study* (HMSO, London, 1971).
15. National Economic Development Office, Distributive Trades EDC, *The Future Pattern of Shopping* (HMSO, London, 1971).
16. National Economic Development Office, Distributive Trades EDC, *Urban Models in Shopping Studies* (NEDO, London, 1970).
17. National Economic Development Office, Distributive Trades EDC, *The Distributive Trades in the Common Market* (HMSO, London, 1973).
18. National Economic Development Office, Distributive Trades EDC, *Career Development in Retail Distribution; Retailing in the Inner Cities; Technology – The Issues For The Distributive Trades* (NEDO, London, 1974, 1981 and 1982).
19. National Economic Development Office, *The Future Pattern of Shopping*, pp. 72 and 73.
20. Cullingworth, J.B., *Town and Country Planning in Britain* (Allen and Unwin, London, 1976).
21. Department of the Environment, *Development Plans – A Manual on Form and Content*, pp. 5 and 18.
22. Ibid., p. 6.
23. Tyne and Wear County Council, *Tyne and Wear Structure Plan Survey of Shopping Patterns in Tyne and Wear – 1975* (Newcastle upon Tyne, 1977).
24. See, for example, City of Newcastle upon Tyne, *Local Shopping in Newcastle: A Survey of Local Shopping Centres* and *Local Shopping in the City: A Discussion Document* (Newcastle upon Tyne, 1976 and 1978).
25. Department of Employment, *Family Expenditure Survey* (HMSO, London, annual publication).
26. Unit for Retail Planning Information, Retail Turnover to Floorspace Ratios, *Information Brief 76/7* and Shopping Centre Turnover to Floorspace Ratios: Variations between the 1971 Census of Distribution Major Centres, *Information Brief 79/4* (Reading, 1976 and 1979).
27. Williams, J. and Arnott, C., 'A New Look at Retail Forecasts', *The Planner*, vol. 63 (1977), pp. 170-3.
28. Huff, D.L., 'A Probabilistic Analysis of Shopping Centre Trade Areas', *Land Economics*, vol. 39 (1963), pp. 81-90.
29. Lakshmanan, T.R. and Hansen, W.G., 'A Retail Market Potential Model', *Journal of the American Institute of Planners*, vol. 31 (1965), pp. 134-43.
30. Wilson, A.G., *Entropy in Urban and Regional Modelling* (Pion, London, 1970).
31. Coelho, J.D. and Wilson, A.G., 'The Optimum Location and Size of Shopping Centres', *Regional Studies*, vol. 10 (1976), pp. 413-21.

32. Openshaw, S., 'Insoluble Problems in Shopping Model Calibration when the the Trip Pattern is Not Known', *Regional Studies*, vol. 7 (1973), pp. 367-71.
33. Some evaluation has been done on individual shopping developments, however. See, for example, Alexander, I., 'City Centre Redevelopment: An Evaluation of Alternative Approaches', *Progress in Planning*, vol. 3, part 1 (1974), pp. 1-81.
34. Gilfoyle, I., 'The Cheshire Shopping Consultative Panel', in *Furthering Local Authority and Retailing Contacts: Report of an URPI Workshop* (Unit for Retail Planning Information, Reading, 1980).

4   AN ALTERNATIVE PLANNING APPROACH

Our basic dissatisfaction with the conventional approach to retail and commercial planning stems from the lack of a clear exposition as to what the aims and central concerns of such plans should be. In seeking to offer some improvement to the form and nature of current practice, therefore, attention is focused in this chapter on identifying what we see as the primary goals and objectives of the field and the major types of problems that ought to be addressed. At the same time, we also want to develop the argument for a general loosening of planning constraints, to treat the distribution system in its entirety and deal with a set of future or emerging problems, as well as those which have long been apparent in the past.

While all this suggests a rather radical or revolutionary stance, in fact the proposals put forward are quite modest in scope and are designed to be incorporated into the existing legislative framework of planning. The goals that are identified are treated in the context of a national set of aspirations and hence refer to those more global issues that need to be confronted by central government. The way in which these goals can be pursued through some practical measures is discussed but this would be contingent, of course, on central government taking a more positive role in the plan-making process than it has hitherto. The objectives that follow through from these goals are directed to the resolution of more localised problems and hence are expected to be dealt with under the auspices of existing Development Plans. The sorts of policies that need to be effected to translate the objectives into workable courses of action are likewise elaborated upon.

The stress that is put on the issues and problems to be faced in retail and commercial planning means that relatively little attention is given to the methodological aspects of plan preparation, particularly the use of those distinctive technical procedures we have outlined before. The view held here is that, whilst these techniques have undoubtedly been important in the past, their development and application has been confined to a limited set of concerns; and in some cases, the methodology itself has come to dominate the content of a plan rather than the subject matter to which it is addressed. We therefore see some diminution of the part played particularly by modelling techniques but at the same time, an extension of the range of analytical tools that might be used to probe a broader spectrum of considerations.

Issues at the National and Regional Level

It was indicated in the Preface to this book that the fundamental aims
of retail and commercial planning should be to promote efficiency in
the operations of the distributive trades and ensure equitability in
opportunities or resources for consumers primarily interacting with
the retail sector. Ideally, this should be a dual responsibility with
neither side taking precedence or priority over the other. In the past,
however, the scales have been tipped in favour of safeguarding consumer interests and there is some justification, in a period of economic
decline, for tilting them in the other direction. The two primary goals,
nevertheless, need to be disaggregated into a number of goal elements,
the most important of which are summarised in Table 4.1. There is no
exact symmetry in the two sets of goal elements listed in the table, but
the various interrelationships that do extend between them have
conditioned the sorts of pairings we have made. It seems desirable to
examine the goal elements in a paired form rather than individually for
there are often inconsistencies and conflicts between them and it is

Table 4.1: The Main Goals of Retail and Commercial Planning

	Demand	Supply
Primary goals	Promote equitability in opportunities	Promote efficiency in operations
Goal elements	Provide choice in facilities Enhance convenience/access Improve comfort/safety Minimise cost of goods (Alleviate job difficulties) (Assist disadvantaged consumers)	Meet locational needs Improve goods circulation Reduce land use conflicts Ensure fair competition (Foster new trades) (Encourage technological change)
Areas for decision-making	Formulation of locational strategies Revision of environmental standards Adequacy of trade regulations Estimates of future conditions (Relations with employment policies) (Relations with consumer protection)	

usually the need to reconcile these that ultimately leads to the imposition of planning controls or regulations over the distribution system. Arising from the general interplay between the goal elements are six main decision-making areas that provide the basis for deciding what types of general regulations to impose. These will be discussed in the second part of this section.

Goals and Conflicts of Interest

Goal formulation, despite its weak development in the retail and commercial field, has received increasing prominence in recent years in the broader aspects of plan preparation.[1] Here, there has been some criticism that the goals put forward are too expansive or all-embracing to provide a suitable framework for guiding the detailed make-up of individual plans. It is largely for this reason that we prefer to treat the business of goal formulation in a national rather than localised context; for we see its purpose, in the retail and commercial field, as setting a course or direction for plans to follow rather than establishing a precise format for local authority endeavours.

Choice and Variety. The first of our national goal elements is the need to provide more choice in types of shopping facilities available to the public and more variety in locational settings from which suppliers can operate. Taking the suppliers' needs first, we have indicated that a combination of strict development controls and rigid organisational blueprints effected during recent years has led to a serious reduction in the kinds of sites which business activities can occupy. Different policies applied to retailing and wholesaling have led to a high degree of centralisation in the former and massive decentralisation in the latter. Services have been variously dealt with according to the planner's perception of where their 'natural' spatial affinities to the other two main categories of trade lie. This simplistic approach to locational needs has meant that a number of activities, many of them new, that do not conform in their requirements to the idealised patterns of organisation assumed have been forced into inappropriate environmental settings and excluded from certain parts of the city altogether. Most seriously affected have been those car-oriented service activities that need prominence alongside main roads and/or cheaper sites on the edge of the urban area. It should be a major goal of retail and commercial planning in the future to be more sympathetic and receptive to inherent market forces rather than antagonistic and largely restrictive towards them.

The same constraints that have hindered the efficient operation of businesses have also deprived consumers of a richer choice in types of facilities to utilise. There has been too much equation in the past between the need to provide equitability in shopping opportunities and the provision of a standardised set of shopping centres. The deficiency is most clearly seen in the context of neighbourhood facilities where the same stereotyped parades or precinct centres have been created, irrespective of wide differences in the socio-economic characteristics and predilections of the population. So long as some basic resource is allocated to each distinctive community group, more allowance should be given to market processes to develop those facilities most in tune with local needs. The emergence of a more diverse range of retailing settings would then allow wider scope in places to visit for those people who do not identify so readily with their 'home-based' provisions. This itself can be fostered by a more liberal planning approach to retail locations alongside major traffic arteries, to which public transport services as well as independent car users are oriented.

Costs and Competition. A further virtue of the loosening of locational constraints is that it is likely to lead to the establishment of a greater number of stores selling goods at the cheapest prices possible to a wider cross-section of the population than is currently found. It would also enable smaller businesses to compete more effectively with the larger companies, especially if there was more relaxation of controls in their favour. Our second key element is concerned with the need for the planning machinery to be used to minimise costs in distribution while at the same time ensuring fair competition amongst different kinds of traders. It is a remarkable fact, however, that neither of these goals has been explicitly employed in the past as the basis to retail and commercial policies, although the latter, in the form of discrimination against large stores, has been implicitly adopted.

Much of the lack of concern over costs has had to do with the special relationship between cheaper prices and large stores and the earlier belief that the introduction of hypermarkets and superstores would lead to unfair trading practices. So far, however, as has been indicated, the fears that were held over these particular innovations have proved to be rather groundless with most of the adverse competitive effects being felt by the smaller branch outlets of chain companies (usually themselves the promoters of large stores) rather than by the small, independent traders. These results have been achieved, nevertheless, against the background of a relatively limited amount of development (at least in comparison to other European countries) and where most hypermarkets and superstores have been integrated into existing shopping centres. It is still necessary, therefore, to consider how much further development can be sustained, and what proportion of this might go into free-standing sites, before there is serious erosion of the traditional retail system. There is little doubt that an unfettered proliferation of hypermarkets and superstores would create immense changes in trading patterns which, if compounded by a widespread increase in out-of-town shopping centres, would threaten not only the viability of small businesses but the health of such important places as the central area as well.[2] Such massive upheavals in the spatial balance of competition must clearly be resisted by the imposition of some form of control. Thus while we advocate a more liberal attitude towards the adjudication of proposals for individual schemes, we recognise that ultimately some limit must be set on the overall pattern and amount of development to be accommodated within an urban area.

Accessibility and Circulation. The third set of goal elements is concerned with improving people's accessibility to shops and shopping centres and facilitating an efficient circulation of goods and services between sources of supply and areas of demand. Accessibility to shopping facilities has been one of the major determinants of past retail planning policies and remains the basis to the use of the hierarchy concept for organising the size and arrangement of shopping centres within most urban areas. It was argued in Chapter 1, however, that this organisational structure is in need of considerable revision to take account of the changes which have occurred both in trading methods and consumer behaviour. There are serious maladjustments in particular at the two ends of the hierarchy. Many of the small local or neighbourhood centres placed in the middle of residential areas have become redundant because of the growth in bulk-buying of grocery goods, increased car usage and more work-based shopping trips;[3] some of the larger towns and city centres, having expanded by virtue of new shopping schemes, are in danger of losing potential trade because their retail investment programmes have not been matched by adequate car parking provisions, improved road conditions and the alleviation of congestion.[4] Those centres that have generally fared best are the newer district centres in outlying areas that have purposely accommodated both large modern stores and the motorist's travel demands.

Many of the difficulties facing the public in gaining access to traditional shopping centres are shared by suppliers when delivering their goods. The problems here are most acute in town and city centres where there are special conflicts with both pedestrians and other vehicular traffic. Some improvements have emerged in recent years with the designation of specified unloading times and the reorganisation of deliveries within the transport trade itself, but much scope exists for further progress to be made.

An additional set of specialised needs can be identified for those disabled and infirm members of the public who have difficulty gaining entry to shopping centres and individual shops.[5] The chief requirement here is to expand upon those facilities such as ramps, enlarged doors and checkout points and special toilets, which have come in with some of the newer shopping developments.

Safety and Orderliness. The fourth set of goal elements we have identified concerns some further longstanding pursuits in retail and commercial planning, namely the quest to provide comfort and safety in shopping environments and ensure a degree of orderliness in the siting of individual businesses so that there will be compatability rather than conflict within the land use pattern. These have often been treated together so that environmental improvement schemes, particularly in the city centre, have gone hand in hand with policies of land use segregation. The clearest expressions have been the development of precincts and pedestrianised streets and the designation, within the central area, of a shopping and office core separate from other quarters devoted to wholesaling, warehousing, education, transport, etc. There is little doubt that these policies have been extremely successful from the point of view of enhancing safety and creating order in the spatial structure of business activities; but it is questionable as to whether they have materially added to the comfort of the shoppers and it may well be that, through stifling new innovations, they have depleted the central area of much of its traditional character and intrinsic interest.

There is a complicated range of issues here which are most prominent in the core area of shopping. On the one hand, purpose-built covered shopping centres afford consumers protection against weather hazards and an attractive interior for family groups of shoppers; on the other hand, externally they often prove to be intrusive elements of the townscape and major contributors to traffic congestion, atmospheric pollution and blight. The exclusion of service activities from principal shopping streets promotes more continuity in shopping provisions but leads to a reduction in the variable appearance of such streets. The concentration of shops into one compact area encourages a much greater consumer usership during the daytime hours but, in the absence of other facilities, tends to create another dead area at night. More generally, the principle of segregating retailing activities from other land uses, while promoting more efficiency for consumers in the actual business of shopping, leads to the dominance of this area by the larger retail firms with smaller businesses forced into the periphery to compete with other activities which they, rather than the larger firms, are less able to withstand. It seems perhaps that a variable set of locational controls is needed to resolve these issues, using the street system as the basis for different management policies to be applied.[6] In some streets, the standards in safety and orderliness will need to be improved; in others, there might be relaxation of constraints to encourage a more diversified environment. The basic dilemma is complicated too by the need to reconcile the claims of today with the likely possibility, in the years ahead, that the city centre will experience a reduction in its shopping role, relative to other land uses, given the impact of computer technology and new advances in retailing techniques.

Employment and Innovation. These subjects have been added to the list of goal elements, although the goals themselves are much more difficult to articulate and have been little discussed before. There has as yet been no deliberate attempt to manipulate the distributive trades for the purposes of job creation or job protection, although a number of policies have had an indirect bearing on this (including the establishment of Enterprise Zones in the former case and the support given to ailing tourist services in the latter). The case for increasing the overall workforce in distribution, especially during a time of declining purchasing power and continued high inflation, is a weak one because of the extra costs that would have to be absorbed and which ultimately would be passed on to the consumer. The case for attacking unemployment in the industry is more complicated with arguments both for and against a comprehensive policy. On the one hand, the loss of jobs within the industry has not been on a scale and with the same degree of permanence as that found within manufacturing; and given that much labour is female, part-time and a secondary occupation for households, it is arguable that the market economy should be left to take care of any redundancies that occur. On the other hand, the pending threat of mass unemployment created by technological changes in the future and the likely importance of secondary jobs to those households where the head may also be out of work, suggest that some positive action should be taken in advance of such events. Two solutions present themselves. Firstly, since the problem of unemployment is always highly localised, encouragement should be given to the development of large stores and other commercial innovations within those areas, such as the inner city, where employment conditions are already poor. While this may not result in an actual growth in the number of jobs, because of the competitive effects on existing businesses, it should lead to a restructuring of the workforce in favour of the young.[7] Secondly, a network of educational and retraining schemes should be identified now to take special interest in the problems likely to develop in the industry so that there will be the nucleus of support facilities when the critical period arrives.[8]

Consumers and Technology. Our last goal elements are also somewhat tentative since they go beyond the bounds of what have usually been included in retail and commercial planning and intrude into the area of consumer protection and social service provision. The rationale for their adoption here is that, in the past, spatial and structural changes in distribution have led to the emergence of distinctive groups of people whom we might describe as disadvantaged (and also neglected) consumers and whose number may increase in size in the future by virtue of technological developments within the field. Most of the consumers who fall into this category are the elderly, infirm, the poor and single-parent households; the types of locality where conditions are most severe are the inner city, certain rural areas and isolated housing estates; the list of disadvantages that have accrued include the loss of essential services, such as post offices and chemists, the replacement of socially-oriented small shops by redevelopment schemes, the lack of convenient access to large stores and the cheaper prices they bring, and the diminution in the vitality of traditional shopping streets. Certain of these problems can be partially resolved by attention to the other goals we have set, but in the matter of access to essential services and large stores some positive discrimination in their favour may be deemed to be necessary. The question arises as to whether central government should encourage local authorities to support the additional provision of essential services in selected areas, or arrange for mobile delivery facilities; and whether it should assist in some way the transport of these groups to large stores (beyond the allocation of bus passes and travel allowances that some already hold). The technological breakthroughs in armchair or teleshopping systems that were referred to in Chapter 2 may provide some alternative solutions to these if an interventionist policy were to be assumed. It would be possible, for example, to link the granting of permission for large store proposals (at the time when such telecommunication systems have come on stream) to the condition that a special service be established by the firm for locally surrounding disadvantaged groups; by the same token, conventional carriers of goods such as dairy companies or the Post Office might find it commercially viable to provide shopping services based on new types of warehouse outlets. While these ideas may sound a little far fetched, a minimum goal for the future must be the containment of consumer disadvantages.

Regulating the Distribution System

The goals to be met for both consumers and suppliers raise a sufficient number of conflicts of interest that some broad regulations must be imposed on the distribution system. The nature of these regulations must be guided and co-ordinated by central government which needs to be more definitive and clear in its direction of local authority policy-making than it has been in the past. A synthesis of the considerations involved in the goals we have discussed suggest six main subject areas where regulatory decisions are required. These are summarised in Table 4.2.

Locational Strategies. The first requirement is for central government to decide what broad locational strategies should be fostered to meet some or all of the goals discussed. There are certain features of the apparent strategies now in force that seem to be desirable and ought to be continued. As far as retailing matters are concerned, the current principle of concentrating the most specialised resources within town or city centres has been relatively successful in maintaining the trading health of these most important areas, subject to the reservations we have expressed on transport and accessibility; likewise, the concept of developing strategically placed district centres has much to recommend it. The ambivalence displayed towards the decentralisation of convenience trades and the growth of large stores in variable locations, however, needs clearing up, with emphasis given to the acceptability of new development in both inner and outer areas.[9] These might be required to be integrated within existing or designated shopping 'areas', as distinct from 'centres', so that while there remained an overall control on the pattern of growth, businesses would be less constrained in occupying their preferred types of sites. The idea of demarcating areas rather than centres for development holds further appeal in commercial as well as retail terms, for certain more important arterials could be set

Table 4.2: Types of Decisions Required from Central Government

Locational strategies

- continued concentration of specialised resources within town centres
- relaxation of locational constraints on arterial services and large stores
- recognition of alternative types of permissible development (e.g. strip developments, trade marts, commercial estates, service plazas)

Recommend advisory document espousing freer development controls in siting but new development to be integrated within existing or designated retail and commercial areas (as distinct from centres).

Environmental standards

- extension of controls on historical legacies and major developments
- loosening of controls on low cost, smaller developments
- continued experimentation with the concept of free enterprise zones

Recommend expansion of the principle of spatial demarcations for variable environmental controls (such as in conservation areas), to designate where both tighter and freer standards will be imposed.

Trade regulations

- reassessment of need for controls on number and sizes of large stores
- consideration of need for controls on growth of corporate organisations
- identification of alternative forms of assistance for small businesses

Recommend panel inquiry into appropriate limits on numbers of large stores in urban areas, their sizes and the future market share of corporate firms; establishment of a consultancy service for small businesses.

Future conditions

- comparative assessments of modern resource endowment by urban regions
- monitoring of growth trends in different sectors of trade
- identification of trading characteristics of business types and centres/areas (e.g. employment, catchment areas, car parking)

Recommend publication of a periodic reference manual on regional stock inventories, sectoral growth trends and characteristics of modern types of development.

Relations with employment policies

(Clarification of role of retail and commercial planning in employment generation and employment protection field.)

Relations with consumer protection

(Clarification of role of retail and commercial planning in consumer protection and general price policy field.)

aside to permit service growth, and vacant land near to the central area promoted for wholesaling and other intermediary activities. Within such areas, too, new forms of development might be encouraged which depart from the conventional, single-purpose centre and allow for some spontaneous, continuous and mixed accretions to take place.[10] These can be referred to as new strip developments, trade marts, commercial estates and service plazas and they will be elaborated upon in Chapter 7.

Environmental Standards. Allied to the requirement to reformulate its locational strategies, central government needs to reassess the suitability of its control on the environmental standards of new development, specifically on aspects of design and construction. In recent years, there have been clear signs of more stringent regulations being applied to the quality of new buildings, particularly in historic towns and places with outstanding architectural legacies.[11] While this must be welcome in these types of localities, one would like to see this type of policy counterbalanced by a loosening of standards in those areas where the environmental heritage is of much less importance than economic revitalisation or social improvement. Just as a freezing of locational constraints can aid many businesses to become more efficient, especially the small independent trader, so a more liberal approach to the aesthetics and built form of establishments can help engender innovation and risk-taking by those with good ideas but slender means. The sorts of development that could be encouraged in this respect are lockup premises for small stockists, market-type halls, new corner shops in residential accommodation and compounds for a variety of transport-oriented services. Both the strengthening and weakening of environmental standards in specific localities, however, require that certain broad directives be given again about appropriate spatial demarcations to be drawn. Precedents already exist in the designation of conservation areas and more recently in the establishment of Enterprise Zones within selected cities.[12] These constitute essentially two extreme forms of control — the one with very high standards to be met, the other virtually free of any encumbrances. In between, there may be two other areal gradations that can be countenanced: the imposition of higher standards in certain localities, such as particular streets in the retail and office cores of a town or city centre, where substantial improvements to the appearance of buildings and the roads themselves may be sought; the acceptance of lower standards in other localities, such as parts of the central area frame and along the inner city arteries. Examples of the sorts of standards to be set would need to be compiled to guide the implementation of such proposals by local authorities; but it should be possible for local authorities to combine the necessary areal demarcations with those made for different locational control purposes.

Trade Regulations. A third subject area for central government consideration concerns the extent to which new trade regulations or influences might further the goals of retail and commercial planning. The focus here remains the relationship between large and small businesses and how the benefits to be derived from both can be reconciled. We have already argued that more scope should be given to the development of individual large stores throughout the urban area but have also admitted that eventually the numbers within any one city may need to be controlled. Linked to this is the question of how large should large stores be allowed to become and whether constraints should be imposed on the comparative growth of firms. The number of large stores, their sizes and the corporate growth of firms are important considerations not only in the context of the spatial trading changes they might bring but also from the point of view of their potential repercussions on the structure and organisation of distribution, employment prospects and the contribution that can be made to cost savings for consumers as a whole. There is no obvious recommendation which can be made on these points. What seems called for is an 'in-house' exercise or special inquiry to determine at what broad threshold levels the existing advantages to be obtained from larger scales of activity begin to be outweighed by their disbenefits. Broad directives might then be established on the desirable limits to set for the number and sizes of stores sustainable in different types of urban areas and the share of trade which can be commanded by individual firms. The way in which central government might intervene on behalf of small businesses should also be subjected to special examination. This was looked at in part in the past (in the Bolton Committee of Inquiry into Small Firms[13]), but little direct action was subsequently taken in the retail and commercial field and the need for remedial help is much greater now than before. There are various forms of help that can readily be identified, although many of these depend on public expenditure commitments that are unlikely to be forthcoming in the present age. The least that could be done is the establishment of a self-supporting consultancy service,[14] backed up by the development of local educational and training programmes of the sort we have referred to before.

Future Conditions. Although we have been critical of the excessive attention given by local authorities to floorspace calculations and projections, it is recognised that some assessment of the future state or capacity of a retail and commercial system is desirable. It seems more important, however, to undertake this type of exercise at a regional rather than local level, under the auspices of central government, to ensure that there is consistency in any estimates produced and to counteract any imbalances that might occur in the expectations of competing places. The appropriate unit for such forecasts might be the urban regions currently being delimited for the 1981 Census of Population.[15] Rather than producing a series of long-range predictions in likely floorspace needs and amounts, it would also be more sensible to concentrate on short-term estimates that are linked to continuous monitoring of recent trends. These in themselves should focus on the more modern trading practices to be found, thus requiring a more appropriate data collection framework than is currently employed, as has been described in Chapter 1. Besides assessing future developments in trading methods and the floorspace implications that arise from these, however, one would also like to see more trend-analysis and projection of a wider set of physical and economic characteristics pertaining to retail and commercial areas. This need not involve a large or comprehensive survey, but could be based on samples of different sizes and locations of shopping centres, wholesaling districts and the like, for which information about employment, car parking provisions, catchment area characteristics, etc., would be obtained.[16] This is a tall order, but we ought to look forward to a day when there is a frequently updated reference manual available to practising planners that provides summary statistics about the changing average conditions of both business activities and the areas or centres in which they are found — much as the developers and larger retail firms already have handbooks on market and trading specifications to guide their expansion plans.[17]

Relations with Employment Policies. Part of the discussion on the formulation of goals in relation to employment, and unemployment, gave an indication of what sorts of affirmative action can be taken by central government to generate new jobs and reduce the threat of redundancies within the distributive trades. What is not clear at this juncture, however, is whether such action should be taken independently within the context of retail and commercial planning or whether it needs to be integrated within some broader programme of employment policies directed at the economy as a whole. Given the uncertainties surrounding the most appropriate way forward, and the lack of attention that has so far been given to this subject, the first requirement to be made of central government perhaps is to determine where the responsibility for policy-making lies and what the scope of this responsibility should be.

Relations with Consumer Protection. A similar conclusion must be reached with respect to the potential role which retail and commercial planning can play in an area which has hitherto been bound up with more general policies directed towards consumer affairs. Here, however, the contributions which planning (in its more narrow sense) can make to a reduction in the prices of goods and a more equitable allocation of essential services, argue more strongly for direct intervention in this field. For this to be channelled through to local authorities and absorbed into conventional planning practice, nevertheless, positive guidelines will again need to be given by central government on how far there should be an overlap in local departmental responsibilities and what degree of collaboration should be achieved.

The Challenge to Local Authorities

Compared to the obligations we have placed on central government's involvement in retail and commercial planning, the obligations we might set for local authorities seem quite modest. The root requirement is a clearer statement of what the objectives in planning should be and how these might be accomplished within the existing organisational structure of plan-making. Our basic ideas are sketched out in Table 4.3. As far as the objectives themselves are concerned, these need to serve two purposes. On the one hand, they need to be a vehicle for translating the broader goals we have conceived, which means they must be defined as a series of operational statements rather than a set of aspirations or value judgements; on the other hand, they must have some reference to local problems to be found that cannot be taken into account at the national scale. This split in the function of objectives is implicitly acknowledged in the division made within existing Development Plans, i.e. between Structure Plans and Local Plans, with the former designed to interpret national goals and the latter to treat more specifically problems of a parochial nature. While there is much that is intended to be different about the existing plans, however, in practice they are often quite similar in the way they are prepared (save

Table 4.3: The Main Objectives of Local Authority Plan Preparation

	[Demand]	[Supply]
Primary objectives	Improve the spatial allocation of resources	Improve the health of the commercial environment
Objective elements	Relate opportunities to changing patterns of demand	Create conditions to enhance local business prospects
	Provide additional resources for disadvantaged consumers	Provide ameliorative measurements for repercussions of change
	Meet new consumer demands and preferences	Allow for the accommodation of new trade forms
	Upgrade deficient local shopping environments	Rationalise and revitalise outworn areas
Areas for decision-making	Analysis of the system General policy proposals Approach to new development Renovation and redevelopment	
Additional specific problems	(System problems) Impact of new centres Small business problems Transport and communication	(Areal problems) Residential area requirements Town centre pressures Rural resource impoverishment

for their scale of coverage, attention to detail and the procedural aspects of implementing development controls). Thus many District Plans resemble Structure Plans in their content and approach; and many Local Subject Plans are mini-replicas of the Subject Plans prepared by counties or certain large boroughs. The reason for this is that both tiers of local government are engaged in preparing general management policies for the distribution system within their areas and both are concerned with resolving special kinds of problems that arise. Unfortunately, the differences in their spheres of responsibility have never been explicitly laid down. The list of topics summarised in the lower half of Table 4.3 is intended to guide discussion on what these could or should be. The four main decision-making areas extracted from the objectives that have been formulated refer to the broader aspects of managing the distribution system and serve as a framework for distinguishing appropriate functions for each tier of local government. The additional special problems that are then cited have been grouped into two kinds, to indicate that there are a set of system problems that are seen as the responsibility of County Councils and a set of areal problems more properly the province of District Councils.

The Background Objectives

The objectives that have been listed are sufficiently self-evident that they require little elaboration. The approach taken to their formulation is similar to that employed in the derivation of goals. There are thus two primary objectives, linked most closely to the goals themselves, which spawn a number of objective elements, only some of which (those with most universal relevance) are reported here. The objective elements are again paired although there is no exact complementarity intended.

On the demand side, our chief interest lies in the adequacy of existing retail and commercial resources for different groups of consumers and what sorts of improvements will need to be made in the future. Conversely, on the supply side, we are concerned with the relative health of the environment in which traders operate and where changes should be made to help raise the efficiency of business practices. These need to be considered both from a sectoral and spatial point of view so that we are seeking to redress any socio-economic as well as land use imbalances that might be found. A first obvious requirement is to develop, within a local context, those freer market conditions that are necessary to enhance a wide cross-section of business prospects, which should in turn, providing there is some direction of new resources to new areas of demand, expand the scope in shopping opportunities available to consumers. Allied to this, and to minimise the deleterious effects of change on weaker sections of the business community and amongst consumers, there must be some supporting services provided, both to assist in the alleviation of any unemployment that may arise and to improve the accessibility of deprived people to the most advantageous shopping resources to be found. New types of trade will need to be accommodated as well as the growth in demand for established activities, such as the fast-food outlets, business services and modern convenience stores. As a general principle, too, local authorities will need to provide those infrastructures and amenities necessary to the revitalisation of existing commercial areas or the generation of new ones, and to continue with their programmes of environmental improvement in run down shopping areas.

Such broad objectives as stated here will clearly need to be narrowed down to be more directly applicable to the circumstances prevailing within any individual local authority. It may also be necessary to specify in more detail the obligations to be met in each separate category of the distributive trades. Some insight into the areal references that will need to be made and particular types of activities that will need to be alluded to is given in the next section.

The Preparation of General Management Plans

We have already pointed to a distinction in our scheme between the requirements facing local authorities to produce what we might call general management plans and a series of more specialised plans directed at specific problems. These will need to be closely integrated; but our primary concern at this point is to clarify what should be expected of the two tiers of local government in the preparation of their common management plans. There are four major considerations that result from a synthesis of the broad objectives we have described, each of which may be conceived as a separate topic or component of the plans. Firstly, clarification needs to be given as to what form and how much analysis of the existing distribution system should be undertaken by the Counties and Districts. This parallels the report of survey already required in Development Plans but we would envisage certain changes here, not least in making the analyses that are undertaken more relevant to the policies that are ultimately applied. Secondly, there must be stronger differentiation between the two tiers of local government in terms of the types of policies formulated to oversee the evolution of the distributive trades. The Counties might be charged with responsibility for determining a broad spatial pattern of development and co-ordinating those services necessary for the protection of minority interests; the Districts should be concerned with the business of land use controls and designating specific areas for socio-economic aid. The policies of the Counties would therefore be oriented to the system as a whole; those of the Districts would be areally based. A third topic, which constitutes a more marked departure from the conventional approach to planning, concerns the attitudes that should be adopted by the two sets of authority towards new or potential development. Large proposals in particular have assumed such importance in recent years that they should be accorded separate and special attention within the preparation of management plans. While the Counties might be given overall responsibility for the adjudication and subsequent monitoring of these, the Districts should provide guidelines on what particular site controls they would impose in different areas. The fourth topic calls for greater prominence to be given also to programmes of renovation and redevelopment; with the Counties in this case being charged with determining the priorities and phasing to be accorded major schemes, and the Districts required to supervise their realisation on the ground.

Table 4.4 suggests in more detail what the different responsibilities outlined above might entail. These suggestions are not intended to be exhaustive, nor is it expected that any one local authority would necessarily follow all of the steps involved. What matters is that there is a clear-cut structure to the separate roles to be performed and that, within the four topics assigned each local government plan, there is a logical progression from one stage to another. This is amplified in the next few paragraphs.

Analysis of the System. The types of surveys and comparative assessments that are seen as appropriate for the Counties to undertake (or some similar upper tier of local government) are quite different from those which are usually found within a Structure Plan. There the emphasis still rests on the accumulation of information about floorspace, the functional composition of shopping centres, the delimitation of trade areas and trends in consumer spending. While these may offer some insights into the relative health of the distribution system and the spatial pattern of resources, they report primarily on the way the environment has been organised in the past and reveal little about new trading needs or the social demands of consumers. The consequence is that policies become formulated which simply expand or contract on elements within the existing environmental organisation rather than dealing with wider socio-economic issues. Our suggestions therefore stress the need for more attention to be given to the diagnosis of consumer needs, than to their shopping patterns, and the advantages and disadvantages to be obtained from different trading forms, rather than their compatibility with a hierarchical arrangement of centres. Special attention should also be accorded to the way in which different components of the distributive trades are integrated within a metropolitan area, the effect which changing channels of distribution are having on locational requirements and the pressures created for new transport services by new physical distribution networks. In addition, there

Table 4.4: Example Contents of an Alternative Set of Local Authority Plans

---

Analysis of the system

Upper-tier functions (e.g. Counties)

1. Comparison of consumer opportunities
   (price surveys; location of essential services; accessibility to major centres)

2. Description of physical distribution networks
   (channels of distribution; transport services; spatial organisation of networks)

3. Appraisal of trading characteristics
   (areas of growth and decline; sectoral trading strengths; floorspace change)

4. Appraisal of employment and business conditions
   (employment shifts; training requirements; rates; rents; trade regulations)

5. Review of past policies

Lower-tier functions (e.g. Districts)

1. Description of retail and commercial areas
   (classification; size characteristics; ownership and organisation)

2. Appraisal of environmental conditions
   (age; blight; congestion; approachability; parking)

3. Appraisal of market characteristics
   (catchment area characteristics; areas of over- and under-provision)

4. Identification of consumers in need
   (disadvantaged minorities; new housing estates; young people)

5. Review of past policies
   (development controls; building regulations; special service provisions)

Policies and procedures

Upper-tier functions (e.g. Counties)
links to national and regional strategies and forecasts

1. Recommendations on investment needs
   (overall floorspace accommodation; new trading forms; support facilities)

2. Spatial indications on growth and constraint
   (relationships between major commercial areas; general locational strategy)

3. Revision of consumer protection services
   (greater publicity; reallocation of offices; links to voluntary groups)

4. Encouragement to commercial training programmes
   (youth programmes; retraining; anticipated technological changes)

5. Co-ordination of local trade policies
   (trading hours; licensing; rating procedures; grant provisions)

Lower-tier functions (e.g. Districts)

1. Designation of the status of retail and commercial areas
   (spatial demarcation of existing areas and appropriate new areas)

2. Specification of variable controls on these areas
   (areas of strict, limited or conventional development and trade controls)

3. Determination of areas for special intervention
   (for renovation or redevelopment; for special urban aid programmes)

4. Demarcation of residential tracts for minor alterations
   (definition of inner, outer city; rural tracts; suburban areas)

5. Promotion of local service needs for disadvantaged groups
   (shopping services for the elderly; mobile provisions; club activities)

Approach to new development
reference to public panel group

Upper-tier functions (e.g. Counties)

1. Adjudication on proposals for new large developments
   (threshold of 50,000 sq ft; locational and trade considerations)

2. Initiation or encouragement to new large schemes
   (markets; trade centres; exhibition halls; multi-purpose centres)

3. Monitoring the performance of existing large schemes
   (trade expectations; employment characteristics; rate returns)

Additional planning attention to specific problems of:
the impact of new large developments
physical distribution problems
small business problems

Lower-tier functions (e.g. Districts)

1. Information on permitted smaller types of development
   (trade types for restricted areas; freer forms in liberalised areas)

2. Site controls on new large development
   (landscaping; access facilities; infrastructures; parking)

3. Recommended support provisions in proposals
   (aids for disabled; amenities; small businesses in tenant mix)

Table 4.4 continued
Renovation and redevelopment
reference to public panel group

Upper-tier functions (e.g. Counties)

1. Concept for the city centre and other major commercial areas
   (anticipated scale of change; relationship to socio-cultural role)

2. Priorities in major area environmental improvement programmes
   (phasing of programmes; emphasis of improvement schemes)

3. Monitoring of commercial repercussions of other major land use changes
   (transport developments; office developments; housing renewal)

Lower-tier functions (e.g. Districts)

1. Specification of variable controls on the city centre
   (areas of strict, limited or conventional development and trade controls)

2. Priorities in minor area environmental improvement programmes
   (phasing of programmes; emphasis of improvement schemes)

3. Alleviation of disrupted and dislocated business activity
   (minimise risk of blight; rent reliefs; new site accommodation)

Additional planning attention to specific problems of:
   residential area requirements
   town centre pressures
   rural resource impoverishment

should be greater scrutiny of the spatial and structural shifts taking place in employment, the educational support facilities provided for those engaged in the distributive trades, and the equitability of local taxes and trade regulations enforced throughout the area. Finally, no future plan should be embarked upon without some critical assessment of how effective past policies have been, including in this scheme an evaluation of the contributions of consumer protection services and estate management practices as well as the conventional land use policies applied.

In contrast, the analytical functions that are recommended for the Districts (or some other appropriate lower tier of local government) resemble more closely those functions already being performed at this level, by virtue of a continuing need to enforce areally-based environmental controls. Surveys will still have to be carried out to determine the physical characteristics of existing retail and commercial facilities and where there is over- or under-endowment in the stock of resources available to consumers. Some greater emphasis might be given in these surveys, however, to measuring the quality of the retail and commercial environment, rather than simply recording numbers of outlets and types of trade found; and likewise, more attention could be focused on identifying specific kinds of consumer disadvantage rather than just the inequalities in accessibility conditions that occur. Besides supplying background information on those localities to which variable development control policies will ultimately be applied, these surveys will be used to support special programmes of planning intervention aimed at revitalising local trading conditions and improving consumer service provisions. How far past forms of development control and the implementation of special planning schemes have been successful in meeting local business and consumer needs will again need to be critically appraised.

Policies and Procedures. The policies to be formulated within our scheme by the Counties will clearly need to be linked to those national and regional strategies which we have already discussed. The same will apply, although to a lesser extent, to the Districts. On the broad matters of locational strategy and permissible development, the upper tier of local government will be primarily concerned with determining the amount and type of new investment to be encouraged throughout the county as a whole and where within the general area there should be particular stimulus to growth or acceptance of decline. This means that some estimates will have to be produced on desirable levels of new floorspace to be accommodated, at least in the relative sense of whether there should be substantial, moderate or only small gains on existing floorspace; and some spatial indication will have to be given as to which shopping centres and commercial areas will be subject to greatest change. These need only be described in broad outline, however, following the format of those Statements of Policy currently issued with Structure Plans, for the Districts would still be left with responsibility to respond to individual proposals and would control the scale and nature of changes in particular localities (through a new code of standards laid down by central government). In order to maintain an effective relationship between the Counties and Districts in the implementation of common spatial organisational concepts, nevertheless, the former will need to be able to exert greater powers of influence over the latter than has hitherto been the case on the acceptability of very large proposals for development or redevelopment. This is elaborated upon in the next two sections of text. The Counties would be able to perform a more complete role on matters of consumer protection, educational and training programmes and trading regulations affecting existing businesses, however, since most of these concerns already fall within the compass of their responsibilities. The need here will be to formulate policies that are more co-ordinated than they have been before and integrated with the wider objectives of retail and commercial planning. The Districts would be called upon to identify areas and groups of people in special need of support in these fields and might (as some already do) supplement the provision of consumer services to elderly and handicapped persons through their Social Services Department.

Approach to New Development. We have argued before that while a more liberal planning attitude can be taken towards individual proposals for large retail or commercial schemes, at some stage limits may have to be imposed on the collective amount that can be supported. A way through this difficult area of decision-making is to concentrate the power of adjudication of large schemes in the hands of the Counties who would be required to seek advice from an independent body or committee of expert opinion. This body might parallel in part the shopping advisory panel established by Cheshire County Council[18] and in part the elected regional committees in France,[19] commanding more influence than the former but not having the statutory functions of the latter. It could be made up of representatives of consumer groups, different retail and commercial traders, informed academics and trade unionists and be expected to advise on other controversial planning matters as well as assist in the formulation of broader planning policies. County officials, with the assistance of this body, might then also take a more active role in generating ideas for future development and would be responsible for monitoring the effects of all those schemes they approve. Special plans may have to be prepared, of the kind we have already referred to, to take account of the impact of new development and also other pressures that have emerged within distribution as a whole, such as in transportation and the decline of small businesses.

The District authorities, meanwhile, might also be obliged to make clearer in their general management plans what sorts of smaller-scale development would be preferred in areas subject to variable environmental and land use controls; what site restrictions they would want to enforce on any large development granted approval from above; and what kinds of supporting services and amenities they would like to encourage in any size of development. The more information that the District planners can furnish developers about the variable trading conditions they would like to create, the better the response will be in applications that conform with these and the less acrimony is likely to result.

Renovation and Redevelopment. An advisory body of retail and commercial experts might also be able to make substantial contributions to the formulation of more sensitive and effective programmes of renovation and redevelopment. Here, it is essential that the Counties give more attention to the creation of ideas about how they see the city centre in the future, both in its environmental form and its functional character, than they have in the past. The potential threats of energy constraints and technological changes in retailing and office activities, together with the likely continuing limitations on public expenditure and private speculation, suggest that very different kinds of problems are going to emerge in the central area compared to those hitherto seen, and these must be anticipated and planned for in advance. The city centre of a large metropolitan area is far too important to the surrounding region to be assigned as the planning responsibility of a District alone. The Counties should also be required to decide on the priorities involved in major improvement schemes to smaller town centres and to monitor the general upgrading of the retail and commercial environment throughout their areas. The Districts, however, will be more closely involved in the day-to-day progress of renovation and redevelopment schemes and, as occurs at the present time through the medium of Action Area Plans, may initiate their own smaller programmes of improvement in a variety of locational settings. It is the variability in problems of declining areas at the local level, in fact, which leads us to suggest that the Districts should prepare an additional set of more specialised plans to complement their general management functions. The subjects which seem most appropriate for these concern the environmental problems of specific residential areas, such as the inner city, the pressures exerted on smaller town centres particularly in the form of traffic and congestion, and the reduction in services to be found in many rural communities.

Special Plans for Specific Problems

Three examples of system-related problems and three types of areally-based problems have already been identified in our discussions, with the former being assigned as the responsibility of the County authorities and the latter to the Districts. The closest parallels to the sorts of plans envisaged here are the Subject Plans of the conventional planning process although the subjects we have selected are probably more specific than those usually adopted. It is not necessary to elaborate on the content or style of these plans in detail for there ought to be considerable flexibility in the way the problems are addressed, but some further reference to the scope of these plans is desirable.

The special plans prepared by Counties would be guided again by central government recommendations on locational strategies and trading regulations. Those new kinds of centres or trade developments whose political impact would be measured would include large store proposals, new shopping centres, trade or exhibition centres and also new warehousing or commercial estates if these were thought to pose some threat to similar existing facilities. The methodologies currently employed by County Planning Departments to assess the spatial repercussions of new schemes would remain relevant here, but additional, more subjective evidence could also be obtained from the advisory panel or committee of retail and commercial experts we have alluded to. The formulation of policies to provide remedial help to small businesses in difficulty might involve the allocation of direct or indirect financial aid to certain essential services; but more generally they would likely be based around the drawing together of, and expansion upon, those elements of the broader management plans that allow for a loosening of locational and environmental constraints and provide for more training and educational support programmes. If central government established a small business consultancy service of the kind we have recommended, then clearly this would also serve as a further nucleus to a special plan, since it would be implemented most effectively at a county or similar size of area. The subject summarised under the heading of transport and communciation would primarily be concerned with various problems of accessibility facing both suppliers and consumers. For suppliers, help is needed in making the business of physical distribution more efficient; for consumers, the main requirement is for greater equitability in the opportunities available to travel to different centres. This is a subject fraught with conflicting interests, however, the chief manifestation of which is the congestion that builds up in central locations and which then does nobody any good. There are issues particularly on the adequacy of goods reception facilities and car parking and bus staging provisions.

The special plans prepared by Districts could be directed at a similar mix of retail and commercial matters within the context of specific areas. The problems of the inner city are perhaps the most obvious ones, ranging from the poverty of the retail and commercial environment to the need to alleviate both unemployment and the relatively high prices of goods to be found; the problems of the middle parts of the urban area have been rather ignored to date, but include the growing antiquity of retail resources, the exodus of large amounts of spending and the need for substantial car parking improvements; the problems of the suburbs are less acute and confined to specific localities, but range from the conflict that often arises between new warehousing or other commercial development and residential growth to the lack of shopping provisions in isolated housing estates. In so far as town centre pressures are concerned, a special plan would need to deal not only with transport problems again but, depending on the type of environment found, the potential threat of intrusive building, the spread of physical blight and the penetration of traditional shopping streets by business services. Rural areas pose a multitude of problems, some stemming from too much pressure for development where tourist interest may be high, but the majority suffering from a general impoverishment in resources due to small business decline. Attempts to provide remedial policies here may therefore have to be dovetailed with those diverted to problems within the small business community as a whole.

Conclusion

This chapter has sketched an alternative approach to retail and commercial planning in Britain to that which is currently pursued by central and local government. The ideas suggested, however, do not call for dramatic changes to the statutory basis or established machinery of planning; rather they look to a reallocation of responsibilities among the existing legislative bodies and professional practitioners and a greater focus on problems to be confronted in place of the emphasis hitherto given to methodology. The root of the approach is a clearer definition of what the goals and objectives of retail and commercial planning should be, with the goals conceived as a national set of aspirations and the objectives the instruments by which policies are formulated at the local level. Achievement of the goals requires a much greater commitment to be made by central government in providing comprehensive strategies to guide the orderly evolution of new development. These strategies should apply to all sectors of the distributive trades and refer to the socio-economic implications of change as well as the land use and physical repercussions involved. Given stronger direction from above, local authorities should find it easier to produce compatible policies on major issues and have more time to identify and deal with those matters of a more parochial kind.

Two types of local authority plans have been distinguished, described simply as general management plans and special plans. The general management plans can be equated with the main functions of both Structure Plans and District Plans in establishing a broad set of policies towards the distribution system; the special plans have some affinity with Subject Plans although they are directed towards problems that have rarely been given separate attention in the past. In making these distinctions, much clearer definition has been given of the different responsibilities to be fulfilled by the upper and lower tiers of local government and how closer co-ordination in their working relationships can be achieved. These ideas provide the essential framework for the chapters that follow in the rest of the book. Part II is concerned with elaborating upon the key elements involved in the general management of the distribution system; Part III is concerned with examining in more detail those specific problems that require more specialised plans. The material presented in each subsequent chapter, however, is intended to be more broadly based than simply an extension of the arguments put forward here.

References

1. See, for example, McLoughlin, J.B., *Urban and Regional Planning – A Systems Approach* (Faber, London, 1969), ch. 6.
2. Gruen has reported on the decline of the American central area in several publications. For example, Gruen, V., *Centers for the Urban Environment – Survival of the Cities* (Van Nostrand Reinhold Co., New York, 1973).
3. Unit for Retail Planning Information, *Local Shopping Centres and Convenience Stores: Report of an URPI Workshop* (Reading, 1980).
4. Thorpe, D., 'Retailing in the City Centre', in Davies, R.L. and Champion, A.G. (eds.), *The Future for the City Centre* (Academic Press, London, 1983).
5. Centre on Environment for the Handicapped, *Access in the High Street – Advice on How to Make Shopping More Manageable for Disabled People* (London, 1981).
6. A basis for this is indicated in Davies, R.L. and Bennison, D.J., 'Retailing in the City Centre: The Characters of Shopping Streets', *Tijdschrift voor Economische en Sociale Geografie*, vol. 69, no. 5 (1978), pp. 270-85.
7. Recent evidence from Scotland, however, suggests that there is usually a net gain to employment within a local economy following the introduction of a superstore. Davies, R.L., *Retail Employment Change in Scotland – With Special Reference to Superstores* (Central Research and Intelligence Report, Scottish Development Department, 1982).

8. A review of training programmes for retailing within various EEC countries is contained in Commission of the European Communities, 'Synoptic Tables of the Specific Measures Taken by the Member States of the European Communities in the Field of Commerce', *Commerce and Distribution Series 3* (Brussels, 1977).
9. Schiller, R., 'The Responsibilities of Retail Planning', in Davies, R.L. (ed.), *Retail Planning in the European Community* (Saxon House, Farnborough, 1979).
10. See the arguments produced by Dischkoff, N., 'Retail Planning in West Germany', in Davies, R.L. (ed.), *Retail Planning in the European Community.*
11. Langton, T. (ed.), *Planning Appeals Volumes 1, 2 and 3* (Ambit, Gloucester, undated).
12. Jones, P.M., 'The Prospects for Retailing – Enterprise Zones', *Estates Gazette*, vol. 259, no. 1037 (26 Sept. 1981), pp. 1037-41.
13. Bolton, J.E., *Small Firms: Report of the Committee of Inquiry on Small Firms* (HMSO, London, 1971); Hall, M., *The Small Unit in the Distributive Trades* (Committee of Inquiry on Small Firms, Research Report 8, 1971).
14. A review of the work of small retailer consultancy services in other EEC countries is given in Dawson, J.A. and Kirby, D.A., *Small Scale Retailing in the UK* (Saxon House, Farnborough, 1979).
15. Coombes, M.G. *et al.*, 'Functional Regions for the Population Census of Great Britain', in Herbert, D.T. and Johnston, R.J. (eds.), *Geography and the Urban Environment: Progress in Research and Applications*, vol. 5 (Wiley, Chichester, 1982).
16. The Unit for Retail Planning Information has gone some way to producing such information in its various reports. See, for example, Jones, P., *Trading Features of Hypermarkets and Superstores* (URPI, Reading, 1978).
17. Urban Land Institute, *Shopping Center Development Handbook* (Community Builders Handbook Series) (Urban Land Institute, Washington, DC, 1977).
18. Gilfoyle, I., 'The Cheshire Shopping Consultative Panel', in *Furthering Local Authority and Retailing Contacts as an Aid to Better Planning* (Unit for Retail Planning Information, Reading, 1980).
19. See, Dawson, J.A., 'Control Over Large Units in France: the Loi Royer and its Effects', *Retail and Distribution Management*, vol. 4, no. 6 (1976), pp. 14-18.

Part II

THE SUBJECTS OF GENERAL MANAGEMENT PLANS

5   EXAMPLES OF STRATEGIC (STRUCTURE) PLANS

It is now 14 years since the need to provide strategic plans for large areas in Britain was formally accepted by central government and a number of local authorities embarked on the preparation of the new Structure Plans in advance of the local government reorganisation that followed in 1972. Some local authorities were more cautious in their response, however, and did not get their plans underway until well into the middle of the decade; and others, of course, where significant county boundary changes had taken place, had to defer their work until a new statistical base was available. At the time of writing, a few local authorities still await approval of their plans from the Department of the Environment but in essence a national coverage of such plans is now complete. The passage of time between the earliest and latest Structure Plans has seen some notable changes in the form and content of these plans, despite their broad approximation to the guiding principles of the Manual on Development Plans.[1] This is most clearly seen in the sections on retailing and commercial activity in terms of a shift away from extensive use of modelling procedures to greater discussion of the problems of individual centres.

The 1980s, however, is expected to be a decade when many of the new initiatives within planning as a whole will come from the Districts rather than the Counties. This has two worrying implications in terms of the legacy of Structure Plans that will be left. Firstly, while some progress has been made in improving the relevance of Structure Plans to the real concerns of consumers and the business community, the majority of them have established a series of policies aimed simply at organising the physical stock of resources rather than addressing questions of a broader socio-economic kind. This may make them outdated as a framework for the production of District Plans although some scope exists to revise and modify them over time. Secondly, if the relative power of the Districts is enhanced at the expense of the Counties, there will in any event be the temptation to ignore the guidelines laid down in Structure Plans, whether these are revised or not. Some disregard already takes place and in the absence of clear directives to the contrary is likely to become more widespread. It is encumbent upon the Department of the Environment (and Welsh and Scottish Offices) to see that the relationships between the upper and lower tiers of local government do not deteriorate still further.

This chapter reviews a small number of the existing Structure Plans to give more insight into their form and content and the way they have evolved. Emphasis is once again placed on their retailing or shopping considerations rather than the full spectrum of the distributive trades, not by deliberate choice over the matter but simply because these are the subjects stressed within the plans themselves. An assessment is then made of the collective strengths and weaknesses of the case studies and indications are given as to where improvements might be made in the future for both the problem identification and policy formulation stages.

The Case Studies

The Leicestershire, Tyne and Wear and Cheshire County Structure Plans have been selected, partly because they reflect on plans prepared at different times in the past and partly for the variety of retail and commercial environments that are embraced. The London Docklands Strategic Plan is also considered for, whilst this reflects on a smaller scale of planning and is addressed to specific problems of an inner city area, recognition should be given to the scope that exists for strategic planning on specialised subjects outside the conventional administrative units. None of the plans should be viewed as representing either the best or worst of strategic plans; they are extracted here simply to show some variable approaches that have been adopted.

The Leicestershire Structure Plan

The Leicestershire Structure Plan was prepared in the early 1970s and was heavily influenced both by the contemporaneous publication of the Manual on Development Plans and the preceding Leicester and Leicestershire Sub-Regional Study.[2] The plan is therefore based around the application of a strong quantitative methodology, incorporating the use of a retail potential model and the testing of alternative strategies for the allocation of future shopping resources. Its rather limited objectives are clearly stated in the terms of reference for the Report of Survey:

> . . . to examine the nature and scale of both durable and convenience goods shopping and make provision for any major increase in shopping which may be necessary. The hierarchy of shopping centres

should be suggested, and the disposition of shopping as between central area and dispersed sites should be considered in relation to the transport pattern of the area.[3]

The steps that were followed to meet these aims are similar to those outlined in Table 3.5 of Chapter 3. They were:

to establish the existing situation at base year; estimate future changes in terms of shopping expenditure and floorspace; set up alternative shopping policies to meet the future demand; evaluate these alternatives; select the preferred shopping policy.[4]

Base year was taken to be 1961 and the main forecast year as 1991. It was claimed that the former time was rather forced on the planners, to the extent that the 1971 Census of Distribution results had not yet been published while the work was underway and sales data were needed to calibrate the model. This meant, however, that other data inputs to the modelling exercise, namely floorspace figures collected in 1967 and 1970, had to be adjusted back to 1961 and one wonders why a forward estimate of sales could not have been made or calibration achieved from some other, preferably trip data, source. The choice of 1991 as the target year can likewise be criticised on the grounds that this was too far forward in time to allow realistic assumptions to be made about changes in consumer behaviour and retailing innovations, which needed to be included in the projected state of the model; but in hindsight, any other earlier data would not have proved to be more satisfactory since the whole exercise pre-dated the inflationary and recessionary economic conditions of the late 1970s. In short, the projections of the model were doomed to be quite erroneous soon after they had been made, for the growth expectations for the 1970s, particularly on consumer spending, were simply not to be realised.

The main purpose of the model, however, as we have indicated before is usually the case, was not to forecast future floorspace requirements as such but rather to indicate what would be the apportionment in particular centres arising from the implementation of different kinds of locational control. A future requirement of 1.1 million square feet (102,225 m^2) of net selling space by 1991 (of which more than 80 per cent would be for durable goods floorspace) had already been determined by ratio methods on an assumed relationship between consumer spending and the sales per square foot (or metre) to be achieved by stores. This total was slightly amended after the final runs of the model had been made but the effect on the resulting spatial allocations was negligible. The general principle followed was to examine the consequences on five types of centre of pursuing six alternative strategies as to where growth should be encouraged or checked. The five types of centre included: the central area of Leicester, the major district centres within Leicester, existing and proposed suburban centres on the outskirts of Leicester, the town centres of the county towns and the hypothetical case of new 'out-of-town' regional shopping centres. The six optional policies comprised: distributing new floorspace on a *pro rata* basis (according to size) throughout all the centres; otherwise concentrating growth on just the county towns, the central area, the inner centres, seven designated suburban developments or on two new regional shopping centres, imagined to be located near motorway junctions on the periphery of Loughborough and Hinckley.

A Lackshmanan-Hansen model[5] was employed to test the outcome of the different policies, which involved changing the potential attractiveness of centres by assumed increases in floorspace (determined from the independent projections which had been made on this). The model then effectively rationalised the likelihood of these assumed increases being met according to the drawing power on consumers which the enhanced centres would have. The results in broad percentage terms are shown in Table 5.1. This indicates the relative likely gains (and sometimes losses) for all centres accruing from each policy up to 1991; but the figures also include the net additions which had been made to the existing stock in 1961 over an intervening 13-year period, so the proportional shifts in many cases are not large. The main significance of the model's output, however, lies not so much with the predicted floorspace changes themselves as with the differences that are found between the predicted amounts and those initially fed into the model. The greater the margin of difference that is found, the more this reflects on the real inherent growth prospects for the variable types of centres. Comparisons which were then made on this basis clearly showed that the central area of Leicester, the county towns and the suburban developments offered most promise, as we might expect. The two hypothetical regional shopping centres would also obviously represent considerable real growth potential, but at this stage in the analysis they were discarded from further consideration on the grounds of their likely debilitating effects on the central area and county towns.

The comparisons which were made between the model's outputs and its inputs constituted a partial evaluation of the acceptability of the six alternative strategies and, after broad appraisal of other conditions

Table 5.1: The Distribution of Retail Floorspace in Leicestershire According to Alternative Strategies

	1961	Policies favouring growth in the following directions by 1991:					
		Present hierarchy	County towns	Central area	District centres	Suburban centres	Regional centres
	%	%	%	%	%	%	%
Convenience							
Central area	13	24	23	32	20	20	22
District centres	23	15	15	13	19	13	14
Suburban centres	5	8	8	8	8	21	8
County towns	23	22	24	21	22	21	20
Regional centres	—	—	—	—	—	—	7
Major centres	64	69	70	73	69	75	72
Minor centres	36	31	30	27	31	25	28
All centres	100	100	100	100	100	100	100
Durables							
Central area	58	54	52	58	47	48	52
District centres	9	7	7	6	13	6	7
Suburban centres	1	7	6	6	6	17	6
County towns	21	21	26	20	20	20	19
Regional centres	—	—	—	—	—	—	6
Major centres	90	89	91	90	87	92	90
Minor centres	10	11	9	10	13	8	10
All centres	100	100	100	100	100	100	100

Source: Leicester County Council, *Leicestershire Structure Plan — Report of Survey* (Leicester, 1974).

within the retail environments of the different types of centre, a new composite policy was formulated which emphasised growth being shared beween the central area, county towns and suburban developments. The consequences of the new policy were again examined via the model and as a result of the findings here a mark 2 version was put forward, incorporating amendments to the relative attractiveness which the different centres would have for convenience or durable goods trade. This revised composite policy was then subsequently accepted as the preferred strategy to guide the direction of new retail floorspace investments up to 1991. The allocations apportioned by the model suggested that, since 1961, the central area would experience a percentage growth of 60 per cent, the suburban developments 349 per cent and the county towns 60 per cent. As a corollary of this, the inner district centres of Leicester would decline by about 3 per cent over the 30-year period. These percentage figures were then converted into actual floorspace amounts and those changes expected to occur from the mid-1970s onwards were embodied as targets to be reached within the Written Statement of the Structure Plan.[6]

Apart from specifying the eventual size or capacity of the retail system in 1991, the Written Statement simply describes in a verbalised way the implications for the different types of centres of pursuing the preferred strategy. The main proposals that stem from these are summarised in Table 5.2. It is arguable, therefore, that the entire content of retail planning for the foreseeable future in Leicestershire has been shaped by a technical exercise which itself was based on highly dubious assumptions. The City of Leicester in fact took issue with the forecasts not long after they had been made stating, in a central area study, that 'the population and income projections were rather high; the viability (retail turnover per square foot) of durable goods floorspace was underestimated; the viability of convenience goods floorspace was overestimated. The conclusion is that the appropriate projection (for overall shopping floorspace) may be too high.'[7] Despite the shaky foundations on which the Structure Plan has been built, however, the spatial policies that were decided upon seem intuitively quite sound. It is significant perhaps that since the plan was published, three major decisions to refuse planning permission for shopping developments that were contrary to the policies have been upheld by the Department of the Environment after going to appeal.[8]

The Structure Plan as a whole, however, can be criticised not only for its limited treatment of retailing issues but also for its scant attention to the other components of the distributive trades. There are brief paragraphs here and there within the Report of Survey on the problems associated with heavy goods vehicles, car parking provisions and entertainment facilities, but there is little substantive discussion of how these could or should be resolved. A survey of 600 wholesaling and warehousing establishments was undertaken, the results of which suggested that most firms were poorly mechanised and had no predisposition to move; but no attempt was made to assess the future impact on these of changes of distribution, the introduction of new technological innovations or the spatial implantation of large branch depots from elsewhere.

Table 5.2: Summary of Shopping Proposals in the Leicestershire
Structure Plan

Leicester city centre

1. To encourage the city centre to continue to provide facilities for the whole
    area and to sustain and increase its importance with regard to durable goods
    shopping.

2. The (city) centre has considerable economic potential, and proposals for
    floorspace growth in the county and city generally, should not be
    encouraged to conflict with this potential.

3. To increase the attraction of the city centre for shopping purposes by
    seeking improvements to the environment such as pedestrianisation, and the
    encouragement of more flexible shopping hours.

4. Some changes in the role of the city centre for convenience goods shopping
    may be expected. . . . (Large supermarkets) need large sites with
    considerable groundfloor parking adjoining, for which city centres are
    unlikely to be the best locations.

District centres within Leicester

5. To maintain existing district centres in Leicester, but to review and where
    necessary rationalise the level and type of provision when redevelopment
    of nearby residential areas takes place. (. . . These are the old established
    shopping areas in the inner suburbs of Leicester, mostly along the main
    radial roads into the city . . . with rationalisation to include concentration
    in particular areas.)

Suburban centres in central Leicestershire

6. To provide for the further growth of existing suburban shopping centres.

7. To give consideration to the provision of additional suburban facilities
    in new locations which satisfy the criteria below:

    a. They should be closely related to the primary road network, with
        accessibility for both car and non-car shoppers.

    b. They should be closely related to the areas which they are likely to
        serve and are likely to be most appropriate near major growth areas
        close to Leicester proposed in the Structure Plan, or to recent major
        new developments.

    c. That adequate and convenient car parking and off-street servicing
        facilities are provided.

    d. The free flow of traffic on adjacent roads should not be impeded, and
        adequate arrangements must be made for access to the site.

    e. They should not lead to any increase in traffic on roads in any adjacent
        residential areas.

    f. They should not be located in close proximity to existing suburban
        shopping centres but rather where additional facilities can be
        demonstrated to be required, because of recent or proposed population
        growth nearby.

(The most appropriate areas are . . . to the north-east, north-west and south-west of Leicester.)

(Edge of town hypermarkets may have their place in the overall pattern . . . but it is unlikely that more than a small number of such centres with an overall total of perhaps 19,000 m^2 (200,000 sq ft) of sales area will be required by 1991.)

County towns

8. To provide for the additional shopping needs of the outer county primarily within the county towns which will continue to provide for the greater part of local shopping needs including those of the surrounding villages.

9. Generally to resist the provision of major new shopping facilities outside existing (county town) centres, but to give consideration to such provision if associated with extensive new residential development.

Local shops and village shops

10. To make provision for local shops in new development areas and villages in accordance with Local Plans where the need cannot adequately be met by existing facilities or those in nearby centres.

Out-of-town shopping centres

11. To resist the establishment of out-of-town shopping centres in Leicester and Leicestershire which cannot be established without seriously damaging the role and undermining the investment in the city and other major centres.

A more redeeming feature of the plan, nevertheless, is a proposal to extend the number of conservation areas throughout the county, particularly in small town and village centres, where problems of environmental conflict are very acute.

The Tyne and Wear Structure Plan

The Tyne and Wear Structure Plan largely followed in the wake of the Leicestershire Structure Plan for work on this was not started until late 1974 and it was not submitted to the Secretary of State for the Environment until the summer of 1979. The course that was set was similar to the extent that much reliance was put on forecasting the future capacity of the retail system, to the same target year of 1991, and a series of alternative locational strategies for guiding new investment were examined before a preferred policy was accepted. The organisation and stages in development of the plan were different, however, by virtue of the fact that the Report of Survey[9] dealt only with trends taking place in retailing and consumer demand and the determination of future floorspace requirements, while a separate volume entitled Choosing the Strategy[10] focused on the spatial allocation of new resources and evaluating the various options available. This split in the application of the general methodology occurred since the alternative shopping strategies that were tested in the Tyne and Wear Structure Plan were bound up with a broader set of strategies directed at the nature of economic development and settlement growth as a whole within the county, while those shopping strategies tested in the Leicestershire case were treated independently of those formulated for other land use activities.

The time at which the Tyne and Wear Structure Plan was prepared, however, gave it some clear advantages over its forerunner. The results of the 1971 Census of Distribution had become available and the Unit for Retail Planning Information had begun publishing its useful analyses of changes in consumer spending and business conditions. Not surprisingly, therefore, the Report of Survey (particularly the earlier interim draft[11]) describes in some detail the various shopping trends that occurred both nationally and within the Northern Region between 1961 and 1971 and it was possible to record the downturns in the economy, affected by increasing inflation and the decline in the birth rate, that became apparent in the mid-1970s. All this enabled a much more accurate assessment to be made of the external factors that would affect trade inside the county in the future; and to this was added the findings of two major surveys which the County Council itself organised to provide further understanding of the internal forces at work. The first of these, conducted in 1975, comprised a postal questionnaire sent to 10,000 households in the county (and from which 2,500 replies were received), aimed at eliciting information about shopping behaviour and attitudes towards shopping centres.[12] The second, undertaken in 1976, involved an inventory of all convenience and durable goods floorspace to be found in centres larger than those of neighbourhood status. The results of the two surveys enabled an up-to-date hierarchy to be described and the catchment areas of its major components to be plotted on maps. (The catchment area for Newcastle's city centre is shown in Figure 5.1.)

The catchment area delimitations were particularly significant in calculating the expected demand for new floorspace provisions in individual centres up to 1991. The future trends in population sizes of these could be fairly easily determined and reasonable assumptions made about spending patterns and turnover to floorspace ratios. The forecasts that were made, however, differed substantially in scale from those produced for Leicestershire because of the general state of the

Figure 5.1: The Catchment Area for Durable Goods Trade in the
City Centre of Newcastle upon Tyne, 1975

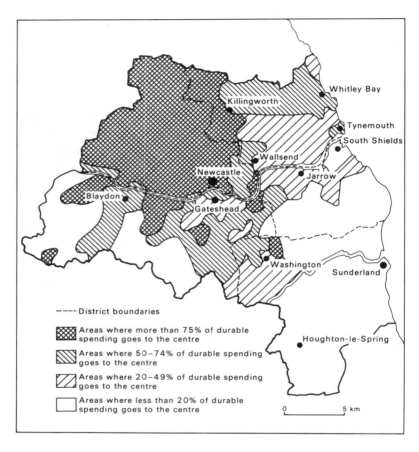

Source: Tyne and Wear County Council, *Structure Plan — Survey of Shopping
Patterns in Tyne and Wear, 1975* (Newcastle upon Tyne, 1977).

metropolitan market and the retail environment. Tyne and Wear has
for long had a depressed economy and seen a depletion of its overall
population base through out-migration. With little improvement
expected in economic conditions during the next decade, and a predicted loss of 7 per cent of the total population, the scope that exists
for real increases in consumer demand is obviously quite small. Much of

the slack in the retail system that existed in the 1960s had also been taken up by the time the Report of Survey was prepared by extensive commercial redevelopment programmes throughout the county. These included the construction of the vast Eldon Square Regional Shopping Centre in Newcastle and the new town centre for Washington, the two schemes together accounting for almost 100,000 square metres of gross floorspace. Given these developments, and the potential adverse effects they were expected to have on other centres, projections for the period 1978 to 1991 suggested that only a further 10,000 square metres of durable goods floorspace could be accommodated throughout the county (or 2.1 per cent of the existing supply); while in the convenience goods sector there would be no net growth at all. Convenience goods floorspace in the inner areas of the conurbation was predicted to decline by 8,300 square metres, that in the intermediate (middle) areas to increase by 5,900 square metres, and in the outer areas there would be a static situation.

The distribution of these small additional amounts of floorspace, together with identification of those centres where likely decline would go unchecked, were considered in relation to five broad strategies that focused mainly on the employment problems and social deprivation of the county. It is not necessary to elaborate on these for in the end a composite policy was once again proposed and accepted. The way in which the alternative strategies were evaluated in shopping terms is interesting, however, for whilst a gravity model was employed as part of this, its role was much less significant than in the case of the Leicestershire Structure Plan, and greater emphasis was given instead to a discussion of the social and economic implications of the different strategies. For example, the benefit of superstores in selected locations on reducing prices of goods was recognised; the over-endowment of Newcastle's central area and other major centres was seen as likely to exacerbate the functional deficiencies of the inner city; the need to take a cautious approach in encouraging new local centres in residential areas was pointed to. This discussion was not based around any quantitative assessment of the pros and cons of each strategy; it simply took the form of a subjective appraisal of the merits and demerits of each.

What materialised in the preferred strategy as a whole was a collection of proposals aimed mainly at giving highest priority to increasing employment in the county and improving the environmental circumstances of the deprived sections of the community. In neither of these two central concerns, however, was retailing seen as being able to play a significant part. Nor were related commercial activities raised in the final conclusions as potential contributors to job creation; and services that might be directed to different disadvantaged groups were generally ignored throughout the report. The chief summary recommendations so far as shopping matters are concerned were that:

a) Growth of shopping in Newcastle, Sunderland and Washington New Town central areas will be limited in scale, and new shops for goods other than food will be concentrated in the other main centres.

b) New local shopping (in district centres and local shops) will be encouraged in areas where population growth is expected to occur. Where population is likely to decline there will need to be action by the local authorities to maintain the service to the public, but some closures will be unavoidable.

c) Out-of-town shopping and developments in existing centres so large as to seem to cause severe losses of trade to neighbouring centres will not be permitted.[13]

The Cheshire County Structure Plan

The Cheshire County Structure Plan is another product of the second half of the 1970s but is noteworthy for having turned its back against the rigid systems approach followed in Tyne and Wear and Leicestershire and adopting instead a much looser, reflective attitude towards the derivation of its shopping policies. There are three particular features that seem to set it apart from the more conventional forms of Structure Plans that emanated during the decade. Firstly, instead of treating shopping matters in isolation from other land use concerns, it attempted to bring several issues together by focusing on the problems of town centres, rather than shopping centres *per se*, and to deal with the consequences of retail, office and commercial developments on traffic, the built environment and the weaker elements of trade. This was only partially successful, however, to the extent that most of the analytical sections of the Report of Survey[14] focus on a comparison of retail and office provisions between town centres in the county and the relationships that should have been shown with traffic congestion, environmental deterioration and adverse economic competition are rather weakly developed. Secondly, the plan gives much less emphasis to the past trends which have been occurring within retailing and to statistical calculations of what future demand may be like and hence the precise requirements in floorspace provisions to be met. Those forecasts that have been made refer only to 1986 and relate mainly to four large sub-areas of the county rather than individual centres. Greater attention is given instead to adjudicating how the planning machinery can be used to encourage growth and improve people's accessibility to shops, and where within the county the greatest priorities in these lie. The third distinctive feature is that much greater reliance has been put on public consultations in shaping the policies ultimately proposed than is found in most other plans. Public participation exercises were conducted at the beginning and end of work on the shopping components of the plan: in the initial stages through a general questionnaire aimed at obtaining people's reactions to alternative possible policies towards town centre development; in the final stages through more specialist advice from official bodies in the county and the Shopping Consultative Panel that had been established (and to which we referred in Chapter 3).[15]

The two main options that were initially put before the public were: 'should just a few major town centres be chosen as centres of expansion or should all town centres be encouraged to improve?'[16] The first implied selecting four main centres, one from each quadrant of the county, encouraging population growth and hence retail spending within their catchment areas, directing investments in public services and partnership shopping developments there, favouring them with environmental 'face-lifting' exercises and giving them priority treatment in the application of traffic management schemes. The second, not quite the opposite of this, was to spread resources throughout the major centres of the county but to give greatest help to those centres in most need of either new retail growth, public service provisions, environmental improvements or traffic relief. Certain subsidiary policy considerations were also raised with respect to the location of shops outside town centres, the nature of conservation schemes and whether the County Council should ensure that people continue to live within town centres. The general response that came back from the public with respect to the two main options was once again rather predictable. Those living closest to three of the four designated centres (Chester, Warrington and Crewe) in a policy of concentrated resource allocations supported this option while those near Macclesfield (the fourth proposed centre) were split either way. People living elsewhere in the county wanted improvements made to their own or nearest other town; the official District Councils, reflecting their own constitutency interests, were divided in their views; the Shopping Consultative Panel seemed rather negative about both options, suggesting that a policy of concentration would have only a marginal effect on private sector investments, and a policy of dispersal (but one favouring the weaker centres) would simply dissipate resources with little real gain to the county as a whole.

Prior to a final decision being made about the spatial strategy to be followed, however, analyses were undertaken of the existing endowment of centres in shopping and service provisions to identify in more detail where strengths and weaknesses were to be found. These exercises departed from the usual practice of ranking centres according to their floorspace size, number of establishments and estimated turnover and dealt instead with the incidence of certain higher-order functions as a guide to the range and quality of facilities available. The functions included several named stores (e.g. Littlewoods, Mothercare, Boots), types of business services (e.g. banks, estate agents, head post offices) and a miscellaneous collection of leisure and recreational activities (e.g. cinemas, hotels and museums). Points were allotted for the incidence of these functions in each town centre of the county according to the following procedure: for each function, the centre with the highest number of representatives scored 100, the centre with the next highest number scored a percentage figure reflecting the proportion of its own number to the highest number, and so on. (Thus if Chester had 10 units of function X and was assigned 100 points, Winsford with 2 units would score 20.) The total of the scores for all functions effectively produced an index of centrality for each centre, as is indicated in Table 5.3. The totals were then also related to the population sizes of assumed catchment areas around each centre so that comparisons could be made of the extent of over- or under-provision of facilities on a *per capita* basis.

This was a simple but effective method of diagnosing the relative health of centres and much of the rest of the appraisal sections of the Report of Survey[17] was concerned with elaborating upon and explaining the level of shopping and service provisions to be found in individual centres. The outcome of these assessments, together with the advice of the special consultative bodies, was a series of proposals that did not follow a single common theme but were rather both pluralistic and particularistic in their nature. In other words, neither of the two original spatial strategies was adopted, although three variable types of centres were singled out for special treatment; instead, a wide range of development control principles was enunciated and considerable specification given as to how the major centres in each quadrant of the county should be dealt with in the future. The main directives that appeared in the Written Statement[18] are extracted in Table 5.4 and

Table 5.3: Centres in Cheshire Ranked According to Incidence of
Higher-order Functions

Centre	Shop types		Local services		Leisure/recreation		Total	
	Score	Rank	Score	Rank	Score	Rank	Score	Rank
Chester	2338	1	1420	1	1255	1	5013	1
Warrington	1340	2	1259	2	759	2	3358	2
Northwich	1021	5	636	6	688	3	2345	3
Crewe	1000	6	687	5	625	4	2312	4
Macclesfield	1024	4	821	3	361	10	2206	5
Runcorn (new town)	1158	3	532	9	455	5	2145	6
Ellesmere Port	510	7	626	7	445	6	1581	7
Widnes	417	9	710	4	393	8	1520	8
Wilmslow	337	12	572	8	388	9	1297	9
Winsford	365	10	444	11	335	11	1144	10
Knutsford	225	14	417	13	440	7	1082	11
Nantwich	365	10	443	12	237	12	1045	12
Congleton	270	13	449	10	211	13	930	13
Runcorn (old town)	495	8	158	17	99	17	752	14
Sandbach	210	15	224	14	153	14	587	15
Alsager	5	18	164	16	119	16	288	16
Neston	32	16	169	15	76	18	277	17
Middlewich	11	17	106	18	136	15	253	18

Source: Adapted from, Cheshire County Council, *County Structure Plan —
Report of Survey, Town Centres* (Chester, 1977).

readers will be able to see for themselves the contrast in rigorousness
with those reported for Leicestershire. As in both the Leicestershire and
Tyne and Wear cases, however, the Written Statement for Cheshire
makes little reference to the intermediary trades, although there is a
significant item in the section on employment concerning their locational requirements, that: '. . . with a growing need to provide more
employment within the County, it is important to have a range of
different types and sizes of sites available for both industrial and commercial development', such that there should be '. . . sites specifically
allocated for wholesale warehousing'.[19]

The London Docklands Strategic Plan

The London Docklands Strategic Plan clearly differs from the others
we have reviewed in terms of the very special problems to which it is
addressed. While there is a general emphasis on ways in which the area
can be revitalised and rehabilitated, however, the shopping studies and
proposals that have been made are fairly conventional in nature and not

Table 5.4: Policies for Shopping and Local Office Services in the Cheshire Structure Plan

General statement of policies

1. Shopping and local office development will generally be concentrated on sites in or contiguous to town centres and strategic sub-centres in Cheshire.

2. The priorities for additional developments for shopping and local offices are the town centres of Warrington, Widnes and Middlewich.

3. No one centre will be allowed to develop commercially to such an extent that any one of the following occurs:
   a. The economic viability of other centres is so affected that the goods and services available in them are reduced to a degree unacceptable to the County Council.
   b. Resources in other centres are wasted.
   c. Traffic congestion in the particular centre reaches a point at which it cannot easily or economically be solved.

Shopping development of strategic importance

4. The County Council will have a material interest in and will act on proposals for shopping development which it considers to be of 'strategic significance'. These will normally be defined as one of the following:
   — an increase in shopping floorspace of the order of 30,000 square feet gross for one shop unit, a shop extension or a group of shops.

5. Shopping developments of strategic significance must satisfy all the following criteria:
   a. They must be in or contiguous to a town.
   b. They must not be likely to result in a loss of significantly more than 10% of annual retail trade from any nearby town centre or strategic sub-centre.
   c. The development must not have a detrimental effect on people living nearby or the general area of the environment of the area.
   d. If public utility services are required they must be available and capable of accommodating the development proposal.
   e. The development must not generate sufficient traffic to cause nuisance or danger, nor require any major improvement of roads.

6. Shopping developments of strategic significance will normally be allowed in town centres and strategic sub-centres provided that they meet all the following requirements:
   a. They are not likely to cause traffic congestion to reach a point at which it cannot be easily or economically solved.
   b. They are not likely to have a detrimental effect on the scale and character of a centre, particularly where a conservation area is designated.
   c. The overall benefits of the developments to people living in the surrounding areas are likely to outweigh minor economic or transport disadvantages.

7. Where the County Council considers that a town centre is already congested and this congestion cannot be easily or economically solved, further shopping development in that centre will be limited.

8. Shopping development of strategic significance will not normally be allowed outside town centres and strategic sub-centres. They will only be allowed outside these centres where one or more of the following applies:
   a. Where a town centre is already congested and this congestion cannot be easily or economically solved.
   b. Where the shopping development is likely to cause traffic congestion to reach a point at which it cannot be easily or economically solved, if the development were located in an existing centre.
   c. Where there is a lack of sites suitable for such development in existing centres and they cannot be easily or economically obtained.
   d. Where the population is expected to grow by more than about 10,000 people in one part of an urban area during the period 1974 to 1986 and this population would not be adequately served by an existing centre.

9. The County Council will object to proposals for shopping developments outside Cheshire if the development seems likely to result in a loss of significantly more than 10% of annual retail trade from any town centre or strategic sub-centre in Cheshire.

10. A maximum of three years from the date of planning permission to the commencement of development will be allowed for a shopping proposal of strategic significance; where planning permission is given, two years will be allowed for the submission of any or all reserved matters not included in the original consent.

11. Until a shopping development of strategic significance has been trading for at least one year the County Council will not normally allow further shopping developments of strategic significance in the town where the development is located. This limitation will not apply where a study indicates clearly that more than one shopping development of strategic significance in the town would be acceptable to the County Council.

12. Planning permissions for shopping developments will not normally be revoked even if they conflict with one or more of the policies set out above.

Policies for retail warehouses

13. The County Council will treat proposals for 'retail warehouse' development in the same way as other shopping proposals.

14. The County Council will ensure that a new wholesale warehouse is not converted, by a gradual change in operational use, to a retail warehouse or other form of shopping.

Policies for 'other uses' in town centres

15. Commercial development in or contiguous to town centres will not normally be allowed if in the opinion of the County Council it leads to a significant net loss of:
   a. Habitable dwellings or houses of visual, architectural or historic merit.
   b. Existing sources of jobs, in a particular service industry.
   c. Recreation, cultural and entertainment facilities.

152 *Examples of Strategic (Structure) Plans*

Table 5.4 continued

Policies for town centres in 5 areas

Example for mid-Mersey area only

16. Warrington: The County Council supports the development of a new strategic sub-centre at Westbrook in Warrington New Town, provided that this is related in scale to the local shopping requirements of the new population, and is substantially for convenience goods.

17. Runcorn: Further shopping development of Runcorn Shopping City should not be detrimental to the town centres of Warrington and Widnes and should not begin trading until after 1982.

18. Widnes: The town centre is designated as an 'action-area'. The particular strategic priorities are:
    a. The development of a shop unit of strategic significance which has an emphasis upon comparison goods sales.
    (b. The development of national, regional or research offices.)

---

unlike those in some of the District as distinct from Structure Plans. The chief departure from, say, the Tyne and Wear Structure Plan that is also strongly oriented to inner city deficiencies, is that the Docklands Plan focuses on improvements to be made in convenience goods shopping rather than the durable goods sector. This is because the area is surrounded by several large regional and sub-regional shopping centres which would themselves be vulnerable to competition from any new major developments; and the linear form of the area together with a dispersed pattern of anticipated population growth suggests there is more logic to building up a healthy network of localised facilities. That there is expected to be significant population growth within several parts of the area, as a result of ambitious redevelopment programmes, also makes the plan different from others concerned with inner city problems for this allows an expansionist policy on shopping to be followed rather than one oriented to contraction of the retail system. It should also be noted that the plan was of a non-statutory kind and substantial revisions might ensue in the future.

The central questions posed in the shopping studies[20] undertaken for the plan were: how large should the new set of local centres be and where precisely should they be located? In answer to the first, four basic size orders of district centres were initially assessed: a large centre (referred to as Type A), where the principal tenant would be a superstore, accompanied by a small supermarket and about 10-15 other shops; a next size of centre (Type B), which would have two large supermarkets and about 30 other shops; a Type C centre, that would have one large supermarket and about 10-15 other shops; and a Type D centre, that would comprise just one small supermarket and about ten other shops. Following up on the second question, a broad appraisal was then made of the suitability of each of these model types for fulfilling the floorspace requirements that had been calculated for four major communities within the Docklands: Wapping; the Surrey Docks area in Lewisham; the Isle of Dogs area of Poplar; and the Beckton, Silvertown and North Woolwich sections of Newham. After further considerations were made of the existing distribution of local shopping provisions within these areas and the phased programme of house-building that was envisaged, it was decided that six potential developments could be accommodated in the general locations shown in Figure 5.2.

All of the potential developments were expected to be quite modest in size, approximating to the Type C category referred to above (with one exception that allowed for later expansion into the Type B category); but subsequent events have seen these expectations raised and at least two of the first four centres to be built will incorporate superstores. These will be in the Surrey Docks area and the Isle of Dogs, with both developments likely coming from Asda, the northern-based firm, who already have planning permission to create a further superstore adjacent to the Millwall football ground which lies just outside the south-western boundary of the Docklands.[21] What seems to have prompted these large investments are the good public transport connections that are offered, the relative cheapness of the sites and the fact that much of the housing redevelopment that was scheduled has been kept on target.

The shopping proposal in the Surrey Docks area has always been the most interesting one since this was originally expected to be developed in conjunction with a large new trade mart. The Strategic Plan[22] itself has little to say about the possibilities of a trade mart, particularly its potential impact on employment; and it may be that the Docklands Joint Committee foresaw the subsequent years of wrangling that has ensued over the idea. The latest position on this story at the time of writing is that a scheme put forward by the Texan businessman, Mr Trammell Crow, to develop 133 acres of permanent exhibition halls and individual manufacturers' showrooms will not now go ahead because of central government's reluctance to provide sufficient grants and loans.[23] The idea offers such promise as being a major catalyst for other developments in the area, however (and independent estimates have suggested that by itself it would create 1,110 new jobs), that it is unlikely to be discarded completely.

The Strategic Plan contains a number of useful statements on other

Figure 5.2: The Initial Proposals for Shopping Centre Development in London's Docklands

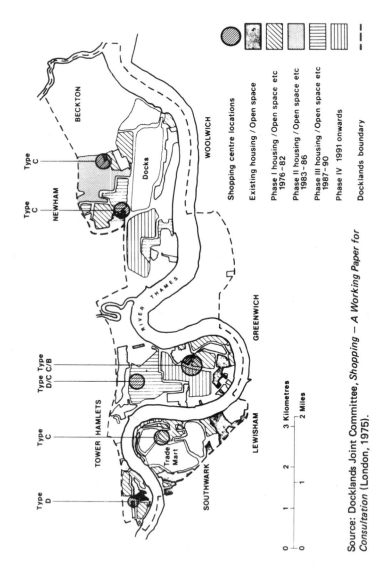

Shopping centre locations

Existing housing / Open space

Phase I housing / Open space etc
1976 – 82

Phase II housing / Open space etc
1983 – 86

Phase III housing / Open space etc
1987 – 90

Phase IV 1991 onwards

Docklands boundary

Source: Docklands Joint Committee, *Shopping – A Working Paper for Consultation* (London, 1975).

forms of commercial activity, nevertheless. It points, for example, to the need to provide small premises at low rent levels in industrial zones to foster embryonic services as well as manufacturing businesses. It recognises that the general redevelopment programme might force out many valuable craft activities and suggests retaining certain older buildings, particularly warehouses, to cater for them. It also takes note of the local authority's duty to help those disabled people in need of assistance, particularly in employment terms, and states its intention to encourage the creation of special workshops. Most important of all, perhaps, it emphasises the need to complement the provision of land for industrial and commercial purposes with the development of training and retraining schemes, not just through the Manpower Services Commission but through the educational system and via major companies as well.

The Missing Components

The four case studies that have been reviewed provide a broad cross-section of the various strategic plans that have been prepared in Britain during the last ten years. While there are numerous points of departure between them, however, they are united by certain common dimensions, most notably the focus of the analytical stages on the existing stock of physical resources and the projections and proposals for the future which deal with the allocation of additional retail floorspace to particular centres. It is relevant in the remaining sections of this chapter to consider how far these similar areas of work meet the underlying objectives of retail and commercial planning and to indicate how any shortcomings that are found can be repaired. The suggestions that are made in this latter regard develop and elaborate upon those alternative approaches to planning outlined in Chapter 4.

The Reports of Survey

Much criticism has already been made of the technical methodologies employed in the case study plans, especially their forecasting and allocation procedures. This is not taken further here, and attention is given instead to the topics that have been addressed. There are three main points of concern:

(a) All of the plans show that a considerable amount of time and energy was expended on an analysis of the retail system but that other components of the distributive trades were felt unworthy of detailed study. There are minor references to an investigation into wholesaling in the Leicestershire Structure Plan; the Cheshire Structure Plan included certain services in its appraisal of town centres; the Docklands Strategic Plan noted the incidence of small commercial enterprises. But there is no comprehensive discussion of the subject of distribution as a whole in any of the plans and little attempt to integrate related transport, office and recreational considerations (even if this required some duplication of material). We have to say, therefore, that none of these plans is directly concerned with the question of how to promote efficiency in distribution.

(b) The need to look at spatial imbalances in shopping opportunities has been attended to in each plan, with that for Tyne and Wear drawing strong contrasts between inner city and outer city areas. The emphasis in each, however, has been on a comparative assessment of the numbers and sizes of shops and shopping centres to be found, using (with the exception of Cheshire that attempted a more qualitative description of different shop types) the outmoded distinction between convenience and durable goods facilities. No comparisons were made of spatial price variations, the incidence of more essential retail services, the locations of more modern shopping provisions or, with some exception for Tyne and Wear, the variable accessibility conditions of shops and centres, as indicated by their trade areas. Nor were the characteristics of existing shopping environments examined in relation to the socio-economic and demographic circumstances of surrounding population groups. The extent to which certain population groups may be deemed to be disadvantaged as consumers has therefore only been partially answered, and little insight has been provided of the real choices available in shopping for communities as a whole.

(c) The relative health of individual large shopping centres and the conditions that exist for potential business investment have likewise been treated in only an indirect way. All of the plans make some reference to the physical problems of centres, particularly their congestion or inadequacies in car parking, but the extent of these problems is usually elaborated upon in some other (mainly transport) section of the Report of Survey. All give some indication, too, of the general growth prospects of centres, and for some cases their susceptibility to decline, but the descriptions here are mainly based on recent changes in floorspace and the birth and death records of firms. There is little discussion of the underlying market forces at work, such as changes in rent levels, functional composition and the ownership of stores, or what the effects of past planning interventions and regulatory measures have been, such as through traffic management schemes, trade opening hours and development control. These matters need not be dealt with in great detail for they can be examined more fully in District Plans; but an underlying objective of the Strategic (Structure) Plans must be surely to provide an overview of business prospects in large centres, not simply in physical or environmental terms to guide a local authority's own response, but also according to those economic criteria of most interest to the private sector.

In seeking ways to redress these shortcomings in the future, we might divide our considerations along the lines of how to improve our understanding of consumer inopportunities and how to provide more insight into the inefficiencies of the distribution system, coupled with the prospects available for business growth. The broad answers lie in a widening and reorganisation of the information that is collected; but this should not be taken to mean an increase in the workload of local authority planning departments. What is envisaged is a reduction in the data collection exercises directed to assessments of the physical state of retailing and an expansion of research into the other components of the distributive trades.

Much of the alternative information that could reflect on consumer inopportunities is readily available. Prices of grocery and household goods, for example, are regularly monitored in most local authorities by the Consumer Services Department. In Tyne and Wear, each District authority records on a weekly basis the prices of approximately 30 (standard) goods offered in four to five supermarkets, and a similar number of small specialist shops, within its largest shopping centres. If the areal coverage is limited in this case to only six centres throughout the Metropolitan County, it would be but a small step to increase the spatial sample for a single week (or month) in a 'one-off' type of survey. Market research firms also regularly monitor prices, often with a much more extensive spatial coverage of stores, and such data might be purchased subject to the agreement of collaborating retail firms. On the matter of the incidence of essential retail services, registers of post offices and chemists can be easily compiled; and information is immediately available for certain types of public services that might be related to these, such as health clinics, libraries and citizens advice bureaux. It is more difficult to obtain a complete list of local grocery stores (which may be seen as being essential stores to certain consumer groups), but the addresses of branch stores of major chains and those independent traders affiliated to the symbol groups can be acquired from the companies concerned. For each of these essential types of service, map plots of their distribution need to be made in relation to the spatial concentration of those sections of the population most dependent upon them, namely, the elderly, younger family groups and the physically handicapped. Accessibility to larger stores and shopping centres, as reflected through catchment area delimitations and public transport provisions, can again be relatively easily measured by using the same techniques or rules of thumb that retail firms themselves employ and consulting the data readily available on bus frequencies, routings and staging points. Catchment areas demarcated for, say, large supermarkets and variety stores, according to average travel distances or travel times of shoppers, modified in relation to the built form of surrounding residential areas and the transport network, should reveal those parts of the general settlement pattern where there is poor proximity and/or limited transport connections to major shopping resources. Finally, information about what new retail developments have occurred in recent years and where these have been placed should be on file within the planning department itself, and map plots made of these in relation to the socio-economic characteristics of surrounding population groups might indicate further spatial biases or inequalities in the shopping opportunities they have brought. A simplistic indication of what might be portrayed on maps from this and the other information sources referred to above is given in Figure 5.3.

When it comes to considering the nature of inefficiencies in distribution and describing those conditions affecting business growth, the information sources we might like to draw on are much less forthcoming. There is a complete dearth of documented statistics, in fact, on the spatial patterns of transactions that take place within any large area for different distribution channels. The main agencies dictating the patterns of flow, however, are relatively few in number and there is a strong case for mounting first-hand surveys of the major retail, wholesale and haulage firms to obtain more insight into the structural organisation of bulk goods deliveries: where most traffic is concentrated, the origins and destinations of goods, the main routes utilised, the attitudes of controllers and drivers to servicing facilities in shopping centres and commercial areas, etc. Much use, too, can be made of the expertise and local knowledge of those people working with distribution problems on a daily basis to build up a picture of where strengths and weaknesses in the intermediary activities occur. For example, estate agents and members of the Estates Departments of

Figure 5.3: Examples of Supporting Survey Information Regarding
Consumer Shopping Opportunities within a County

PRICE INDICES

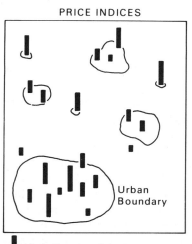

- ▌ High Grocery Prices
- ▪ Medium Grocery Prices
- ▪ Low Grocery Prices

ESSENTIAL SERVICES

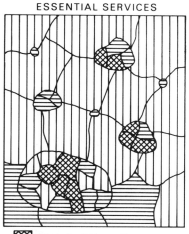

- ▨ High Incidence Rate
- ▤ Medium Incidence Rate
- Ⅲ Low Incidence Rate

ACCESSIBILITY CONDITIONS

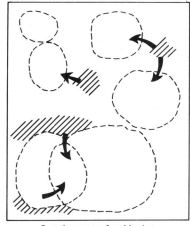

- ◌ Catchments for Variety
  Stores
- ⁄⁄⁄ Areas Under-Penetrated
- ➤ Poor Transport Connections

RETAIL DEVELOPMENTS

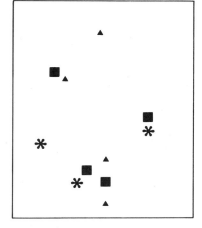

- ■ New Shopping Centres
- ✳ New Superstores
- ▲ Large Supermarkets

local authorities can furnish fairly accurate assessments of the relative health of new commercial and trading estates and those with long experience may be able to quantify the amount of decline that has occurred in outworn, inner areas. Their appraisal abilities will enable them to determine average rent levels in different localities and records will be available of rates that are charged. A comprehensive survey of rents and rates, the changing directions of these and where special grants may be obtainable on a county-wide basis would be of great help to potential investors, especially those whose headquarters offices were some distance away. The transport managers of firms, their drivers and the recipients of regular shipments of goods should also be able to give useful information on the relative degree of congestion found in various places throughout a large area, whether the congestion is related to inadequate road conditions, conflicts between different kinds of vehicles or the inadequacies of loading and parking facilities. Similarly, transport planners within the public sector ought to be in a position to pinpoint where there is most demand for certain basic service provisions, such as lorry parks and access routes into shopping centres, and where the chief hindrances to efficient goods circulation arise. Some suggestions on how these more subjectively derived information sources might be conveyed in map form are given in Figure 5.4.

In addition to the accumulation of further data about spatial processes at work, however, there is the need to gain more insight into the structural changes affecting business conditions and to evaluate how far past and present trading regulations have been effective in meeting their original aims. In our proposals for an alternative planning approach, outlined in Chapter 4, it was suggested that some of these studies might be better undertaken by central government, perhaps through their regional offices. This would apply particularly to the monitoring of shifts in sectoral trading strength amongst all three components of the distributive trades and possibly to examining changes in the structure of employment characteristics. Trade regulations, applying to licensing measures, opening hours and health controls, are rarely aired in the context of Structure Plans, but a listing of these and discussion about them might yield a greater response from interested parties on how appropriate they are for the future conduct of business. Likewise, the inclusion of information about educational and training schemes for those engaged in the distributive trades might contribute to a growing awareness of the important role which these facilities should and will play in retail and commercial planning in the future.

Figure 5.4: Examples of Supporting Survey Information Regarding
Commercial Operating Conditions within a County

COMMERCIAL ESTATES

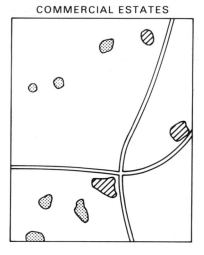

=== Motorways
▨ Growth in Wholesaling
▩ Decline in Wholesaling

RENT LEVELS

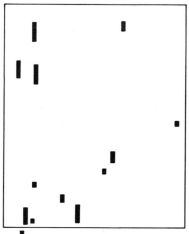

▐ High Rents/Rates
▮ Medium Rents/Rates
▪ Low Rents/Rates

DEGREE OF CONGESTION

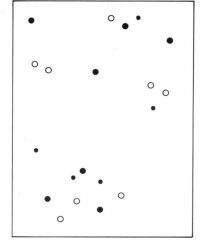

● Severe Vehicle Congestion
○ Moderate Vehicle Congestion
• Slight Vehicle Congestion

ASPECTS OF HAULAGE

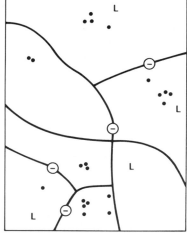

⊖ Roads with Heavy Vehicle
    Restrictions
L   Lorry Parks
•   Distribution of Haulage
    Contractors

The Written Statement

A number of the suggestions that have been made about improving the information sources for the Reports of Survey of Structure Plans imply an extension of the role of public consultations, particularly in drawing upon informed opinion within distribution itself. All of the four plans reviewed in this chapter involved some form of public consultation in their preparation but, with the exception of that for Cheshire, these were directed to obtaining opinions about alternative strategies that might be employed rather than the identification of problems as such. The Shopping Consultative Body established by Cheshire was unique in the significant contributions it made to both the analytical and policy-making stages of this particular plan; but its terms of reference were still confined to the retailing field and it would be desirable, in future applications of the model by other local authorities, to include representatives of the other distributive trades or to form parallel bodies for the intermediary activities and services.

Our criticisms of the main content of the Written Statements of Structure Plans again partly focus on the lack of attention devoted to the intermediary activities and services. While detailed forecasts of how much shopping floorspace can be accommodated in selected centres during the next decade have been provided in each of the case study plans, no projections of the likely needs in services or future states of wholesaling and warehousing have been given, despite the fact that in some segments of these trades there are likely to be more profound changes than within most aspects of retailing itself. The same sorts of omission are to be found in the spatial policies put forward in these plans although the related topics of industrial and recreational development are accorded much importance. Apart from providing estimates of how much retail floorspace can be supported in the future and where this should be distributed, however, the plan proposals say little else even on the subject of shopping. There are no deliberations on the likely effects of high energy costs, the impact of technological developments or potential changes in consumer needs and tastes. Nor is there much discussion on how the basic disadvantages of certain population groups can be improved, save in the Docklands case; and, in the absence of analyses directed towards the operational difficulties facing small firms, how business conditions might be enhanced for weaker traders through the manipulation of various trade regulations and development controls. It may be, as we have said before, that some of these considerations need fuller guidance from central government, either directly or through its regional offices; but the local authorities could also provide some initiatives through the Monitoring Reports that are now being prepared.

Many of the other features that we would like to see referred to in Monitoring Reports or incorporated into the Written Statements of future Structure Plans follow from the recommendations that have been made regarding the development of the information base for Reports of Survey. This implies diversifying the nature of policies put forward to include not only a broader range of subject concerns but also a number of aspatial measures that can be taken to improve consumer opportunities and business conditions. The route we are advocating is one leading to a corporate approach to planning, where policies oriented to the management of the physical stock of resources are allied to those aimed at developing consumer protection, commercial education and the effectiveness of trade regulations. While corporate planning has ostensibly emerged as a general ethos for planning in several local authorities, it has not yet been widely practised in the retail and commercial fields.

Conclusion

When Strategic (Structure) Plans were originally conceived in the mid-1960s, they were seen as the basis to a radical change in the plan-making process, enabling a much more comprehensive approach to be taken to problem-solving than had hitherto been the case. The prospects envisaged in the retail and commercial fields, however, have only been partially realised for, while the areal coverage of study has been enlarged, the range of problems addressed has not been substantially expanded upon. The root focus of most Structure Plans remains the determination of how much retail floorspace an area can support in the future and where within the area additional shopping provisions should be allocated.[24] There has been no broadening of the base of study to include the other components of the distributive trades; nor has there been much development, except in a cursory way, in the formulation of social and economic objectives directed to reducing social disparities in shopping opportunities and improving the efficiency of various retailing practices.

The four case studies reviewed in this chapter suggest that retail planning at the strategic level has been guided less by the problems inherent within retailing itself than by the preoccupations of planners with broader doctrinal concerns. The Leicestershire Structure Plan is a classic example of the application of a systems approach to retail planning and epitomises the way in which this methodology tended to govern all aspects of structure planning in the early 1970s. The Tyne and Wear Structure Plan retains some of the same methodological influence but also shows the renewed interest in urban development programmes that emerged in the middle part of the decade with particular reference to the plight of the inner city. The London Docklands Strategic Plan is obviously a more complete response to the concerns expressed over the inner city but also gives some recognition to the fact that the administrative units established for the preparation of Structure Plans are not always appropriate to conditions on the ground. The Cheshire Structure Plan perhaps comes closest to rejecting the original guidelines laid down for the preparation of Structure Plans but, in down-playing the role of modelling techniques, gives emphasis to the part played by public participation exercises in the decision-making process. In each of these plans, retailing is viewed as rather a passive consequence of change, the outcome of other policies effected particularly in the employment and housing fields, and is not used as an instrument which could itself contribute to job generation and significant social improvement. While the record on retail planning at the strategic level is therefore somewhat modest and uninspiring, nevertheless, one consolation is that the changes which have occurred within the nature and content of Structure Plans have been made in the right direction; and, if substantial revisions are permitted in the 1980s, we may yet see the basis to a more imaginative and relevant treatment of the distribution system being laid down.

References

1. Department of the Environment, *Development Plans – A Manual on Their Form and Content* (HMSO, 1971).
2. Leicester City Council and Leicestershire County Council, *Leicester and Leicestershire Sub-Regional Planning Study* (Leicester, 1969).
3. Leicestershire County Council, *Leicestershire Structure Plan – Report of Survey* (Leicester, 1974), p. 58.
4. Ibid., p. 59.
5. Lakshmanan, T.R. and Hansen, W.G., 'A Retail Market Potential Model', *Journal of the American Institute of Planners*, vol. 31 (1965), pp. 134-43.
6. Leicestershire County Council, *Leicestershire Structure Plan – Written Statement* (Leicester, 1976).
7. Leicester City Council, *Central Area Study – Report of Survey* (Leicester, 1978), Appendix 4.

8. Leicestershire County Council, *Leicestershire Structure Plan — Monitoring Report* (Leicester, 1979).
9. Tyne and Wear County Council, *Tyne and Wear Structure Plan — Report of Survey* (Newcastle upon Tyne, 1978).
10. Tyne and Wear County Council, *Tyne and Wear Structure Plan — Choosing the Strategy* (Newcastle upon Tyne, 1978).
11. Tyne and Wear County Council, *Tyne and Wear Structure Plan — Report of Survey, Interim Draft* (Newcastle upon Tyne, 1976).
12. Tyne and Wear County Council, *Structure Plan — Survey of Shopping Patterns in Tyne and Wear, 1975* (Newcastle upon Tyne, 1977).
13. Tyne and Wear County Council, *Tyne and Wear Structure Plan — Choosing the Strategy* (Newcastle upon Tyne, 1978), p. v.
14. Cheshire County Council, *County Structure Plan — Report of Survey, Town Centres* (Chester, 1977).
15. Cheshire County Council, *County Structure Plan — Report of Survey, Methodology* (Chester, 1977).
16. Cheshire County Council, *County Structure Plan — Report of Survey, Town Centres* (Chester, 1977), p. 45.
17. Ibid.
18. Cheshire County Council, *County Structure Plan — Written Statement of Policies and Proposals* (Chester, 1977).
19. Ibid., p. 73.
20. Docklands Joint Committee, *Shopping — A Working Paper for Consultation* (London, 1975).
21. Ognijenovic, D., 'Asda Pushes South', *Shop Property*, November (1980), pp. 28-9.
22. Docklands Joint Committee, *London Docklands Strategic Plan* (London, 1976).
23. *Financial Times*, 3 February 1979.
24. Some further case studies of Structure Plans are contained in Shaw, G. and Williams, A., 'Structure Plans and Retail Planning', *Retail and Distribution Management*, vol. 8, no. 1 (1980), pp. 43-7.

6 EXAMPLES OF LOCAL (DISTRICT) PLANS

It is more difficult to generalise about the record of local plan preparation than has been possible in the case of Structure Plans for the work of the District Councils has so far been extremely varied. Relatively few comprehensive District Plans have materialised, at least in the sense of containing broad statements of policy on how a wide range of problems and issues will be approached, for such plans are meant to complement and develop upon the Structure Plans, many of which have themselves only relatively recently been approved. What we find instead, for the most part, therefore, are a number of Interim Plans for individual topics, many of which are rather short documents giving official acceptance to the recommendations made in advisory reports prepared by consultants or other outside bodies. Where there has been more progress of a formal kind at the local level, it is to be found in the numerous Action-Area and Subject Plans prepared, the majority of them dealing with environmental improvements to town centres and the inner city. These more specific types of plans are not considered in this chapter, however, but will be referred to later in Part III of the book which is devoted to special planning concerns. Our attention here remains focused on those plans, or more correctly the supporting studies, that are aimed at managing affairs throughout a District's (or large urban centre's) territory as a whole.

The wider local studies we can refer to suffer the same limitations as Structure Plans in being almost exclusively concerned with shopping matters rather than the full spectrum of the distributive trades. Within this context, nevertheless, some of the studies have proved to be quite innovatory in terms of the problems and issues addressed, adopting a stronger socio-economic perspective than that displayed by most plans at the county level. This may not be too surprising, given the small areal units which are involved and the greater recency of such work; but it must be seen as encouraging in view of the fact that Local Plans will be the dominant mode of planning in the next decade. Local Plans will inevitably remain heavily preoccupied with the business of development control, however, and it is in the linking of these procedures to the more enlightened objectives that now seem to be held that the greatest challenge to planning at this scale really lies.

This chapter looks at the emerging trends in local planning by reviewing a small selection of case studies once again. These are then critically evaluated in the light of the needs of the 1980s and the establishment of formal, comprehensive District Plans. Finally, some suggestions are made on the subject of development control which elaborate upon those outlined in Chapter 4 and argue for a more flexible approach to be taken to environmental change.

The Case Studies

Five case studies are described in varying degree of detail in this section, with most attention being devoted to those for Gateshead, Bath and Tower Hamlets, and more minor treatment being accorded those for Southend and Telford New Town. The studies for Bath and Southend were undertaken by consultants, respectively Drivers Jonas and Nathaniel Litchfield and Associates; those for the other places by the local authorities themselves. It should be noted that the study for Telford, as well as those for Bath and Southend, do not refer to the Districts in which these places are found; but they are sufficiently wide-ranging, in terms of dealing with the urban retail system as a whole, that they fall into the category of general management plans rather than being specialised pieces of work. Nevertheless, each study does give prominence to a particular set of considerations.

The Gateshead Study

This study is titled *A Shopping Policy for Gateshead – A Consultative Report*[1] and refers to the District of Gateshead within Tyne and Wear rather than just the old town of Gateshead itself. The study is effectively a Report of Survey on shopping matters and provides an integral input to the preparation of a full District Plan; but pending the completion of other subject-area studies, its recommendations have been adopted as a Statement of Policy too. Since its publication in 1978 also virtually coincided with the appearance of the final volumes of the County Structure Plan, it makes relatively little reference to the detailed nature of strategies to be applied throughout the metropolis, although it notes the main principles that are expected to be adhered to. In several respects, the study is therefore a rather self-contained one and can be singled out as a prototype for a particular kind of Local Plan.

The study aimed at deriving a shopping policy that would meet two central objectives: 'the physical distribution of shops of the right type in the right place to meet people's needs and desires', and 'the physical distribution and organisation of those shops to allow efficient and profitable trading'. But 'These two requirements cannot always be be satisfied together, and it is often the case that the need for profitability prevents the provision of all the shops that people might want.' Therefore, 'The Local Authority's role is to strike the correct balance between these competing forces to form a basic shopping provision for day-to-day needs and to facilitate cheap shopping in larger stores and the purchase of durable goods at inevitably more distant but strategically sited centres.'[2] Such objectives clearly have a strong socio-economic flavour and might be deemed to be of universal relevance, but while admirable in themselves, it seems curious perhaps that they were not backed up by additional considerations relating to the special conditions prevailing in Gateshead, namely the concentration of a large number of disadvantaged consumers in a designated inner city area and the poverty of the retailing environment caused both by past planning mistakes and the proximity of Gateshead to two major growth centres (namely Newcastle and Washington New Town). The past planning mistakes relate essentially to a massive commercial redevelopment programme in the town centre which split the traditional high street into two separate parts and created a new purpose-built shopping scheme that has been an abject failure both in its physical form and functional attunement to local consumer and retailer needs.

Although the study is weak in not stressing the seriousness of these legacies however, its analysis of the retail system in general, and particularly the shopping conditions to be found in smaller centres, has much to be commended. The analytical sections begin with a conventional appraisal of the organisational structure of retailing, noting the exceptionally high incidence of independent shops (85 per cent of the total) and a description of the hierarchy of centres according to both floorspace size and functional components (which reveals five district centres, 17 smaller neighbourhood centres and a myriad of individual corner shops and small parades). Using these only as broad background material, rather than as a major feature of the work, however, the study proceeds to a more extensive assessment of the physical environment associated with 23 more significant centres. In this, a series of maps are presented that summarise surveys undertaken of the quality levels, traffic hazards and car parking provisions to be found in each centre; with quality levels being measured in terms of physical layout, visual appearance, noise and fumes and degree of weather protection afforded. These are reproduced in revised form in Figure 6.1. The methods

Figure 6.1: Environmental Conditions of Shopping Centres in Gateshead, 1978

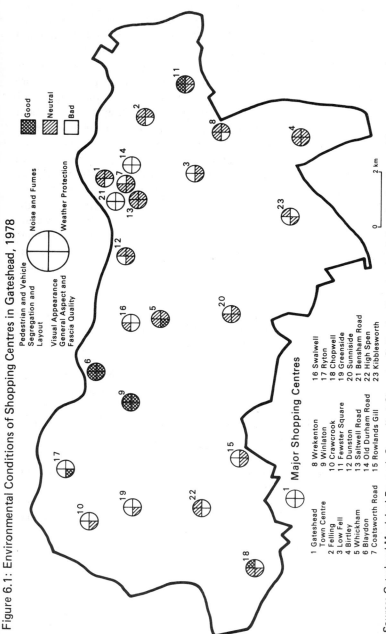

Source: Gateshead Municipal Borough Council, *A Shopping Policy for Gateshead — A Consultative Report* (Gateshead, 1978).

employed in the surveys are not reported upon, but presumably involved local authority officers making fairly subjective field observations for most of the criteria utilised. Although it might be possible to find limitations here, such criticism should not detract from the overall usefulness and relevance of the approach. It is precisely the condition of the physical environment to which a major part of local planning efforts should be addressed and this type of appraisal provides a meaningful basis for pinpointing where and in what ways future action should be taken.

Another, major part of the analysis focuses on the incidence of more essential local facilities, namely the distribution of chemists, post offices and grocery shops. Here the results were surprisingly encouraging, allowing the conclusion to be drawn that 'Despite the decline in shops over the last 15 years, the overall picture of essential shopping facilities is at present quite good.'[3] The District contained a total of 46 chemists in 1978, or approximately one for every 5,000 people; and this is a ratio that is better than the minimum standards suggested by the Pharmaceutical Society.[4] Only in the south-western part of the District was there a marked weakness in incidence, and this is a rural area where those surviving chemists should be eligible for central government support on the basis of their limited dispensing functions.[5] Post offices were even more widely distributed, with approximately one for every 4,000 people and there being but a single residential tract that was thought to be poorly served. Grocers were highly concentrated in the inner city and shortfalls occurred in several newer housing estates but not on a scale that was considered to be of serious concern. In sum, this was a further exercise that gave useful insights, although there are perhaps stronger grounds for suggesting that the investigations did not go far enough. The distance to these essential facilities for more housebound consumers is extremely important and some assessment of their locational pattern in relation to concentrations of the very elderly, the handicapped and single-parent households might have been undertaken. Likewise, it could be argued that spatial variations in the prices of goods should have been inspected and the distance relationships to the cheapest sources *vis-à-vis* concentrations of the poor might have been explored.

Following from these assessments of existing shopping provisions, however, the study turns to a discussion of what changes can be expected to occur in the future. This shift in time perspective is accompanied by a shift away from more localised issues to a consideration of what might happen to trading conditions as a whole. At this stage, the unfortunate location of the town centre in relation to Newcastle and

Washington is brought into account[6] and statistics paraded to demonstrate the enormous outflow of consumer expenditure that already takes place. Of £69.3 million that was spent on all retail goods in 1976, only £35.9 million went to shops in the District or approximately 66 per cent of convenience goods expenditure and 40 per cent of durable goods. Given the recent development of new shopping schemes in the major competing centres, and a decline in Gateshead's population of 7,800 by 1985, it is not anticipated that this loss of trade will be checked during the next few years, although there are some encouraging signs that there may not be a worsening situation. These include the re-opening of the market in the Trinity Square Shopping Centre and the renovation of an old department store by Tesco, which has been converted into a multi-unit operation trading under the name of Shopping City. Against these positive developments, however, there is the prospect that the opening of a Metro station in Gateshead will enhance the accessibility of Newcastle, thus undermining whatever new gains the town centre realises in the shorter term.

The study ends with a fairly detailed specification of what policies should be effected in the future. Only three of the six main proposals made, however, follow directly from the analyses undertaken and the others appear to be extensions of the recommendations emanating from the County Structure Plan. These latter proposals include: the restriction of 'out-of-town' hypermarkets and superstores, although scope might exist for equivalent 'in-town' developments; limiting the establishment of retail warehouses to either the town centre or district centres; encouraging the growth of district centres wherever this might be possible. For the three main issues discussed in the report and reviewed above, the conclusions were that:

(a) the town centre should be conceived as being complementary to, rather than a rival of, Newcastle and that 'Its success as a centre providing convenience and "down-market" durable goods should be used to advantage and expanded.'

(b) essential shopping facilities should be fostered in areas deficient in local shopping centres and 'Council-owned shops should be let to tenants who will provide the best service rather than the highest rent, with in appropriate cases rent free periods or reduced rent, while the shopkeeper builds up custom.'[7]

(c) individual district and neighbourhood shopping centres require a variety of environmental improvement schemes, for one of which (Felling) a special Town Centre Local Plan has been prepared. An elaboration of the specific recommendations made for the smaller centres is extracted in Table 6.1.

Table 6.1: Schedule of Policies for Local Centres in Gateshead

---

Group A: Centres to be encouraged and upon which future facilities should be centred

Ryton: Further facilities to meet rising demand necessary. Sites to be determined by Ryton-Crawcrook District Plan. Suitable off-street parking needed to maintain appearance of conservation area.

Swalwell: Additional floorspace required to meet local needs, preferably a small supermarket.

Coatsworth Road: Authority to take lead in improving centre by providing off-street car parks, environmental improvements and the declaration of a Commercial Improvement Area, covering the whole centre, to enable financial assistance to be given to retailers to improve their property.

Wrekenton High Street: Continue work of improving centre and encourage redevelopment and improvement by existing retailers.

Group B: Centres likely to decline or change their relative function

Bensham Road: Very old units on a busy road, reversal to a few corner shops with growth in Coatsworth Road.

Group C: Centres to remain little changed

Chopwell: Commercial viability of existing shops should improve and possible re-opening of vacant units when new housing schemes take place.

High Spen: Proposed new housing should reverse decline; some consolidation may be needed depending on location of new housing.

Rowlands Gill: Some consolidation possible if suitable site arises.

Winlaton: Continue work of improving centre with possible very small-scale infilling and redevelopment.

Crawcrook: New housing should strengthen commercial viability. Centre would benefit from small off-street car park and rear servicing.

Old Durham Road: Function little changed, but some consolidation and environmental improvements necessary.

Fewster Square: some environmental improvements required.

Greenside; Dunston; Sunniside; Kibblesworth; Saltwell Road: Little change envisaged in these centres.

The Tower Hamlets Study[8]

This study is a contemporary of that for Gateshead and refers, of course, to a similar type of urban area, containing a large inner city population and rather outworn shopping centres that are overshadowed by stronger competitors just outside its boundaries. So, too, part of the area falls within the compass of the Docklands Strategic Study which, like the Tyne and Wear Structure Plan, we have already reviewed. Given these same sorts of circumstances, it seems instructive to compare the work of the Borough of Tower Hamlets with that for Gateshead and to highlight where there have been notable differences in approach. The main report for the study is described as a Topic Paper on Shopping and again appears essentially as a Report of Survey, although in this case there are not the same clear set of objectives and concluding Statement of Policy that are found in the Gateshead report.

A further distinction in the format of the report is the outline provided on the scope of powers available to the Borough Council for the control of retailing activities. In addition to the expected reference to zoning and development control through the Use Orders, mention is made of: the role of the local authority as a landlord and regulations that can be applied through leases and covenants; the use of compulsory purchasing powers; the ability of the local authority to modify the general rules applying to trading hours; implementation of the public health legislation; and the development of consumer protection through enforcement of the Weights and Measures, Trades Description and Consumer Protection Acts. While all this suggests that the study that follows will then take stock of the effectiveness of these powers in the Borough to date, and how they might be better effected in the future, in fact the study reverts to the usual spatial-analytical theme of examining the demand for and supply of shops.

The analyses that were undertaken in this study, however, while less comprehensive than those for Gateshead and specifically in reference to the physical conditions of shopping centres, are noteworthy for the attention given to the special needs of the Borough. A separate chapter, for example, is devoted to the role of street markets and their evolution over time. Twelve markets were still actively trading in 1975, comprising a total of 2,495 stall pitches, of which 1,980 were used on a regular basis. Their turnover is somewhat difficult to assess but rough estimates suggest that they account for about 13 per cent of total trade in the Borough, a figure that puts them on a par with the leading variety and chain store operators. Separate treatment has also been accorded a wide range of designated 'special issues' discussed under the headings of: do the poor pay more?, transport, council shops, employment in shops, the physical environment, cash and carries, non-shopping uses in shopping areas, chemist shops and sub-post offices. There is not room here to recount all the main points raised but the following might give some indication of the contents involved. On the question of whether the poor pay more, the discussion revolved around the fact that the cheapest stores were found in the largest centres, often some distance away from those most seriously disadvantaged consumers. One way to assist pensioners who could not easily reach these stores would be to establish special shopping outlets in community centres, perhaps run by the Council. Transport was an issue in the sense that the extremely low car ownership rates in the Borough meant that a preponderance of shopping trips are made by bus or foot (estimated at 90 per cent of all trips); hence shopping provisions must be related to such travel patterns, requiring a highly localised distribution of centres with good public transport connections. Since nearly one-third of all shops in the Borough are owned by the council (562 out of a total 1,816), the majority of which are located in smaller centres, it is also clearly necessary for such shops to be managed efficiently but in a way that the council as landlord might improve the social as well as economic health of individual centres. Employment in shops is a significant consideration given the loss of jobs in the manufacturing sector, and there was some expectation that this would increase in the future, albeit with a shift in numbers from the convenience to the durable goods trades. Discussion about the physical conditions of centres ranged over the general needs for improvements in servicing, safety and cleanliness, but also gave emphasis to the particular requirements of the handicapped and young mothers with prams for improvements in layout and approachability. Cash and carries were raised in the context of the potential abuse that can occur by unscrupulous operators using them as retail outlets. Non-shopping uses in shopping areas referred to the universal phenomenon of the growth in business services, although this was not yet seen to be a major problem in the Borough. Chemist shops and post offices were considered again from the valuable social role they perform; but, somewhat interestingly, the density of chemist shops resembled that reported upon in Gateshead, with approximately one store serving 5,000 people.

Much of the rest of the study was preoccupied with looking at the quality and quantity of shopping provisions in the Borough in comparison with surrounding areas. Thus a number of statistics were produced to show that Tower Hamlets has amongst the lowest *per capita* spending characteristics of all the London boroughs; the limited amount of commercial redevelopment that has so far taken place means that it has an exceptionally high number of small, independent shops; there is a marked lack of large chain outlets which, together with the absence of a dominant centre in the area, means that there is a significant outflow of trade, particularly to Stratford and the City of London. Forecasts for the future tend to be more optimistic than those calculated for Gateshead, however, for whilst there has been a loss of about one quarter of the Borough's population during the last decade there is expected to be more stabilisation in the 1980s and it is felt the outflow of trade can be significantly checked. The key to this is a new shopping centre development to be built in Whitechapel, currently estimated at 550,000 square feet (51,115 m²), which will therefore be of sub-regional status (and comparable to the strategic centres of other London boroughs identified in the Greater London Development Plan[9]). An earlier proposal, dating back to 1972, for a new large centre at Gardiner's Corner, has only been partially fulfilled, for whilst a vast office complex and sports facilities have been built, the shopping component totals only about 50,000 square feet (4,650 m²).

The last feature of this study that is worth reporting on concerns the relationships between the Borough's planning views and those of the Docklands Strategic Study Team. Of three proposals made in the Docklands Plan[10] regarding shopping provisions in Tower Hamlets, two were disputed by the Borough and one accepted. The first point of disagreement arose over the proposal for a new district centre at the Isle of Dogs and in particular the choice of its site. The Docklands Plan assumed that the Millwall Docks would shortly close and the release of land could be used for new housing that should then be accompanied by a new development at Mudchute. The Borough felt the future for the docks was more uncertain and any new development should go into the existing shopping area of Christchurch. As events have unfolded, the docks will in fact now close and a new district centre at Mudchute will be constructed (incorporating a superstore as we have indicated before). The second difference of opinion concerned the provision of corner stores in new housing development, which the Docklands planning team regarded as undesirable and the Borough strongly advocated. The third matter, where agreement was reached, involved the proposal for a new large supermarket in Wapping.

The Bath Study[11]

This study provides an interesting contrast with those for Gateshead and Tower Hamlets not only by virtue of an entirely different kind of urban setting but also because it was undertaken by private consultants rather than by the local authority itself. The setting is clearly one of a relatively prosperous city, with the retail system heavily dominated by the city centre, and where the city centre also contains a number of important historic legacies in terms of its buildings and intrinsic functional character. The study produced by the consultants exhibits a different type of approach from those for Gateshead and Tower Hamlets, but this is largely a result of the different kind of philosophy held or alternative interpretation of the planning process. It may be viewed once again as something akin to a Report of Survey, although like the Gateshead study it contains a set of recommended policies for the future as well.

There were six specific terms of reference established for the study:

(a) an assessment of the present functions and relationships of the city centre in the context of the sub-regional hierarchy of shopping . . .

(b) the present relationship of the city centre shopping to the fringe and suburban centres in and adjacent to the city.

(c) quantitative and qualitative analyses of the present composition of shopping within the city.

(d) examination of the 'pull' towards the southern end of the city centre and whether a counter magnet in the northern part would be beneficial . . .

(e) the likely impact in terms of diversion of trade which would result from implementation of various proposals for new shopping . . .

(f) the effects (of these proposals) in relation to conservation, traffic and car parking.[12]

The stages followed in the study did not correspond with these terms of reference, however, for implicit within them are several other considerations that needed to be made, most notably an assessment of future shopping requirements and anticipation of new pressures that might arise. Much of the preamble to the report is therefore devoted to recent and emerging trends in retailing and a separate chapter is devoted to estimates of future consumer demand. As part of both these exercises, the findings of a number of other previous studies were examined and drawn upon and in particular an alternative consultant's forecast[13] as to how much new floorspace could be accommodated in the years ahead. This earlier study used a gravity model projection which the new study rejected on the grounds that it did not satisfactorily take into account significant amounts of tourist expenditure; but it was able to modify the results through more subjective methods and arrive at the figures shown in Table 6.2. The process of converting estimated turnover

Table 6.2: Step-by-Step Approach to Forecasting Retail Floorspace Requirements in Bath in 1986

---

1. Estimated turnover by 1986 (based on 1971 prices)

	Convenience trade £m			Durable trade £m		
	C.A.	Non-C.A.	City		C.A.	Non-C.A.	City
1971	6.3	9.3	15.6		17.8	5.3	23.1
1971-86			0.4				12.9
1986			16.0				36.0

2. Floorspace utilisation changes

This allows for changes in floorspace utilisation in existing shops of −1.3% per annum for convenience trade and +1.7% for durable trade, i.e. this is the 1986 turnover which existing floorspace would support.

Convenience trade: £12.8 m turnover; Durable trade: £29.7 m turnover.

3. Post-1971 retail developments

Surveys of the city showed a net floorspace gain of approximately 80,000 sq ft between 1971 and 1977.

Convenience trade: approx. 10,000 sq ft; Durable trade: approx. 70,000 sq ft.

4. Floorspace utilisation on new shopping floorspace

On the basis of floorspace utilisation factors of £90 per sq ft for new convenience shops and £55 per sq ft for new durable goods shops, the following turnover would be supported:

Convenience trade: 10,000 × 90 = £0.9 m

Durable trade: 70,000 × 55 = £3.9 m

5. Shopping capacity in 1986

This is based on existing shops, having allowed for changes in floorspace utilisation, plus post-1971 developments:

Convenience trade: £12.8 m + £0.9 m = £13.7 m

Durable trade: £29.7 m + £3.9 m = £33.6 m

6. Floorspace deficiency in 1986

This is 1986 forecast turnover compared to 1986 shopping capacity.

Convenience trade: £16 m − £13.7 m = £2.3 m
                       £2.3 m ÷ £90 per sq ft = 25,500 sq ft, sales floorspace

Durable trade: £36 m − £33.6 m = £2.4 m
                       £2.4 m ÷ £55 per sq ft = 43,600 sq ft, sales floorspace

---

figures into retail floorspace requirements is extracted in full since this seems to be a particularly clear example of the steps which other researchers often go through. A further, but useful, apparent departure from the terms of reference was a comparison of the retailing characteristics of Bath with those of five other like kinds of cities: Cambridge, Chester, Cheltenham, Oxford and York. The most significant point of difference that emerged from this was that, with the exception of Cheltenham, Bath was the only major historic city to exhibit an increased concentration of convenience goods shopping as well as durable goods trade within its central area over the previous decade. Between 1961 and 1971, in fact, the share of overall trade within the city commanded by the central area grew from 59.5 per cent to 62 per cent.

Not unexpectedly, much of the rest of the study was concerned with examining the spatial structure of the city centre, particularly its changing functional composition and the likely locations of new development. Although the city centre is very compact, it contains a number of distinctive sub-areas of activity with major differences, especially between its northern and southern parts. In the north, based around Milsom Street, there is a high concentration of specialist shops and business services, while in the south, there is a greater preponderance of multiple shops and the new Southgate Shopping Centre. Recent trends suggest a reinforcement rather than weakening of these zonal contrasts but there is some concern that business services may continue to grow at the expense of smaller retail outlets in the north while too much large convenience shopping floorspace might accrue in the south. Substantial environmental improvement schemes have been effected during the last few years, including the pedestrianisation of Union and Stall Streets, the main shopping streets in the middle of the city centre, and the council has been actively acquiring the ownership of buildings for itself (to the point where it now owns 51 per cent of all retail properties) to ensure protection of their architectural value. Six so-called 'soft areas' were identified in the study as being the most likely targets for future development, with one location in particular, at Green Park Station, the subject of competing proposals for a new large store from Sainsbury and Tesco. After considering the potential trading effects and visual intrusiveness of the schemes, the authors of the study concluded that neither should be permitted.

A fairly detailed appraisal was also made of local shopping provisions in the rest of the city, with attention being given to both the physical conditions of individual centres and their accessibility to particular communities. A significant feature of the former set of analyses was the distinction drawn between centres in a proper sense and ribbon developments described in this study as fringe shopping areas. The two main fringe areas of London Road and Walcott Street are characterised by a high proportion of services and so-called secondary furnishing, clothing and antique shops; and the form they take seems to be unsatisfactory to the eyes of the authors, such that '... the present shopping frontage, interspersed with residential properties, does not reach the general standards expected of a modern shopping centre.'[14] On community needs, the broad catchment areas of existing centres were inspected in relation to bus services to identify where there might be inadequacies in basic shopping support; but few serious deficiencies were found and the only major proposal to emerge was the recommendation that a new district centre be built on the western side of the city, but this was to help ease the pressure for new convenience-shopping floorspace being exerted on the central area as much as to improve local shopping supplies.

The final point of interest in this study concerns the way in which future policies were arrived at for the city as a whole. Several preliminary objectives were enunciated which, because of the interrelationships between them, could be synthesised into two main sets of policy options: retaining the present dominance of the city centre and planning for some expansion of this; or encouraging a greater decentralisation of the convenience goods trade. In the event, the second set of policy options was recommended as being most desirable, but where the strength of the city centre for specialist and durable goods shopping would be maintained. The precise policies advocated to meet this strategy are listed in Table 6.3.

The Southend Study[15]

This study is worth noting since it exhibits a much stronger areal approach to the identification of shopping problems than any of the others so far reviewed. This is particularly accentuated in the public consultation document that summarises the main findings and recommendations of the consultant's report.[16] The town of Southend was effectively split up into four parts: the central area, mid-Southend, east Southend and west Southend; and for each area, a series of issues were raised followed by a set of suggestions on how they could be resolved. The study, or more exactly its summary of conclusions, therefore demonstrates a more pragmatic approach to local planning but where the emphasis is very much on the physical components of the retail system rather than more controversial themes.

A brief précis of the findings for one of the study areas, east Southend, will perhaps be sufficient to indicate the general nature of the work. Three major problems were diagnosed that collectively

Table 6.3: Recommended Shopping Policies for Bath

General policies

1. To maintain and enhance the city centre's functions as a sub-regional shopping centre.

2. To maintain the dominant role of the city centre in the general retailing structure of the city and to encourage and augment its durable and specialist trades functions.

3. To take measures to diminish the incidence of local car-borne trips to the city centre for convenience shopping.

4. As a corollary to this (3 above), to extend and improve local facilities for convenience shopping.

5. To monitor the commercial 'mix' of retailing in order to take such measures as may be necessary and feasible to avoid imbalances.

6. Generally, to supplement the authorities' planning powers by the use of appropriate estate management measures.

Policies for the central area

7. To maintain the compact nature of the city centre by resisting proposals for peripheral expansion for shopping uses.

8. To monitor the commercial 'mix' of retailing to enable such measures, as are feasible and economically possible, to be taken to avoid imbalances, particularly in those areas where there are significant numbers of small units currently occupied by convenience and specialist trades.

9. To maintain its function as a local convenience centre for the immediate close support residential population, but to discourage the introduction of large convenience trades shopping units.

10. To maintain, as far as is practicable and economically feasible, the presence of small shop units for uses appropriate to their location in the central shopping area.

11. In general to prevent the disruption of existing continuous shopping frontages by the intrusion of inappropriate non-retail uses.

Policies for non-central area shopping facilities

12. Establishment of new district centre: In accordance with item 4 above, to initiate locational, design and feasibility studies for the establishment of a new district centre, preferably in the area of the Windsor Road Bridge.

13. Local centres: To take measures to encourage the augmentation and improvement of retailing facilities in the following local centres: Bear Flat; Larkhall; Odd Down and/or Coombe Down.

14. Fringe shopping: Generally, to resist the physical extension of the present fringe areas of shopping.

related to deficiencies in local shopping provisions. The first concerned the absence of shops in two new large housing estates; the second concerned the lack of large supermarkets throughout the area, to cater for car-borne bulk food purchases; the third referred to the absence of a district shopping centre and the attendant community facilities that might go with a fairly wide range of shopping opportunities. Inspection of the existing shopping centres in the area suggested that none of these offered sufficient potential growth that they could be enlarged and hence meet some or all of the needs described above, although modest improvements could and should be made to both their physical condition and approachability. Instead, it was favoured that a new purpose-built district centre be developed, close to the new housing estates so that their specific shopping requirements would be met, but of a size large enough, and incorporating social and service activities, that it would act as a focal point for the area as a whole. A precise location in North Shoebury was proposed and it was recommended that the main retail magnet should be a superstore of 50,000-60,000 (gross) square feet (4,650-5,575 m^2).

This 'matter-of-fact' style to the presentation of findings characterises the rest of the contents of this study. It can be convincing because it sounds authoritative and is not complicated by wider discussion of the possible impact of such a scheme, the advantages that might be offered by alternative kinds of development or whether certain consumers might be disadvantaged by the location selected. The fuller consultant's report offers more justification; but one wonders when things are put as baldly as this in a consultation document directed at the public, whether the problems identified and solutions proffered really are as cut and dried as are intimated.

The Telford Study[17]

The reader's attention is drawn to this study because, while it comprises an assessment of areal needs, it looks much more at the workings of the retail system as a whole and seeks to determine whether the system is functioning in the way in which it was intended. The research singled out for special consideration, a survey of the localised centres of the shopping hierarchy, is in fact but one of a trilogy of studies, the others to be based on an examination of the central area and appraisal of what the policies for the future should contain.[18] This example is therefore a much more technical study, amounting essentially to a monitoring exercise on how consumers actually utilise the structure of shopping facilities provided them. It is open to criticism on a number of technical aspects and should not be viewed as the best of its kind; but it has been fairly comprehensively written up and is selected for epitomising a large amount of similar work which is often undertaken but not widely reported.

The immediate rationale for the study was concern that the basic form of the hierarchy (a three-tier system of local centres, district centres and the town centre), laid down in the 1960s, was steadily being eroded. In particular '. . . . local centres now in design are much smaller in relation to their catchment population than were the initial centres . . . also several district centres have been dropped or downgraded.'[19] This prompted a review of the hierarchy to adjudicate particularly from the point of view of expenditures on different levels of centres whether they were being supported in the sorts of proportions originally envisaged; but also, as a corollary consideration, to see whether a decline in the servicing provisions of local centres was adversely affecting the location of alternative land uses (such as the siting of dwellings for the elderly). Two sets of surveys were undertaken to achieve these dual aims: the first involving residents of four selected areas keeping diaries of their shopping behaviour and spending over a period of one week; the second comprising interviews of shoppers in the four local centres that fall within the same areas. A sample of one in six households was selected for the diary survey which, with a fairly high response rate of 60 per cent, yielded a return of 500 completed diaries; the in-centre surveys netted 120 completed interviews in the Brookside shopping centre and between 70 and 80 interviews in each of the other three centres.

While a considerable amount of information was collected in these surveys, however, the results were difficult to synthesise in the light of the original objectives set. Figure 6.2 indicates that there is considerable variability in patterns of spending between the areas and that rather than the local and district centres being the weakest elements in the shopping hierarchy, it is the town centre that is most in need of improvement. An extension to the town centre is in fact now being built which will presumably have some effect on the district centres, although the main intention is to check the outflow of trade to other competing places. Once the town centre can fulfil a more dominant role, the rest of the shopping hierarchy is expected to be utilised in a more evenly balanced way. The detailed implications of this for the four areas studied, however, are not really of interest here; what is of most significance about the study in general is the fact that the behaviour of shoppers has been scrutinised to see where there are strengths

Figure 6.2: Variations in Spending at Shopping Centres amongst
Different Areas of Telford, 1977

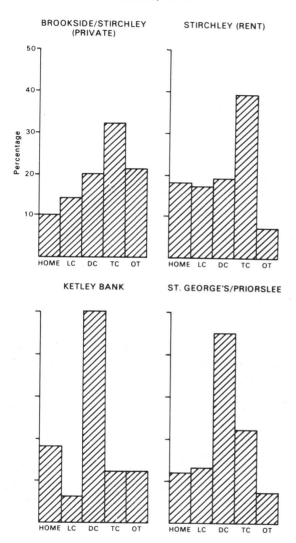

LC Local Centre, DC District Centre, TC Town Centre, OT Outside Telford

Source: Telford Development Corporation, *Shopping Study in Telford, 1977*
(Telford, 1978).

and weaknesses in the retail system as a whole.

The Scope for Improvement

Each of the five case studies that have been reviewed above is clearly quite different in its form and content from the others. As yet, there does not appear to be a consensus approach to the preparation of local management plans, at least to the same degree as has characterised the production of Structure Plans. Nor perhaps should we expect that there will be a single, stereotyped outcome, for the problems encountered at this scale of inquiry will vary considerably from one areal setting to another. Where there needs to be a closer harmony of views, however, is in the basic principles of what the plans should be striving to achieve and what should be the most appropriate procedural measures to adopt to meet the underlying objectives which have then been set.

Since Local Plans are meant to develop and elaborate upon Structure Plans, there must obviously be some compatibility between them in the nature of their objectives and we shall take as our terms of reference here those common objectives suggested in Chapter 4. In translating such objectives into a series of policies, however, a major difference arises by virtue of the different obligations of the two tiers of government. While the Districts are statutorily committed to using development control procedures as their main form of intervention into the distribution system, the Counties, in being more advisory in their functions, will generally use other means. This rather implies that both the problem identification and policy formulation stages of Local Plan preparation will be much more spatially based than those at the Structure Plan level. At the end of the plan-making process, in fact, the Districts are expected to produce a detailed map which will show where future changes are likely to take place.

Given the necessity of a spatial or geographical approach, the case studies reported on might themselves point to where other common denominators in Local Plan preparation are desirable. All of the studies recognised that some fairly detailed description needs to be given of the retail (and we should add, commercial) system, in order to serve as the basis for more specific inquiries, such as an examination of the physical deficiencies of particular centres. The Gateshead study perhaps exemplifies this most fully, although the Bath study is notable for stressing the importance of providing protection as well as initiating change within certain kinds of environment. All the studies likewise assumed that an assessment should be made of the spatial pattern of retail supplies in relation to source areas of consumer demand, with the Southend study giving most attention to the adequacy of supplies in particular areas and the Telford study questioning, in a more conceptual sense, the accepted notions of what constitutes an evenly balanced distribution of shopping provisions. The special requirements of certain categories of consumers, namely the housebound and seriously disadvantaged sections of society, were less widely referred to, but the Tower Hamlets study gave considerable prominence to their needs. Each of these points on the direction of analytical work happens to fit with those suggestions made in Chapter 4 as to what the Reports of Survey of a Local Plan might embrace (although reference was also made there to the need to review the outcome of past policies). On the policy-making side, however, the case studies have less to offer in the way of guidelines for the future since only three of them provided concrete proposals and these were intended to serve as interim measures pending the production of full District Plans. Since many of the proposals were also concerned with points of detail regarding particular centres, our later discussions on the procedural aspects of local planning in this section will relate more completely to those suggestions made in Chapter 4.

The Analytical Stages

The first step in the analytical stages of Local Plan preparation is, as we have indicated, to establish a descriptive framework of the system of activities to be dealt with. The usual approach has been to delimit only a hierarchy of shopping centres which then ignores both important commercial elements and the mixture of retail and service activities to be found in ribbon developments. In order to gain a more comprehensive insight into the varied locational needs of all types of activity, a much broader classification is required that makes reference to the differences in forms and functions of business configurations as well as their variations in size. This can be achieved via a multivariate statistical analysis of the kind referred to in Chapter 1, or more modestly by inspecting map plots of the incidence of a wide range of businesses.

Once such a classification has been derived, an appraisal can then be made of the various conditions accruing within or around individual business configurations. The appraisal should encompass those matters of concern to the public at large, such as the adequacy of parking provisions and bus connections, the extent of traffic congestion or safety hazards and the like; but it should also refer to the relative trading health of places, as indicated by the proportions of vacant premises to be found or the recent history of new development, to be useful to prospective investors. A composite measure of the socio-economic well-being of certain places, especially shopping centres, might be attempted in order to show where there is an accumulation of problems in special need of solution. Several geographical studies have pointed to a way forward on this by ranking centres according to the quality levels of businesses, where the quality levels themselves are determined by subjective rating scales of the range of merchandise provided, the prices of the goods, the physical upkeep of premises, their degree of cleanliness, etc.[20] Basically, several persons are employed to evaluate independently all the business establishments found in a centre according to several criteria reflecting on differences in quality or image; the recorded scores are then averaged and a mean total is worked out for the centre to be compared to others included in the analysis.

The determination of catchment areas for all types of business configurations will serve a variety of purposes. Firstly, it will demonstrate more clearly the different functional roles of these places, as between shopping centres in a strict sense and ribbon developments, and between different kinds of commercial areas. Secondly, it will provide further insight into the relative trading health of individual places, where the actual sizes of trade areas are compared against expected sizes. Thirdly, the pattern as a whole will indicate where there are apparent deficiencies in the provision of goods and services within the District. The catchment areas themselves can be determined, of course, by a variety of methods, but the ideal way, where resources allow, is to build them up from surveys of consumer behaviour, conducted in people's homes (or, in the case of commercial activities, at the source origins of clients). Home-interview surveys, especially those including a 'diary' component, are particularly useful for shopping studies, since they enable a detailed picture of the pattern of expenditure to be obtained. In addition, questions directed to the attitudes and preferences of consumers can provide information not only on traditional concerns, such as the support given to local shops, but also on the receptiveness of people towards new retailing elements, such as fast-food outlets, discount stores and petrol stations that combine other convenience trades. The public's attitude towards new shopping provisions, particularly with respect to the different locations that these facilities will seek to adopt, should be a much more important component in the implementation of development controls than is currently the case.

The special needs of deprived consumers must also be a more important consideration in future policy-making and some guidance on where there are major deficiencies in accessibility to the cheaper prices of modern shopping facilities should be forthcoming in the Reports of Survey of Structure Plans (as we indicated in the last chapter), but greater specification will have to be given at the local level as to where there are signifant concentrations of deprived consumers, and what precisely constitutes the deprivation we are alluding to. Consumer deprivation should be seen in terms not only of poor access to essential shops for the elderly and other minority adult groups, but also as the absence of entertainments and catering services for teenagers in isolated communities and more widely, perhaps, in the lack of proximity to major wholesaling outlets of small, independent traders. It is a subject which, in a broader sense, has been little researched in the Local Plan context.

The Framework for Policy-making

Although most local authorities will have to confront a range of problems that are unique to their areas, there will be three underlying requirements that appear to be common to all; the maintenance of the stability of those parts of the distribution system that appear to be in equilibrium with their surrounding client groups; the accommodation of new forms of growth in locations where these can be absorbed (and where the locations themselves may be different in kind from those hitherto provided); and the replacement or removal of outworn features of the distribution system where these no longer make a positive contribution to either the consumers' or business community's needs. The development control procedures that will have to be involved to meet these requirements will perforce need to be effected within some spatial design framework. This means extending in some way those geographical classifications deemed suitable for analysing existing patterns of activity to make them appropriate for incorporating change. Some indications of how this might be achieved have been given by the author in a separate paper[21] and are summarised in Figures 6.3 and 6.4.

Figure 6.3 refers to the city-wide system of retail and commercial activity and contrasts the type of design framework employed for policy-making in the old style of Development Plans with an alternative proposal that seems more radical in appearance but is actually more in tune with those market processes that continue to operate within the urban environment. In essence, the traditional design framework

Figure 6.3: A Possible Development of the Spatial Framework for Retail and Commercial Planning Policies within a City

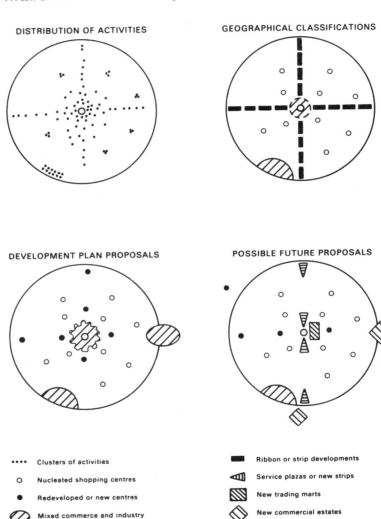

DISTRIBUTION OF ACTIVITIES

GEOGRAPHICAL CLASSIFICATIONS

DEVELOPMENT PLAN PROPOSALS

POSSIBLE FUTURE PROPOSALS

•••• Clusters of activities

○ Nucleated shopping centres

● Redeveloped or new centres

⬭ Mixed commerce and industry

▬ Ribbon or strip developments

◀ Service plazas or new strips

▨ New trading marts

◇ New commercial estates

Source: Davies, R.L., 'A Framework for Commerical Planning Policies', *Town Planning Review*, vol. 48 (1977), pp. 42-58.

Figure 6.4: A Possible Development of the Spatial Framework for Retail and Commercial Planning Policies within the City Centre

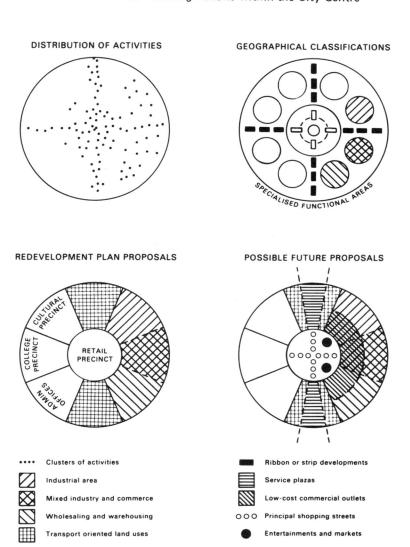

DISTRIBUTION OF ACTIVITIES

GEOGRAPHICAL CLASSIFICATIONS

SPECIALISED FUNCTIONAL AREAS

REDEVELOPMENT PLAN PROPOSALS

CULTURAL PRECINCT
COLLEGE PRECINCT
RETAIL PRECINCT
ADMIN OFFICES

POSSIBLE FUTURE PROPOSALS

•••• Clusters of activities

▨ Industrial area

⊠ Mixed industry and commerce

◺ Wholesaling and warehousing

▦ Transport oriented land uses

■ Ribbon or strip developments

▤ Service plazas

◺ Low-cost commercial outlets

OOO Principal shopping streets

● Entertainments and markets

Source: Davies, R.L., 'A Framework for Commercial Planning Policies', *Town Planning Review*, vol. 48 (1977), pp. 42-58.

provides only for a hierarchy of shopping centres and various mixed commercial and industrial areas, thereby making the presumption that all new forms of development within the distributive trades will have to conform to the locations epitomised by these. The alternative proposal, while recognising the need to maintain a hierarchical structure of nucleated shopping centres, also allows for a wide range of services to be located alongside major roads in a set of newly designated strip developments (which might be upgraded ribbon developments) and service plazas; and, at the same time, it provides for different kinds of locational settings for the assortment of intermediary trades in so-called trading marts and special-purpose commercial estates. Examples of what the physical characteristics and functional constituents of these new business complexes might be like are given in the next chapter.

Figure 6.4 makes a similar set of adjustments to the type of design framework that has hitherto been applied specifically to the city centre. We have stated before that the pattern of retail and commercial activity inside the central area is effectively a microcosm of that to be found in the rest of the city, but that planning policies to date have removed much of the variable character of the older districts through redevelopment and applying strict policies of land use segregation. It is not possible to alter those parts of the spatial structure of a city centre which have been affected in this way (and some changes have clearly not been undesirable); but it should be feasible to reduce the scale of redevelopment and rigid zoning in the future to encourage a renewed diversification of trade, especially in the fringe zones of the central area. In order to maintain some orderliness in this, the diagram again suggests the designation of new business complexes using the terms service plazas and trading marts. Inside the retail core of the city centre, too, greater recognition should be given to the variable nature of shopping streets, rather than presuming that this zone can be treated as a single homogeneous entity. An elaboration of how a design framework can be constructed around the variability of shopping streets and what sorts of detailed requirements need to be met in the frame is given in Chapter 8.

In addition to establishing more flexible and relevant design frameworks for the implementation of planning controls, however, two other major procedural changes could and should be effected to ensure that policies formulated in local plans are capable of meeting the underlying objectives that have been set. Firstly, instead of demarcating on maps the physical extent of various kinds of business complexes according to the existing or (in the case of new developments) projected distribution of activities, it seems preferable to prescribe broader areal boundaries around them to suggest fields of potential retail or commercial change. The idea would be to deflect attention away from occupation of the most central sites (particularly in healthier shopping centres) to help reduce competition and encourage a reduction in rents. This should then be of benefit to smaller businesses who might find it easier to penetrate the traditional high street or alternatively who wish to establish modest operations in a fringe position; likewise, it might aid certain multiples seeking larger premises with accompanying car parking facilities. Secondly, to ensure that the broader areal designations do not lead to unbridled change and the physical deterioration of particular places, such areas should be subject to varying levels or degrees of development control along the lines suggested in Chapter 4. In those situations where one might want to promote the revitalisation of, say, a decaying inner city business district, the development controls (and associated trading and building regulations) might be very lax. In contrast, for those places which contain important historical legacies or are surrounded by extensive green tracts, such as in part of the town centre or an outlying district centre, there may need to be a strengthening of controls. For the broad mass of business areas to be found, of course, the existing forms of development and other regulatory controls might remain sufficient, especially where there seem to be few grounds for additional planning intervention.

The determination of different levels of development control for particular business areas would also need to be accompanied in certain Districts by the designation of further, larger areas in need of special policies by virtue of particular, but extensive problems to be found. We might envisage here the problems associated with rural tracts, large suburban areas or inner city areas that fall within the Inner Area Partnership Schemes (and might contain free Enterprise Zones within them). Such areas would probably qualify for being the subject of special plans at the local level to be taken up in Part III of this book; and they would resemble of course some of the Action-Area Plans which a number of local authorities have already embarked upon.

A final consideration is that, while Local Plans might be generally preoccupied with establishing a new set of spatial principles to govern the evolution of the distributive trades, there will be certain policies that will need to be formulated that are essentially aspatial in nature. The development of special services to aid deprived consumers might fall within this compass although such services might need to be organised on a geographical basis. The sorts of services we have in mind, however, include not only support for local, essential shops in particular neighbourhoods, but the use of modern technological resources to improve the communication links between relatively housebound people and large stores. It is unlikely, of course, that the local authorities themselves will be able to provide much financial backing for experimentation along these lines, which means that the goodwill and assistance of firms will have to be sought. An alternative possibility, as we have indicated before, is to make the granting of future planning permission to build large stores conditional on the firms involved developing a service facility for disadvantaged people.

Conclusion

The preparation of District Plans (or other local equivalents) is still in its infancy as only a very few of these plans have yet been completed. The vast majority of District authorities have embarked upon the analysis of retail problems within their areas, and some have even formulated interim policy measures to deal with these; but to date most of the studies have been *ad hoc* in nature and there are none of the full statements of intent that characterise the Structure Plans. Much of the work that has been undertaken, however, has been encouraging for, despite a concentration on shopping matters and a neglect for the other components of the distributive trades, there has been a greater emphasis on examining the quality rather than the quantity of the physical stock of resources than is to be found in the county plans. Typical of the more wide-ranging studies produced so far are those for Gateshead, Tower Hamlets and Bath. These appear much like a collection of Reports of Survey, but while the first two are similar in the types of problems addressed, the Gateshead study goes further than that for Tower Hamlets in recommending future policies; and the Bath study, while not unlike the structure of the others, is different by virtue of having been prepared by outside consultants. Two other studies have been reviewed in this chapter, for Telford New Town and Southend, not for any special merit to be found, but simply to illustrate the diversity in methodologies that are being employed, particularly in the analytical stages of plan-making. The Telford study included an ambitious household diary survey to assess the functional use of existing shopping centres; the Southend study, adopting a more traditional approach, considered the balance of shopping provisions to be found throughout the town from a detailed area by area land use appraisal.

The major challenge facing local planning in the next few years, however, is how the problems that are currently being identified will be dealt with through the machinery of development and other regulatory controls. Given that the local authorities will have to show in detail how their policies will be translated on the ground, much thought will need to be given to appropriate spatial design frameworks and the suitability of the controls to be implemented within these. Our concern with this scale of planning lies not so much with the objectives guiding the exercise, which should emanate from those drawn up for Structure Plans, nor with the policies that are formulated since these will vary considerably from one District to another. Rather, it lies with the spatial principles and strength of controls that will operate which, if conceived more imaginatively and executed more flexibly than has hitherto been the case, could give planning a much more constructive stance. We have to admit, however, that the suggestions made along these lines in this chapter are quite upstart and might need to be tested on a limited basis before being widely adopted.

References

1. Gateshead Municipal Borough Council, *A Shopping Policy for Gateshead — A Consultative Report* (Gateshead, 1978).
2. Ibid., p. 1.
3. Ibid., p. 17.
4. Ibid., p. 16.
5. Ibid., p. 16.
6. The impact of new shopping centres in Newcastle and Washington on Gateshead's town centre is discussed in Bennison, D.J. and Davies, R.L., 'The impact of Town Centre Shopping Schemes in Britain — Their Impact on Traditional Retail Environments', *Progress in Planning*, vol. 14, part 1 (1980), pp. 1-104.
7. Gateshead Municipal Borough Council, *A Shopping Policy for Gateshead*, p. 35.
8. London Borough of Tower Hamlets, *Shopping — A Borough Plan Topic Paper* (Tower Hamlets, 1977).
9. Greater London Council, *Greater London Development Plan* (London, 1976).
10. Docklands Joint Committee, *London Docklands Strategic Plan* (London, 1976).
11. Drivers Jonas, *City of Bath — Shopping Study 1977* (London, 1978).
12. Ibid., pp. 1-2.
13. Nathaniel Lichfield and Partners, *Bath — Minimum Physical Change Study* (London, 1976).
14. Drivers Jonas, *Bath Shopping Study*, p. 70.
15. Southend Borough Council, *Southend Shopping Study — A Consultation Report* (Southend, 1978).

16. Nathaniel Lichfield and Partners, *Southend Shopping Study* (London, 1977).
17. Telford Development Corporation, *Shopping Study in Telford, 1977* (Telford Development Corporation Planning Department, 1978).
18. While a study of the central area was completed in 1977, the appraisal of policies for the future has yet to appear.
19. Telford Development Corporation, *Shopping Study*, p. 2.
20. See, for example, Potter, R.B., 'Spatial and Structural Variations in the Quality Characteristics of Intra-Urban Retailing Centres', *Transactions of the Institute of British Geographers*, vol. 5, no. 2 (1980), pp. 207-28; Davies, R.L., 'The Retail Pattern of the Central Area of Coventry', *Institute of British Geographers Occasional Publication*, no. 1 (1972), pp. 1-42.
21. Davies, R.L., 'A Framework for Commercial Planning Policies', *Town Planning Review*, vol. 48, no. 1 (1977), pp. 42-58.

7   RETAIL AND COMMERCIAL DEVELOPMENT

A major feature of both Structure Plans and Local Plans, as the collective term Development Plans denotes, is the emphasis they purport to give to the accommodation of new development. It may be, as we have suggested before, that not enough attention has so far been given to the accommodation of different forms of new development in a variety of locations, but, in principle, the Written Statements of Policy and the maps that accompany these are very much concerned with the questions of what sorts of innovations should be encouraged within an area and where should these ideally be placed. For this reason, most plans contain within their Reports of Survey a special section devoted to recent trends within the distributive trades, and discussion particularly about the characteristics of large new shopping facilities. This separate consideration for the main agents of change is extremely important and deserves to be broadened out, as we indicated in Chapter 4, to a full description of all the elements involved rather than just those that are apparently most controversial.

This chapter therefore takes stock of the larger developments that have emerged in recent years and provides some pointers as to what kinds of further innovations might occur in the future, including a few ideas that the local authorities could themselves promote. A wide range of new retail developments are dealt with first since these have been extensively studied and reported upon. Our treatment of these is limited to a commentary on their physical, locational and trading characteristics for the effects they have on more traditional retail environments is a subject taken up in a later chapter. This section is then followed by a similar description of new commercial developments which, because of the poorer source material available, is limited to certain more prominent examples. Our speculations about the future come next, drawing in part on the experiences of other countries and in part on a set of personal convictions regarding the desirability of experimenting with some radical alternatives to the conventional forms of planned development seen to date. Finally, the chapter concludes with some suggestions as to how the obligations of local authorities, in meeting pressures for new development and implementing a set of development controls, might be better fulfilled during the next decade.

Retail Developments

It has been indicated before that there are two main groups of new retail developments, the purpose-built shopping centres and the individual large stores. Both groups contain a variety of retail forms, with most of the variability in the former occurring where they have been built in traditional town or city centre locations and that in the latter in the more residential parts of the city. Both groups are also intertwined, of course, so that large stores, such as superstores, may be part of a town centre shopping scheme or an outlying district centre, as well as sometimes being free-standing. In view of the complexity, rather than treating the two groups in a strict systematic way, we shall examine them in the context of the prevailing areal settings in which they are found, distinguishing first the town centre shopping schemes and later the residential area shopping schemes.

Town Centre Shopping Schemes

Much of the variation to be seen in town centre shopping schemes in Britain is the result of changes which have occurred over time in the underlying development process.[1] It was suggested in Chapter 2 that, since the end of the last world war, there have been two distinctive eras in shopping centre development. The first, roughly occurring between 1950 and 1965, encompassed a relatively small amount of building but where the initiative for new schemes came from the local authorities. It was they who ushered in the precinct idea, seeking to accommodate a modern set of shopping resources within a much safer and more attractive environment than had hitherto been found. The City of Coventry pioneered the way with its large cruciform-shaped precinct at the heart of its programme to reconstruct a central area that had been severely bombed; the New Towns, such as Crawley and Basildon, followed suit in using square or rectangular-shaped precincts as the foci of their new town centres; subsequently, a number of the local authorities in the older conurbations of the North implemented the idea into certain of their decaying town centres (such as Jarrow and Wallsend in Tyneside) in an attempt to rejuvenate them and improve their appearance.

From about 1965 to 1980, however, a second era of more prolific building can be recognised which has largely been orchestrated by the property development companies, who had earlier been preoccupied with speculative ventures in the office and housing fields. Their primary objective has been, not to contribute to environmental improvement as such, but to meet the rising pressures from the multiple retailers for new sites in favourable trading circumstances. Essentially, what they have sought to do is to recreate the conditions to be found in the traditional high street, which in most towns and cities has for long been unable to cope with all the demands placed upon it. The most satisfactory way of achieving this proved not to be through developing spacious precincts but through copying the enclosed shopping malls that had already been widely established in outlying locations in the United States. The last 15 years or so has therefore been characterised by a massive injection of new specialised retail floorspace, the greater part of which has been housed in covered shopping centres.[2]

This second era of development, nerverthless, also exhibits some distinctive variations in types of covered centres that were built, as Figure 7.1 tries to suggest. The initial schemes were fairly small copies of the classic American 'out-of-town' centres, where they approximated a so-called 'dumb-bell' shape, with a single mall connecting two large

Figure 7.1: Distinctive Stages in the Evolution of Town Centre Shopping Schemes

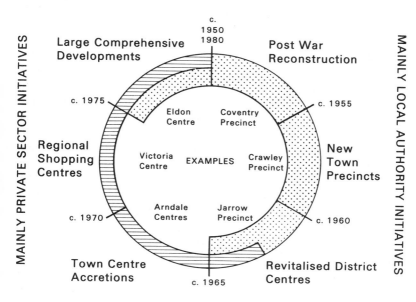

Source: Bennison, D.J. and Davies, R.L., 'The Impact of Town Centre Shopping Schemes in Britain — Their Impact on Traditional Retail Environments', *Progress in Planning*, vol. 14, part 1 (1980), pp. 1-104.

attractor stores at each end. Such schemes as the early Arndale centres were slotted into a central area almost as appendages to the high street, adding a major stock of new resources but without distorting too much the established patterns of trade. By the middle of the 1970s, however, several developments had appeared that, by virtue of their size (which was often in excess of 500,000 square feet (45,500 m^2) of retail floorspace) and the number of large attractor stores found (which may have included two or three variety stores in addition to one or more department stores or superstores) made claim to being regional shopping centres as distinct from the earlier centres which fulfilled a district-level function. The most celebrated examples are the Victoria and Broadmarsh Regional Shopping Centres in Nottingham, which, while still resembling the form of American counterparts in suburban locations, inevitably display some irregularities in their layout because of the confined nature of their sites. Such developments have had a much more significant impact on the traditional patterns of trade within a central area, especially where they have been established in more peripheral positions as essentially new loci of activity.[3] This trend to increasing sizes of shopping centres, nevertheless, culminated in the late 1970s in the construction of exceptionally large schemes (the Eldon Square centre in Newcastle, the Arndale centre in Manchester and the new town centre for Milton Keynes), which represented a further departure in the development process to the extent that these could only be realised with considerable local authority help. This help included both financial contributions and assistance in acquiring the sites and additionally, in a more indirect way, in the provision of extensive infrastructures to cope with major changes in traffic and pedestrian flows. The Eldon Square centre, in particular, because of the key part it has played in a wider programme of redevelopment throughout the central area of Newcastle, reflects almost a return to the local authority aspirations of the early post-war years when new shopping schemes were conceived as the focal points of comprehensive development plans. Needless to say, these giant centres exhibit their own unique forms with the Manchester Arndale centre comprising several malls that span across two existing roads.

The first part of the 1980s may therefore prove to be a watershed in the recent history of town centre shopping schemes for a variety of reasons. Firstly, the involvement of local authority participation in the development process seems to have turned full circle over the last 30 years, but the political and economic climate for the future suggests there will now likely be a further diminution of this role. Secondly, the growth in numbers of large schemes seems to have peaked and we can expect that proportionately more schemes in the next decade will be both small in their own size and more commonly built in smaller sizes of settlements.[4] Thirdly, the shape or form of centres is likely to become much more varied, partly because of the increasing difficulties in obtaining expansive sites but also because there has been some reaction against the provision of stereotyped malls. Fourthly, the fact that many of the earliest developments have now reached a mature age means that we shall enter a period of refurbishment and renovation with perhaps some of the more successful open precinct schemes being converted to covered centres. There are also signs, as was indicated in Chapter 2, that Britain might follow the example of the USA again in experiencing the establishment of new shopping facilities in former warehouse and factory buildings on the periphery of the central area.

The four main variables referred to in the above paragraph, the type of developer, and the size, form and age of centres, are the critical determinants of further differences in town centre shopping schemes that can be recognised throughout the country. Some of these differences, cross-tabulated against the four main variables, are shown in Table 7.1. This is derived from a detailed survey of 172 schemes built since 1963 and which represent approximately 55 per cent of the total number of new developments which have been enumerated since that time.[5] Over the 15-year period (to February 1979), the new centres tended to become not only larger in size but also much more specialised in their functional roles. This is to be seen not only in a reduction in the number of schemes which incorporated housing provisions and other associated social facilities but also in the proportional decline in the number of business services that have been accommodated. Commensurate with the increased emphasis on purely retailing activities, however, has been a marked improvement in the commercial or trading success of centres. The survey, which had been conducted with local authority planning departments, showed that over time only 13 per cent of all schemes had failed to reach the trading performances expected of them but, of those that might be deemed to be failures, the majority are to be linked with the speculative ventures of the 1960s. The different sizes of centres that have been built bear an obvious set of relationships with the differences to be found in such things as costs of construction, site acreages utilised, average numbers of shop units provided and the vertical dimensions of schemes. Most growth in the individual size categories of centres, however, has taken place at the intermediate levels where there has been a somewhat countervailing

Table 7.1: Mean Characteristics of Town Centre Shopping Schemes in Britain

	% No. of schemes built	Gross floorspace (000s sq ft)	Ground area (acres)	Cost (£ million)	% borne by local authority	No. of shop units	No. of non-retail units	Office floorspace (000s sq ft)	No. of housing units	Car parking spaces	Distance to peak shopping (yds)	No. of shopping levels
Age												
1963-66	10	197	6.6	2.9	2.5	79	7.7	50	14	690	229	1.5
1967-70	31	154	7.1	2.9	18.6	55	5.1	41	18	474	101	1.4
1971-74	31	214	6.9	6.0	13.8	53	3.5	35	68	654	121	1.5
1975-79	28	239	5.6	9.6	26.8	49	1.9	40	2	695	89	1.4
Size (sq ft)												
50-99,000	35	69	3.0	2.2	6.2	32	2.7	20	13	301	138	1.2
100-199,000	24	139	6.9	4.4	28.3	45	3.3	21	21	528	145	1.5
200-499,000	35	316	9.1	6.2	21.6	77	5.4	73	33	869	81	1.6
500,000	6	655	11.4	36.2	47.8	110	5.6	45	139	1172	98	1.9
Form												
Enclosed	32	272	6.2	10.7	22.5	62	3.3	49	22	798	131	1.6
Partly covered	41	185	7.2	4.5	18.2	57	4.6	39	28	566	63	1.4
Open	27	149	6.3	4.3	15.3	47	4.0	35	37	485	178	1.3
Developer												
Private	56	149	4.9	3.5	0.5	48	4.1	38	14	486	130	1.4
Local authority	8	282	11.1	9.0	93.0	74	3.7	21	69	710	71	1.5
Mixed	36	264	8.1	8.1	29.9	63	3.8	49	38	781	109	1.6
All schemes	100%	201	6.6	6.7	18.5	55	4.0	41	28	614	118	1.4

Source: Bennison, D.J. and Davies, R.L., 'The Impact of Town Centre Shopping Schemes in Britain — Their Impact on Traditional Retail Environments', *Progress in Planning*, vol. 14, part 1 (1980), 1-104.

trend towards the provision of fewer but larger retail outlets housed in proportionately smaller ground areas. The effects of enclosure on construction costs are particularly clear in the table as are the associations with vertical development and a number of transport conditions. By and large, the enclosed centres are more likely to have underground or rooftop servicing facilities than their open precinct counterparts, they are more likely to have second- and third-floor levels of shopping, they have better average allocations of car parking spaces and more frequently incorporate a bus station. Over time, of course, the enclosed centres have become the preferred type of shopping scheme because of the attractive internal environment that is usually found; and, as the local authorities have increasingly involved themselves in the development process, the standards of their exterior appearances have also been substantially improved. The partnership arrangements in development that are now commonplace between local authorities and property companies have also worked to the advantage of both groups in providing a much higher guarantee for the commercial success of a scheme. This has been made possible not only through the sharing of financial risks but through the greater ability to secure favourable sites close to the traditional nexus of trade within a central area.

With so much apparent systematic variation in the characteristics of town centre shopping schemes, one might expect that it would be relatively easy to provide a comprehensive typology or classification to summarise their major differences. This is far from the case for there seem to be several underlying dimensions that separately may be very discriminating but when combined together have a blurring effect. Apart from the four variables discussed above, we have previously referred to the distinctions that may be drawn in terms of functional role, as between those that are of regional and perhaps supra-regional status and those equivalent to a district level of centre. Elsewhere, we have sought to distinguish between schemes that are essentially core-replacement schemes and others that are peripheral accretions.[6] An attempt to provide a classification from a principal components analysis of 28 sets of characteristics associated with the 172 schemes that have been surveyed in detail failed to add much further help.[7] This drew a distinction initially between schemes in nodal and peripheral locations and then divided the former into those occupying either constricted or larger sites and the latter into those having either significant or limited amounts of housing related to them. The nodal centres, being the largest group, could also be further subdivided according to their degree of accessibility to public transport facilities

202 Retail and Commercial Development

and the quality of their exterior physical appearance. Town centre shopping schemes in Britain therefore seem to retain a high degree of individuality despite their apparent similarities when compared according to a single criterion. Some selected examples to illustrate this are described in an abbreviated form in Table 7.2.

Table 7.2: Profiles of Three Town Centre Shopping Schemes

Luton Arndale centre

History: Built in two main stages, with first part opened in 1972. Some collaboration from the local authority, particularly over the redevelopment of the site, but principal developer was Town and City Properties.

Physical characteristics: Gross retail floorspace of 816,000 sq ft; fully enclosed scheme; 110 shop units; 2,300 car parking spaces but no integrated bus station; single long mall at one level; underground servicing facilities; mainly brick structure.

Functional status: Large size suggests regional status but no major department store. Woolworths, Marks and Spencer, Littlewoods, C & A, Tesco and Sainsbury represented. Some associated office activities, a market and hotel.

Location: Parallels the traditional high street with most of the attractor stores opening onto both the street and mall.

Swindon Brunel centre

History: Developed by the local authority and first opened in 1972. Awarded architectural prizes for its overall design.

Physical characteristics: Gross retail floorspace of 517,000 sq ft; partially enclosed scheme; 106 shop units; 107 car parking spaces and no integrated bus station; square/rectangular layout; two shopping levels; rooftop servicing facilities; extensive use of glass in its physical form.

Functional status: Sub-regional or equivalent to large district centre. Major tenants are Marks and Spencer, Sainsbury, Boots, Co-op, 72 housing units, a market and some services.

Location: Fronts onto principal shopping street but extends back at right angles to it. Approximately 100 yards from traditional peak point of shopping; established second locus of shopping.

Edinburgh St James centre

History: Developed by Murrayfield Real Estate Co., opened in 1971 in association with extensive office development.

Physical characteristics: Gross retail floorspace of 395,000 sq ft; fully enclosed scheme; 58 shop units; 556 car parking spaces, plus bus station; several short malls at one level; underground servicing facilities; concrete structure.

Functional status: Extension to high street. John Lewis department store and several small fashion/household goods branch outlets. Hotel as well as 327,000 sq ft of associated office floorspace.

Location: Frontage onto Princes Street, but 200 yards from main area of traditional shopping activity.

Source: Adapted from Davies, R.L. and Bennison, D.J., *British Town Centre Shopping Schemes — A Statistical Digest* (Unit for Retail Planning Information, Reading, 1979).

Residential Area Shopping Schemes

There is considerable individuality, too, amongst the numerous shopping schemes that have been developed elsewhere in the city, although historically these have been subject to much more rigid planning controls as to what their prevailing forms and functional roles should be like. Throughout the post-war period, as we have seen, the general intention has been to integrate them into an urban hierarchy of centres, although there has been a change in emphasis over time from promoting the lower levels of the hierarchy to strengthening the middle and then upper levels. In recent years, however, the introduction of new design concepts and the growth in size of the stores themselves has led to an erosion of the traditional structure of the hierarchy so that we need to consider the nature of modern developments in terms of their own variable characteristics rather than how far they conform to out-dated, preconceived ideas. For convenience, we shall distinguish between four main types of schemes; outlying strategic centres, district centres, local centres and free-standing large stores.

Outlying Strategic Centres. There are relatively few centres in Britain that can be described under this heading, but they represent a close counterpart to those 'out-of-town' shopping centres to be found in other countries. There are two prominent kinds of examples that can be given and a third that is more questionable. The first includes the Brent Cross shopping centre in north-west London, and perhaps one or two other large schemes developed in relatively virgin sites some distance away from established town centres, such as the Hempstead Valley scheme in Rochester. The second includes certain of the new town centres for the New Towns which, while serving as a central shopping place for their own local populations, also act as satellite centres for people living in a nearby conurbation. The new town centre for Washington New Town is a good case in point. The third, more doubtful, set includes some of the centres built in very large outlying estates, such as the Yates shopping centre on the outskirts of Bristol. and the Crossgates Arndale centre outside Leeds, which have otherwise been described as District Centres. Collectively, the centres are a very miscellaneous group, representing 'one-off' projects within the urban environments in which they are found.

The Brent Cross shopping centre deserves special attention because it is almost an exact replica of a North American 'out-of-town' regional shopping centre implanted into an area of extensive inter-war housing in London. Somewhat surprisingly, the original application for its development by the Hammerson group in the early 1960s was quite sympathetically received by the Planning Department of the Greater London Council, but it was refused at that time (and in several revisions throughout the decade) on traffic grounds. Its site lies to the north of the North Circular Road, and between the A5 and what is now the M1, and there was rather obvious concern over the additional congestion it would create on roads already heavily laden. Its merit in retail planning terms, however, lay in its providing for the first time a major shopping focus for this part of London to complement those large, established shopping centres serving most other suburban tracts around the city.[8] Permission for its development was finally given in 1970 and it opened in 1976. Physically, it compares with the largest of the town centre schemes constructed in Britain. It comprises a total of one million square feet (93,000 m^2) of covered floorspace, of which 790,000 square feet (74,000 m^2) is given over to shops (on two levels), the principal tenants being John Lewis, Fenwicks, Marks and Spencer, Boots, Waitrose, C & A and W.H. Smith. The two department stores are located at each end of the single malls, with Marks and Spencer approximately in the middle. It is an extremely attractive shopping development, with a high quality of 'finish' to its interior artefacts, and it conveys an atmosphere of the more successful American schemes. Seventy per cent of the customers travel to the centre by car on a Saturday and more than one quarter of them are drawn from beyond a 20-minute driving-time band.[9] Awaiting them are 4,500 car parking spaces, as well as the 100 or so high fashion shops.

The Washington New Town development offers an interesting contrast to this, for while it has again been designed to serve mainly a carborne shopping population (for which there are about 3,000 car parking spaces), its chief attraction lies in its convenience goods provisions rather than the more specialised stores. The centre was first opened in 1973 when it comprised a covered, square-shaped precinct and an adjacent Woolco superstore, the whole totalling approximately 250,000 square feet (23,000 m^2) of gross floorspace. In 1977, however, a Savacentre hypermarket was added to the other end of the Galleries precinct which, in the years since, has also itself been enlarged (Figure 7.2). Collectively, the scheme now measures about 500,000 square feet (46,500 m^2) in size and, since it contains a large supermarket as well as the hypermarket and superstore, it is obviously hugely endowed, and some would argue over-endowed, in the food and household goods sector. The centre, however, lies only about five miles

Figure 7.2: Layout of the Town Centre of Washington New Town

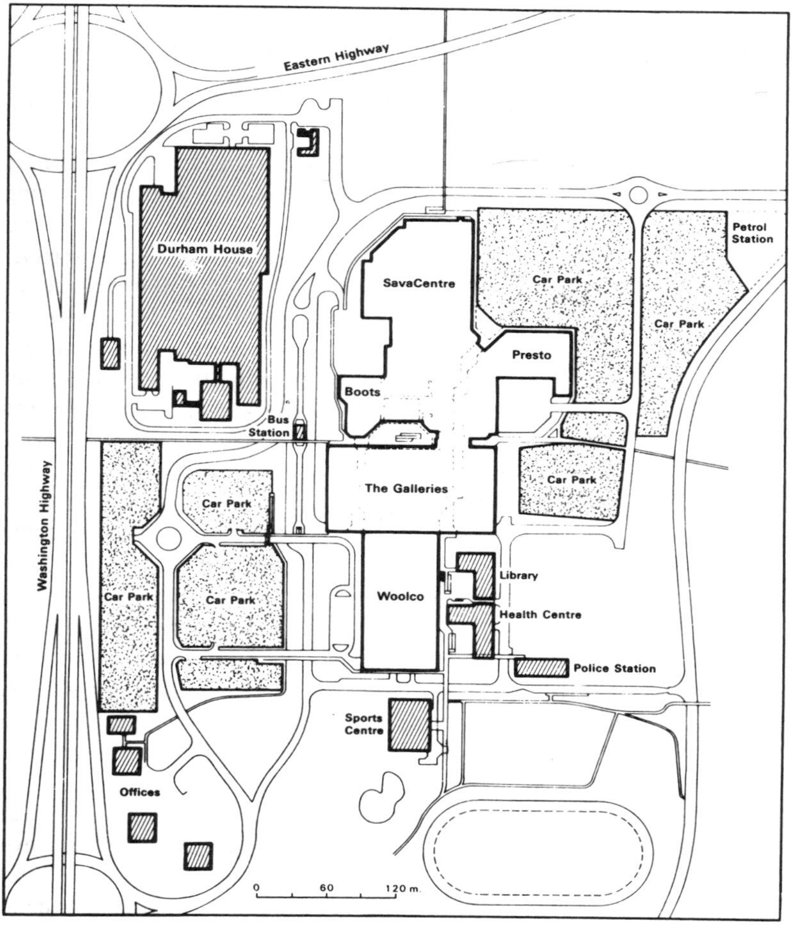

Source: Washington New Town Development Corporation.

from the south bank of the River Tyne; hence its catchment area includes much of Gateshead, Hebburn and Jarrow as well as Sunderland to the east. It therefore serves, to all intents and purposes, as an 'out-of-town' centre for the Tyneside conurbation.

District Centres. The concept of the district centre was first promulgated in Sir Wilfred Burns' book on British shopping centres in the late

1950s.[10] Burns recognised that the early post-war proliferation of neighbourhood centres would quickly become outdated by the growth in car-borne shopping; hence he advocated the development of much larger centres, still placed in the midst of new housing estates, but serving two or three rather than single neighbourhoods. At the time, he contemplated a catchment area of about 20,000-40,000 people and the provision of between 100 and 150 shops. Several district centres were built around the country during the ensuing decade, including such schemes as the Cowley centre in Oxford and the Bell Green centre in Coventry (the city to which Burns was attached at the time); and the new concept was also adopted in certain early inner city redevelopment programmes, as indicated by the Aston New Town development in Birmingham and the Cruddas Park shopping centre in Newcastle (to which city Burns later moved). The new schemes were expensive propositions, however, largely financed at this time by the local authorities themselves, and it was not until the 1970s and the injection of private money into their development that they became common features of the urban scene.

The second wave of development was particularly associated with retailer-sponsored schemes, initially from Asda[11] and more recently from Sainsbury. The intervening years and the changes in retailing techniques that had occurred led to a dramatic alteration to the size, tenant mix and appearance of the new schemes, with the chief attraction now being the presence of a superstore rather than a large number of shops. Schemes ranging from 50,000 to 250,000 square feet (4,600 to 24,000 m^2) were constructed, serving catchment area populations of 30,000 to 150,000, some of them enclosed centres and all of them with a greatly reduced number of small, independent shops. At the present time, the ideal appears to be a scheme of about 100,000 square feet (10,000 m^2) where about half of this is taken up by a superstore, there are three other main attractor stores (such as a 'do-it-yourself' store, modern convenience store and a furniture store), and perhaps ten other small units (such as a butcher, chemist, post office, launderette or dry cleaner, baker, restaurant or café, a radio/TV shop, a bank, boutique and pub).[12] The emphasis, therefore, still lies on the provision of mainly food and household goods but with some lower-order durable goods too.

The large retailing firms have been attracted to the district centre concept since it enables them to establish large stores in relatively outlying locations without being seen to be radically altering the established urban hierarchy or creating major changes in the overall pattern of trade. Having formerly been rebuffed by many local authority planning departments in their attempts to develop free-standing superstores or hypermarkets in true 'out-of-town' sites, the retailers found the same planners more than sympathetic to the idea of developing 'edge-of-town' centres so long as these were in areas of relative population growth, would accommodate certain other stores and represented an extension to, rather than replacement of, the hierarchical system of shopping provisions within the town or city as a whole. Many contemporary developments, in fact, like the town centre shopping schemes, are partnership ventures between a retailing company and a local authority. This is desirable from both points of view for, apart from sharing the financial risks involved, there is considerable scope for compromising over the separate commercial and social interests that may be held. In particular, a retailing firm might be given preferential treatment in the choice of a site in return for collaborating in the development of a wider service centre rather than a purely shopping complex.

It was always envisaged from the early days that district centres would provide a wide range of community facilities as well as retail functions but relatively few schemes have lived up to these expectations. Some of the first local authority centres accommodated a branch library, health centre and one or two other welfare outlets, but over the years the social service inputs tended to be discarded. The emergence of more collaborative efforts between retailers and local authorities has seen a reawakening of the ideal, with certain modern developments, like the Estover centre in Plymouth and the Dyce centre in Aberdeen, offering a considerable number of provisions. The former contains a branch library, health centre, community hall, day-care centre, church, housing office and old people's home; the latter, a school, games hall, swimming pool and theatre. The question of whether such services should be concentrated in this way or dispersed throughout a community, however, has not been widely discussed in the planning literature or examined from a research point of view. Duerden[13] has recently compiled a list of all those types of facilities that could conceivably be associated with a district centre (and others more appropriate for a local centre), as Table 7.3 indicates; but these need to be more closely evaluated as to which are the most suitable ones. The principle of concentrating social services within district centres, nevertheless, seems intuitively quite sound, especially since it allows for a combination of trips to be made to the same focal point, where there can then be a sharing of car parking, bus staging and other

Table 7.3: Community Facilities that could be Integrated with Shopping Centres

Facility	District centre	Adjacent to district centre	Local centre	Other locations
Social security offices	*			
Job/recruitment centres	*			
Public health inspectorate	*			
Housing offices	*			Large estates
Special planning agencies	*			
Probation offices	*			
Education welfare office	*			Schools
Further education	*			
Social services office	*		*	
Home help office	*			
District nurses office	*			Health centre
Swimming pool	*	*		
Youth employment office	*			
Transport information centre	*			Transport terminal
Private sports provision	*	*		
Evening institute	*		*	Schools
Police station		*		
Fire station		*		
Ambulance station		*		
Day-care services	*		*	
School health clinic		*		
Health clinics	*	*		
Secondary school		*	*	
Health centre	*		*	
Libraries	*		*	
Youth services	*		*	
Community centres	*		*	
Laundry-wash house	*		*	
Indoor sports provision	*		*	
Luncheon clubs	*		*	
Doctors	*		*	
Dentists	*		*	
Chiropodists	*		*	
Primary school			*	Residential areas
Pre-nursery class			*	Residential areas
Play centre			*	Schools
Recreation centre			*	Schools
Day nursery			*	Residential areas
Residential services			*	Residential areas
Welfare teams			*	Schools

Source: Duerden, B., 'Community Facilities and District Centres', in *District Shopping Centres — Report of an URPI Workshop* (Unit for Retail Planning Information, Reading, 1977).

supporting infrastructures. At the same time, there is no reason why this diversification in the functional role of such centres should not also include a greater provision of services from the private sector as well, particularly in the business, leisure and catering fields.

Local Centres. The term 'local centre' has come to embrace a variety of small shopping provisions from the single corner store upwards to the neighbourhood centre. In all cases, there has tended to be a serious erosion of their economic viability in recent years because of the competitive effects of larger centres and the poor business returns to be made on limited scales of operation. An URPI workshop on these centres in fact concluded that the local parade of shops was now extinct as a contemporary development since neither local authorities nor property development companies were prepared to finance them any more.[14]

Certain modern equivalents to the old corner shops are beginning to assert themselves, however, as we have indicated before. The so-called modern convenience stores (such as those in the 7-Eleven chain), which have hitherto been located in Britain in town centres, are now being experimented with in residential areas. The development of retail outlets in petrol stations is expanding and the Mobil Oil Company that first introduced these in 1969 is moving towards the provision of groceries, toys, magazines and off-licence products as well as the confectionary, tobacco and motor accessory goods it now mainly sells. Some local authorities, too, are seeking to create a more versatile type of shop in new housing estates, building a selected number of properties that can be easily converted to a retail use if there appears to be demand for them but otherwise serving as dwelling units.

The future for neighbourhood shopping centres, those larger than the local parades, is much more uncertain. It is likely that in some parts of the city, where substantial new housing takes place but where a district centre cannot be supported, there will still be sufficient latent demand for convenience goods shopping that a modern neighbourhood centre could be supported. It is likely to require a large supermarket as the key tenant, however, perhaps of a size order of 15,000-20,000 square feet (1,400 m² to 1,800 m²) or one that represents the contemporary operating threshold for a regional supermarket firm (as distinct from a national company). This may then be accompanied by up to half-a-dozen small units, so that it becomes in effect a mini-version of a district centre. At the other end of the scale, however, it is doubtful whether a small neighbourhood centre could survive in the old accepted sense of a precinct serving populations of about 5,000 people. The key to the future prospects of these and other local centres, however, lies more in a shift in locational settings than meeting theoretical optimum sizes, either in the store operating sense or for catchment areas; for positions alongside main roads rather than concealed in the middle of housing estates would allow for the potential capture of passing trade as well as that indigenous to the surrounding area.

Free-standing Large Stores. Most of the superstores and hypermarkets that have been established in Britain have been absorbed into existing town centres or made the cornerstone of new district centres. A few are free-standing in generally outlying locations, however; for example, the Carrefour hypermarkets in Caerphilly and Chandlers Ford, Hampshire, Tesco's superstore at Irlam, Greater Manchester and Asda's superstore in Huntingdon, York. It is difficult to disassociate the physical and trading characteristics of these from the total set of superstores and hypermarkets (summarised in Table 7.4) but, if

Table 7.4: Mean Characteristics of Hypermarkets and Superstores in Britain, 1976-1977

Mean total turnover	£4.56		
Food sales	£3.74	Non-food selling areas	£0.77
Gross floorspace	64,300 sq ft (5,970 sq m)	Net floorspace	39,100 sq ft (3,630 sq m)
Food selling areas	18,300 sq ft (1,700 sq m)	Non-food selling areas	17,900 sq ft (1,660 sq m)
Turnover to gross floorspace	£74 per sq ft (£800 per sq m)		
Site area	6.22 acres	Car parking spaces	575
Full-time staff	122	Part-time staff	95

Source: Jones, P., *Trading Features of Hypermarkets and Superstores* (Unit for Retail Planning Information, Reading, 1978).

anything, they are likely to cater to slightly higher levels of car-borne shoppers and to draw from a broader territory in a town or city than their integrated counterparts.[15] To all intents and purposes, however, these free-standing stores serve as the equivalents of small district centres in the goods they provide and the numbers of people they cater for. Several studies have examined their comparative price advantages and the types of customers to which these accrue, but these are taken up in a later chapter dealing with their impact on the traditional retailing environment.

By contrast, there is much less documentation available on discount retail warehouses and other large retail units, such as home improvement centres, nurseries and leisure centres (in the sense of those selling caravans, camping equipment, boats, etc.). Many of these are again integrated into traditional shopping areas, including town centres and district centres, and some operate from converted cinemas, industrial warehouses and even former churches, as well as being purpose-built. The varied locational characteristics reflect in part on the different types of trading activities embraced within this group but also on the effects of planning interventions that have guided them to particular localities. Thus proportionately more electrical goods and domestic appliance outlets prefer to locate in town centres while the home improvement, garden and leisure centres usually prefer outlying locations; but representatives of all these are to be found in industrial trading estates and the inner city. A recent URPI workshop took stock of the diverse requirements of all these outlets and produced a check-list of the advantages and disadvantages accruing to particular sites (summarised in Table 7.5).[16] In the main, for those types of trades preferring outlying locations, sites along major radial roads in the built-up parts of the city were seen to be more advantageous than truly 'out-of-town' sites. The ideal type of operation for a home improvement or 'do-it-yourself' centre was seen to be a store about 25,000 square feet (2,300 m^2), aligned alongside a major radial road, providing about 150 car parking places and where there is a catchment population of 100,000 within ten minutes' travelling time. It seems to make little difference whether these are truly free-standing or associated with other compatible land uses, but inclusion in district centres and industrial estates is not considered desirable.

Commercial Developments

Our earlier discussions on recent changes within the intermediary trades focused on the decline of traditional wholesaling pursuits and the emergence of what we called 'bulk transference activities'. Apart from the cash and carry depots, whose main period of growth now appears to be over, and warehouses used for longer-term storage purposes, or where the term 'warehouse' can be used in a conventional sense, we have had little to say about the form and functions of the new developments. This is because there have been no comprehensive surveys that have distinguished between their physical and trading characteristics

Table 7.5: Advantages and Disadvantages of Different Locations for Discount Retail Warehouses

	Town centres	Inner cities	District centres	Industrial estates	Radial roads	Out of town (car *owners only)
Advantages						
good accessibility to consumers	*	*	*		*	*
town centre trade maintained	*					
local authority infrastructure safeguarded	*					
relatively low land values		*				
aid to regeneration of inner city		*				
traders' requirements met			*			
availability of larger sites				*	*	*
relatively low rents and rates				*	*	*
adequate car parking				*	*	*
easier servicing and deliveries				*	*	*
better trading margins				*	*	
attraction good — advertising costs less					*	
Disadvantages						
high rents and rates	*	*	*			
promotes traffic congestion	*	*				
limited car parking	*	*				
limited sites available	*	*				
poor accessibility to individual stores	*	*				
adverse effect on retailing in town centre			*	*	*	*
high land values			*	*		
attraction poor — advertising costs more				*		
loss of industrial land use				*		*

Source: Abbreviated from Unit for Retail Planning Information, *Discount Retail Warehouses — Report of an URPI Workshop* (URPI, Reading, 1978)

or analysed their variable sites and locations. There are certain labels given to the new developments, to which we have made passing reference, nevertheless, that ought now to be given broad definition. We shall concentrate on those names attributable to new developments linking suppliers to retailers.

Firstly, there are *trans-shipment depots* which may be operated by a private company or occasionally by a local authority.[17] They are points to which a variety of goods are brought from several supply sources, to be trans-shipped to a range of retailing destinations. They vary in so much as some act as receivers of large deliveries which are then broken down into smaller quantities to be despatched by smaller vehicles whereas others make up bigger loads from the variety of source materials obtained. A variant type of this latter facility is the so-called *consolidation depot*, operated by a haulage firm on behalf of a single retailer or groups of retailers. For example, BOC Transhield operates consolidation depots for most of the foodstuffs destined for Marks and Spencer's stores with BOC making the final deliveries. National Carriers Ltd operates a similar service for many of the high street fashion stores. Secondly, there are *distribution* or *redistribution centres*, usually owned by the larger retail firms themselves, which act as the main stock control facility for particular lines of goods.[18] The goods may be brought in from several sources and there may be some packaging, bottling or other treatment of them but they are then usually despatched to other, smaller, more localised warehouses rather than direct to shops. These smaller warehouses are then often known as *field depots* which provide a final delivery of smaller quantities of goods on a more regular basis to the firm's branch stores within their areas. Such field depots, however, may receive their goods from more than one distribution centre. A third category of distributional facilities is the so-called *transit depot*, usually operated by hauliers, who provide a rapid delivery service to retailers for specific orders placed with a manufacturing firm or distribution centre.[19] In other words, they retain no stocks of their own and differ from the trans-shipment depots in fulfilling a limited number rather than multiplicity of needs.

In addition to these new developments that effect the distribution of goods on the ground, there have recently emerged a few extremely large facilities concerned more with the generation of trade particularly from an export point of view. These include so-called trade centres and exhibition centres, some of which command national prominence and have been inspired by the public and private sectors working together. The two most important are the International Trade Centre proposed for London's Docklands, and still in the development stage, and the National Exhibition Centre on the outskirts of Birmingham. The differences between them are rather implied by their names, with the former to contain a more permanent set of agents and showrooms for different activities and the latter hosting temporary exhibits, conventions and a miscellaneous collection of events.

The need for a new National Exhibition Centre was first mooted in the later 1950s and during the 1960s serious consideration was given to redeveloping the former site of the Crystal Palace (home of the 1851 Great Exhibition) in London.[20] For various reasons, partly concern over communication problems and escalating likely costs, this idea was abandoned and a further inquiry conducted by the Labour government under Lord George-Brown, suggested that an alternative site should be found outside the London area. Shortly thereafter, the Birmingham Chamber of Commerce and Birmingham Corporation jointly persuaded the government to endorse a proposal for the centre to be built adjacent to Birmingham airport, at a point that would be close to a major intersection of motorways (the M6 and M42) and other trunk routes (the A45 and A452) and which also lay alongside the main London-north west rail link. The site itself was acquired from two farms and, following the granting of planning permission in 1972, the scheme was finally opened in 1976. The general layout of the scheme is shown in Figure 7.3 and the statistics which accompany its main features rather speak for themselves: six halls provide a total of approximately one million square feet (93,000 m^2) of exhibition space; a seventh hall is a dual-purpose convention room or arena allowing for up to 12,000 seated spectators; there is parking for 15,000 cars and 200 coaches; a central piazza provides shops, offices and service outlets; there are two hotels, numerous restaurants, an artificial lake, and the entire site area (excluding the access roads) amounts to 310 acres.

The National Exhibition Centre is clearly a major achievement in planning terms but it represents but one large resource directed to the promotion of British industrial goods, and there are other countries, most notable West Germany, Holland and the United States, that have several, similar-sized schemes. The urban settlement pattern in Britain is such that perhaps only one or two giant centres can be supported; but there is a strong case for the development of smaller sizes of centres in such places as Glasgow, Newcastle, Liverpool and perhaps Bristol. These might take the form of a combined exhibition and trade centre, and could perhaps play a significant part in the regeneration of those cities with depressed local economies. Two outline planning proposals

Figure 7.3: Location and Layout of the National Exhibition Centre, Birmingham

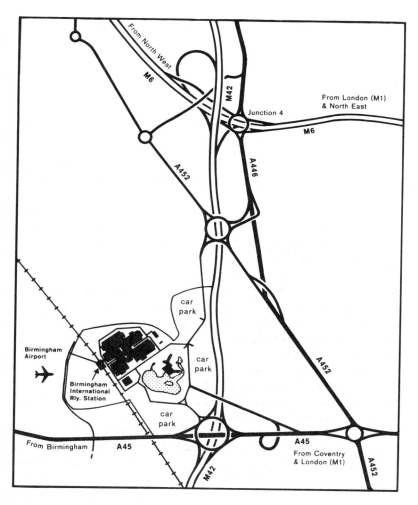

Source: Mills, E.D., *The National Exhibition Centre* (Crosby Lockwood Staples, London, 1976).

were submitted to the councils of Liverpool and Glasgow for schemes along these lines a few years ago,[21] but they appear to have been shelved for the time being, presumably in part because of the poor financial climate. Several major convention centres have been built or are in process of development in smaller-sized places, however, including Brighton and Harrogate, and a new complex directed at staging international conferences has recently been opened at the Barbican in London.

A further set of important commercial developments are the new wholesale green markets that have appeared in such places as Newcastle, Birmingham and Manchester. Chief amongst these is the new Covent Garden Market at Nine Elms in London. Like the National Exhibition Centre, this saw more than a decade of discussions and research before a site was finally selected and the scheme opened in 1974. Nine Elms in fact was originally discarded as a suitable location for the new market in a study of five prospective sites by the Fantus Company in 1963,[22] mainly on the grounds of the limited amount of space to be found on land to be released by British Rail Preference was expressed for a site at Beckton, close to the docks through which so much of the fruit, vegetable and flower produce are imported. Nine Elms came back into the reckoning a year later, however, when British Rail offered to release a larger block of land (approximately 80 acres) and the Market Authority itself felt that the scheme should be located closer to its main area of customer demand (the west side of central London, where most of the major hotel and catering facilities are to be found) than to its principal source of supply.[23] The final result has been an impressive scheme where the wholesale outlets are arranged in two parallel sets, each divided by a central concourse or mall wherein most of the trading takes place, and with service vehicles entering and exiting from the sides (Figure 7.4). The general principle is therefore not unlike that for a major shopping centre development, except that greater accommodation has had to be given to commercial vehicles rather than cars.

At the root of the relocation of Covent Garden Market, as with those that have occurred elsewhere, of course, was the need to reduce the severe traffic congestion that had built up at the former site and to create a spacious, modern environment where the latest loading and handling machinery could be used. Most new markets around the world have been established in relatively outlying locations, including the early, influential developments at Paris (Rungis), Hamburg and Philadelphia. The new market serving Tyne and Wear best illustrates this in Britain, where a new site was taken on the Team Valley Trading Estate in 1968, close to the A1(M) and the London-Newcastle rail link. The relocation was planned and financed by the wholesalers themselves

Figure 7.4: Layout of the Covent Garden Market at Nine Elms, London

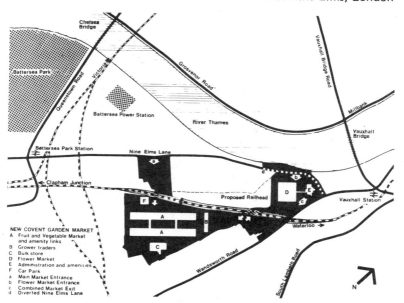

Source: Covent Garden Market Authority.

(although with assistance from development grants) and left a valuable, central site in the city centre of Newcastle which has subsequently been occupied by the Eldon Square shopping complex. The layout of the market is similar to that for Covent Garden, and it comprises 16 major units together with a few associated commercial activities, such as a packaging plant and banana-ripening rooms.

Some Radical Alternatives

While most of the new retail and commercial developments we have reviewed have brought significant improvements to both the business community and various groups of consumers, through increasing the efficiency of trade practices and enhancing the environment in which shopping is undertaken, there are two major criticisms that can be made and to which we have pointed elsewhere. Firstly, most of the developments are single- rather than multi-purpose in function and, in those cases where two or more land uses have been linked together, one usually predominates and the others are seen as relatively minor appendages. This is somewhat surprising given the extensive local authority involvement in the planning and often financing of schemes and in view of the increasing integration of the distributive trades. Secondly, most of the developments have been expressions of the demand for new facilities from the larger business organisations and the bulk middle-class sections of the population, with few modern facilities being tailored to the needs of weaker, minority groups. Even among those schemes which serve a more powerful set of interests, however, the developers have usually been constrained to establishing only those sorts of facilities, in particular types of locations, that the local authorities deem acceptable.

Superficially, the two criticisms appear somewhat contradictory, for it is being suggested on the one hand that local authorities ought to seek to promote a greater mixture of activities and on the other that the local authorities should give developers a freer hand in what they set up. The objectives, however, are the same in each case, namely to create more variability in the scope of opportunities available to all elements of the business community and population. The need to provide more multi-purpose developments is probably easier to treat in respect of shopping centres; the need to allow more freedom in types and locations of developments is better discussed in relation to commercial schemes.

Multi-purpose Developments

A large number of shopping centres in Britain have incorporated either housing complexes, offices, hotels or sports facilities but there has rarely been a full combination of these and other types of land use activities, except in relation to the new town centres of the New Towns or certain smaller centres at the neighbourhood level. In large, heavily redeveloped central areas, such as those of Birmingham and Newcastle, each major land use activity (as we shall see in Chapter 8) has been assigned its own special quarter. Contrast with this the physically integrated redevelopment schemes to be found in Lyons or Utrecht or dozens of cities across the United States.[24] In Utrecht, a large shopping centre has been enjoined with a trade centre, convention halls, an hotel, a new railway and bus stations, sports facilities and offices, all collectively referred to as the Hoog Catherinje project. In Detroit, the Renaissance Centre comprises extensive office provisions, a large hotel, conference facilities, a theatre, together with its shopping centre. Both schemes are an attempt to create a mixture of activities so that there will be a sharing of support infrastructures and consumers can utilise the centres for more than one purpose. In the more critical need to promote a greater social interaction between people, or to provide opportunities for all socio-economic and age groups of the population, however, these schemes seem just as wanting as the more special-purpose shopping centres established in Britain. Hoog Catherinje draws on a substantial business and shopping clientele, but for most people it is an avenue through to the medieval core of Utrecht where there is a much more varied environment to be found. The Renaissance Centre sits like a fortress in downtown Detroit, catering predominantly to a white, middle-class population and completely separate, socially, from surrounding shopping streets.

The two foreign examples share with most British schemes a lack of an important land use which is not generally recognised to be such, i.e. an amenity space, where a wide cross-section of people can simply rest, look at exhibits or organise their own events. This is essentially the function of the old market square which continues to provide a meeting place in many towns and cities, except where it has been given over completely to car parking. In Denmark, a radical experiment has been conducted with the shopping centre known as City 2 on the outskirts of Copenhagen to try to recreate this condition. The centre has been built in a square form, with a large amenity space in the middle and shops and services arranged on three levels around it. The amenity space provides extensive seating, a miniature Tivoli Gardens for children (including a boating stream), an amphitheatre for local dramatics or school productions, and room for advertising and exhibitions. On this ground level, most of the surrounding businesses are cafés, bars and food outlets, with the fashion stores being arranged above. The scheme has been extremely successful in the social sense; unfortunately, for the developers, the expected growth in population in the surrounding suburbs has not materialised and the retail provisions have ended up being too large for the catchment support available. In commercial terms, it has therefore been a rather dismal failure.

Free-form Developments

We have repeatedly argued throughout this book that a large number of intermediary and service activities are restricted from obtaining appropriate sites alongside main roads and that, in addition to the development of purpose-built shopping centres and large warehousing facilities, there needs to be some modern equivalents to the old ribbons of towns and cities.[25] At various stages we have talked in terms of the need for planned strip developments where these recreate the locational advantages of old ribbons but without the associated problems of congestion and safety hazards. In the last chapter we also introduced the notion of service plazas and trading marts which might be conceived as special forms of strips, with the former containing a high concentration of entertainment and leisure activities and the latter a mix of wholesaling and retail discounting functions.

Some examples of how these ideas might be translated into practice are shown in Figure 7.5. A 'convenience' strip can be contemplated, located in an outlying position alongside a major highway, that supersedes the traditional role of the local parade. It might comprise a bank, modern convenience store, 'do-it-yourself' and car accessory shops, a dry cleaner and fast food outlet − all, or most, of which are growth elements in the retail service sector. To avoid traffic problems, there might be access via slipways with car parking provisions in the rear. Alternatively, a larger 'auto' strip might be envisaged, located closer to the city centre, that draws together a range of car-oriented activities, such as petrol stations, car dealers, car accessory and repair shops. These are conspicuous in an unplanned form in many North American cities and are emerging, in an embryonic form, on the outskirts of several British central areas. Access here might simply have to be controlled through conventional traffic lights. Service plazas could be built in either strategically placed outlying locations or intruding into the city centre, and might embrace the sorts of activities identified on the diagram itself. There could be a sharing of car parking facilities which, during day-time hours, might also serve some nearby shopping streets. Trading marts could be enjoined to service plazas or developed separately but they would provide space for both those types of intermediary activities where there is frequent customer contact and those bulk shopping activities that usually prefer peripheral city centre sites.

The schemes presented in these diagrams, however, exhibit the same limitations of purpose-built shopping centres and large warehousing facilities to the extent that they would constitute relatively fixed entities to be developed in an instantaneous way. What needs to go with them is the designation of areas appropriate to mixed retail and commercial activities wherein a more gradual coalescence of firms can take place in a less rigid form. In other words, one ought to be providing a series of general settings where small businesses in particular can grow up incrementally without being forced into some grandiose or tightly controlled environment. There is no reason, nevertheless, why these areas should not be designated around specific developments, whether these are of a shopping, warehousing or service kind.

Figure 7.5: Some Hypothetical Forms of Alternative Retail and Commercial Developments

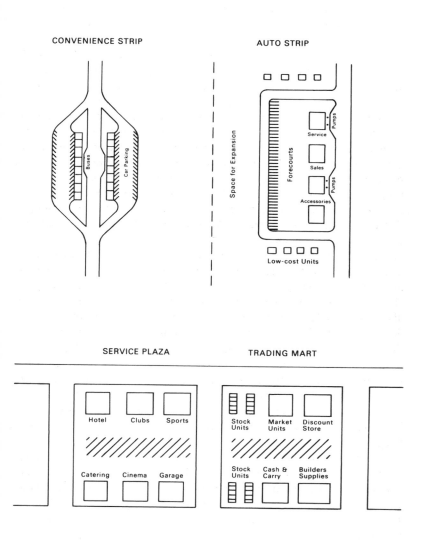

The Control of Development

It was indicated in Chapter 4 that there needs to be a reorganisation of the responsibilities and powers of the various branches of government with respect to the control of new development. In summary, what was suggested was that central government should continue to be the final arbiter over controversial schemes or where there is disagreement between local authorities but that a more positive role should be played in recommending a range of control standards to be adhered to. This may take the form of a series of policy notes or directives over the conformity of new developments to locational strategies, trade regulations, environmental standards and the future requirements of an urban area, but in seeking to promote an improvement in the developments themselves might also involve the publication of one or more handbooks recommending desirable objectives to be fulfilled. Such handbooks could include a set of definitions and classification of the various types of retail and commercial developments to be found; appropriate numbers of car parking spaces and servicing facilities for different sizes of schemes; proportions of amenity space and amenity provisions to accompany new shopping centres; suitable sizes of units for small, independent businesses and recommendations regarding their inclusion in large developments; and so on.

The Counties, however, would mainly be responsible for the adjudication of large developments, those over a suggested size threshold of 50,000 square feet (5,000 m^2). This should ideally be effected through reference to a consultative body of experts, or indeed two or more bodies with special knowledge of the different sectors of the distributive trades. At the same time, the Counties, through their advisory panels, might initiate or encourage the introduction of new developments, particularly those that might be instrumental in improving their local economies: such as a trade centre or exhibition hall, redistribution centres, or even service plazas and trading marts. A final area of responsibility would lie in monitoring the performance of existing large schemes and assessing the potential impact of new ones. This latter function would then be tied in with the preparation of special plans devoted to the consequences of new developments and which will be elaborated upon in a later chapter.

The District Authorities would primarily be concerned with the detailed aspects of development control, as they are already of course. They would have responsibility for ensuring that large developments met the site requirements placed on them and that those standards advocated by central government were approximated in so far as was possible; they would initiate and adjudicate in their own right on smaller schemes; and perhaps most importantly they would designate those areas where small-scale development would be permitted to grow up in an incremental and relatively unencumbered way. In addition, as we shall go on to discuss in the next chapter, they should ideally be empowered to designate other areas, particularly within established town and city centres, where stricter planning controls would apply than is normally the case.

Conclusion

The reaction of local authorities to proposals for new development is often regarded as the cornerstone of retail and commercial planning. Although in the day-to-day work of an office the implementation of development controls may be viewed as a less challenging task than the formulation of policies, ultimately it is the way in which recurring decisions are made that a plan can be seen to be taking effect. During the last two decades, in fact, it is arguable that an entrenched, consensus approach to the implementation of development controls has itself shaped the policies of local authorities, rather than vice versa, and as a consequence most new forms of development have simply reinforced an existing system of distribution rather than making radical alterations to it.

This is clearer in the case of retail developments than commercial developments, however. While much publicity has accompanied the containment of outlying superstores and hypermarkets, vast numbers of shopping centres have been built in central area locations mainly on the basis that here they would presumably be more easily absorbed and have less deleterious effects on traditional retailing activities. Many of these developments have brought significant improvements to the business of shopping but others are rather sterile appendages to the high street that fulfil only a limited social role. In the residential parts of the city, the planners, having sought to promote a continuing set of conventional centres, of the local neighbourhood and district kind, are now finding that the smaller ones are no longer viable and a serious legacy will be left behind.

The treatment of large warehousing facilities appears to have been more positive, for here a wide range of new developments has occurred which seem to have had a more profound effect on the distribution system. One suspects in this case, however, that the planners have largely been acting in the dark, for they have had virtually no factual information available to suggest what the trading characteristics or repercussions of alternative schemes might be. A broad acceptance seems to have been reached that, so long as such developments do not intrude into residential or shopping areas, they will be tolerated in whatever locations they seek, especially if these conform with industrial estates.

There are certain types of activity, nevertheless, which do not seem to be housed in their own distinctive, modern developments, partly because the local authorities have resisted them and partly because the private sector has been loath to accommodate them. These include a wide range of services and intermediary activities that traditionally have occupied the ribbons and twilight areas of towns and cities. These represent a special challenge for the future that some enlightened planners might like to take up, using development control procedures in a much more constructive way than has hitherto been the case.

References

1. Northen, R.I. and Haskoll, M., *Shopping Centres: A Developer's Guide to Planning and Design* (College of Estate Management, Reading, 1977).
2. Gosling, D. and Maitland, B., *Design and Planning of Retail Systems* (Architectural Press, London, 1976).
3. Bennison, D.J. and Davies, R.L., 'The Impact of Town Centre Shopping Schemes in Britain — Their Impact on Traditional Retail Environments', *Progress in Planning*, vol. 14, part 1 (1980), pp. 1-104.
4. Hillier, Parker, *British Shopping Developments* (Hillier, Parker, London, 1979).
5. Davies, R.L. and Bennison, D.J., *British Town Centre Shopping Schemes: A Statistical Digest* (Unit for Retail Planning Information, Reading, 1979).
6. Davies, R.L. and Bennison, D.J., 'The Planning Repercussions of In-Town Shopping Schemes', *Estates Gazette*, vol. 246 (1978), pp. 117-19, 121.
7. Bennison, D.J. and Davies, R.L., 'The Impact of Town Centre Shopping Schemes in Britain'.
8. Shepherd, I. and Newby, P., *The Brent Cross Regional Shopping Centre — Characteristics and Early Effects* (Retailing and Planning Associates, Corbridge, 1978).
9. Lee, M. and Kent, E., *Brent Cross Study* (Donaldsons, London, 1977).
10. Burns, W., *British Shopping Centres* (Leonard Hill, London, 1959).
11. Asda, *Developing and Financing District Centres — The Role of Asda Superstores* (Asda, Leeds, 1975).
12. Wakefield, I.B., 'District Centres — A Retailer's View' in *District Shopping Centres — Report of an URPI Workshop* (Unit for Retail Planning Information, Reading, 1977).
13. Duerden, B., 'Community Facilities and District Centres', in *District Shopping Centres*, ibid.

14. Unit for Retail Planning Information, *Local Shopping Centres and Convenience Stores: Report of an URPI Workshop* (Reading, 1980).
15. Jones, P.M., *Trading Features of Hypermarkets and Superstores* (Unit for Retail Planning Information, Reading, 1978); Bruce, A., 'Shopping Trips to Superstores and Other Centres – Some Comparisons', *URPI Information Brief* (July 1978).
16. Unit for Retail Planning Information, *Discount Retail Warehouses: Report of an URPI Workshop* (Reading, 1978).
17. See, for example, Battilana, J.A. and Hawthorne, I.H., *Design and Cost of a Trans-shipment Depot to Serve Swindon Town Centre* (Transport and Road Research Laboratory, Crowthorne, 1976); McDermott, D.R. and Robeson, J.F., 'The Role of Terminal Consolidation in Urban Goods Distribution, *International Journal of Physical Distribution*, vol. 4, no. 3 (1973), pp. 166-75; Lorries and Environment Committee, *Report on Trans-shipment* (London, 1976).
18. Wytconsult, *Retail Deliveries in Urban Areas and the Relevance of Trans-shipment* (Wytconsult, Document 602, 1975).
19. Freight Transport Association, *Planning for Lorries* (Freight Transport Association, London, 1974).
20. Mills, E.D., *The National Exhibition Centre* (Crosby Lockwood Staples, London, 1976).
21. 'Plans for Two Trade Centres', *Guardian*, 4 July 1975.
22. *Study for the Re-location of Covent Garden Market, London* (The Fantus Co., London, 1963).
23. *A New Site for Covent Garden Market – The Nine Elms Area* (Covent Garden Market Authority, London, 1964).
24. Gruen, V., *Centres for the Urban Environment* (Van Nostrand, New York, 1973); Redstone, L.G., *The New Downtowns* (McGraw-Hill, New York, 1976).
25. Davies, R.L., 'A Framework for Commercial Planning Policies', *Town Planning Review*, vol. 48, no. 1 (1977), pp. 42-58.

8 RENOVATION AND REDEVELOPMENT

Many of the developments described in the previous chapter are the result, not of investments in virgin sites, but of the clearance and renewal of the older parts of the urban environment. This is particularly true of the new shopping schemes built in traditional town and city centres and some of the inner residential areas of the larger conurbations. Such schemes are therefore part of a broader process of change affecting a wide mixture of land use activities which itself needs to be given careful planning consideration. There are perhaps two primary contributors to this process of change: the small, often imperceptible but ongoing rehabilitations of individual buildings and streets, which we might collectively call renovation; and the larger, more dramatic and instantaneous reconstructions of properties and sometimes whole areas that are more commonly known as redevelopment. Both these components, however, represent attempts to improve or modernise the environment and therefore take place against a background of relative decline in the physical and functional well-being of areas.

This interplay of growth and decline, particularly within central areas, must be looked at in a more holistic way than most of the other topics treated in this book, i.e. that the special concerns of retail and commercial planning cannot be divorced from what goes on in the transport, office or leisure fields. We shall therefore deal with the concepts of renovation and redevelopment in this chapter in very broad terms. We begin with an outline of the attitudes which planners themselves have adopted towards urban renewal and show how these have altered quite substantially in recent years, from a position where any change seemed to be desirable to one that gives greater recognition to the importance of conservation. Within this discussion, however, a distinction is drawn between those policies that have been applied to the central area and those directed at the inner city, where the need for renewal has been bound up with wider social and economic concerns. The second section goes on to describe the shift in planning philosophies regarding the central area in more detail, illustrated by two case studies of Newcastle upon Tyne and Covent Garden in London. The third section then moves away from an examination of the content of past and present plans to raise questions about what should be the conceptual basis to planning the city centre of the future; and at the end, we once again try to indicate how and where there might be significant improvements to the future control of change or management of the renewal process.

The Historical Background

In tracing the history of urban renewal it is possible to distinguish between a set of formative influences that have conditioned the mood of planning at any one time, particularly government legislation and the reactions of the public at large, and what actually seems to have taken place on the ground in the form of physical or functional change. In other words, there is a time lapse between thought and its translation into practice so that we can either consider a sequence of ideas or look at the events as these unfold. The former is easier for often before a plan can be realised there will have been a change of opinion that has then affected what has been built or not. This first section is primarily concerned with the intent rather than the outcome of plans and we shall leave it to the case studies to shed more light on the complicated results that usually ensue.

The Evolution of Central Area Plans

Renovation and redevelopment have obviously occurred continuously, on a piecemeal basis, throughout history. The idea of co-ordinating and manipulating these changes on a large scale, through a plan, however, is relatively recent. There are certain towns and cities in Britain, for example Edinburgh and Newcastle, for which ambitious schemes were first conceived in the early nineteenth century and others, such as London and Birmingham, where this was a necessary prerequisite to the provision of major transport systems shortly after the First World War. But for most places, the introduction of a distinctive body of policies, put forward by the local authority and designed to cope exclusively with the problems of the central area, is a product of just the last 30 years or so. The impetus to this was again the 1947 Town and Country Planning Act which gave to local authorities the power to acquire land through compulsory purchase orders and embark on programmes of slum clearance and the alleviation of congestion. The mechanism by which land was obtained and these programmes pursued was the designation of Comprehensive Development Areas, which remained subject to the approval of central government and wherein compensation had to be given to the previous landowners.[1] Although CDAs could be established in any part of a town or city, they clearly provided a special opportunity for planning the central area since local authorities, at long last it seemed, could now deal with a complexity of land use problems in a much more expansive way.

Two important documents were also produced around the time the legislation was passed. The first, called *The Design and Layout of Roads in Built-up Areas* and published by the Ministry of Transport,[2] referred to the projected increase in city centre traffic and advocated the building of ring roads to alleviate congestion. It was assumed that the principal shopping streets in most towns and cities would continue to act as major traffic arteries, but tacit recognition was also given to the need to separate vehicles from pedestrians through such recommendations as the provision of underpasses. The second, more directly influential, publication was *The Redevelopment of Central Areas*, put out by the new Ministry of Town and Country Planning,[3] which essentially enunciated the aims of city centre plans (as seen at that time) and how local authorities should prepare them. There was further emphasis on the improvement of traffic conditions and the idea of segregating land uses, partly through slum clearance and partly through conventional development controls, was introduced. The plans should show 'the proposed location and size of the various zones in the central area, the density of building accommodation within them, and provision for the convenient circulation of pedestrian and vehicular traffic'.[4]

Despite the aspirations of these documents, however, and the subsequent formulation of a number of plans, relatively few places experienced much redevelopment until the late 1950s. The most notable exceptions, of course, were the blitzed cities we have referred to before. There were several reasons for this: the limited resources of both the public and private sectors in the aftermath of the war; the higher priority given to the housing rather than commercial market; the deterrent effect on speculation provided by the betterment levies and to some extent the building licences that had to be obtained. These latter regulations were in fact subsequently revoked in 1954 which sparked off a considerable amount of speculative development over the next few years, particularly in office construction in central London. But towards the end of the decade local authority interest in initiating change seems to have waned for there was a significant decline in the number of CDAs submitted for approval.[5]

During the 1960s, however, the improvement in the economy and a more confident outlook on what could be accomplished, brought a new wave of central area plans and much greater investment in commercial development throughout the country. Somewhat curiously, there were again two major publications, based around the transportation and planning themes, which had a considerable effect on local authority thinking. This time the planning guidelines appeared first: a series of bulletins published jointly by the Ministry of Housing and Local Government and the Ministry of Transport under the headings: *Town Centres – Approach to Renewal* (1962), *Cost and Control of Redevelopment* (1963) and *Current Practice* (1963).[6] These advocated adopting a much more comprehensive approach to renewal than had so far been seen, effectively providing for planned change throughout the central area rather than in selected localities only; and, in addition, they set out in greater detail than the earlier document had done the precise steps to be followed in implementing a city centre plan. Of particular note in this latter regard were some example diagrams illustrating, in spatial terms, the likely outcome at different points in time of a phased programme of renewal. Shortly after, there appeared the so-called Buchanan report, published under the title *Traffic in Towns*,[7] which also argued for extensive redevelopment to take place but in this case to facilitate the introduction of multi-level circulatory systems. These were seen as desirable both to cope with the unprecedented growth in vehicles and to ensure greater safety for pedestrians. The notion of underpasses had been taken a stage further, but in many of the grand designs to follow, pedestrians were allocated to a network of walkways above the main vehicular routes rather than below them.

A further influence on the new comprehensive renewal plans that emerged in the 1960s was the growth in civic societies around the country that followed the establishment of the Civic Trust in 1957. These societies represented the beginnings of organised pressure groups which later on often clashed with the local authorities but in the early days received a fairly sympathetic hearing, at least from the professional planners. The combined efforts of the Civic Trust, various independent societies and individual government officers in fact led to the Civic Amenities Act of 1967 which enabled local authorities to designate large areas, important for their historical legacies or townscape values, as conservation zones. Special measures were made available to protect existing buildings within such conservation zones; hence there was a presumption against redevelopment here although renovation was to be encouraged where this conformed to the essential character of an area.

At the root of both the advisory publications on central area planning and the introduction of special conservation legislation, however, was the enormous pressure for new development that was by now building up within the private sector. The property development companies had begun to submit proposals for large shopping schemes as well as office complexes and, in some cases, were seeking ways of collaborating with local authorities in the development of multi-purpose projects. There were, too, development pressures arising from a number of public bodies: for new polytechnics or extensions to other educational establishments, for sports and recreational facilities, for new buildings to house the burgeoning government bureaucracy, and so on. All of this had to be managed or controlled in some spatially efficient form and the general principle adopted was the first advocated just after the war, namely the segregation of land uses. This in itself required a design model that could be approximated in the new comprehensive plans; and a successful format seemed to have been found in the reconstruction of Coventry's city centre. Broadly speaking, shops and offices were to be concentrated in the core of the central area, but physically separate within this, and other distinctive land uses were to be allocated their own quarters in the surrounding frame. The whole would be bounded by a motorway box or inner ring road which would siphon off through traffic; but feeder routes would lead local traffic to strategically placed car parks and bus stations near to the core. The core would then be largely pedestrianised to allow shoppers and office workers to reach their destinations in greater comfort and safety.

Most of the large provincial cities in Britain conceived new comprehensive plans for their central areas in this way in the 1960s.[8] Birmingham was the forerunner and ultimately saw more of its plan fulfilled than the others; but vestiges of this period can be seen in the present townscape of such places as Liverpool, Leicester and particularly Newcastle. London, because of its greater size, was never circumscribed to the same basic model. The central area here seemed to be treated from two quite different points of view. Firstly, the earlier pressures for office development, and on a scale much greater than that found elsewhere, led to the Labour government's legislation to curtail further redevelopment in the City (through the issue of Development Certificates) and to try to channel such investment into other parts of the country, particularly the marginal regions. Planning in the central area of London in the mid-1960s was therefore in part bound up with a national regional development policy. Secondly, the fact that the central area effectively encompassed three distinct cores (the City, the West End based on Oxford Street and the newer shopping focus established around Kensington High Street) meant that existing land use patterns were far more complicated than in other cities and could not be reallocated in quite the same holistic way. A more empirical or patchwork approach was called for, reinforced by the extremely high land values that made extensive redevelopment, over large areas, prohibitive. In the two retail cores, the problems that seemed to command most attention were the growth in congestion, the deterioration of the physical environment and the accommodation of new services, related in part to the increase in tourists. A number of relatively modest road schemes were therefore planned, a few environmental improvement schemes were contemplated (most notably for Piccadilly) but to little effect, and attention was given to the need for additional hotels and related service activities. The various aspirations held for these and other parts of the central area of London, however, seemed quite humble at this time compared to the visions of certain provincial cities.

As the new comprehensive plans for the central areas of the provincial cities began to be implemented, and also emulated in smaller towns, however, so there appeared the first signs of a public reaction against them. People who had hitherto been swayed by the rhetoric of local politicians suddenly had second thoughts once familiar buildings started to come down. The backlash was fomented by the construction of the urban motorways and the displacement of small businesses from the larger shopping and office schemes. Indirectly, the Town and Country Planning Act of 1968 also contributed to further criticism and a re-examination of the plans by encouraging greater public participation in the decision-making process; and later, as a result of local government reorganisation, many of those city-based local authorities that had championed the plans found their planning powers considerably reduced. In the first part of the 1970s, too, a number of academics produced articles advocating the abandonment of the comprehensive redevelopment approach and arguing instead for a wider emphasis on renovation.[9]

Two other factors emerged in the 1970s to alter professional attitudes towards the city centre, however. One was the change in the birth rate and a growing concern that the demand for future retail and office floorspace would eventually be reduced. The other, and linked to this, was the deteriorating economic circumstances of the country which was quickly reflected in public expenditure cut-backs by successive governments. The first meant that a second generation of central area plans to be implemented in the 1980s should have more modest targets in the amount of new commercial development; the second, that any major proposals in the transport, educational or cultural fields would not likely be funded, at least in the short term. Reinforcing the need for a more cautious planning stance were two further, more specific events that occurred in the first half of the 1970s: another spectacular office boom in London following the relaxation of building constraints in the City; and the potential threat of the Community Land Tax which subsequently was repealed by the present Conservative government. The former led to an over-provision in offices and much vacant property; the latter to fears that the commercial property market would become depressed sooner rather than later. As events have unfolded in recent years, too, the uncertainties that now exist over the effects of energy costs on people's travel behaviour, the pending impact of technological change and the growth in unemployment, all suggest that a careful, gradualist approach should be taken to the preparation of a new set of central area plans.[10]

Renewal Elsewhere in the City

Much of what has been reported above about the shifts in planning attitudes towards the central area over the last 20 years is equally applicable to renewal in other parts of the city, particularly the inner city. Many Comprehensive Development Areas were designated in inner cities in the 1960s, primarily to remove slum housing conditions but also to improve the retail and commercial environment. The scales of the commercial redevelopment programmes were usually much smaller than those envisaged for the central area, but the social consequences that followed, taken in conjunction with the population upheavals that accompanied the housing schemes, were often more serious both for traditional businesses and the consumers they served. The emphasis on the eradication of ribbons at this time literally removed scores of small, independent traders from a single locality and the clearance of housing in surrounding side streets led to both the displacement of numerous corner stores and the breakdown of well-established customer links for those who somehow managed to survive. The purpose-built shopping centres that came in to fill the new voids were, as we have stated before, largely disastrous experiments that could neither accommodate locally based firms, because of the high rents involved, nor attract many national chains, because of the erosion of the trade areas that had occurred. The result was a series of white elephants that remain a visible legacy to the present day and, over the intervening years, have deterred alternative shopping investments that might have been made in a smaller, incremental way.[11]

The 1970s witnessed much more circumspection about the planning approach to renewal in the inner cities, just as they did in the case of the central area. But the inner cities collectively became a much bigger issue, both politically and professionally, than the central area had ever been, though the concerns again were over broader socio-economic matters than simply the poverty of the retail and commercial environment. Thoughts turned to a more human scale of aid programmes that included devoting more resources to educational improvements and job stimulation as well as encouraging more renovation in place of redevelopment. Two of the later central government initiatives that were taken, however, had particular relevance to the retail and commercial field. Firstly, the Inner Urban Areas Act of 1978 which established a selected number of Inner Area Partnership Schemes between local authorities and central government enabled much more financial support to be given to the development of new business premises and a variety of recreational and leisure facilities than had hitherto been possible. Secondly, the designation of a trial set of Enterprise Zones in 1981 gave some encouragement to a wide range of services, often excluded from conventional retail or commercial sites, that at long last they might be able to locate more or less where they would like. This new concept, however, has been extremely controversial, both within the business community as a whole and amongst the professional planners partially responsible for creating the zones. Criticism has come from the former in terms of the discrepancy in aid that will arise between businesses sited either side of a dividing line; the concerns of some planners are that larger firms will move into the areas more quickly than small ones and, in utilising the advantages to be gained by building mainly warehouses, will contribute relatively few new jobs. Special fears have also been expressed by both groups that a number of superstores and hypermarkets will come in which, while generating more employment locally, may erode the economic health of established shopping centres elsewhere in the inner city and thus contribute to further unemployment there. On these grounds, some local authorities have been pressing for the exclusion of large stores from Enterprise Zones or special planning regulations to be applied to them.[12]

While most renewal outside the central area has so far been directed at the inner city, the recent decline of many small local centres in the middle parts of the city and also some suburbs raises the question, of course, as to what action should be taken in these cases in the future. It may be that the solutions here are not to be found in the form of retail and commercial policies as such but that centres which have become seriously degenerated should be converted to other uses, perhaps community facilities or housing accommodation or simply play area space. Small town centres and village cores that might have been absorbed into a metropolitan area will likely remain more economically viable but contain a further set of problems related to the age of their buildings and the narrowness of their streets. Conservation and pedestrianisation will play an important role here but other aspects of planning, particularly in the transport field, will be necessary to support them. These concerns of a more local kind are taken up in the third part of this book where similar problems to be found in rural areas are also discussed.

Newcastle upon Tyne and Covent Garden, London

The changes which have occurred over time in professional attitudes towards urban renewal and the effects these have had on both the preparation and implementation of plans, particularly with respect to the central area, are well illustrated in two contrasting case examples, for Newcastle upon Tyne and Covent Garden in London. Newcastle is an interesting case from the standpoint that two distinctive plans have been produced in the last 20 years, the first epitomising comprehensive redevelopment taken to an extreme and the second, just recently released, reflecting the complete opposite to this with its emphasis on infilling and gradual renovation. Covent Garden provides a more parochial but nevertheless dramatic example of how a plan conceived in the intervening years of the early 1970s failed to gain public acceptance because its proposals were too far removed from the shifting values of society. This plan had to be substantially revised and ended up, in fact, resembling an alternative 'people's plan' that the local opposition groups had themselves suggested. In both case examples, however, most of the reaction to large-scale change that had set in was induced less by concern over future retail and commercial development than by what might occur in other land use activities.

Plans for the Central Area of Newcastle

Besides the two specific plans for the central area of Newcastle referred to above, there have been two other occasions in the past when the city centre has come under special scrutiny and a considerable amount of planned renewal has taken place. The first occurred almost 150 years ago when three leading dignitaries of the city, named Grainger (an architect), Dobson (a builder) and Clayton (the Town Clerk), set about redeveloping vast tracts of the central area contained within the former medieval wall.[13] The ramshackle of later medieval and seventeenth- and eighteenth-century buildings was removed, a ravine containing the Lort Burn (a tributary to the Tyne) filled in, a new network of roads laid down and impressive new houses, shops and office premises constructed, partially segregated from each other and all conforming to a new Regency style of architecture. Most of the results of this enormous programme of work have survived through to the present day and have therefore become the basis to the designated conservation zone. The second, much later assessment of central area needs accompanied the publication of a Development Plan for the city as a whole in 1953.[14] This proposed the development of a new highway on the east side of the city centre to reduce traffic on Northumberland Street, the most important shopping street, but at this time also part of the A1; and it further envisaged the construction and concentration of a new set of public buildings, including extensions to the university and new civic centre, to the north. Little actual building took place until well into the 1960s, however, by which time these ideas had been subsumed into a far more ambitious plan for redeveloping virtually the entire city centre, save for the more significant parts of the Regency legacy.

Behind the plan were again three visionary individuals: T. Dan Smith (leader of the Labour council at this time), Arthur Gray (leader of the subsequent Conservative council) and Wilfred Burns (the city's first Planning Officer). Their aspirations for the city centre were first aired in a document entitled *Central Area Redevelopment Proposals – First Report of the City Planning Officer*, 1961, and these were shortly, formally adopted in the Newcastle upon Tyne Development Plan Review of 1963.[15] There were three main sets of proposals (Figure 8.1):
1. The establishment of a new transport system. At the heart of this were to be two new motorways aligned in a north-south direction, on the east and west sides of the central area and which would be inter- connected to the north and south by two further 'free-flow' roads. These would cater for through traffic but local travellers to the city centre would be diverted into an inner distributary network; and it was expected that there would be a tripling of short- and long-stay car parks as well as improvements in public transport services. Three pedestria- nised or precinct areas were to be designated, one based around the northern shopping focus, another to the south-west (centred on Clayton Street and Westgate Road) and the third on those streets of most historical interest to the south-east (namely Grey Street and the Bigg

Figure 8.1: The Redevelopment Plan for the City Centre of Newcastle upon Tyne, 1962

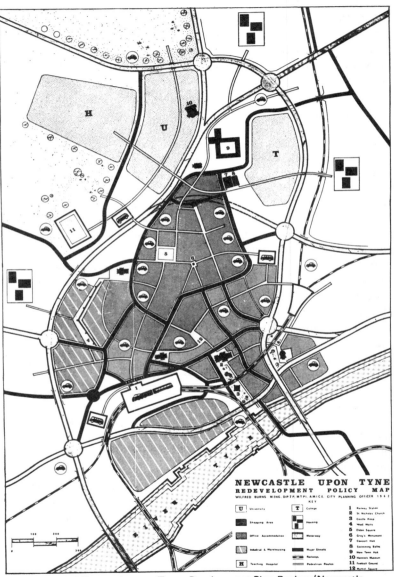

Source: City of Newcastle upon Tyne, *Development Plan Review* (Newcastle, 1963).

Market). Pedestrians would be able to move safely between these via a system of elevated walkways.

2. The provision of a new regional shopping centre and major office complex. The plan envisaged that shopping resources would become concentrated in the northern half of the city centre with Northumberland Street complemented by a new purpose-built centre, originally projected to be 400,000 square feet (38,000 m²) in size. A large hotel and entertainment facilities would also be integrated with this. Concern was expressed over the potentially deleterious effects of the new development on small businesses but compulsory purchase orders were subsequently taken out on 3.64 hectares (9 acres) of land containing buildings that were regarded as obsolete. Offices were to be concentrated in the southern half of the city centre, in part adjacent to the traditional business quarters in the historic core but extending also to a new area around the Tyne Bridge. Forecasts suggested that a total of 731,000 square feet (68,000 m²) of new office floorspace would need to be met by 1981.

3. The designation of other land use zones. Further concentrations of distinctive land uses were to be encouraged in the peripheral parts of the central area, including the development of an educational precinct embracing the university and polytechnic to the north, a wholesaling and warehousing district to the west and a mixed commercial and industrial quarter to the south. These zones would become possible in part by the migration of business firms out of the central area altogether; for, in wholesaling alone, it was estimated that two million square feet (190,000 m²) of activity would be removed to outlying industrial sites. New development seeking a central area site would then be directed to the appropriate zone using the normal development control procedures. Cultural facilities, however, such as a new library and art gallery, were to be dispersed throughout the core of the city centre; and there would be four preservation areas focused on the most important remnants of earlier times, namely the castle and Cathedral, the Guildhall (at the quayside), St John's Church and those streets epitomising best the former Grainger-Dobson-Clayton era.

The plan was pursued with much vigour during the late 1960s and early 1970s but, although considerable redevelopment took place, it was only partially realised before a new set of socio-economic conditions in the country at large and a new climate of opinion locally led to substantial revisions in its underlying objectives and ultimately to the formulation of quite different ideas. The proposed shopping centre, Eldon Square, was built at almost double its projected size; all of the new office floorspace expected to be accommodated up to 1981 was constructed by 1975 (most of it within the All Saints complex); the designated peripheral land use zones emerged in a conspicuous form, following the anticipated migration of many wholesale firms (although much of this proved to be enforced relocation); and the four preservation areas were subsequently absorbed into one large conservation zone, within which an extensive 'face-lifting' exercise was carried out. The proposals that saw the greatest change were those in the transport field. By the end of the 1960s, a suggestion to build a Metro system had been taken up[16] and the plan's original intention to provide equally for the needs of private motorists and public transport users were then altered in favour of the latter's interests. Car parking provisions were cut back (although two new car parks were built in association with Eldon Square and one for the All Saints complex); a 'park 'n ride' service introduced; and the western spinal motorway, together with the two 'free-flow' roads, were (and remain) deferred because of the vast expenditures incurred elsewhere. In addition only parts of the elevated walkway system for pedestrians have been completed and, since most of the malls in Eldon Square were built above ground level to integrate with this, there are now effectively two separate levels of shopping within the central area. Part of Northumberland Street has been closed to motorists, though not buses or taxis, and three side streets have been paved over; but none of the major pedestrianisation schemes that were envisaged has yet been accomplished.

Transport considerations are again a central feature of the new draft plan for the city centre, published in 1981,[17] but already there is evidence of considerable uncertainty over the policies put forward. In particular, there is little reference in the plan to the future form of the public transport network despite this being the subject of much discussion during the preparatory stages. In its more general content, and the way in which it was conceived, however, the plan differs from its predecessors in two fundamental respects; the modest nature of the proposals that have been made; and the extensive public consultation that was carried out to arrive at these.

There were two steps involved in the public consultation programme. Firstly, prior to any substantial 'in house' work being embarked upon, notice was given of the intention to produce a plan and a leaflet and discussion paper were circulated to interested parties inviting their preliminary comments. Secondly, following the completion of a Report of Survey, a series of policy alternatives were formulated and described in a publication entitled *Choices for the Future* which was again distributed to informed groups and, in a shortened pamphlet version, to the population at large.[18] The alternatives were presented in terms of variable amounts of change that could be effected with respect to eight major topics (mainly sets of activities) and different types of land use and movement opportunities that could be made available in 15 separate areas. For example, on the topic of shopping, two choices were given: that there could either be little growth in new shopping floorspace over the next few years with encouragement directed at small shops and large stores being allowed to develop only in the southern, weaker part of the central area; or alternatively, there could be a medium level of growth, up to about 260,000 square feet (24,000 m^2) of new floorspace being accommodated, where large developments would be permitted in the north, including a possible extension to the Eldon Square shopping centre. For an area designated Blackfriars and Clayton Street, the main land use opportunities lay in utilising a defunct college as either a locus for workshop activities or a new housing complex; and as far as movement improvements were concerned, no direct options were provided as such but opinions could be conveyed on whether there should be limited vehicular access to Clayton, Grainger and Newgate Streets. The exercise yielded some 2,000 responses from the public[19] and the prevailing views that were aired for each of the main topics are summarised in Table 8.1. As the city Planning Officer states, these clearly showed 'a desire on the part of the public for a period of respite' from further large-scale redevelopment.[20]

The policies that were finally arrived at, however, were conditioned not only by public opinion but by the results of the Report of Survey which had indicated some worrying trends. In particular, and partly as a consequence of the previous era of planning, there had been a decline in employment in certain types of occupational groups, most notably in the 'blue-collar' services; the southern part of the central area, especially those parts embraced within the conservation area, had suffered a depletion of trade and exhibited much vacant property as a result of the large shopping and office developments elsewhere; traffic congestion had become worse, despite the motorway construction and the imposition of rigid traffic management schemes; and many fringe areas of the city centre had continued to deteriorate both physically and functionally, most noticeably in the vicinity of the Quayside. Not surprisingly, therefore, these problems form the key issues of the plan with the main remedial solutions being further encouragement to substantial office and commercial growth as employment generators;

Table 8.1: Summary of the Public Response to Future Options for Newcastle's City Centre

Topics

1. Commerce and administration

   Respondents have voted for low growth, and some for medium growth; at the same time comments have been made about excessive vacancy and the need for refurbishment of older office buildings.

2. Manufacturing industry

   The majority of respondents have chosen modest growth. . . . The choice implies that Manors Goods Yard and Station, and the Bath Lane College area should not be developed for industrial purposes.

3. Blue-collar services

   There was general agreement that little could be done directly to halt a decline in employment. Some hope was expressed that tourism and related activities might create job opportunities.

4. Shopping

   Respondents have indicated a desire for an improvement in shopping facilities. While opinion was split on the question of growth, it is clear that respondents want to see development which helps the older shopping area and which increases choice. . . . Redevelopment of the Haymarket area was not a popular option.

5. Housing

   Respondents have called for action to create more housing accommodation in the city centre by a variety of means in a variety of locations.

6. Leisure, recreation and tourism

   Respondents have indicated strong support for the development of tourism.

7. Movement

   (a) Broad principles

        The principle of removing traffic from the heart of the city centre and giving priority to pedestrians, buses and cyclists, was strongly supported. However, . . . respondents expressed concern about the environmental effect of new road construction.

   (b) Pedestrian facilities

        Respondents have indicated a positive desire for more areas of pedestrian priority . . . specifically in relation to Northumberland Street and the Monument area.

   (c) Highways and traffic

        The idea of directing general traffic onto a ring road was well received, but concern was expressed about possible environmental damage . . .

(d) Public transport

Respondents have not given a clear lead as to the future of Marlborough Crescent and the bus services currently using it.

(e) Parking

There was a division of opinion on this topic with a significant minority view in favour of no more, or less, parking in the city centre.

8. Character and environment

The main elements of the response — the desire for increased conservation action, concern about the impact of new development, concern about appearance of modern development, the desire to keep old buildings — all go hand in hand together.

Source: City of Newcastle upon Tyne, *Local Plan for the City Centre — Choices for the Future — Public Response* (1979).

---

the restriction of major shopping investments to magnets that might be introduced into the southern area (although a small extension to Eldon Square is envisaged); the improvement, through road widening and some new road sections, of the ring route skirting the city centre; and extensive renovation of the decaying buildings near the Quayside, together with much landscaping of derelict open space.

An example of the detailed proposals that were made to effect these policies is given in Table 8.2. The case of shopping has been selected since it well illustrates the mix of broad statements of intent and fine rulings to be applied in particular instances that characterise the entire plan. A particularly controversial set of proposals are those that refer to the development controls to be applied to business services seeking to enter different categories of shopping streets. Thirteen principal shopping streets (and malls) have been demarcated where the introduction of non-retail frontage will not be permitted and a further 34 streets are to be carefully monitored. The arguments for and against such impositions are finely balanced, as we have indicated elsewhere, and it is interesting to note that they were omitted from consideration in the public consultation exercise.

Despite the fact that in these instances the plan seems to be strengthening rather than relaxing its development controls, from a more general point of view it displays a much greater sensitivity to local activities on the ground than was found in its predecessors. For some time to come there will likely be little further dramatic change within the city centre although pressures for a new wave of redevelopment may build up towards the end of the decade. At this point, of

Table 8.2: Shopping Proposals in the Newcastle Draft City Centre Local Plan, 1981

---

1. The shopping area (as defined on the proposals map) will be consolidated and expansion of floorspace limited.

2. A range of measures will be adopted to support and improve shopping facilities within the southern part of the shopping area.

3. Shopping redevelopment will be encouraged in Newgate Street.

4. The development of a new mall for shoppers on the east side of Eldon Square, crossing Blackett Street by means of a new bridge would, in principle, be welcomed.

5. No large-scale shopping development will be permitted in the Haymarket area.

6. Shopping development will be allowed as part of the 'opportunity' development on the site to the west of central station.

7. The local authority will consider, on merit, proposals to expand existing stores.

8. Small-scale shopping developments will be encouraged in the Blackfriars and Quayside, in the context of mixed use development in these areas.

9. Redevelopment of the temporary buildings on the west side of Percy Street will be encouraged, with ground floor shopping use.

10. The environment of the shopping area will be improved.

11. The introduction of non-retail frontage into the principal shopping streets and malls will not be permitted.

12. The introduction of additional non-retail frontages into (secondary) shopping streets will be considered on merit.

13. The introduction of retail frontage into predominantly non-retail streets will be considered on merit.

Source: City of Newcastle upon Tyne, *Local Plan for the City Centre — Draft Proposals* (1981).

course, there will also be a different set of socio-economic conditions to contend with so that the thrust of any future redevelopment might not be in accommodating additional growth but simply the reallocation of existing resources into a more desirable and efficient form.

Plans for Covent Garden

The plans that have been produced over the last decade for the area known as Covent Garden differ from those for the city centre of Newcastle in two major respects. Firstly, they have been more narrowly conceived in serving the interests of the area itself and those areas immediately adjoining it rather than the city as a whole. This is because

Covent Garden is a rather specialised functional area sandwiched between the retail core of the West End focused on Oxford Street and the office core of the City. Secondly, the interests to be served have been difficult to interpret mainly because of a conflict between local community needs and pressures for development extending into the area from outside. This has meant that any plan produced has met with fierce opposition from some quarters and, although there have been serious attempts in recent years to improve relations between the politicians and planners on the one hand and residents and business groups on the other, the general experience has been one of acrimony in contrast to the rather quiescent atmosphere that has prevailed in Newcastle.

The need for a comprehensive plan for the area was first mooted in the early 1960s following the decision to relocate the green market to Nine Elms. A series of objectives were drawn up (Table 8.3) and almost 100 acres (40 hectares) of land earmarked for designation as a Comprehensive Development Area. Draft and revised plans were then published in 1968 and 1971.[21] In both cases very extensive redevelopment was envisaged, although the historical legacies of the area, particularly those associated with Inigo Jones' St Paul's Church and Piazza and the distinctive character of the Seven Dials neighbourhood, dictated a considerable amount of conservation too. The main thrust of the plans, like so many elsewhere at this time, appeared to be the clearance of outworn property to ease congestion within and around the area, to provide new buildings for residential, office, entertainments and arts activities, and also to concentrate policies of renovation on selected streets that demonstrated the best of architectural and townscape qualities. In the original proposals there were to be two major spine roads, sunken below ground and aligned along the northern and southern perimeters, to remove through traffic; 4,000 off-street parking places; an international conference centre and hotels; sufficient new housing to increase the residential population from 3,000 to 7,000; an extensive network of elevated walkways; and a special 'character' route that would be the main focus of a facelifting operation. The vast costs to be incurred by these proposals, however, led to some revision of the more ambitious elements, particularly on the transport side; but there was relatively little change to the underlying principles involved.

During the five-year period over which these plans were prepared, there was mounting criticism of the underlying principles not only from the local community but from within the ranks of the politicians

Table 8.3: Objectives Behind the Covent Garden Plans, 1966-1973 and 1973-1978

Objectives 1966-1973

1. The incorporation of a complex of uses to create a vigorous and interesting environment by day and night both as a place to live and as a centre for entertainment and cultural activities.

2. A substantial increase in residential accommodation.

3. The provision of new public open space in addition to amenity open space within individual sites.

4. The easing of congestion in central London, in particular by the avoidance of major employment generators and major traffic generators.

5. Separate but integrated systems for pedestrian and vehicular movement within and immediately adjoining the area, including specifically proposals for efficient co-ordination with public transport and for car parks on a scale recommended based on a study of traffic generation following redevelopment and of the capacity of the approach roads.

6. The integration of new development with existing uses and some provision for the retention of suitable mixed uses which are appropriate to the area's special location and character.

7. The retention of those groups of buildings, including buildings of architectural and historic importance, which contribute substantially to the variety and character of the area and are the physical embodiment of its past history.

Objectives 1973-1978

1. To safeguard the existing residential community and provide for a substantial improvement in housing conditions.

2. An increase in the residential population achieved through an increase in the stock of rented accommodation and a greater provision of family accommodation.

3. Improvement in local services to meet the needs of the residential and working populations.

4. To strengthen the economic character and vitality of Covent Garden by promoting the growth of new and traditional uses appropriate to the area.

5. Urgent re-use of buildings and land previously in market use with activities that will give the area a new vitality and focus.

In addition:

6. Safeguard and improve the existing physical character and fabric of Covent Garden.

7. Restrict vehicular traffic and give much more emphasis to pedestrians and access to public transport.

and also the planners themselves.[22] It was estimated that about 60 per cent of the existing floorspace in the area would be demolished and the traditional street pattern fundamentally altered. Twenty-five of 50 listed buildings would be removed together with half of the 652 art and craft activities that had been enumerated in 1966. The transport proposals seemed contradictory for whilst the spine roads would divert much traffic the parking provisions would attract other visitors to the area whose business might be in adjoining districts. The new residential accommodation was expected to benefit outsiders too, for the rents and rates to be levied would be beyond the means of the indigenous, mainly low-income, population. In addition, the plans seemed to have little to say on matters of school provisions, play facilities and amenities that would serve the local population itself.

Academics also joined in with the general arguments with Alexander, in particular, producing an important quantitative assessment of the relative costs and benefits to be derived from the extensive redevelopment envisaged.[23] Using both cost-benefit analysis and the 'planning balance sheet' technique, he showed that the collective proposals would still be extremely expensive and with fewer advantages accruing to the community than if a more gradualist, piecemeal approach to renewal was followed.

Following a public inquiry on the Revised Plan, in 1973 the Secretary of State for the Environment (then Geoffrey Rippon) returned a curious verdict on its overall suitability. The basic concept of a comprehensive redevelopment programme was accepted, by virtue of the recommended Comprehensive Development Area being approved, but most of the additional proposals that had been made were rejected and a new plan was called for that was to be prepared with much greater public participation. This was set in motion almost immediately and a year later a Report of Survey had been published by the new planning team and a Public Forum (made up of 30 elected members from the community) established to represent the views of various factions. A home interview survey was also conducted in 1974, directed at every household (and leading to responses from 70 per cent of the resident population), to ascertain the opinions of individuals on a wide range of socio-economic matters. From all of this came a new set of objectives, summarised in the lower half of Table 8.3, which clearly gave much greater emphasis in the second set of plans to dealing with local needs rather than outside pressures and which elevated the role of renovation beyond that of redevelopment.[24]

However, although there appeared to be a new spirit of harmony between the former protagonists, this was quickly dispelled in 1976 when the planning team announced a series of policy alternatives[25] and the Covent Garden Community Association denounced them as returning too much to the old approach. The Association produced its own set of proposals[26] and, perhaps somewhat surprisingly, the Greater London Council's Planning Committee accepted these over the suggestions of its own officers. Relations improved somewhat for a further short period of time and culminated in the publication of the Action Area Plan in 1978.[27] Since then, nevertheless, the CGCA has again become extremely critical of the planners, this time for ignoring the basic objectives agreed upon in the way the Action Area Plan is being implemented.[28] In particular, it feels that too many resources have been devoted to the renovation of the Piazza area (and especially to the restoration of the Central Market Building) at the expense of Seven Dials; that two formerly derelict parcels of land had been taken up for unnecessary housing and office developments; and that the erosion of traditional craft activities is continuing, as exemplified by the recent withdrawal of the printing and publishing trades, and despite the introduction of many new small businesses which it sees as being mainly transient 'fashion-based' firms. Underlying these specific points is a more general concern that the Conservative-led council that was elected in 1977 has adopted a more liberal attitude towards new development than was formerly being shown.

From the planners' point of view, however, much comfort must have come from the plaudits received elsewhere for its work in renovating the old green market area and especially for the fact that the Action Area Plan has been nominated as one of Britain's four contributions to the Council of Europe's 'Campaign for Urban Renaissance'. It is a plan, nevertheless, that has emerged with much professional acclaim because of its absorption of many ideas first mooted by the local people themselves. Like the new plan for the city centre of Newcastle, it symbolises a different philosophical approach with its basic content having been willed from below rather than imposed from above. But the fulfilment of this new breed of plan carries with it a number of problems, not least the absence of a background theory or set of concepts for translating the underlying thoughts into efficient results on the ground.

Concepts for the City Centre

In the past, the grand designs for city centres have been able to draw on two distinctive types of concepts. The first and most fully developed have been the schematic spatial models put forward by both geographers and planners that have described an idealised pattern of land uses within the central area. Horwood and Boyce promulgated the idea of a core and frame, where the core is made up of concentrations of retail and office activities and the frame comprises specialised groupings of wholesaling, educational, industrial, residential and transportation land uses.[29] (The schematic form of this was shown earlier in part of Figure 6.4.) The core-frame concept is interesting from the standpoint that it was originally conceived to represent the spatial structure of the city centre as this would arise through the interplay of relatively free market forces, specifically with reference to the North American case; and its adaptation to planning in Britain therefore suggests an attempt to reinforce or accentuate what might occur anyway but through a more orderly process of change. Whether the concept has been consciously applied in this way or not, it bears a striking resemblance to those models put forward by Keeble[30] and Buchanan[31] as to what the ideal future form of the city centre should be and, apart from matters of detail regarding the layout of streets, is not unlike the blueprint used in the reconstruction of Coventry.

The second type of concept relates to the functional role of the city centre and its importance with respect to the rest of the urban system. There has been little careful articulation of this, but an underlying assumption of most of the comprehensive redevelopment plans was that the central area should be strengthened as the main commercial hub of the city and an environmental showpiece for the general population. What seemed to be lacking was what sort of social as distinct from economic objectives should be fulfilled, although there was much wishful thinking that the night-time gaiety to be associated with other European city centres could be generated within Britain. From the mid-1960s onwards, however, a group of Danish planners had been arguing that the central area should be viewed primarily as a cultural rather than business centre and that the main thrust of planning should be directed at improving its attractions as a meeting place for the exchange of ideas and experiences rather than the purchasing or selling of goods.[32] The Institute for Center Planlaegning recently published an Ideplan for the city centre of Copenhagen that suggests the development of a series of 'theme' quarters (such as for music, theatre and other arts activities) in certain of the side streets adjoining the main shopping artery.[33] These quarters would comprise shops and commercial agencies as well as studios and facilities made available for social organisations. The main shopping artery itself, known generally as the Strøget (literally 'the main stretch'), was pedestrianised as early as 1962 and is extensively used during non-shopping hours as simply a pleasant street along which to walk.

The retail core is perhaps the most important and sensitive part of the central area to deal with in planning for it is here that there is the greatest infusion of different types of people and a variety of needs and preferences have to be catered for. The comprehensive redevelopment plans of the 1960s, however, had no specific concepts behind them to guide the massive changes they envisaged in this quarter beyond the notions that the shopping area should become more compact and a safer environment created. There is little doubt that these broad objectives have been fulfilled but in hindsight there have also been a number of deleterious effects that we have touched on before. In global terms, what seems to have happened is that the mixed character of the traditional shopping area has become replaced by a set of specific-purpose building blocks supposedly integrated by the old high street. We can trace the detailed nature of these effects through Figure 8.2. This shows in schematic form how the locational characteristics of the three component sub-systems of retailing activity in the city centre have each been altered by different types of planning action.[34] The areal stratification of domestic shopping activities that formerly arose through relatively free market forces has been interrupted by the transplantation of new shopping centres in fairly peripheral positions, with other locational changes arising through pedestrianisation schemes and the penetration of offices; the ribbons of service activities, extending out of the core area of the city centre along major traffic arteries, have often been truncated; many of the old specialised retailing and service districts, such as markets and side streets with small, independent businesses engaged in repair activities, have been removed through redevelopment projects, either to create new shopping resources or alternatively other land uses. In the bottom left-hand part of the diagram, one can see how the superimposition of the three component sub-systems of activity in their pre-planning state has led to an extremely complicated retail pattern, that then provided the visually mixed character of the traditional shopping area; to the right, the superimposition of the new elements introduced by various planning interventions suggests a much more orderly spatial structure, but one

Figure 8.2: The Effects of Planning Interventions on the Traditional
Pattern of Retailing and Commercial Land Uses in the Central Area

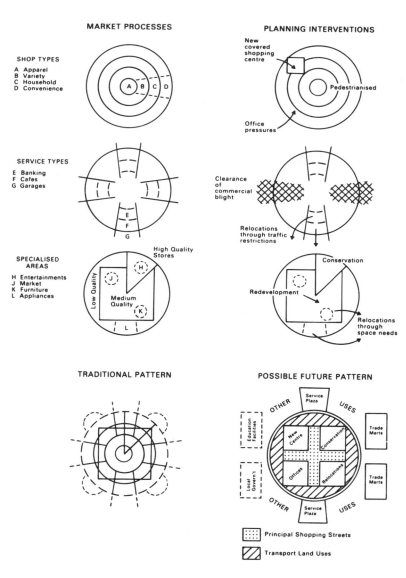

Source: Davies, R.L., 'A Framework for Commercial Planning Policies', *Town
Planning Review*, vol. 48 (1977), pp. 42-58.

where retailing has become concentrated in particular blocks in a rather sterile fashion.

This type of model, however, while useful in demonstrating how past planning interventions have altered the traditional pattern of retailing in the city centre, provides little guidance on how present and future planning policies should be directed to emerging conditions on the ground. A further conceptual approach has been suggested that seeks to relate geographical and planning considerations to a smaller scale of inquiry, namely at the level of individual streets.[35] The idea is to distinguish the inherent characters of streets and then identify specific problems that may be associated with these and put forward solutions to alleviate them. In other words, a street classification is derived which then serves as a framework for both monitoring and controlling change in a way that is appropriate to the new spirit of planning the city centre on a gradualist or incremental basis.

An example of the street classification has been worked out for Newcastle, and those parts of a more comprehensive scheme that are relevant to this particular central area are shown in Figure 8.3. Three broad categories of streets can be designated, under the headings activity, access and special streets. These related in part, of course, to the three sub-systems of retailing recognisable at a macro-scale, but the classification is intended to refer to other land use components as well. Activity streets are essentially those streets, primarily shopping streets, wherein most business within the city centre is conducted. They can be differentiated into principal shopping streets (further subdivided into primary and supporting shopping streets) and subsidiary shopping streets (again, perhaps, subdivided into those that are major or minor streets in terms of relative importance). Access streets are those which, while they may contain a wide variety of businesses, are predominantly used by consumers as routeways through to the activity streets. These may be differentiated into principal routeways (where some will be major and others minor thoroughfares) and subsidiary routeways (subdivided into major and minor link streets). Special streets tend to be those that are distinctive because of prominent functions to be found within or around them. They may be special forms of activity streets, where there is a concentration of entertainment, office or service establishments (which can then be described as major or minor adjunct streets, adjunct in the sense that they provide additional functions to the main types of retailing activities to be found); alternatively they may be special forms of access streets, where, for example, there are several bus staging points, car parks or other

Figure 8.3: A Classification of Streets by their Functional Roles in the City Centre of Newcastle upon Tyne

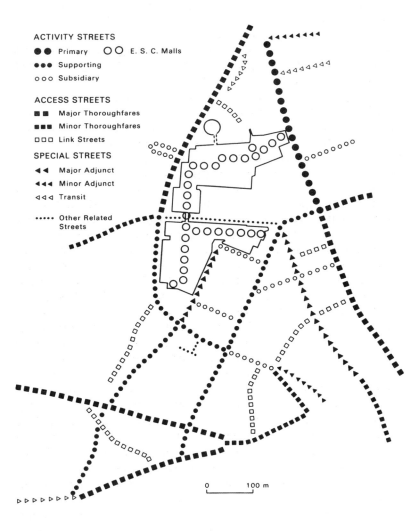

Source: Davies, R.L. and Bennison, D.J., 'Retailing in the City Centre: The Characters of Shopping Streets', *Tijdschrift voor Economische en Sociale Geografie*, vol. 69, no. 5 (1978), pp. 270-85.

transport provisions (hence these are subdivided in terms of major or minor transit streets). Clearly, the terms used throughout the classification are simply summary notations, and not every type of street referred to here will be represented in any one city centre. The broad differences in functional roles that the terms suggest were analysed in some detail in the Newcastle case, involving multivariate statistical analyses of the business composition of streets, map plots of pedestrian flows and trip structure characteristics, and studies of consumer perceptions about the characters of streets.

The perception studies undertaken in this research also enabled an assessment to be made of the extent to which certain streets exhibited pronounced problems or important attributes. Three sets of problems and attributes were concentrated upon: those of a functional, environmental or traffic kind. An example of a functional attribute would be the presence of unusual shopping attractions along a street; for environmental attributes, a fine architectural legacy; for traffic attributes, the relative safety and comfort provided by a pedestrianisation scheme. Representative of a functional problem would be the high incidence of non-retail uses or 'dead frontages' along a major shopping street; for environmental problems, blighted or decaying property; and for traffic problems, the high degree of congestion found along a particular street. Clearly, there will again be a variable scale of relative states or conditions that can be applied to these broad groupings, but streets which exhibited either very strong attributes or severe problems in Newcastle were once more portrayed in map form, as shown in Figure 8.4. Generally speaking, there is a close relationship to be found between the nature of the attributes or problems associated with particular streets and the type of functional role they perform as indicated by the street classification.

When the two schemes described above are used in conjunction, there appears to be a more rational basis for the implementation of development and management controls over particular streets, or indeed sets of streets. The street classification has in fact already been used by Newcastle City Planning Department as a framework for monitoring the intrusion of business services into shopping streets and the derivation of a policy to deal with this particular problem.[36] Essentially, three different categories of streets have been identified, along the lines suggested, within which there now applies three different levels of development control over applications for new non-retail businesses. Conservation policies and traffic management schemes could also be implemented in a similar way, as examples of treating the

Figure 8.4: Categorisation of Streets by Attributes and Problems in
Newcastle's Central Area

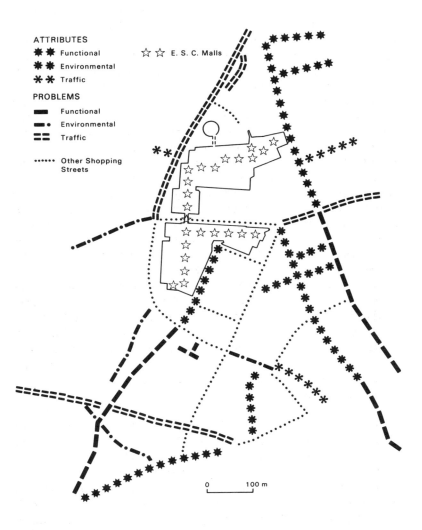

Source: Davies, R.L. and Bennison, D.J., 'Retailing in the City Centre: The
Characters of Shopping Streets', *Tijdschrift voor Economische en Sociale
Geografie*, vol. 69, no. 5 (1978), pp. 270-85.

environment and traffic problems we have referred to before.

The need to have some conceptual basis to the implementation of development controls and specific policies in the core part of the city centre is equally applicable to the frame. Unfortunately, there have been few academic studies directed at this area and our starting-point is weak. Nevertheless, there are certain special challenges within the frame that could be met with ideas taken from elsewhere. Firstly, the area could be looked at in social terms to see the potential for recreation and amenity space that derelict land might afford. It may be, too, that there are opportunities here to establish focal points for craft and small-scale cultural activities along the lines of the Copenhagen model. Secondly, there is considerable evidence that the frame remains a major source of employment within the city as a whole, particularly for lower skilled jobs, and this important role must be protected from further erosion in the future. This means adopting a much more careful approach to redevelopment despite the pressing claims for environmental improvement and the use of this area for new roads. Thirdly, although many planning departments have now reversed their previous policies of deterring commercial and industrial activities from expanding within this area, there is still little evidence of positive steps being taken to make the area an attractive investment proposition. One does not envisage the creation of a set of mini commercial or industrial estates, but the designation of certain parts of the frame as appropriate locations for new mixed activities, perhaps under the headings of trade marts and service plazas that we have raised before, might lead to new pockets of growth within an area that is generally in decline.

The Control of Change

So far, within this chapter, no definition has been given as to what constitutes a city centre or, more to the point, what differentiates this from a town centre and should one really be making distinctions between the two. The questions have been avoided because there are no clear-cut answers; but broadly speaking the term city centre is appropriate to use for the central areas of large provincial cities, say those over 250,000 in population size, where there is a much greater complexity of activities than in smaller places and their trade areas encompass several other urban communities that might have a substantial retail and commercial focus of their own. Alternatively, one can view the city centre, in the sense in which we have been using this term, as the apex to a regional hierarchy of centres and as such it does not require a precise size specification.

The importance of a city centre to its surrounding region, as well as the settlement in which it is found, however, means that it must command the attention of all three tiers of retail and commercial planning. There will be central government interest in ensuring that the balance of resources, as distributed within the hierarchy, are not unduly affected by changes taking place in the city centre; the County Council, to which the city centre relates, will be concerned with its special relationship to other large town centres in close proximity to it; the District Council, responsible for managing the supporting services of the city centre, will have particular regard for the repercussions of change in one part of the city centre on its other parts and other areas within the local environment.

Central government's contributions to the actual control of change within the city centre will again be largely advisory, however. It was indicated in Chapter 4 that these should mainly refer to the scale of change deemed to be acceptable for the future in any city centre and what sorts of variable controls would be appropriate to implement under different environmental conditions. This would mean in the first case giving guidelines on how much additional retail and commercial floorspace could be accommodated over a certain time period; and in the second case, providing examples of the sorts of criteria to be used for strengthening or relaxing locations and trading regulations governing particular categories of trade in specific areas. Central government has already gone some way to fulfilling the latter requirements, as we have said before, in its suggestions over the designation of conservation areas (in an inner city context) and Enterprise Zones.

The Counties' contributions, in our view, should focus on determining the future functional role of the city centre, in a conceptual context, and in relation to those roles to be performed by other surrounding large centres. Over the specific matters of renovation and redevelopment, they should have responsibility for identifying in which centres and in which parts of the city centre encouragement should be given to major renewal schemes and what should be the priorities, phasing and broad form of these. Likewise they should be prepared to monitor shifts in the retail and commercial health of both the city centre and other large centres that arise from such major renewal schemes and from other substantial changes that involve development of one kind or another. To assist with these tasks, it would be desirable to draw once again on expertise of a consultative body of the sort that we have described in Chapter 4.

The District authorities should then be charged with implementing the recommendations that have been made by the upper levels of government and also complementing them with initiatives of their own regarding smaller-scale aspects of change. This would mean designating on maps the boundaries within which variable levels of development or trade controls apply; ensuring that appropriate building and safety regulations were being met in major renewal schemes; and encouraging minor environmental improvement programmes to be undertaken according to their own specifications both within and without the central area. In addition, they should be concerned to see that business prospects, particularly for the smaller firms, are enhanced wherever appropriate and adequate compensation is directed towards those which may be unwittingly but adversely affected by the process of planned change. Superficially, all these tasks might be seen to be of secondary importance to those assigned to the other tiers of government; in fact, in an age when the accent will be very much on cautious, incremental change, the contributions of the District authorities may well be viewed as the most important of all.

Conclusion

It seems rather extraordinary that, within the space of ten years, there should have been such a dramatic change in the basic planning approach to urban renewal. Just at the time when we are about to witness the full impact of the new technological revolution, there seems to have been an abandonment of those grandiose ideas for creating an environment suited to a computer age. In their place have come a modest set of proposals that suggest a hankering for the past and a belief that perhaps, after all, the traditional form of the city centre is best. There are many reasons, of course, for the *volte face*: the public reaction to the insensitivity of many new schemes, the increase in public participation within the planning process itself, the feeling that some central areas may now be over-endowed with modern shopping and office provisions, and the underlying straightened economic circumstances of our time; but none of these factors can fully dispel the unique shift in professional attitudes that has occurred, unforeseen a decade ago and quite unprecedented in the post-war era.

While it is difficult to be critical of the new approach, there are two concerns that should be raised about it in these final paragraphs. Firstly, one hopes that the greater emphasis to be placed on renovation will not be taken to such an extreme that every proposal for large-scale redevelopment will be automatically met with fierce resistance. We shall all want to see more pedestrianised streets and facelifts given to historic buildings, but there must continue to be substantial improvements to the efficiency of traffic circulation and encouragement given to the construction of new facilities that are major employment generators. Secondly, one hopes that the greater emphasis to be placed on gradual, piecemeal change will not be made without some recourse to an underlying set of concepts as to the long-term direction of this change. This in turn means that there must be some prognostication about the likely future needs to be met in the city centre towards the end of the century and how these might be best fulfilled during the passage of time.

The two new plans reviewed in this chapter, for Newcastle and Covent Garden, are forerunners of the types of central area plans that we can expect to see being prepared elsewhere during the next decade. The Newcastle plan provides an example of how there might be an adjustment to a past period of massive redevelopment; the Covent Garden plan suggests what are likely to be the main types of initiative that can be taken in areas that have hitherto experienced relatively little disruption. Both are very similar in their basic methodology, however, with a strong reliance on seeking to involve the public in as much decision-making as possible, although this has arguably been more successful in the former than in the latter case. Neither of the local authorities involved appears likely to countenance extensive new development in the short term; neither displays a clear vision as to what will be sought in the distant future. As such, the two plans emerge rather as holding operations, intent on protecting and upgrading the legacies of the past, but with few pointers as to how the city centre will deal with the new social and economic problems of the 1990s.

References

1. For a full discussion on the use of CDA powers, by case study example, see: Hart, T., *The Comprehensive Development Area*, University of Glasgow, Social and Economic Studies, Occasional Paper no. 9 (Oliver and Boyd, Edinburgh, 1968).
2. Ministry of Transport, *The Design and Layout of Roads in Built-up Areas* (HMSO, London, 1946).

3. Ministry of Town and Country Planning, *The Redevelopment of Central Areas* (HMSO, London, 1947).
4. Ibid., p. 7.
5. Hart, T., *Comprehensive Development Area*.
6. Ministry of Housing and Local Government, *Town Centres – Approach to Renewal*, Planning Bulletin 1 (HMSO, London, 1962); *Town Centres – Cost and Control of Redevelopment*, Planning Bulletin 3 (HMSO, London, 1963); *Town Centres – Current Practice*, Planning Bulletin 4 (HMSO, London, 1963).
7. Buchanan, C.D., *Traffic in Towns* (HMSO, London, 1963).
8. Five case studies are described in Holliday, J. (ed.), *City Centre Redevelopment* (Charles Knight, London, 1973).
9. Much of this criticism and the articulation of a new approach to central area renewal is reflected in a later collection of essays: Cresswell, R. (ed.), *Quality in Urban Planning and Design* (Newnes-Butterworth, London, 1979).
10. Davies, R.L. and Champion, A.G. (eds.), *The Future for the City Centre* (London, Academic Press, 1983).
11. See, for example, Benwell Community Development Project, *From Blacksmiths to White Elephants – Benwell's Changing Shops* (Newcastle upon Tyne, 1979).
12. Restrictions will be placed on large store developments in the Enterprise Zones of Dudley and Salford/Trafford but not in Wakefield or Newcastle/Gateshead. Town and Country Planning Association, *Planning Bulletins*, 6 February 1981 and 22 May 1981.
13. This period of redevelopment is described in Wilkes, L. and Dodds, G., *Tyneside Classical – The Newcastle of Grainger, Dobson and Clayton* (John Murray, London, 1964).
14. City of Newcastle upon Tyne, *Development Plan for Newcastle* (1953).
15. City of Newcastle upon Tyne, *Central Area Redevelopment Proposals – First Report of the City Planning Officer* (1961); *Newcastle upon Tyne Development Plan Review* (1963).
16. Voorhees, A.M. and Associates, *Tyneside Rapid Transit Analysis, Summary and Conclusions and Technical Reports* (London, 1972).
17. City of Newcastle upon Tyne, *Local Plan for the City Centre – Draft Proposals* (1981).
18. City of Newcastle upon Tyne, *Local Plan for the City Centre – Choices for the Future* (1978).
19. City of Newcastle upon Tyne, *Local Plan for the City Centre – Choices for the Future: Public Response* (1979).
20. City of Newcastle upon Tyne, *Local Plan for the City Centre* (1981), p. 8.
21. Greater London Council, *Covent Garden's Moving – The Covent Garden Area Draft Plan* (1968); *Covent Garden: The Next Step – The Revised Plan for the Proposed Comprehensive Development Area* (1971).
22. Christie, I., 'Covent Garden – Approaches to Renewal', *Town Planning Review*, vol. 45, no. 1 (1974), pp. 30-62.
23. Alexander, I., 'City Centre Redevelopment – An Evaluation of Alternative Approaches', *Progress in Planning*, vol. 3, part 1 (1974), pp. 1-81.
24. Greater London Council, *Covent Garden Local Plan – Courses of Action* (1975).
25. Greater London Council, *Covent Garden Local Plan – Policy Options Report* (1976); and *Draft Plan* (1976).
26. Covent Garden Community Association, *Keep the Elephants Out of the Garden* (1976).
27. Greater London Council, *Covent Garden Action Area Plan* (1978).

28. Covent Garden Community Association, *Covent Garden – Putting the Record Straight* (1980).
29. Horwood, E. and Boyce, R., *Studies of the Central Business District and Urban Freeway Development* (University of Washington Press, Seattle, 1959).
30. Keeble, L., *Principles and Practice of Town and Country Planning* (Estates Gazette, London, 1961).
31. Buchanan, C.D., *Mixed Blessing* (Leonard Hill, London, 1958).
32. Agergaard, E. and Allpass, J. *et al.*, 'Centres – Places for Distribution or Public Meeting Places?', *Build International*, vol. 6 (1973), pp. 463-9.
33. Institut for Center-Planlaegning, *Hvad Med City? (Ideplan 77, for City)* (Copenhagen, 1977).
34. Davies, R.L., 'A Framework for Commercial Planning Policies', *Town Planning Review*, vol. 48, no. 1 (1977), pp. 42-58.
35. Davies, R.L. and Bennison, D.J., 'Retailing in the City Centre: The Characters of Shopping Streets', *Tijdschrift voor Economishe en Sociale Geografie*, vol. 69, no. 5 (1978), pp. 270-85.
36. City of Newcastle upon Tyne, *Local Plan for the City Centre – Interim Shopping Policy* (1977).

PART III

SPECIFIC PROBLEMS AND SPECIFIC PLANS

9   THE IMPACT OF NEW SHOPPING SCHEMES

The development of large stores and purpose-built shopping centres has been the dominant issue of retail and commercial planning throughout the last decade. Their propensity to cause enormous changes to the traditional pattern of retailing has meant that virtually every application has received special scrutiny, particularly those for new facilities within suburban locations. It is right that this should have been so, although there are questions to be asked as to whether the most appropriate types of criteria have been used in the adjudication process and whether some of the evaluation techniques employed have been capable of providing sufficient objective evidence. There has tended inevitably to be much stress on the potential trading shifts that might follow from the introduction of new schemes and less attention given to the contributions they might make to job generation within local economies or their fulfilment of demands from the bulk of the population. Too much emphasis in the past was put on the results of simulation models that had a doubtful conceptual basis; more recently forecasts have been made from data that are themselves of little contemporary relevance. The fact is that the arguments for and against new developments are extremely complicated and need to be carefully assessed both nationally and at the individual local authority level. For this reason, there should continue to be the preparation of special plans directed at their accommodation, with inputs provided from central government over the cumulative effects of the new developments and vetting procedures administered by the Counties and Districts under the guidance of consultative bodies.

This chapter takes stock of the variable forms of impact which large stores and new shopping centres can have. It also points some way to what the content of a special plan or separate body of policies might be. It begins, however, with some international comparisons regarding the effects of new developments under different kinds of planning conditions. Many lessons have and will be learned in Britain from the experiences of North America and continental Europe and there are signs that other countries are now seeking to benefit from the history of regulatory controls imposed over here. The next sections deal with the different sets of effects to be associated with outlying shopping schemes and those established in town centre locations. These focus in the former case mainly on hypermarkets and superstores and in the latter case on the larger covered centres. A brief discussion is then given of various methods that have been used to measure the scale and extent of different forms of impact, but particularly from the point of view of trading shifts that occur. Finally, the chapter concludes with some observations on desirable courses of planning action in the future.

Some International Perspectives

The cautious attitude adopted towards new suburban shopping schemes by professional planners in Britain arose in part because of the limited territorial size of the country and the need to contain urban sprawl whenever possible but also because of the visible scars that resulted from an excess of decentralisation over earlier periods of time in North Amercia and continental Europe. In particular, the serious decline in trade of major American downtown areas by outlying regional shopping centres made a deep impression, largely accounting for the total ban that seemed to be placed over these developments in Britain during the next 15 years. There were mitigating circumstances within the United States itself, of course, that explain their greater acceptability there, including the higher rates of car ownership, more profligate suburbanisation of the population and the social divides between the black and white communities; but it nevertheless remains astonishing that new centres were still being built throughout the 1970s at the rate of about a thousand per year.[1] The continued proliferation has finally met with pockets of resistance, however, some of it engendered by local politicians and pressure groups concerned about the environmental impact of large schemes on small town centres and the depletion of tax revenues, some of it stoked by state and federal government officials alarmed at the drain of energy resources.

A widely publicised example of this new-found resistance was a decision by the Vermont District Environment Commission in 1978 to deny approval for the development of a regional shopping centre on the outskirts of Burlington. Amongst the evidence submitted to a public hearing, the City of Burlington had estimated that $24.4 million of projected retail sales up to 1983 would be deflected from the downtown and consultants had forecast that, whilst 516 jobs would be created by the scheme, 617 jobs would eventually be lost elsewhere because of trading ramifications.[2] The public hearing proved to be something of a test-case for the nation as a whole and the resulting decision buoyed many other civic authorities to take a tougher line. An independent New York organisation known as Downtown Research and Development Center has also sought to promote a backlash through a publication entitled *Strategies for Stopping Shopping Centers.*[3]

Federal government initiatives were also taken under the Carter administration. A document was produced at the White House called 'Community Conservation Guidance',[4] the main thrust of which was to curb the future spread of suburban shopping developments and encourage more investment in the central city. A set of guidelines was laid down on how controls could be exerted through a stricter allocation of public money for those infrastructures and services necessary for the support of new developments. 'The primary objective of the guidelines . . . is to encourage, through appropriate Federal, state and local action, the targeting of limited resources on the redevelopment and/or development by the private sector of older commercial areas. In order to accomplish this, they are aimed at discouraging major Federal actions that will directly lead to the construction of those, and only those, large commercial developments that clearly and demonstrably weaken existing communities, particularly their established business districts.' The intended policies were never presented to Congress, however, and they appear to have been abandoned by President Reagan.

Similar, tentative steps have also been taken in Canada and Australia to check the further growth of suburban shopping centres. In 1979, Prince Edward Island placed a two-year moratorium on further developments, Nova Scotia passed a special Act to regulate them and New Brunswick instituted the procedure that any applications for new developments in unincorporated urban areas will be subject to Provincial Cabinet approval. At about the same time, the Town and Country Planning Board and Melbourne and Metropolitan Board of Works were commissioning studies to find an appropriate retail planning framework within which they too could exercise greater control over such developments.[5]

This trend towards a more critical view of outlying shopping centres in the newer countries of the world has been paralleled in continental Europe by a stricter stance towards large stores, namely hypermarkets and superstores, as we have indicated before. During the 1960s and early 1970s, and taking the variable sizes of countries into account, there seemed to be as much rampant growth in these developments in France and West Germany as occurred in shopping centres in North America.[6] The same local resentments and official concerns emerged, however, when smaller town centres became seriously affected, not just from the presence of a single large store, but from two or three of them competing against each other. France introduced its special legislation, known as the Loi Royer, to check the pace of development in 1973; but in the following three years, 223 applications for new hypermarkets were filed with the new adjudicating committees, 39 per cent of which were granted approval.[7] Some tightening up of the vetting procedures has occurred since then, but so great has been the recent alarm over local effects being felt that the new socialist government shortly after taking office announced a total embargo to be placed on all hypermarket proposals over the next 12 months.

The change in attitudes displayed by other member countries of the European Community is summarised in Table 9.1.[8] Belgium has followed most closely in the wake of France as we have stated elsewhere, while West Germany has sought a similar retraction of its earlier *laissez-faire* policies though opting to do this through its existing planning machinery. Luxembourg and Italy have for long been able to use restrictive trade laws and licensing requirements to prevent large stores from assuming a commanding position within their retail economies; and the Netherlands, also displaying a restrictive stance from the beginning, has now put the onus on the store companies themselves to prove that they can be satisfactorily accommodated in certain urban situations by requiring them to conduct their own impact assessments during an intervening period of two years from the date of submission of an application to when it is approved or rejected. Denmark remains something of a special case: the controlled decentralisation policies operating in Copenhagen allowing for the absorption of large stores in the new satellite shopping centres; but elsewhere, in the mainland, there has been a creeping growth in large stores that many planners would like to keep in stronger check.

We now witness the curious state of affairs where Britain, in its current attitude towards hypermarkets and superstores, once more seems out of step with the rest of Europe, but this time because of a greater recognition of their positive rather than negative attributes. The change in attitude has been in part political but it has also permeated the planning profession and reflects to a large degree the outcome of several careful monitoring studies conducted in the first half of the 1970s. The planning profession also continues to give the

Table 9.1: Changes in Attitudes of EEC Countries towards Outlying Shopping Developments

Policies towards outlying shopping developments in the 1960s	Policies towards outlying shopping developments in the 1970s	
	Controls	Size limits
Britain .... Resistance	Planning directive	10,000 m² (UK)
Netherlands	Planning directive	1,500 m² (Neth)
Italy	Special law	1,500 m² (Italy)
Eire	Planning constraint	– (Eire)
Luxembourg	Legal constraint	600 m² (Lux)
Denmark .... Controlled decentralisation (Copenhagen)	Regional planning extended	(Den)
Belgium	Special law	3,000 m² (Bel)
France .... *Laissez-faire*	Special law	3,000 m² (Fr)
West Germany	Planning directive	1,500 m² (Fed)

impression that it is still firmly in charge of events, that the large stores will not be allowed to develop in a willy-nilly fashion and will generally be guided to certain locations only. This may well be the case, but few local authorities have formulated specific policies with regard to large stores and they remain responsive to individual proposals as they arise rather than identifying them in advance as essential features of a plan.

Effects of Outlying Shopping Schemes

Hypermarkets and Superstores

The debate that has ensued in Britain for almost two decades over the relative benefits and disbenefits to be derived from hypermarkets and superstores was coloured in the initial stages by much factual misunderstanding and the pursuit of various self-interests. Doom and gloom was preached on the one hand by local chambers of commerce, the representatives of many high street multiple firms and some professional planners too; on the other hand, certain local politicians, prospective developers and of course the major food retailers themselves exaggerated the improvements in shopping that would accrue and downplayed the idea of there being any adverse consequences at all.[9] Experience has brought us nearer the truth, but the evidence compiled so far relates to a different situation from that found in France and other continental European countries. By comparison, there have been far fewer stores built in suburban locations in Britain, their sizes have tended to be smaller and they have mainly been guided into existing residential areas rather than occupying greenfield sites. Bearing these factors in mind we can trace through what seem to be the major considerations involved in their entry into the retail environment from a planning point of view.

Economic Considerations.   (a) To the retailer or developer, the development costs in establishing a large store in an outlying location will usually be much less than those associated with a town centre site. This then allows for increased profits to be made and/or significant advantages to be passed through to consumers in the form of cheaper goods, the provision of special services and a more attractive environment. The drawback to these types of site acquisitions is that the public may have to pay proportionately more for supporting servicing and infrastructure costs, they will generally yield lower levels of rates and they may deflect from the value of alternative town centre sites that might be suited to a similar use.

(b) The prices of goods offered in hypermarkets and superstores are usually significantly lower than those offered in smaller stores, including supermarkets, and with savings to be achieved for those purchasing small quantities of goods as well as in bulk. Fears have been expressed in some quarters that these price advantages may only be temporary and that when a large store assumes a monopoly position within an area, through perhaps the closure of weaker competitors, it might start charging artificially high prices.[10] There is little evidence to substantiate these fears, either in terms of large stores assuming the type of monopoly position envisaged or in pricing abuses occurring where stores have a relatively strong captive market.

(c) Large stores make a substantial contribution to employment within local areas, generating between 100 and 500 jobs when they are first opened. What is not yet clear is how much employment contraction takes place amongst smaller stores through competition and whether, over a period of years, there is a net gain or loss in jobs. Over time there will likely be significant shifts in the structural characteristics of employment, towards more younger, female and part-time workers; and the presence of large stores may have an inhibiting effect on potential job generation in other forms of retailing.

(d) The developers of large stores are particularly attracted to suburban locations where there is a trade vacuum; hence they will often cater to new localised sources of demand and communities which are relatively far removed from traditional shopping centres. However, because of the size of their catchment areas, it is inevitable that they will deplete trade from traditional shopping centres and of these, neighbourhood shopping centres and small district centres, by virtue of the composition of their retailing activities, are most at risk. It does not follow, nevertheless, that in the absence of large stores, the smaller traditional centres will flourish.

(e) The specific types of retailers who are most adversely affected by hypermarkets and superstores are the smaller branches of multiples engaged in convenience goods trade. Since these, mainly supermarkets, often serve as the anchor tenants of neighbourhood and smaller district shopping centres, however, their demise can have a delayed, ripple effect on other small independent shops. Generally, nevertheless, corner shops are little affected by large stores. There are also few adverse effects on all types of shops engaged in durable goods or specialist goods trade, especially those located in larger district shopping centres or town centres.

Environmental Considerations. (a) It is clearly much easier to acquire expansive sites of a suitable shape for large store development in outlying areas than within the central city. In consequence, more extensive car parking can be provided at ground level, entry and egress points can be made more approachable, conflicts between shoppers and delivery vehicles can be reduced and the collective store operations can be made more efficient. In contrast, the acquisition of such expansive sites may contribute to the general process of urban sprawl or alternatively, if obtained within existing residential areas, take up land that could be devoted to other uses. Bearing in mind that some shopping uses are usually seen as a desirable feature of all communities, however, there would likely be little difference in the amount of land occupied by a single large store and its equivalence in functional provisions, as represented by two or three neighbourhood centres or a district centre.

(b) A particularly sensitive issue regarding the development of suburban sites is whether a proposal might intrude into green belt land. Green belts are designated to protect the countryside from too much penetration of urban land uses and clearly any proposals that fall within these must be viewed with some prejudice. But green belts are not always uniformly attractive areas of land and sometimes contain run-down tracts that could be improved by a tastefully designed large store. Likewise, within the city proper, much derelict land can be found in some inter-war suburbs as well as the inner city which could be designated as appropriate sites for large store development.

(c) Hypermarkets and superstores are often criticised for their poor external appearance and their visual intrusion into residential settings. This is a matter that could and should be relatively easily resolved between developers and local authorities through an upgrading of architectural design standards and greater attention to landscaping. Less easy to contend with are the audible nuisances and safety hazards that may arise from increased traffic along local roads.

(d) The growth in traffic along local roads is also contentious from the point of view of the adequacy of an existing road network to support it.[11] The possible need for new pavements, turning points, traffic lights or indeed new roads is also bound up with the economic question as to whether the local authority should pay for such improvements. The issue usually centres on the overloading of relatively minor roads; however, occasionally there can be a wider conflict between local traffic mixing with through traffic on major or ring-roads.

(e) The physical and cultural properties associated with particular sites will also be important considerations to both a prospective developer and the local authority. Clearly, there will be reluctance on the part of a local authority to grant approval for a large store on land that might have high agricultural potential, scenic value or strong historical connections. On the other hand, the developer too will have requirements in terms of relative flatness, an open aspect, good drainage and ready access to utility services.

Social Considerations. (a) The opening of a hypermarket or superstore, in whatever location it might occupy, will not only usually bring cheaper prices and a greater selection of goods but will also add to the choice in shopping opportunities available to the majority of consumers. This element of choice is important not simply because the store is large but because it offers a different style and mode of shopping to that available in traditional shopping centres. That a majority of consumers welcome the choice is attested to in their use of the stores.

(b) Hypermarkets and superstores have a special appeal to certain groups of consumers, notably the younger, more mobile and more affluent sections of the population who shop relatively infrequently and typically buy in bulk. The greater proximity of these groups to large stores in suburban locations can mean that the older, less mobile and poorer sections of the population become disadvantaged in a comparative sense in not sharing in the same opportunities. The approach to this dilemma, as we have argued before, should not be the curtailment of choice in the suburbs but rather the promotion of large stores in inner city areas or the improvement of local accessibility conditions there to large stores found in the town centre.

(c) For other minority groups in the population, such as the disabled, hypermarkets and superstores in suburban locations can provide superior forms of shopping assistance over other stores in more congested sites, through wider aisles and checkout points, ramps and special toilet facilities. In the largest stores, crèches and play areas have been provided for the convenience of mothers with young children.

(d) Special concern has been expressed about the isolation of immobile consumers in suburbs which fall within the catchment areas of hypermarkets or superstores and where there are poor alternative local shopping opportunities and inadequate bus connections to the large stores. The solutions to this will be circumscribed by how much demand exists. Special bus services could be organised, as they sometimes are,

Table 9.2: Major Factors Involved in Inquiry Decisions Over Large Stores

Proposal	Result	Planning process	Designation	Intrusion	Nuisance	Need	Effective retailing	Hierarchy impact	Site access	Network impact	Other
Morrison Darlington	App	os	or		as	as		os			AP
Woolco Bulwell	Dis		OP		on			os		os	
Sainsbury Chichester	All	on	as			as	ar	on	or	os	
TCS Wilnecote	All		os			as	AP*	os		os	
Asda Turnford	Dis		OP	OP		os	AP	on			
Asda Bilton	All	on			os		as	os	or	os	
FineFare Chichester	Dis	on	on		OP*		AP	as		or	
SavaCentre Calcot	All			as	on	an	as	os	or	or	
International Redruth	All*		as		or		AP	os	or	on	on*
PIMCS Bedhampton	All			an	os	an		os	or		
Enfield Highway CS							AP	os		os	
Waltham Cross	Dis		OP	OP	os		as	os		os	

Asda Boldon Colliery	Dis	or	OP	OP	os	as	os	or
Asda Harrogate	Dis	Dis			ar	an	OP	
NECS Monkton	Dis	os			os	as	OP	

Key

*   Inspector's recommendation rejected by the Secretary of State for the Environment.

OP   AP   Objectionable or acceptable in principle, when for example presumption against green belt development is upheld, or the inspector describes an issue as critical or the deciding factor.

or   ar   Objectionable but remediable by conditions or detailed planning; acceptable but already provided by alternative plans or facilities.

os   as   Objectionable or acceptable but of secondary importance where the factor is overriden by issue of principle.

on   an   Objectionable or acceptable but treated as of minor importance in the decision; a matter noted.

Source: Lee, M. and Roberts, C., *Planning Inquiry Study Three* (Donaldsons Research Report 8) (Donaldsons, London, November 1981).

by the retail companies themselves; alternatively there may be scope for encouraging visits by mobile delivery vans. In such cases, the size of demand could be quantified by a local authority and brought to the attention of different retail traders.

(e) There has been relatively little assessment of how hypermarkets and superstores in outlying locations will change or respond to future patterns of shopping behaviour, given the trends to higher petrol costs, increasing levels of unemployment, a greater elderly component within the population and the introduction of more sophisticated technology into the retail industry itself. The evidence to date suggests that there may well be some reconvergence of consumers on traditional shopping centres, including town centres, for convenience goods, but that large stores placed at strategic sites throughout the urban area will be most desirable.

While the above paragraphs suggest that there is an extremely wide assortment of considerations to take into account in assessing the effects of outlying hypermarkets and superstores, the adjudications of proposals that have been made in practice have tended to give more weight to certain criteria than others. Lee and Kent and Lee and Roberts[12] have provided extremely useful summaries of the main sets of evidence used by inspectors at Planning Inquiries to approve or reject 80 proposals for such stores between 1970 and 1980. The most important criteria involved in decisions over some of the more recent cases are listed in Table 9.2. Broadly speaking, the main focus of attention throughout the decade has been on purely shopping matters, i.e. the relative benefits accruing to consumers through lower prices and increased opportunities versus the disbenefits to other traders and the impact felt on the traditional hierarchy of centres. However, land use issues have assumed particular importance when there has been potential penetration of green belt land; and traffic considerations have often been discussed in some detail in the preliminary stages of an inquiry while not being stressed as a major factor in the final outcome. Other socio-economic considerations, such as employment and the potential social divisiveness of new schemes, have hardly been raised at all (although the employment implications are likely to become more important in the future). An additional feature noted by these researchers has been the extent to which any proposal has fitted in with the overall planning policies being pursued by a local authority; but they concluded that few inspectors have taken much notice of the evidence presented on this theme, although in the earlier years much of this would have referred to interim policies pending the later publications of Structure Plans and Local Plans.

Studies which have been undertaken of stores subsequently built have likewise focused on their relative price advantages and trading repercussions. There has been some variability in results because of the different sizes, locations and urban settings for the cases involved, but in the main the conclusions have been much the same. Thus, on prices of goods, a study of the Carrefour hypermarket at Caerphilly showed these to be 12 per cent lower on average than those of competitors in the first year of trading but 9 per cent lower during the second year; prices at the Eastleigh Carrefour were 6 per cent below those of competitors after three months of trading; prices at an Asda town centre site in Coatbridge were 11.3 per cent lower than elsewhere; but a Sainsbury superstore in Cambridge showed a differential of only 2 per cent.[13] More generally, comparisons of a limited basket of small standard goods between six superstores in Tyne and Wear and 150 supermarkets in Newcastle showed the superstores to be consistently cheaper.[14] What has not been taken into account in any of these studies, however, is the erosion of cost savings achieved by extended journey lengths and the greater usage of cars for shopping purposes.

On the subject of trading effects, most studies agree that the main casualties are the smaller branches of the multiple food retailers, most of which are themselves the developers of hypermarkets and superstores. A comparative study of the competitive effects of three large stores in York, Northampton and Cambridge showed that specialist independent food retailers, like butchers and greengrocers, were little affected.[15] Detailed monitoring of conditions in the Eastleigh Carrefour catchment area showed substantial losses in turnover were experienced by a wide range of shops engaged in the convenience goods trades, but that no shop closed within the first year of the hypermarket's opening and only one in the second year.[16] During the first year, total turnover declined by 9 per cent in the local shopping centre nearest the hypermarket and in Shirley, a district centre four miles away, there was a decline of 17 per cent in food turnover but an increase of 15 per cent in durable goods sales. At the nearby Eastleigh district centre, the reported results were complicated by the opening of a large Tesco supermarket there. In Caerphilly, extensive shop closures were recorded in and around the town centre, but after monitoring events over a five-year period, Lee and Kent concluded '. . . there is no evidence to suggest that the hypermarket has had a widespread adverse impact upon the established hierarchy ... there have been substantial changes ... yet these relate more closely to the normal evolution of centres ...'[17]

Overall, much of the concern that was expressed during the early years of the hypermarket debate has proved to be unfounded. We ought to reiterate, however, that most of the studies undertaken to date have looked at large stores operating in relative isolation from each other. There is considerable variance between the experience so far gained in Britain and the more alarming stories reported from France. This will have something to do with the different organisational characteristics of retailing in the two countries, particularly the higher incidence of small independent shops in France compared to the entrenchment of multiples in Britain, and there are differences in the prevailing sizes and characters of settlements; but it will also reflect on the greater numbers of hypermarkets and superstores operating in France and a careful watch should be kept in Britain to ensure that the marginal benefits so far obtained should not eventually be outweighed by a relative overpopulation of these stores.

Outlying Shopping Centres

While hypermarkets and superstores have dominated the public inquiry process during the last two decades, there were in the late 1960s several proposals for out-of-town shopping centres, following the North American models. In hindsight, these proposals can be seen as test-cases of central and local government opinion towards such developments. There were five applications in particular that went to appeal and which have been widely reported upon. These were for centres at: Haydock Park (between Manchester and Liverpool); Wolvercote (on the outskirts of Oxford); Cribb's Causeway (on the outskirts of Bristol); Toton (on the outskirts of Nottingham); and Stonebridge (between Birmingham and Coventry). The proposed centres varied in size but all, with the possible exception of Wolvercote, could be viewed as applications for regional-level shopping centres. All were refused planning permission, primarily on the grounds of their potential adverse trading effects on surrounding town centres and, in three cases, for the additional reason that they would penetrate into green belt land.[18]

Brent Cross was a different case as we have indicated before. While clearly exhibiting many of the classic features of the North American out-of-town centre, including its dumb-bell shape and position at the intersection of two limited-access highways, it does not occupy a greenfield site and sits in the midst of an extensive residential area. Since its opening in 1976, it has of course been extensively monitored, particularly in terms of its trading effects.[19] These appear to have been slight and widely dissipated, in part because there is no comparable competing centre nearby and in part because much of its custom has been drawn from people who would otherwise shop in the West End of London, itself such a large retailing focus that any trade deflections have been hardly noticed. Some specialist and durable goods stores in Harrow, Golders Green and Hendon reported a reduction in their turnover immediately following the opening of Brent Cross but there have been no store closures directly attributable to competition from the new scheme. Needless to say, convenience goods stores in the smaller, more localised shopping centres have been virtually unaffected.

In addition to Brent Cross, there have also been certain district centres and the town centres of New Towns which have acted as sub-regional or satellite centres to the central areas of conurbations, as we have stated before. The mixed functional role and relatively small size of these centres in comparison to the central areas, however, makes it difficult to perceive a distinctive pattern of effects. Where they can make a more pronounced impact is when they combine with a town centre shopping scheme to divert trade away from an inner city shopping centre. This has occurred in Tyne and Wear where Gateshead has been seriously affected both by the hypermarket and superstore developments in Washington New Town and by the Eldon Square Regional Shopping Centre in Newcastle. We turn now to a wider consideration of the effects emanating from such town centre schemes as Eldon Square.

Effects of Town Centre Shopping Schemes

General Forms of Impact

In this section, no distinction is made between hypermarkets and superstores on the one hand and shopping centres on the other since, within town centre locations, the two types of development are commonly associated together. In looking at the relative benefits of town centre shopping schemes, however, we must be mindful again of their variable sizes and urban settings and recognise that in some central areas there is now more than one scheme. Much of the evidence we can draw upon is unfortunately limited to the largest schemes[20] but some analogies can be made with the outlying developments discussed before, as is indicated in Table 9.3. These need qualification particularly in terms of the redevelopment process that is involved and the fact that

Table 9.3: Major Forms of Impact of Town Centre Shopping Schemes

Economic		Environmental		Social	
Positive	Negative	Positive	Negative	Positive	Negative
Adds new stock	Reduces old stock	Modernises outworn areas	Changes traditional character	Allows for efficient shopping	May favour car-borne shoppers
Accommodates larger modern stores	Discriminates against small independents	Reduces land use conflicts	Creates new points of congestion	Provides new shopping opportunities	May limit choice to stereotypes
Increases rates and revenues	Increases monopoly powers	Scope for new design standards	Intrusive effects on older townscapes	Provides more safety	Creates new stress factors from crowds
Creates new employment	Changes structure of employment	Provides weather protection	Creates artificial atmosphere	Provides more comfort and amenities	Attracts delinquents and vandals
Improves trade on adjacent streets	Reduces trade on peripheral streets	Leads to upgrading of some streets	Causes blight on other streets	Concentrates shopping in one area	Breaks up old shopping linkages
Enhances status of central area	Affects status of surrounding centres	Integrates new transport	Causes pressure on existing infrastructures	Potentially greater social interaction	Becomes dead area at night

Source: Bennison, D.J. and Davies, R.L., 'The Impact of Town Centre Shopping Schemes in Britain: Their Impact on Traditional Retail Environments', *Progress in Planning*, vol. **14**, part **1** (1980), pp. 1-104.

the forms of impact felt relate much more to durable goods than to convenience goods trades.

In contrast to an outlying development, the *economic* effects of a town centre shopping scheme begin far in advance of its opening through the disruptions caused in the acquisition of its site. Small retail businesses in particular often suffer directly from being displaced in the redevelopment process, some 3,050 shops having reportedly been cleared away to make room for 125 new centres in the last 15 years, of which only approximately one-fifth were subsequently able to relocate within a scheme.[21] Other small shops may be adversely affected by changes in pedestrian flows related to work on a site or through the later relocations of larger attractor stores. On the brighter side, the trading shifts which eventually take place within a central area may lead to considerable increases in turnover for those small businesses adjacent to a new scheme, although these may be counteracted by reductions in trade for those in peripheral positions. The general experience, however, is that small, specialist retailers, wherever their location might be, suffer less in direct competition with stores in a new scheme than the multiples found on the traditional high street or important secondary shopping streets.

Shifts in the centre of gravity of trade within a central area, nevertheless, are complicated by a number of factors. While new schemes may alter the general pattern of pedestrian flows and consumer trip structure characteristics they will usually increase the overall volume of trade available within a central area by virtue of their enhancement of the stock of resources. New types of stores and branches of multiples previously unrepresented in the central area might come in and accessibility might be improved by the provision of new bus stations and/or car parks. The reorganisation of transport facilities, however, can then in itself cause major changes in consumer behaviour leading to a contraction of the action space in which most consumer spending is concentrated, while the general activity space may remain much the same. Schiller[22] has also shown that whilst new schemes may initially add to the range of shopping opportunities, their presence can have an inhibiting effect on the future introduction and development of smaller, specialist stores.

The consequences of town centre shopping schemes for shopping centres in the wider trade area are less well known. Much will depend on the particular trade mix of a new scheme and/or the relative strength of surrounding shopping centres as competing centres. Large schemes will generally compete with town centres as a whole although, since most of these will have their own new schemes, there will likely be some counterbalancing of effects if the schemes are of a similar size order. Town centres are most directly threatened where they lie within the shadow of a major city centre that has an exceptionally large development, as in the case of Gateshead in relation to Newcastle. Smaller schemes, with hypermarkets or superstores as their major tenants, are more likely to affect district and neighbourhood shopping centres within the same urban area, and particularly those within the inner city.

As far as environmental issues are concerned, most argument has focused on the design and appearance of town centre shopping schemes and their contributions to blight and congestion within and around the central area. A distinction can clearly be drawn between the relative achievements found in the internal environment of many of the covered schemes and their external intrusion into a surrounding townscape. The Victoria centre in Nottingham is a good example of this, as is the Manchester Arndale centre and the Birmingham shopping centre. In some instances, however, and more commonly with the open precincts, the new schemes have been disastrous from both points of view: as in the cases of the Tricorn centre, Portsmouth, the Trinity Square centre, Sunderland, and the early form of the Elephant and Castle centre, in London. Yet again, some schemes appear to be pleasing both inwardly and outwardly, especially smaller-scale developments implanted into historic towns, as with the Dairygate centre in York, the Lion Yard precinct in Cambridge, and Millburngate centre in Durham.[23] The record has obviously been mixed although most observers might conclude that generally architectural standards have not been high and the majority of schemes lack warmth and sensitivity. It is no real consolation to think that the record has been worse in housing and office development.

The issue regarding blight and congestion has been no less contentious but the effects that may have been realised here are difficult to separate from those brought on by other land use developments. Blight may be caused as a relatively temporary phenomenon during the early stages in planning a scheme and as a more lasting feature it may be exacerbated by the opening of a scheme; but the emergence of large run down parts of a central area will usually be due to a complex set of economic factors that have as much to do with structural changes within retailing as a whole as to localised shifts in trading conditions. It can be argued, too, that many new shopping schemes in fact reduce the amount of blight to be found since they are often built in the backyard areas of shopping streets and stimulate growth within their immediate surroundings. Congestion is also usually the result of a combination of processes at work, not least the general growth in traffic, the more intensive use of land within parts of the central area and planning interventions aimed at reducing severe conflicts between vehicles and pedestrians at particular points. There is no doubt, however, that the concentration of new shopping resources within a city centre will by itself lead to increased trip generation and this may be further facilitated by improvements in accessibility, through the widening of approach roads and in some cases the provision of urban motorways. Attempts to deal with these additional trips to the city centre, either through increasing the amount of car parking or through traffic management schemes directed at encouraging a greater usage of public transport systems, have so far proved rather unsuccessful. In many of our larger central areas, there are serious problems of congestion at certain times of the day in and around the new shopping schemes, with safety conditions worsening particularly on a Saturday. A further contribution to this congestion is the inhibiting effect which the new developments have had on investments in shopping schemes elsewhere in the urban region.

The social effects of town centre shopping schemes are mostly quite different in kind from those described for outlying developments although there is the same general improvement in choice and range of opportunities made available to the public. Town centre shopping schemes tend to attract slightly higher proportions of car-borne, younger and more affluent consumers than are typically found along traditional shopping streets but there is a much greater mixing of socio-economic groups than would occur in suburban shopping centres or free-standing large stores. Crowd convergence is usually correspondingly higher and conditions can become claustrophobic and even antagonistic. There tend to be greater problems with security, although whether there is more vandalism and anti-social behaviour than in outlying developments is difficult to judge. The largest schemes, by virtue of their size, tend to attract a hooligan element and it is sad to see a scheme like the Victoria centre, designed to appeal to the young, being patrolled during daylight hours by guards with dogs. For the young, as well as other sections of the population, there are relatively few amenity spaces as we have pointed out before and, apart from the odd play sculpture or decorative artefact, there is little to interest the passer-by beyond the shops themselves.

This leads us back to our earlier criticism in Chapter 8 that town centre shopping schemes, together with other land use developments, seem to be contributing to a greater authoritarianism and conformism in the conduct of life within large tracts of the central area. The malls of the shopping schemes are not usually public rights of way and certain forms of behaviour are not permitted within them as they might be on traditional shopping streets; they are usually closed off at night and on Sunday and, because of their inward-looking design, become desolate, inhospitable parts of the city centre during these times; they seem uniform in the types of shops that are found, which will often reflect on discriminating tenant policies that have been applied. Much of this has had to do with the growing monopoly powers of large firms and also the local authorities, but it may be that during the next decade, within a climate of harsher economic constraints and more modest planning objectives, this trend will be arrested to some extent.

The Eldon Square Shopping Centre

Most of the above generalisations have been substantiated in a detailed case study of the effects of the Eldon Square shopping centre in Newcastle upon Tyne.[24] When the Eldon Square centre was first opened in 1976, it was the largest purpose-built scheme in Britain (with 782,000 square feet (73,000 m^2) of gross floor space) and arguably the largest in Europe. It contains a large department store (Bainbridges), openings to a second department store (Fenwicks) and Marks and Spencer, large branches of Boots and W.H. Smith, a market and over 100 mainly durable goods and fashion goods stores. Its extensive network of malls broadly approximates the three sides of a rectangle in shape, with two east-west prolongations linking up with Northumberland Street, the most important traditional shopping street in the central area, and Grainger Street, the second most important traditional shopping street. The scheme therefore has the effect of channelling consumers around in a large circuit, although there are of course many additional entry and exit points at various positions within it.

The enormous site of the scheme and its location adjacent to the main nexus of trade meant that it carried the potential for quite dramatic changes in shopping patterns at both the local and regional level. In its first year of opening, it generated a turnover of approximately £63 million, equivalent to about 30 per cent of the total trade available within the central area, although this had itself grown by some 12-13 per cent as a result of the introduction of the centre. The net shift in local trade that took place, that diverted from other streets in the central area, was estimated at £23 million. A similar amount of trade was deflected from other major centres within the region, with the surplus gain in Eldon Square being accounted for by the capture of expenditure that would otherwise have gone outside the region, shifts in trade from smaller centres and the general growth in consumer spending at this time. A special input to this additional trade was the spending by Norwegian shoppers.

Within the central area, massive changes did take place in the pattern of pedestrian flows and consumer trip structure characteristics and a high proportion of retailers along the traditional shopping streets experienced considerable reductions in turnover, as the first part of Figure 9.1 indicates. Most of the effects felt in trade competition, however, were borne by the variety and fashion stores along Northumberland Street which, because of the increased spending overall within the central area, were relatively easily sustained. Most concern in the initial year of impact focused on the trade depletion in the smaller shopping streets of the conservation area. Within the ensuing three years, nevertheless, a quite remarkable improvement in trading performances seemed to occur throughout the central area, as the second part of Figure 9.1 suggests. This no doubt reflected in part on an adaptation by retailers to the presence of Eldon Square and some re-establishment of customer loyalties after the novelty attractions of the scheme had worn off; but other evidence indicated that there was a slight but continuing growth in consumer expenditure and that much of this represented a catching-up on trade deficiencies that had existed within the city centre over previous years. During the extensive planning and construction phases of Eldon Square, the city centre was relatively under-shopped and a number of major multiple firms were not represented. It is significant, in particular, that by the end of 1979 there were only 27 vacant shop units within the central area compared to 51 just prior to the centre's opening and 69 at the end of 1977, after its first year of trading. It needs to be noted, however, that 113 small retail businesses were cleared away to make room for the scheme and only five independent traders became tenants within it. There was therefore a considerable reduction in the stock of cheap premises available within the central area and much of the apparent revival of economic health within peripheral shopping streets in the last three years has been due to the take-up by small businesses of units previously occupied by multiple firms that relocated into the scheme. This process has purportedly been aided by the City Planning Department's restriction on non-retailing activities entering certain shopping

Figure 9.1: Changes in the Trading Health of Streets in the City Centre of Newcastle upon Tyne, 1976-1979

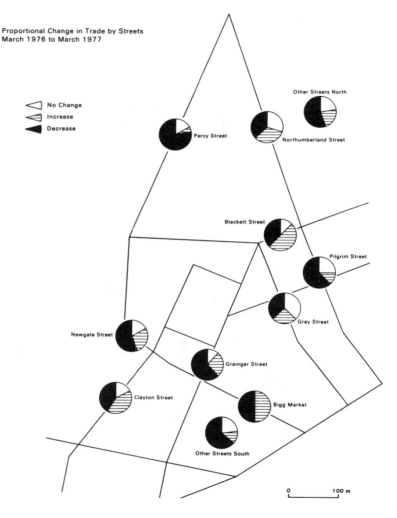

Source: Bennison, D.J. and Davies, R.L., 'The Impact of Town Centre Shopping Schemes in Britain: Their Impact on Traditional Retail Environments', *Progress in Planning*, vol. 14, part 1 (1980), pp. 1-104.

Figure 9.1: Continued

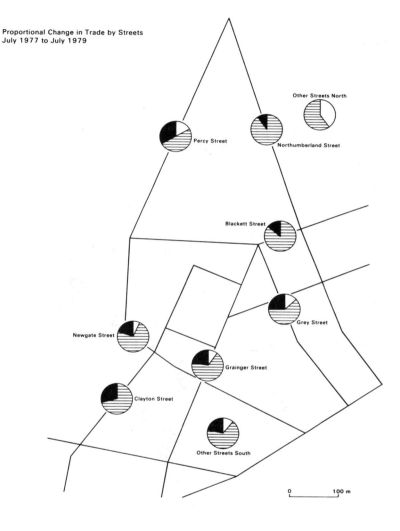

Proportional Change in Trade by Streets
July 1977 to July 1979

streets, which has had the effect of depressing rent levels and making larger shop units there more viable propositions for smaller retailers.

Within the wider region, most of the trade drawn by Eldon Square has naturally come from within the metropolitan county although, somewhat surprisingly, proportionately higher levels of customer support, relative to the population sizes of communities, has come from surrounding market towns and dormitory suburban areas. Inside the conurbation, the major district shopping centres experienced collectively a 9 per cent decline in their durable goods turnover in the year following Eldon Square's opening, but this constituted a relatively small fraction of their total trade, the greater part of which is made up of convenience goods shopping and which was virtually unaffected by the new scheme. Three of the shopping centres closest to Eldon Square were closely monitored from 1976 to 1979 and in none of them could any shop closures be directly attributed to the scheme. Of the various centres that properly qualify in their own right as being town centres only Gateshead seems to have been seriously affected and here, as we have indicated before, it is difficult to dis-associate the effects of Eldon Square from other factors at work. In outlying places, such as Durham City, Morpeth and Hexham, most of the initial depletion of durable goods trade that occurred has been compensated for in recent years by fairly rapid population growth and high average levels of spending within their own local trade areas. The general impact of the new scheme has therefore been widely dissipated throughout the region and, as in the case of the central area, accommodated with remarkably little serious erosion of the traditional retail environment. It may be, however, that some of the longer-term disbenefits of the scheme have yet to be realised for planning policies within Tyne and Wear are now oriented towards prohibiting any further large-scale retail developments that might have their own impact on the scheme and this could well inhibit the introduction of new innovations in the outer parts of the county or the regeneration of the older inner areas.

On the question of its relationship to the built environment, Eldon Square has been more controversial. By dint of its size, it could not but emerge as a massive, dominating edifice within the central area but its design was originally quite carefully conceived to integrate its various external frontages with the scale of building around it. That this integration has not been wholly achieved is due to the changes which have occurred in local planning circumstances.[25] On the western side of the scheme, a vast blank exterior was intended to act as a buffer against the noise and pollution from a proposed motorway but, as we have indicated in Chapter 8, the motorway itself has not been built and is unlikely to be constructed for many years to come. Inside the scheme, at this point, the malls are elevated above ground level for they were intended to link up with a series of elevated walkways spanning the motorway and other distributary roads. The subsequent curtailment of the development programme for the walkway system has now left the malls suspended as it were above the traditional street network which is itself devoid of any shops despite continuing to channel much consumer movement. In the north section of Eldon Square, however, the main mall has been graded towards the east so that it joins Northumberland Street at ground level and the overall height of the scheme has been restricted to that of the surrounding department and variety stores. In the south section, too, whilst two levels of malls are accommodated, there is direct street access to the lower level and the façades of buildings displaced to make room for the scheme have been retained so that it abuts the conservation area in a relatively unobtrusive way. Part of this conscious effort to blend in with the Regency style of architecture in the conservation area, nevertheless, followed from a local outcry over the clearance of buildings on two sides of the old Eldon Square, leaving a third side completely surrounded by towering brick-faced structures.

A second subject of controversy has been the accumulation of traffic congestion, particularly on the west side, and relating in part again to the abandonment of the motorway proposal. The problem has been exacerbated, however, by mixed policies towards the provision of public versus private transport facilities. At the time that the Eldon Square shopping centre was conceived, it was recognised that it would have a special appeal to car-borne shoppers, particularly those from the outer parts of the regions. Two car parks were subsequently built into the scheme itself, but proposals to give additional support to these were shelved as interest was taken up and a commitment later made to the construction of a Metro system. It may be that when the Metro system becomes fully operational the high levels of congestion sustained over the last five years will be reduced; but observation of the relief given to date by the first section that has been opened suggests that the reduction will likely be quite small. Continued congestion may well have to be tolerated therefore simply as a social cost in the attempt to improve public transport services which, on many other grounds, can be strongly supported.

On other matters to do with the physical environment, Eldon

Square has proved to be less contentious, particularly in relation to the spread of blight. Relatively temporary forms of blight appeared on the western side of the central area in the first half of the 1970s but in response mainly to the uncertainties of the motorway proposal at that time rather than the construction of the shopping centre. More lasting pockets of blight have emerged in the conservation area but, whilst the new scheme has been a contributor to these, other factors have again been more significant, especially the development of the All Saints office complex and the implementation of traffic management schemes.

In terms of its social effects, Eldon Square epitomises much of what we have said before. It has been extremely successful commercially and must therefore satisfy a considerable range of demands from within the population. The mall layout has been deliberately designed to keep people moving through the scheme, however, and there is no large focal area where they can easily congregate for non-shopping purposes. A recreation centre above the scheme caters for mainly special-purpose sporting activities. In its internal appearance it might be construed as a paragon of its time, but like any other shopping centre, it lacks the intricacy and character of a traditional shopping street.

Impact Assessment

While the impact of any new retail development, whether a single large store or complex shopping centre, needs to be looked at from several points of view, most interest at the local planning level and from within the business community focuses on its actual or potential trading repercussions. There are a number of ways in which these can be assessed and, despite the similarities in findings about the general form and scale of effects that we have referred to before, there has been little systematic repetition in types of methodologies utilised. Our review here distinguishes between four main lines of approach: the use of costing procedures; survey methods; modelling techniques; and (for want of a better term) area-based calculations.

Costing Procedures

Superficially, one might think that techniques such as cost-benefit analysis and the planning balance sheet would be particularly suited to weighing up the economic arguments for and against a new retail development but in practice they carry several limitations particularly in terms of the quality of data that is required. Alexander[26] has shown that such techniques can be applied but his work was directed at the broader question of what form renewal should take in Covent Garden rather than at the likely consequences of a new shopping centre. There has in fact been no authoritative case study of a retail development that has followed this approach, although cost aspects have been important elements in critical pieces written about the Victoria centre in Nottingham[27] and the proposal for an out-of-town centre near Burlington in Vermont.[28] This approach, however, would seem to have further relevance in relating purely economic considerations to social and environmental matters and in this respect Guy[29] has indicated how something akin to the planning balance sheet might be used to evaluate alternative locations appropriate to superstores in the preparation of a plan. The broad framework for this is shown in Table 9.4 and while Guy has not provided any quantitative examples of the relative costs and benefits involved it is an attractive and logical idea that ought to be tested more fully. He suggests himself that the framework can be expanded upon to treat the costs and benefits accruing to different geographical areas and for different socio-economic categories of consumers and that, using the conventional mechanics of the technique, these can also be weighted to reflect the wider policy interests of a plan, such as in regenerating the inner city or encouraging growth in particular outlying localities.

Survey Methods

Most of the detailed studies which have been undertaken of the trading effects of hypermarkets and superstores have been based on surveys of one kind or another. Three principal kinds of survey can be recognised. Firstly, and perhaps most commonly, a series of consumer questionnaire surveys have been conducted before and after a store's opening. Sometimes these have involved interviewing shoppers at centres in a surrounding area, and subsequently at the hypermarket or superstore itself, as in the case of the Caerphilly and Eastleigh studies,[30] where land use changes were also monitored; others have involved questionnaires posted to people's homes, as in Bridges' study of the York Asda;[31] Rogers[32] persuaded a panel of 172 consumers to keep short diaries of their shopping behaviour in a study of the Sainsbury superstore at Bretton in Peterborough. In each case, comparisons have been made between the two sets of survey findings to trace changes in consumer behaviour and especially changes in expenditure patterns. A second type of approach has involved conducting consumer questionnaire surveys only after a store, or centre, has been opened and asking

Table 9.4: A Matrix Presentation of Costs and Benefits Incurred in Superstore Location Policies

	Locations					
	City centre site	Existing district centre	Proposed district centre (inner)	Proposed district centre (outer)	Other urban site	Edge of town
A. External costs						
Minimise economic impact on town centre shops	×					
Minimise economic impact on suburban shops		×	×	×	×	
Minimise economic impact on proposed new centres			×	×		
Minimise traffic congestion	×	×				
Minimise disturbance to local residents by traffic	×	×	×	×		
Minimise intrusion into urban fabric	×	×				
Minimise intrusion into countryside						×
B. Social benefits						
Maximise accessibility by car	√		√	√		
Maximise accessibility by public transport	√	√	√	√		
Maximise accessibility by foot	√	√	√	√		
Maximise potential for multi-purpose trips	√	√	√			
C. Economic benefits and costs						
Maximise catchment population	√					
Maximise ease of car access and car parking				√		
Minimise land costs	×	×	×			√
Minimise costs of site preparation	×	×				√

Key:
√   advantageous location in principle
×   disadvantageous location in principle
(blank)   advantages or disadvantages slight
Source: Guy, C.M., *Retail Location and Retail Planning in Britain* (Gower, Farnborough, 1980).

people to recall earlier patterns of behaviour. Thorpe and McGoldrick[33] have applied this method in home interview surveys of consumers within the catchment area of the Caerphilly hypermarket and in pavement-based surveys at four centres in North Manchester. Lee and Kent[34] have used it in a study of the impact of Brent Cross, interviewing consumers as they left the shopping centre. The third type of approach has involved conducting questionnaire surveys of retailers in the vicinity of a new development, either on a postal or personal interview basis or through a mixture of these. Thorpe and his associates[35] have undertaken comparative assessments of the changes in trade recorded by retailers following the introduction of superstores in York, Northampton and Cambridge; Dawson and Kirby[36] investigated the views of retailers towards a new superstore in Cwmbran prior to its opening.

Similar kinds of surveys have been conducted to determine the trading effects of town centre shopping schemes, although there are fewer examples to cite. The Eldon Square study[37] involved a combination of pavement-based consumer questionnaire surveys, retailer interviews and land use inventories, undertaken both before and after the scheme opened and subsequently repeated on an annual basis over a three-year period. In addition, bi-annual counts of pedestrians passing 128 control points throughout the central area of Newcastle were taken; and addresses and expenditure amounts recorded on some 16,500 cheques and charge accounts were processed to assess the trade area characteristics of the scheme. A modelling exercise of the type described below was also used in this work to examine some aspects of Eldon Square's regional impact.

Modelling Techniques

Spatial interaction models were widely used in the first half of the 1970s to forecast the potential sales of new retail developments and to assess their competitive effects on surrounding centres, as has been indicated before. Disenchantment with these models set in during the second half of the decade, however, partly as a result of the Department of the Environment's revised Development Control Policy Note 13[38] which reported upon conflicting results submitted at appeals when simulation exercises had been conducted by both a local authority and retail company, or agents on their behalf, and partly because of growing criticism from within the ranks of academic model-builders. Some of this criticism focused on the technical limitations in applying the models, particularly during the calibration process,[39] and some of it on a more fundamental concern that the models are conceptually unsound in predicting radical changes in consumer behaviour, which usually ensue from the introduction of a hypermarket or superstore.[40] Where the models can be based on an extensive data set of existing trip patterns and applied to a large urban area within which new retail developments can be expected to be integrated into the traditional hierarchy of centres, however, there remain certain grounds for continuing to use them. It has been argued, for example, that the effort involved in applying a model will itself impose a sense of discipline on the person seeking to make predictions about future behavioural change and that the model, despite its imperfections, will show the broad directions in which such change will likely take place.[41] Taken in conjunction with other evidence regarding future shopping conditions and perhaps the utilisation of other forecasting techniques of the kind described below, interaction models might still therefore play a useful role in pointing to the consequences arising from new retail developments and more generally, in the context of Structure Plans, suggesting preferred locational strategies for the accommodation of growth. The Unit for Retail Planning Information has undertaken several studies in recent years for County Planning Departments using a hierarchical form of gravity model where distinctions can be drawn between large and small developments and different strategies examined in terms of future changes in durable goods and convenience goods shopping.[42]

Area-based Calculations

Prior to the advent of spatial interaction models into the business of forecasting, most local authorities used a so-called step-by-step approach to predicting the future sizes and trading relationships between centres and particularly, in the context of the 1950s and 1960s, for assessing the future share of trade that might be captured by a town centre. This essentially involved defining an existing catchment area for the town centre, estimating its areal expansion and population growth for some future time period, relating likely consumer expenditure levels to the enlarged catchment area and, from assumptions regarding the split between spending on durable goods versus convenience goods, calculating how much trade would accrue to the town centre and how much would be diverted to other, mainly localised centres. The methodology resembles that commonly followed by retail companies in determining the market share likely to be captured by opening a new store in a particular shopping centre.

This older approach has recently been resurrected and modified in an interesting study undertaken by Breheny and others[43] for Gloucestershire County Planning Department, specifically to assess the potential impacts of new hypermarkets and superstores. Instead of dealing with the trade likely to be generated within a preconceived catchment area, however, it looks at trade in relation to a series of arbitrary isochrones drawn around the potential location for a new store, where the isochrones refer to approximate distances covered at average driving times. Otherwise the steps involved are not unlike those described above except that more refined procedures can be used to derive forecast figures than were available in the past. Briefly the process entails: determining initially future levels of available expenditure on a *per capita* basis (from URPI sources related to local conditions); estimating likely population numbers and total expenditure that would be forthcoming from each isochrone (based on other planning information concerned with residential development); assessing the likely turnover of the store itself (by analogies with comparable stores already operating); calculating the proportion of the store's turnover that is likely to be accounted for by consumers in each isochrone (using a method devised by Donaldsons and based on surveys undertaken of the source origins of customers patronising hypermarkets and superstores); relating the proportion of turnover accountable to each isochrone to the likely total expenditure forthcoming in each isochrone (linking the last mentioned step to the second step); and finally, adjudicating where the expenditure that is expected to be captured by the store would have gone if the store had not been built (involving an examination of existing patterns of consumer behaviour and the use perhaps of spatial interaction models). A worked example of the sequence of steps is shown in Table 9.5.

Conclusion

The impact of large stores and shopping centres will continue to be a major focus of research within retail and commercial planning in the future. We might expect, however, to see three kinds of changes to the nature of this work. Firstly, there is likely to be less emphasis on the purely trading repercussions of such developments and a greater interest in their employment effects and social consequences for the population at large. Secondly, greater attention will probably be given to the introduction of discount retail warehouses, for which there has been increased pressure for new, alternative sites to their traditional

Table 9.5: Worked Examples of the Gloucestershire Impact Assessment
Procedure

Step 1.	Expenditure rates				
	Convenience goods 0.0% = £148				
	Comparison goods 2.0% = £170				
	Total at 1981 = £318				

Step 2.	Isochrone expenditure		Isochrones (minutes)		
			0-10	10-20	15-25
	(in £000s)				
		Convenience goods	24,420	11,100	21,460
		Comparison goods	28,050	12,750	24,650
		Total	52,470	23,850	46,110

Step 3.	Store turnover	
	(Lower estimate)	
	Convenience goods	= £5.32 m
	Comparison goods	= £2.28 m
	Total	= £7.60 m

Step 4.	Isochrone contribution	Isochrones (minutes)		
		0-10	10-20	15-25
		45%	20%	25%

Step 5.	Isochrone impact		Isochrones (minutes)		
			0-10	10-20	15-25
		Convenience goods	9.75%	9.59%	6.20%
		Comparison goods	3.64%	3.57%	2.30%
		For all goods	6.49%	6.37%	4.10%

Step 6.	Centre impact		Convenience goods	Comparison [goods]	Total [goods]
		Gloucester	13.9%	4.7%	7.6%
		Cheltenham	10.2%	3.0%	4.9%
		Stroud	6.9%	2.4%	4.4%
		Cirencester	5.3%	1.0%	2.7%
		Tewkesbury	6.7%	1.9%	4.5%
		Suburbs	19.0%	—	—

(Repeated for upper estimate of store turnover)

Source: Breheny, M.J. *et al.*, 'A Practical Approach to the Assessment of Hyper-market Impact', *Regional Studies*, vol. 15, no. 6 (1981), pp. 459-74.

locations in recent years. Thirdly, the shift in investment in town centre
schemes from large to small places is likely to be accompanied by a
greater concern for what happens to the retail environment of smaller,
localised communities as well as those of the larger, metropolitan areas.
One hopes, nevertheless, that future research initiatives will also take a
more broadly-based or comprehensive approach to the impact of new
developments. Too often in the past, studies have been specific to a
single set of benefits or disbenefits arising from a single type of large

store or shopping centre. It is time to take stock of what the cumulative effects of several schemes have been across a wide variety of urban settings and from various socio-economic points of view. Both the local authorities and retail companies ought now to be questioning whether there are optimum amounts of floorspace to be devoted to certain types of development beyond which a series of negative effects begin to outweigh any positive advantages that may previously have been found. In the late 1960s, a number of extensive shopping surveys were undertaken to obtain a broad insight into patterns of behaviour and consumer attitudes towards various retailing provisions. It would be instructive to repeat some of these surveys during the next few years to determine by how much and in what ways people's behaviour and attitudes have changed since the proliferation of superstores, discount retail warehouses and town centre shopping schemes.

References

1. Golledge, R.G., 'Overseas Trends in Retail Centre Development', *Paper Delivered to the Town and Country Planning Board* (Melbourne, Victoria, 1979).
2. Muller, T., *The Economic and Fiscal Effects of a Proposed Shopping Mall on the State of Vermont* (Vermont State Planning Office, Burlington, 1978).
3. Alexander, L.A. (ed.), *Strategy for Stopping Shopping Centres* (Downtown Renewal and Development Center, New York, 1980).
4. The White House, 'Community Conservation Guidance' (unpublished document, Washington, DC, 1979). See also, Dennis Lord, J., 'Governmental Intervention in Retail Development: The Community Conservation Guidance Policy in the US', *Planning Outlook*, vol. 24 (1981), pp. 33-7.
5. Golledge, R.G., *Consultant's Report on Retail Centre Policy* (Town and Country Planning Board, Melbourne, 1979).
6. See, for example: Evely, R., 'Superstores in West Germany', *Retail and Distribution Management*, vol. 6, no. 5 (1978), pp. 27-9; Dawson, J.A., *Commercial Distribution in Europe* (Croom Helm, London, 1982), ch. 3.
7. Fries, J., 'Government Intervention in France. How has it Affected Development?', *Retail and Distribution Management*, vol. 6, no. 2 (1978), pp. 41-5.
8. See, also, Davies, R.L. (ed.), *Retail Planning in the European Community* (Saxon House, Farnborough, 1979).
9. The debate was extensively aired in such journals as *Built Environment, Estates Gazette* and *New Society*. See, for example, Hillman, M., 'In the Market Place: The Hypermarket Debate', *New Society*, 21 Sept. 1972, and Cole, H., 'Up the Hypermarket', *New Society*, 4 Dec. 1975.
10. Pickering, J.F., 'Economic Implications of Hypermarkets in Britain', *European Journal of Marketing*, vol. 6 (1972), pp. 257-69.
11. Harris, M.R. and Andrew, H.R., 'The Traffic Implications of Hypermarket Development', *Traffic Engineering and Control*, vol. 20 (1979), pp. 2-8;

Maltby, D. and Johnston, I., 'Traffic Implications of Hypermarket Development', *Traffic Engineering and Control*, vol. 20 (1979), pp. 261-2.

12.   Lee, M. and Kent, E., *Planning Inquiry Study, One and Two* (Donaldsons, London, 1976 and 1978); Lee, M. and Roberts, C., *Planning Inquiry Study Three* (Donaldsons, London, 1981).

13.   Seale, S., *The Impact of Large Retail Outlets on Patterns of Retailing – A Synthesis of Research Results in Great Britain* (Scottish Office, Edinburgh, 1977).

14.   Davies, R.L. and Champion, A.G., *Social Inequities in Shopping Opportunities – How the Private Sector Can Respond* (Tesco Stores Ltd., Cheshunt, 1979).

15.   Shepherd, P.M., Bates, P. and Thorpe, D., *Food Retailers and Superstore Competition – A Study of Short Term Impact in York, Northampton and Cambridge* (Manchester Business School, Retail Outlets Research Unit, 1976).

16.   Wood, D., *The Eastleigh Carrefour – A Hypermarket and its Effects* and *The Eastleigh Carrefour Hypermarket After Three Years* (HMSO, London, 1976 and 1978).

17.   Lee, M. and Kent, E., *Caerphilly Hypermarket Study* and *Caerphilly Hypermarket Study Year 2* and *Year 5* (Donaldsons, London, 1973, 1975 and 1979).

18.   Lee, M. and Kent, E., *Planning Inquiry Study Two.*

19.   Lee, M. and Kent, E., *Brent Cross Study* (Donaldsons, London, 1977); Shepherd, I. and Newby, P., *The Brent Cross Regional Shopping Centre – Characteristics and Early Effects* (Retailing and Planning Associates, Corbridge, Northumberland, 1978); Downey, P., *The Impact of Brent Cross* (Reviews and Studies Series no. 2) (Greater London Council, 1980).

20.   Two notable exceptions are: Scottish Development Department, *The Impact of a Town Centre Superstore* (HMSO, London, 1978); Thomas, C., *Retail Change in S. Wales – With Special Reference to Redevelopment in Small Towns* (Retailing and Planning Associates, Corbridge, Northumberland, 1978).

21.   Davies, R.L. and Bennison, D.J., *British Town Centre Shopping Schemes – A Statistical Digest* (Unit for Retail Planning Information, Reading, 1979).

22.   Schiller, R., 'The Impact of New Shopping Schemes on Shops in Historic Streets', *The Planner*, vol. 61 (1975), pp. 367-9.

23.   See also, for example, Amery, C., 'Brunel Centre, Swindon', *Architectural Review*, vol. 160 (1976), pp. 146-55.

24.   Bennison, D.J. and Davies, R.L., 'The Impact of Town Centre Shopping Schemes in Britain: Their Impact on Traditional Retail Environments', *Progress in Planning*, vol. 14, part 1 (1980), pp. 1-104.

25.   Galley, K., 'Eldon Square: The Planning Aims', *The Planner*, vol. 64 (1978), pp. 71-2.

26.   Alexander, I., 'City Centre Redevelopment: An Evaluation of Alternative Approaches', *Progress in Planning*, vol. 3, part 1 (1974), pp. 1-81.

27.   McDougall, M.J. *et al.*, 'Nottingham's Victoria Centre', *Town and Country Planning*, vol. 42 (1974), pp. 124-8.

28.   Muller, T., *Effects of Proposed Shopping Mall on Vermont.*

29.   Guy, C.M., *Retail Location and Retail Planning in Britain* (Gower, Farnborough, 1980).

30.   Wood, D., *Eastleigh Carrefour Hypermarket*; Lee, M. and Kent, E., *Caerphilly Hypermarket Study.*

31.   Bridges, M., *The York Asda. A Study of Changing Shopping Patterns Around a Superstore* (Manchester University, Centre for Urban and

Regional Research, 1976).

32. Rogers, D., *Bretton: Peterborough* (Manchester Business School, Retail Outlets Research Unit, 1974).

33. Thorpe, D. and McGoldrick, P., *Carrefour: Caerphilly – Consumer Response to a Hypermarket* (Manchester Business School, Retail Outlets Research Unit, 1974).

34. Lee, M. and Kent, E., *Brent Cross Study*.

35. Shepherd, P.M., Bates, P. and Thorpe, D., *Food Retailers and Superstore Competition*.

36. Dawson, J.A. and Kirby, D.A., *Retailers' Reactions to Cwmbran Woolco* (St David's University College, Lampeter, 1975).

37. Bennison, D.J. and Davies, R.L., 'Impact of Town Centre Shopping Schemes in Britain'.

38. Department of the Environment, 'Large New Stores', *DOE Circular 96/77* (HMSO, London, 1977).

39. Openshaw, S., 'Insoluble Problems in Shopping Model Calibration When the Trip Pattern is Not Known', *Regional Studies*, vol. 7 (1973), pp. 367-71.

40. Roe, P.E., 'An Appraisal of Shopping Models', *Paper Presented to PTRC* (University of Warwick, July 1974).

41. Talbot, J. and Brockman, R., 'The Practical Uses of a Shopping Model in Structure Plan Preparation', *Paper Given to the Regional Science Association* (1977).

42. Moseley, J., *Cumbrian Shopping Model: Preliminary Calibration* and *Shopping in Berkshire: The Shopping Model* (Unit for Retail Planning Information, Reading, 1976 and 1977); Alty, R. *et al.*, *The South Yorkshire Shopping Model* (Unit for Retail Planning Information, Reading, 1979).

43. Breheny, M.J., Green, J. and Roberts, A.J., 'A Practical Approach to the Assessment of Hypermarket Impact', *Regional Studies*, vol. 15, no. 6 (1981), pp. 459-74.

10 SMALL SHOPS AND RELATED SMALL ACTIVITIES

Small shops and related small activities have become a subject of special concern to planners in recent years by virtue of their diminishing role in the distribution system. Two facts are clearly apparent. Firstly, there has been a substantial decline in the overall number of small retail outlets during the last two decades and this is likely to continue into the 1980s. Secondly, and perhaps more significantly, there has been a quite dramatic depletion of their trading strength to the point where they now account for less than half of the total sales that are generated in retailing. This demise can be associated in part with the growth of larger scales of activity but is more properly to be explained by the changes in consumer behaviour that have occurred and some deep-seated problems in the operating circumstances of small-unit retailers themselves.

The literature that has been built up around this subject, however, has perhaps become too overly preoccupied with the trends taking place rather than the conditions existing within the small business community. There seems to be a widespread assumption that the demise of the small-unit retailer is necessarily a bad thing and something to be avoided if at all possible. This stems in part from a sentimental attachment to the small shop and a nostalgia for past forms of retailing activity; but it also reflects on a concern for the growth of monopoly powers amongst the large corporate groups and the loss eventually of important localised services. Such a viewpoint tends to ignore the need to inject a higher degree of efficiency into the small business community and that a further reduction in the number of more marginal traders might in fact be to the benefit of those with inherent growth potential. Improvement in the relative trading health of a leaner, but fitter, set of small retail outlets might then become the basis for improving the working conditions of owners and employees and improving the scope in shopping opportunities available to consumers.

This chapter seeks to project and substantiate these arguments in its focus upon the problems facing the small business community. It begins, however, with an elaboration of the trends in numbers and market shares of small retail outlets, pointing to some evidence of pockets of growth within the overall pattern of decline. There then follows a fuller discussion of the causes of decline, including reference to the part played by past planning interventions as well as market processes. The next section considers some of the problems confronting the small business community in more detail using case studies to illustrate the diversity of trading conditions to be found. The final section indicates which types of business are likely to fare best in the future and whether and in what form governmental assistance should be given to those businesses whose prospects are poor.

Recent Trends in Growth and Decline

The terms small shop, small retail outlet and small retail unit have been used interchangeably so far but there are subtle distinctions between them that are sometimes important in interpreting the published statistics available on their number and market share. Generally speaking, a small shop is a fixed premise from which goods or services are sold; but a retail outlet will include market stalls, mobile shops and also traders that call on customers at their homes. The term small retail unit might then refer either to some kind of establishment or to a business which includes several operations but remains relatively small in scale. A further complication can be introduced when different forms of ownership and methods of organisation of businesses are considered. The majority of businesses will contain but a single shop or outlet and are deemed to be independently owned (although the 1971 Census of Distribution classified independents as including businesses that contain up to nine branch establishments). Other businesses, with large numbers of shops or outlets, are referred to as multiples; but some of their establishments may be very small in size and occasionally smaller than those which are independently owned.

While these distinctions are worth noting, we shall talk most commonly in this chapter about the small shop. The definition ascribed to this is that given by Dawson and Kirby: of 'a retail establishment of any form of organisation (but most commonly independently owned) with an annual sales figure of less than approximately £100,000 [perhaps to be raised to £150,000 at the present time] and having fewer than ten employees'.[1] Our chapter title suggests, however, that we are also concerned with related small activities, by which is meant a wide range of retail and commercial services, many of which are intermingled with conventional shops but which operate from premises usually identified in some other way. These might include small post offices, public houses, cafés, garages, hairdressing salons and the like.

Table 10.1: The Decline in Numbers of Retail Units, 1961-1980

A. 1961-1971	1961	1971	% change
Independent shops	446,204	390,793	−12.4
Co-operative shops	29,396	15,413	−47.6
Multiple shops	66,701	66,785	+0.1
Total shops	542,301	472,991	−12.8
B. 1971-1980	1971	1980	% change
Single-outlet retailers	338,210	197,884	−41.5
Small multiple retailers	83,966	76,920	−8.4
Large multiple retailers	87,642	73,797	−15.8
(Co-operative outlets)	(16,480)	(8,556)	−48.1
Total outlets	509,818	348,601	−31.6

Sources: A. *Census of Distribution*, 1961 and 1971; B. Business Monitor, *Retailing*, 1976 and 1980.

It is not possible to provide a comprehensive and consistent statistical analysis of the trends which have been taking place in small-scale activities during the last two or more decades for the methods of compiling and reporting information about them have changed so markedly in the publications of the Business Statistics Office in recent years. Some broad indication can be given, however, by comparing the results of the Censuses of Distribution for 1961 and 1971 with those of the special Business Monitor publications on retailing for 1976 and 1980. Table 10.1 shows the numerical and proportional decline in first the independent sector of trade and then for single-outlet retailers. Two significant features are apparent: firstly, that the rate of closure has quickened over the two decades and that by the end of the 1970s the overall number of small shops in Britain was probably only half that at the beginning of the 1960s; secondly, that the percentage decline was still less than that amongst co-operative outlets, and there is additional evidence that in more recent years it has been less than that for certain kinds of small multiple retailers.

Table 10.2: The Decline in Retail Units by Trade Type, 1976-1978

	1976	1978	% change
Grocers and general food			
Single-outlet retailers	52,780	39,851	−24.5
Small multiple retailers	8,168	4,101	−49.8
Large multiple retailers	8,884	8,336	−6.2
Other foods retailers			
Single-outlet retailers	42,035	40,633	−3.3
Small multiple retailers	15,316	14,887	−2.8
Large multiple retailers	15,365	12,387	−19.4
Confectioners, tobacconists, newsagents			
Single-outlet retailers	36,664	35,772	−2.4
Small multiple retailers	5,415	6,438	+18.9
Large multiple retailers	6,437	7,281	+13.1
Clothing, footwear, textiles			
Single-outlet retailers	30,772	27,663	−10.1
Small multiple retailers	22,253	16,033	−27.9
Large multiple retailers	18,965	16,567	−12.6
Household goods			
Single-outlet retailers	33,800	32,159	−4.8
Small multiple retailers	14,208	12,186	−14.2
Large multiple retailers	12,575	12,014	−4.5
Other non-food goods			
Single-outlet retailers	33,119	28,813	−13.0
Small multiple retailers	12,842	12,111	−5.7
Large multiple retailers	4,420	4,439	+0.4
Mixed retail businesses			
Single-outlet retailers	1,940	3,132	+61.4
Small multiple retailers	468	2,175	+364.7
Large multiple retailers	14,709	13,059	−11.2

Source: Business Monitor, *Retailing*, 1976 and 1978.

This additional evidence comes from the detailed figures available on changes in numbers of shops by kinds of business as well as by organisational groups for 1976 and 1978 (Table 10.2). In 1976, the total number of singly-owned outlets stood at 231,110 but in 1978 had become reduced to 208,023 (a decline of 10 per cent). The comparable figures for outlets belonging to small multiple retailers were 78,670 and 67,931 (a decline of 13.7 per cent); and for co-operative outlets on their own, 11,117 and 10,207 (a decline of 8.2 per cent). Amongst the independents, the greatest numerical decline was experienced by the grocery and general food trades, which showed a net loss of 24 per cent; but for the small multiple retailers, the greatest numerical decline was sustained in clothing, footwear and textiles where there was a net loss of 28 per cent of shops. These are quite astonishing changes to occur over such a short time interval and the magnitude of such changes must reflect in part on slight differences in the classification procedures that have been used. There is the possibility, too, of errors in the reporting since the figures quoted for total numbers of small multiple outlets in 1978 do not gel with those for 1980.

The same volumes, however, provide some pointers to the erosion that has taken place in the trading strength or market share of small shops. By 1978, singly-owned grocery and general food outlets commanded only 22 per cent of the total sales generated within this trade group. The branches of small multiple retailers fared even worse in capturing only 7 per cent of sales. Other poor performers amongst the independents were those in the alcoholic drinks, footwear, men's wear, radio-television and electrical goods, and radio-television hire trades. Small multiple retailer outlets also performed poorly in these trades but were distinctive, too, for their low market shares in motor accessories, confectionery, tobacco requisites and general repair activities. On the brighter side, the independents still seemed to hold a dominant market share in antiques, gifts, cut flowers, newspapers, cycles and second-hand goods. The small multiple retailers seemed strongest in household goods and specialised items but in no individual line of trade were they able to command a higher proportion of sales than either independents or larger multiple firms.

What these and other statistical sources do not reveal, however, are the growth rates that have been achieved in recent years in a variety of small shops and related small activities that have been established by the larger multiple firms. The sorts of examples we have in mind here are the small fast-food outlets, the small limited-line discount outlets, mini-markets and modern convenience stores, new off-licences, and travel agencies. These are in part a response to the generation of new consumer demands but they also reflect in some cases on the scope to penetrate traditional markets previously dominated by independent shops. This latter fact relates to the creation of vacuums in trade in localised communities, where the closure of large numbers of small shops which might have been collectively weak businesses enables the entry and successful operation of fewer, more modern, enterprises. Such a process is explained more generally in the polarisation theory.[2] This assumes that over time, the increasing trend to larger sizes of stores, spaced more widely apart from each other and concentrating on the sale of bulk quantities of goods, leaves behind the opportunity for new small businesses, based at the neighbourhood level and oriented to convenience shopping, to take up a residual trade available. The new small stores then fulfil a role which is essentially complementary to that of the large ones, rather than acting in competition with them. The best expression of this theory to date is the phenomenal growth in modern convenience stores which has taken place over the last ten years in the USA and during which period the average size of new supermarkets or superstores that were opened has almost doubled.[3] Some support for the theory is also seen in Britain in terms of the fact that superstores and hypermarkets appear to have little direct competitive effects on traditional grocers or corner shops.

The chief concern that arises over these recent growth trends amongst small shops is that the contribution of the independents looks to be rather poor. The 1960s held much promise in the rise in number of independent household and specialist goods shops and saw the introduction of the boutique and record shops as well as such initially small firms as Mothercare and the television-hire companies.[4] The 1970s seemed to produce far fewer innovations and what there were came largely from the established multiple retailers. Looking to the 1980s, therefore, one cannot expect to see a renaissance of the small business community, induced at any rate by new modes of independent trading; but it may just be that there will occur a reformation in the more conventional forms of trade brought about by a further rationalisation of those weaker stores both in the independent sector itself and amongst the multiples.

The Causes of Small Business Decline

We have indicated that the decline in numbers and trading strength of small shops and related activities has been due less to direct competition with larger business establishments than to underlying changes in consumer behaviour and the operating circumstances of small unit retailers themselves. The central problem appears to have been the failure by many small businesses to adapt to the evolving trends in demand and supply, particularly the trends to bulk purchasing by the population and to mass distribution by the producers of goods and services. In some cases, the necessary adaptation required has simply been impossible to achieve by virtue of the limited sizes of the businesses concerned; but for others the difficulties of adjusting to new market processes have been exacerbated by unfavourable planning interventions which, while often unintentional, have hindered their modernisation or expansion.[5] These limitations, however, must also be considered against the fact that, given the trends to larger scales of activity, there have been too many small shops that have remained as vestiges of past forms of retailing. The surfeit of small shops in recent years has led to increasing competition amongst themselves at a time when the demand for the sorts of goods and services they offer has been diminishing.

Changing Demand and Supply Factors

The diminishing demand for small shops can be recognised in three ways. Firstly, the role of the small shop within most communities has changed during the past two decades from being an institution that was essentially the primary source for most household shopping requirements to one that is now just supportive to the larger retail outlets that have emerged. In other words, for a majority of consumers, it has become a source of topping-up or supplementing the main basket of goods which is obtained elsewhere. This will be true not just for food items, but for hardware, electrical, clothing and many other goods as well. Secondly, loyalty to the small shop in terms of continuing to use it as a major source of shopping has remained strongest amongst the poorer, more elderly and more immobile sections of the population. These are clearly the weakest consumer groups within the population with most of their spending being directed at lower-quality products where profit margins are low. Their loyalty is in any case a dubious one, determined more by their lack of access to larger stores than by a genuine concern to support small shops. The third way in which a reduced demand for small shops can be seen is in the changing relationship between their prevailing patterns of location and those of the population as a whole. Small shops tend to remain more dominant forms of trading in those two parts of the environment, the inner areas of cities and more isolated rural areas, from which there has been the greatest proportional population decline in recent years. In absolute terms, the greatest shift in consumption has taken place from the inner urban areas to the suburbs; but the erosion of the population base in many outlying rural areas has created particularly serious problems for small shops in these localities. Looking at the three trends in demand collectively, therefore, small shops have found themselves increasingly oriented to selling small quantities of goods to customers with generally low levels of purchasing power and under circumstances where their trade areas are steadily being eroded.

These trading difficulties, however, are further compounded by the physical conditions in which most small businesses have to operate. The basic problem is the small amount of selling space which is generally available within a shop which restricts the range of goods that can be displayed, hampers customer access and internal movement and limits the scope for presenting goods in attractive and variable ways. Most premises, too, by virtue of their age, and whether or not they are converted houses or purpose-designed units, are poorly laid out to receive deliveries of goods and difficult to enlarge. These strictures of size then constrain the volume of stocks that can be held which in turn means that frequent acquisitions of goods must be made, involving either direct shipments from supplier firms or the shopkeeper himself visiting cash and carry and other wholesaling depots. This leads not only to high transport costs being incurred but also to an inability to buy large quantities of goods at discounted prices. For some independent retailers these distribution problems have become particularly acute through the restrictions placed by larger supplier firms and also larger cash and carry operators on the amount of goods that can be delivered or purchased in any one transaction.[6] Such restrictions mean that small retailers then have to work through a small intermediary firm to obtain relatively modest supplies which will inevitably cost more (in proportional terms) than those available through other, larger channels. In comparison to larger retail outlets, small shops may also incur disproportionately higher overhead costs in terms of the amount of money tied up in interest payments on bank loans for stock, on rents paid as a percentage of both turnover and profits and from the expenditure incurred in the physical upkeep of ageing premises. Finally, there is the burden of paperwork to endure, particularly related to the filing of VAT returns, which tends to be a much more time-consuming and difficult undertaking for the smaller businessman than for chain companies. Adding all these considerations together means that the owner or manager of a small shop can only offer a limited range of goods to his customers and the prices of these will generally be considerably higher than those found in larger stores. Over time the range of goods is likely to become still further reduced and prices to continue to escalate as other factors on the demand side affect the general scale of the operation. A deterrent effect on consumers may set in which, coupled with the attractions of larger stores elsewhere, will ultimately lead to the closure of the small shop. The accumulation of problems which typically produce such a result is summarised in Figure 10.1.

Figure 10.1: The Process of Decline amongst Small Shops

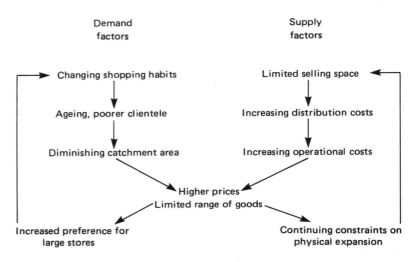

This general process of decline, however, will be complicated in individual circumstances, not least by the resilience and determination of a store's owner or manager. Too often, nevertheless, the owner or manager is insufficiently experienced or knowledgeable about the root problems that confront him to do more than stave off closure until a later day. Several studies have pointed to the lack of training and expertise amongst independent retailers,[7] particularly in the field of business methods, and perhaps not unexpectedly it is financial difficulties incurred that such retailers themselves perceive as the main contribution to their demise. Dawson and Kirby,[8] in a survey of small shops in Derby, Exeter and Port Talbot, found that it was the very smallest businesses (those with an annual turnover in 1976 of £15,000 or less) which experienced the greatest financial strains and that these were particularly marked amongst household goods shops, confectioners, tobacconists and newsagents, and the census category of 'other non-food' shops. When questioned about the causes of their difficulties, however, the main response was to cite the national economic situation, which presumably encompassed a number of considerations ranging from depressed consumer demand to inflation and relatively high interest rates. The second most important reason cited was the general cost of overheads.

The same survey confirmed the findings of many of the impact studies that the factor of supermarket and/or superstore competition was not seen to be a particularly significant problem amongst the vast majority of small (mainly independent) retailers. While this may be true, however, we ought at this stage to make three qualifications regarding the general evidence obtained about trading effects. Firstly, we have pointed to the fact that over time the increase in sizes of new large stores introduced into the retail system has led to a shift in the direction of competition away from the smaller independent shops to the smaller branches of the multiples. While the number of smaller multiple outlets adversely affected may be few, and of relatively little concern to the parent companies, the consequence of their possible closure in particular localities may be much greater than that of any independents. This will be due to the fact that, as their share of market trade indicates, they will be serving on average a larger proportion of customers. Secondly, and linked to this, the upper limit that has been taken to define what constitutes a small shop ought perhaps to be raised over time, in relation to the increased sizes of new large stores, to include those now relatively smaller intermediate-sized shops that are bearing the brunt of direct competition. Thirdly, most of the evidence about the competitive effects of new large stores has been based around the introduction of either supermarkets or superstores and our understanding of what has taken place *vis-à-vis* the discount retail warehouses or other large innovations is sketchy to say the least.

Effects of Public and Private Policies

In various chapters throughout this book, we have also referred to the way in which government interventions into the retail system and the actions of corporate organisations have contributed to the decline of the small shop. These effects have been both general and specific. At the general level, one of the by-products of town and country planning policies has been a reinforcement of the changing pattern of consumer demand, especially the shift in population concentration from the inner city to the suburbs; and the abolition of resale price maintenance has been seen to have given the larger retail companies an unfair trading advantage over smaller firms. More specifically, a number of planning measures can be itemised which have led directly to the closure of small shops and these can be matched in three instances by the adverse consequences arising from corporate growth. They are listed quite baldly here since they have usually been elaborated upon elsewhere.

Planning Effects. (a) Urban redevelopment programmes. These have led to the clearance of large numbers of small shops and related small activities in both the inner city and central area. Such clearance may have made way for new housing, new shopping centre developments or a variety of other new land uses. Numerous other small shops may also have been forced to close as a result of planning blight, created perhaps by redevelopment in a nearby area or through the expectation that they might eventually themselves be displaced.

(b) Development control policies. In this case the effects are more complex and difficult to trace but relate to the emphasis on the centralisation of retailing by planners. By encouraging most retailing activity to be concentrated in town and city centres, competition for the most accessible sites within the central area has been intensified over time and multiples have come to dominate the high street. Small shops have therefore been relegated to secondary positions where their potential for trade has become eroded as the main action space for consumers (influenced by the location of magnet stores) has contracted.[9] Elsewhere in the city, small shops have been forced to take up sites in highly centralised shopping centres, but where the principle of centralisation has been linked to the idea that people should be able to walk to shops. The lack of foresight regarding the increased use of cars for shopping and the strictures placed against shopping centres evolving alongside main roads have led eventually to the decline of small shops in residential areas.[10]

(c) Traffic management schemes. There has been very little study of the deleterious effects on small shops of traffic management schemes but it is safe to assume that a combination of parking restrictions along main roads, the closure of many side streets joining arterials, the barrier effect on local movement created by some urban motorways and the introduction of one-way systems will have depleted the trading base of many small businesses, particularly in inner city areas. Many services, such as garages, cafés and public houses will have been particularly affected. As in the case of redevelopment, however, the closures that will have taken place might be seen as a necessary sacrifice for achieving more important goals in the planning process.

Company Effects. (a) Company rationalisation programmes. Most of the large corporate groups in retailing have implemented extensive rationalisation programmes during the last two decades to rid themselves of relatively uneconomic small units. Some of these units have been closed not by virtue of a record of trading losses but rather on the basis of their future anticipated weakness given changes in the company's distribution system or new merchandising policies to be effected. In many cases, the sale of the properties involved has been used to finance new large-scale developments. The co-operative movement has been instrumental in the largest number of closures (40 per cent of their outlets being closed between 1961 and 1971) and this has been bound up with the broader attempt to create an organisation of regional rather than locally-based societies.[11] During the first half of the 1970s, Tesco closed 182 of their small shops and Sainsbury 52.

(b) Mergers and takeovers. A further example of rationalisation takes place when there are mergers between firms or one takes over another. Here, small branches of either company involved may be closed down not so much because of inherent economic deficiencies but because of a duplicity in functions or the over-representativeness of the new group in a particular area. At the root of this will often be a general decline in consumer demand for the types of goods which the two companies are selling. Thus Burtons and Jackson-the-Tailor came together and released many of their smaller properties against a background of reduced demand for made-to-measure suits. The acquisition of Timothy Whites by Boots in 1968 occurred at a time of diminishing profits on pharmaceutical goods and when there was growing competition from other stores in the trade for cosmetics and 'soft' household goods.

(c) Shopping centre tenancies. The high rents commanded by most purpose-built shopping centres will often put at risk a number of small multiple branch outlets which are opened up with the expectation of realising high turnovers but fail to reach them. Among many of the chain companies operating from small outlets, fine adjustments are made to the amount of stock carried and number of employees engaged in relation to turnover, so that rent becomes a critical determinant of success. If a certain threshold on sales cannot be achieved, or if there is a sudden and sustained drop in trade or the rent itself is increased, then closure of a particular store can quickly follow. Some stores have in fact been known to have their rents deliberately increased by centre owners in order to force them out and have them replaced by alternative, more promising performers. High rents and also in some cases discriminatory tenant-mix policies have, of course, deterred many small independent retailers from occupying the more successful purpose-built shopping centres but these facts are difficult to tie in with the general process of decline. They are more properly part of a series of problems that confront those small businesses which might be relatively healthy but have difficulty in expanding or finding more ideal sites.[12] We shall move away at this juncture from examining the broad factors that lead to the closure of small shops and consider some of the variable trading characteristics of particular types of small shops.

Characteristics of Small Shops

The small business community is extremely heterogeneous and some emphasis should be given to the individual personalities projected by small shops operating in highly localised circumstances. Instead of providing a systematic account of the different conditions to be found among the principal trade groups, therefore, this section offers some comparisons by way of case examples. The typical characteristics of the traditional corner shop are examined first; followed by those for a grocery shop affiliated to a voluntary trading group, the independent pharmacist, and branch owners of a chain organisation of confectioners, tobacconists and newsagents.

The Traditional Corner Shop

There have been several studies of the traditional corner shop focusing in particular on the social aspects of its operation and the precarious nature of its trading base.[13] The majority of these businesses are family managed, typically a husband and wife team who live on the premises and own both the shop and flat. Male involvement in the business of selling is therefore high in relation to other forms of retailing and there is a greater proportion of full-time employment, with usually but one part-time assistant engaged. Long hours are worked, one survey reporting an average of 54 hours per week with 47 per cent of shops being open on a Sunday, this necessitated in part by a meagre turnover returned but also by the essential role of the shop as a convenience outlet and the ability of the owners to be on hand to open up at unusual times.[14] The commitment required to endure these working conditions for a low level of income means that the average age of owners has been increasing over time, with fewer sons and daughters being prepared to take over the running of a shop when parents have died or retired. A notable exception concerns the acquisition of corner shops by Asian immigrants who, perhaps by cultural background, appear to be more willing to work longer hours at a younger age. Comparisons of independent grocery shops operated by immigrants with those operated by English-born persons show the former to be even more heavily characterised by male employment, but where premises will be more typically rented, of slightly larger size and generating higher levels of sales.

The term 'corner shop' is a vernacular one that is not strictly synonymous with a particular line of trade; hence it is difficult to provide an accurate statistical assessment of the economic performances and problems experienced by this group. If we assume that the majority function principally as grocery shops, however, then the survey quoted above shows that the mean annual turnover realised in 1974 was £34,700 from an average floor space size of 422 square feet (40 m²). Only 35 per cent of the sample (of 816 shops) operated their business on a self-service basis; and most relied on secondary lines of trade (such as confectionery, fruit and vegetables and toys) to supplement their sales. Stocks were acquired in a variety of ways, but 41 per cent of shops were members of voluntary trading groups (principally the larger ones operated by younger owners) and only 26 per cent of shops obtained more than 90 per cent of their goods from cash and carry depots. The acquisition of stock and stock shortages were seen as a significant problem by some operators, but the majority blamed high rates, inflation and VAT for most of their trading difficulties. Somewhat surprisingly, despite the historical record of a high rate of mortality amongst corner shops, most operators were also generally optimistic about the future viability of their businesses.

A Voluntary Group Grocery Shop

Symbol chains have brought a number of significant advantages to independent grocers, particularly the ability to have large quantities of stock delivered frequently at relatively low cost and to be able to sell own-label goods to customers at cheaper prices.[15] In addition, they have helped to improve the physical appearance of shops, by providing fascia boards and display materials, and to assist in financial and management matters, by arranging for advertising, loans, training programmes and incentive schemes for high sales achievement. The obligations to the retailer are relatively few, mainly to show some loyalty to the general merchandising policies of the organisation and to place regular stock orders of a certain minimum required size.

This latter constraint on a minimum size of order has become increasingly significant over recent years in two respects. Firstly, it has enabled a symbol chain to keep down its delivery costs and contributed to a more efficient buying process in the acquisition of goods from agricultural and manufacturer sources. Secondly, it has been useful as a screening device in the recruitment of members to the organisation, to distinguish those independent retailers who will likely enhance the overall trading strength of the group. Not unexpectedly, therefore, the majority of affiliated symbol stores are larger in size than the average corner shop and have turnover levels sufficient to allow for the recruitment of several staff.[16] The thrust of their operation will be directed at competing with the smaller supermarkets and capturing a high proportion of weekly bulk orders of grocery goods rather than relying simply on convenience trade. The following example has been quoted by the Chairman of VG as to what he considered (in 1980) to be an ideal type of affiliated food retailer:

he has 1,600 square feet (150 m^2) (gross) and a net sales area of 1,250 square feet (120 m^2). His sales in 1978 were £260,000. The store has the full range of grocery requirements, the full range of provisions, a good produce section, a bakery section, and an off-licence. His hours are 8.30-5.30 and a late night on Friday. The staff, outside his wife and himself, one full-time, 14 part-time. The market that he is serving is a 1,000 house estate and these 1,000 houses are within a half-mile radius of his store. The parade that his store is in contains a hairdresser, wool shop, CTN, butcher and hardware shop. The socio-economic group that he is serving is C1, C2 and D which is the very best you can serve as a grocery retailer. Parking, 15 cars which is inadequate but better than nothing. The competition consists of another Spar store about a mile away, the town centre is a mile and a half away, and includes Tesco and Sainsbury, and then 5 miles away an Asda Superstore — typical competition for this kind of store.[17]

The Independent Retail Pharmacist

Retail pharmacy is a trade category in which there has been little development of voluntary trading organisations (Numark being an exception with 2,000 members) and in which relatively little use is also made of cash and carry facilities. Most distribution is effected via traditional wholesalers which, together with the need for variable deliveries of small quantities of goods but over a wide range of specialised commodities, leads to high costs in the acquisition of stock. This is but one of several trading difficulties that the independent pharmacists have had to contend with, the others relating to increased competition from both large stores and new health centres, legislative restrictions on their mode of operation, and an extremely variable pattern in their locational characteristics. The collective effects of these problems led to an average decline in number of outlets by 2 per cent per annum between 1966 and 1976, although since then there has been a diminution in the rate of closure and 1980 saw a net loss of only 28 establishments.[18]

Adverse competition has developed in two directions: firstly, from the growth in dispensing functions performed not only by health centres and by some doctors but also from a new wave of drugstores, although recent legislation has curtailed the range of proprietary medicines that the latter may prescribe; secondly, through the increased share of trade on cosmetics and toiletries that supermarkets and superstores have commanded in recent years. It is from these 'over the counter' sales, of course, that the independent pharmacist will normally obtain his highest profit margins. Like the corner shop and unaffiliated grocery store, however, the traditional chemist suffers from being too tradition bound. The age structure of registered independent pharmacists is dominated by those in advanced years, 20 per cent being over 60 in 1977, and while every pharmacist has had to become qualified in the profession, few have had training in the commercial aspects of retailing as such and it does not necessarily follow that a skilled chemist will have a good business acumen as well.[19] Proposals that pharmacists might capitalise more on their professional skills, such as taking over some of the routine diagnostic functions of medical practitioners, have always been frustrated by central government; and such activities as running a mobile dispensary are still illegal under present regulations. Finally, there are the problems of location which stem from the conflict of seeking to trade as a shop as well as being a focus of basic health needs. Considerable imbalances in the incidence of chemists have arisen at both the regional and local levels. Bates has shown that in 1974, Wales had the highest density of chemists, with each shop serving an average 3,830 people, while East Anglia had the lowest density of one per 6,710 people.[20] Broadly speaking, he found that low densities were also associated with areas of recent high population growth and which are relatively prosperous with high levels of personal mobility while high densities were characteristic of older, declining industrial areas, tourist areas or areas which had fragmented markets. Close study of the closures of pharmacies in Greater Manchester and Lincolnshire also indicated that few local areas suffered a loss in accessibility to chemist shops for most of the closures represented a rationalisation of duplicated outlets trading from the same location. Combining these findings with the population shifts that had taken place in Lincolnshire, Bates concluded 'any increase in the difficulty of reaching a pharmacy in the country arises not so much from the changing distribution of outlets as from general transport problems'.

Branch Outlets of Multiple Confectioners, Tobacconists and News-agents

The branch outlets of multiple CTN companies combine many of the characteristics of the three types of shops described above. Like the grocery shop affiliated to a voluntary trading group, they will be subject to some central organisation of their operations, particularly on the distribution side but also in this case more closely on their selling techniques. Like the unaffiliated corner store, however, they will also be required to concentrate on the provision of a convenience trade and experience all of the unsociable hours of opening that this entails. Being purveyors of small, often specialised goods they will resemble too the independent pharmacist, carrying perhaps thousands of lines but where 90 per cent of sales will be generated from just a few hundred standard items.

Their own uniqueness stems perhaps from the fact that they engage in essentially very small-scale activities within the framework of a large organisation. Like the sub-post offices, with which they are often linked as a single trading outlet, they carry a special social role within the community. Sometimes as much as a third of a CTN's sales will be obtained before eight o'clock in the morning, in part from the delivery of papers and in part from shop purchases by people on their way to work.[21] Further peaks in trade occur at other times during the day as other special groups within the community drop by: children on their way to or from school, mothers and retired people in the mid-morning, passers-by and perhaps a local workforce during the lunch period. On Sunday morning, especially, the local CTN often becomes a collecting point for large numbers of the population, when the purchase of papers is combined with a stroll, exercising the dog or simply getting some fresh air. A small brigade of boys and girls will be employed each day, forging still closer links with the community.

Such local integration, however, has to be achieved within relatively strict codes of efficiency and profitability. The operators of the stores are usually managers who will be guaranteed a certain level of income whatever the customer support that is gained. Not unexpectedly, therefore, we find that the trend in new CTN outlets that are opened by the multiple companies is once more to larger sizes of stores and to a reduction in the standardisation of the stock that is held. To some extent too, however, the larger sizes of the newer stores have been dictated by a relative saturation of the traditional locations preferred by CTNs, namely the neighbourhood centre of an estate of say 1,000 houses where they can establish a virtual monopoly on trade. Increasingly, the multiple companies have looked to sites in town and district shopping centres where both an overall greater amount of competition, not just from other CTN businesses but from variety stores and superstores as well, and the greater amounts of pedestrian traffic to be found tend to dictate a diversification in the trading effort and the promotion of keener prices, which comes down to achieving larger scales of economy again.[22]

Possible Forms of Assistance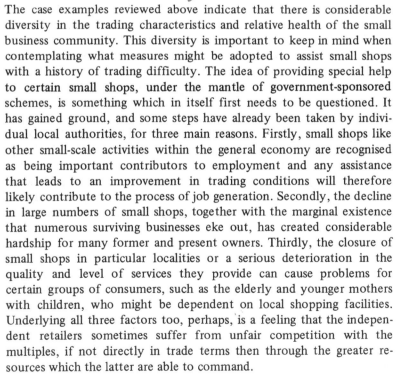

The case examples reviewed above indicate that there is considerable diversity in the trading characteristics and relative health of the small business community. This diversity is important to keep in mind when contemplating what measures might be adopted to assist small shops with a history of trading difficulty. The idea of providing special help to certain small shops, under the mantle of government-sponsored schemes, is something which in itself first needs to be questioned. It has gained ground, and some steps have already been taken by individual local authorities, for three main reasons. Firstly, small shops like other small-scale activities within the general economy are recognised as being important contributors to employment and any assistance that leads to an improvement in trading conditions will therefore likely contribute to the process of job generation. Secondly, the decline in large numbers of small shops, together with the marginal existence that numerous surviving businesses eke out, has created considerable hardship for many former and present owners. Thirdly, the closure of small shops in particular localities or a serious deterioration in the quality and level of services they provide can cause problems for certain groups of consumers, such as the elderly and younger mothers with children, who might be dependent on local shopping facilities. Underlying all three factors too, perhaps, is a feeling that the independent retailers sometimes suffer from unfair competition with the multiples, if not directly in trade terms then through the greater resources which the latter are able to command.

Given these justifications for why there should be some form of governmental assistance to small shops, the next question that arises is which ones should be eligible or should qualify for help? Should the assistance be directed at just the very smallest of shops, in which case some size definition will need to be invoked? Should it be aimed at just the independent and, if so, what will be the cut-off point at which a growing business joins the ranks of the multiples? More important than either of these perhaps is the consideration as to whether all types of trade categories should be eligible for assistance or whether it should be available only for those who can demonstrate that certain positive benefits would accrue to society as a whole.[23] There are two particular dimensions to this. Firstly, it has been indicated that there is considerable variability in the growth potential of small shops. Some of the more traditional forms of retailing, such as the draper, haberdasher, shoe repairer and barber, have been among the more vulnerable small shops and are likely to continue to decline in the future. Other small shops, affiliated to voluntary trading groups or operating on a franchise basis, receive considerable assistance already from their parent organisations. Still others might be deemed to be the new innovative small shops, like the boutiques of a generation ago, the unisex hair stylists and mini-markets. It is this latter group which holds most promise for growth in the years ahead and arguably, where they encounter trading difficulties, especially in their formative stages, are most deserving of help. The second point that needs to be made is that small shops vary considerably in terms of the consumers that they serve. On the one hand, there are many that are community-based and make up the predominant trade types of our neighbourhood centres. Some of these, like the grocery shop, chemist and post office, might be seen to be essential components of the retail system, especially in these locations, and again are therefore deserving of assistance whenever this may be genuinely required.[24] On the other hand, there are other small shops, like the off-licence and fish and chip shop, which are frequently found in neighbourhood areas but which command support from only certain sections of the surrounding population. More questionable as candidates for governmental assistance are small betting shops, second-hand shops and the burgeoning number of sex shops. A summary of the different types of trade categories that would need to be considered in any comprehensive policy to assist small shops is given in Table 10.3.

There are three main ways in which governmental assistance could and, in some instances, has been provided: through a set of financial provisions, the removal of various restrictive legislation and by extending the special advisory and support services that have been established to help small manufacturing businesses. The more specific options available along these lines are summarised in Table 10.4.

Table 10.3: Variable Types of Small Shops and Related Small Businesses

	Convenience	Specialist	Service
Traditional	Fish shop	Draper	Shoe repair
Affiliated	Grocery shop	TV rental	Petrol station
Innovative	Mini-market	Boutique	Hair stylist
Essential	General store	Chemist	Post office
Acceptable	Off-licence	Bookshop	Fish and chips
Questionable	Second-hand shop	Sex shop	Betting shop

Table 10.4: Possible Forms of Assistance to Small Shops

Subsidies and grants	Relaxation of regulations	Research and training
Rent relief	Planning controls	Consultancy service
Special loans	Tax controls	Training programmes
Subsidised incomes	Trade controls	Pensions/qualifications

Subsidies and Grants

Probably the most common form of assistance seen to date in Britain has been the rent and rate relief given to many small shops occupying premises owned by a local authority. Rents and/or rates have been lowered below accepted market values when shops deemed to be desirable to retain in a local area have experienced considerable trading difficulties. Small multiple branch outlets, as well as independents, have been subsidised in this way in many of the failed shopping centre developments of the inner city. It is doubtful, however, if any small shops have been given rent or rate relief to enable them to trade competitively in the large, successful shopping centres to be found in central areas. As a general principle, the main advantage of using this form of relief is that particular shops deserving of some form of assistance and being important to a local community can be singled out for special treatment. On the debit side, it is a policy that inevitably props up the weaker elements of retailing and often covers up for serious planning mistakes over the spatial allocation of shopping facilities.

The provision of special loans and grants to small retail businesses is a second potential way in which financial assistance may be given. Apart from a few very specific funds made available, such as by some local authorities to assist in environmental improvement schemes, however, there has been no general source of funding in Britain to help either new businesses to get started, growing businesses to expand, or older businesses to overcome temporary trading difficulties. This is in contrast to other countries in the European Community where, for example in France, Italy and Denmark, special loans are available for modernising shop premises, installing new equipment and establishing particular new trading activities.[25] The Enterprise Zones in Britain, of course, provide generous grants for all forms of industrial activity but their location, in the decaying parts of cities, are hardly attractive to potential shop investors.

Guaranteed minimum levels of income are a further way in which certain, presumably specially selected, small shops might be given financial assistance. To some extent, the National Health Service payments made to pharmacists for the prescriptions they make up and the base salaries accorded to sub-post office operators by the PO constitute two forms of income subsidy that are already in practice in Britain. In Norway, attempts have been made to ensure that surviving stores in remote localities are given every possible means of assistance to enable the operators to earn an adequate living.[26] Besides grants being available for modernisation and the purchase of new equipment, grants can be obtained to defray the everyday running costs of a store. To qualify, a store 'must play an important role in the community by providing a sufficient range of goods to provide the local community with a balanced diet, by being open throughout the year and by being at least four kilometres from the next general store', as well as being below a certain threshold on turnover size.[27]

Relaxation of Regulations

While financial problems are often a major cause of concern to small businesses, the chief complaint of most operators when drawn to the subject of government intervention is that there is too much interference in their trading practices. It is frequently asserted that if planning and building regulations were relaxed, VAT abolished or substantially reduced, corporate taxes and national insurance contributions brought down and some of the trade licensing laws revoked, then many of the financial difficulties which retailers incur would simply disappear overnight and there would be no need for the sorts of governmental assistance schemes identified above. Such reasoning is rather compelling if somewhat glib, but it is difficult to see how small shops can be treated differentially from the rest of business over such broad areas of legislation. A loosening of trade controls and lessening of the tax burden applied to all forms of retailing might ultimately be to the disadvantage of small shops. However, in so far as planning is concerned and especially development controls, we have indicated before that there could and should be much scope for improving the choice of sites and allowing most retail firms a greater freedom to locate where they want. The designation of certain parts of the city where this might occur was outlined in Chapter 4. If coupled with a set of freer environmental and building controls, small shops would find it easier to occupy cheaper premises in more accessible positions than they do at present.

Research and Training

Bates' study of the independent grocery trade indicated that 65 per cent of present owners of small shops had not previously had any experience of retailing and entered into business simply to gain more personal independence, to change the nature of their work or fulfil some family obligation. Since we might surmise that few will also have had any formal education in business methods, the majority would seem to be ill-equipped to make the most of whatever trading opportunities present themselves or to overcome trading difficulties when these might arise. Although there are several professional persons, such as accountants, solicitors and bank managers, to whom they can go for general advice, there is no official body in Britain that oversees the provision of specialist retailing advice. This is again in contrast to several other EC countries where there is an assortment of institutes that offer consultancy services directed specifically at assisting the small shopkeeper. In the Netherlands, the Central Small Business Institute (CIMK) and the Economic Institute for Small Business (EIM) tend to focus on the dissemination of information and undertaking research for individual clients; in France, so-called 'modernisation instructors' are trained at the Centre de Formation des Assistants Techniques du Commerce (CEFAC) and made available to businesses to assist on practical problems; in Denmark, the Technological Institutes at Copenhagen and Arhus oversee the activities of approximately 100 trade consultants who offer advice of both an educational and practical kind.[28]

A further way in which the business skills of small shopkeepers, and their staff, can be improved is through the provision of more formal educational and training programmes. However, the extent to which, say, a national programme of short and long courses on retailing offered at further education and technical colleges would ultimately lead to significant, visible improvements in the efficiency of small shops is difficult to assess. The increase in 'in-house' training programmes offered by the large multiple firms and the concomitant growth in their economic success in recent years suggests that over time the benefits might be considerable. Unfortunately, Britain currently offers few practical courses in its colleges, either on a full-time or part-time basis, to which young aspiring small retailers might be attracted and there is virtually nothing available to the established independent trader. The Distributive Industry Training Board and the College for the Distributive Trades have made some contribution to the overall training and educational process, but the DITB is shortly to be closed.

Concern over the low levels of efficiency amongst small shops, together with their high rate of birth and decline, has been one of the factors behind the maintenance of licensing controls in Italy and the Netherlands. Over time, the granting of licences to establish a new small business has increasingly become contingent on obtaining a certificate of proficiency in retailing, usually derived from completing a vocational training programme. France has likewise encouraged its younger entrants into retail ownership to undertake preparatory courses, offered through the auspices of Chambers of Commerce as well as technical colleges, but has also actively sought to entice more elderly shopkeepers to retire, by offering them special pensions and the chance, if appropriate, to retrain.[29] In each of these cases, an attempt is being made, albeit indirectly, to shift the balance in composition of the small business community away from entrepreneurs who are ageing, tradition-bound and relatively unskilled to those who are younger, more innovative and hopefully better prepared.

Taking stock of all the various forms of assistance that could be provided for small shops it would seem that Britain has lagged behind other European countries in terms of committing itself to a clear-cut programme of action. The argument against this is that the problems of small shops have often been more severe in other countries and therefore the need for major government initiatives in Britain has been that much less. The rationale behind the need for policy-making is in any case complicated by the fact that market processes have already proved to be a fairly effective regulator of the amount of small-scale business activity in Britain; and that where government intervention has occurred in a more indirect way, such as through planning controls, it has tended to exacerbate rather than alleviate the problems of small shops. Perhaps the best line of approach to be taken in the future is to assist in the promotion of those sorts of conditions in which the small business community can do more to help itself. This would require a combination of some relaxation in the nature of regulatory controls and the provision of special training schemes and consultancy services to improve the business expertise of store operators. The case for providing direct forms of financial assistance at the local level is really applicable only to certain types of essential community-based shops.

Conclusion

The problems of small shops and related small activities have commanded a great deal of attention in recent years but little progress has been made in identifying the most appropriate ways in which these problems should be addressed or action taken to help resolve them. There is a general reluctance on the part of both central and local government to intervene and the various agencies representing the small business community, including chambers of commerce and trade, seem powerless to halt the decline of their membership. The public, too, appears to be fickle in its general attitude towards the independent trader. On the one hand, most people would profess to find the small shop a beneficial and even necessary feature of the retail environment; but on the other hand, a clear majority are no longer loyal in the sense of patronising them in preference to the larger multiple stores. For the mass of the population, the small shop has been relegated to fulfilling a secondary role, except when circumstances prevent a choice being made. It is in this context, however, that the retail and commercial planner is faced with a dilemma: that the small shop will often be seen to be indispensable and for certain minority groups can be of inestimable value. This means that special regard must be given to their spatial incidence and especially to those that offer more essential services. The chief obligations are to meet their locational requirements as they would perceive them and to allow them to trade in as unfettered a way as is practicably (and responsibly) possible.

References

1.   Dawson, J.A. and Kirby, D.A., *Small-Scale Retailing in the UK* (Saxon House, Farnborough, 1979).

2.   Kirby, D.A., 'The Convenience Store Phenomenon: the Rebirth of America's Small Shop', *Retail Distribution and Management*, vol. 4, no. 3 (1976), pp. 31-3.
3.   Ibid.
4.   Schiller, R., 'What the Census Says About Shops', *Chartered Surveyor*, vol. 109, no. 6 (1977), pp. 190-2.
5.   Davies, R.L., 'The Recent History and Problems of Small Shops and Related Small Businesses', in Jones, P.M. and Oliphant, R. (eds.), *Local Shops: Problems and Prospects* (Unit for Retail Planning Information, Reading, 1976).
6.   Kirby, D.A., 'Supply Problems of Small Unit Grocers: A Case Study', *International Journal of Physical Distribution*, vol. 4, no. 5 (1974), pp. 276-85.
7.   See, for example: Bates, P., *The Independent Grocery Retailer: Characteristics and Problems – A Report of a Survey* (Manchester Business School, Retail Outlets Research Unit, 1976); Berry, R.K., *Public and Private Policies Towards Small Shops* (Retailing and Planning Associates, Corbridge, 1978).
8.   Dawson, J.A. and Kirby, D.A., *Small-Scale Retailing*, 1979.
9.   Seeley, L.E.S., 'The Decline of Small Shops', in Jones, P.M. and Oliphant, R. (eds.), *Local Shops: Problems and Prospects*.
10.   Maroney, A., 'The Decline of Small Shops in Liverpool and the Problems Involved in Providing New Facilities', in Jones, P.M. and Oliphant, R. (eds.), *Local Shops: Problems and Prospects*.
11.   Berry, R.K., *Policies Towards Small Shops*.
12.   Bechofer, F., Elliott, B. and Rushforth, M., 'The Market Situation of Small Shopkeepers', *Scottish Journal of Political Economy*, vol. 18 (1971), pp. 161-80.
13.   For example: Burns, W., 'The Despised Corner Shop', *The Surveyor*, vol. 113 (1954), pp. 823-4; Cheer, J.S., 'The Isolated Corner Shop in Residential Areas', *Journal of the Royal Town Planning Institute*, vol. 44 (1957), pp. 16-18.
14.   Bates, P., *Independent Grocery Retailer*.
15.   National Economic Development Office, Distributive Trades EDC, *Voluntary Group Trading: Six Case Studies* (HMSO, London, 1971).
16.   Economist Intelligence Unit, *Retail Distribution in Britain* (London, 1976).
17.   Branston, R.A., 'The Grocery Voluntary Group View', in *Local Shopping Centres and Convenience Stores: Report of an URPI Workshop* (Unit for Retail Planning Information, Reading, 1980).
18.   A.C. Nielson Co. Ltd., 'How Healthy are Retail Pharmacies?', *Nielsen Researcher*, no. 1 (1981).
19.   Bates, P., *Retail Pharmacies: Their Changing Distribution* (Manchester Business School, Retail Outlets Research Unit, 1977).
20.   Ibid.
21.   Schweitzer, R.G., 'The View of a CTN Retailer', in *Local Shopping Centres and Convenience Stores*.
22.   Ibid.
23.   Davies, R.L., 'Planning Solutions to the Problems of the Small Shop', *Town and Country Planning*, vol. 44 (1976), pp. 215-20.
24.   Planning and Transportation Committee of the Association of Metropolitan Authorities, 'The Preservation of Essential Shopping Facilities', in *Local Shopping Centres and Convenience Stores*.
25.   Commission of the European Communities, 'Synoptic Tables of the Specific

Measures Taken by the Member States of the European Communities in the Field of Commerce', *Commerce and Distribution Series 3* (Brussels, 1977).

26. Kirby, D.A. *et al., The Norwegian Aid Programme to Shops in Sparsely Populated Areas – An Assessment of the First Four Years* (Norwegian Fund For Market and Distribution Research, 1981).
27. Dawson, J.A. and Kirby, D.A., *Small-Scale Retailing.*
28. Commission of the European Communities, 'Synoptic Tables of Specific Measures'.
29. Beaujeu-Garnier, J. and Bouveret-Gauer, M., 'Retail Planning in France', in Davies, R.L. (ed.), *Retail Planning in the European Community* (Saxon House, Farnborough, 1979).

11 ACCESSIBILITY, TRANSPORT AND COMMUNICATIONS

This chapter is somewhat shorter than others in this book but has been included to indicate that transport considerations are a special concern of retail and commercial planning. Obviously, these considerations will normally come within the compass of transport planning; but transport planning is itself a broad field and too often in the past the interests of retailers and both their suppliers and customers have received only scant attention. There is a case, as we have argued in Chapter 4, for a specific plan to be formulated that deals with these interests separately, although the overall planning context within which such a plan is placed is perhaps immaterial.

There are two traditional problem areas that warrant greater scrutiny. The first relates to the concept of accessibility and the differing degrees of ease with which suppliers and customers can visit individual shops and shopping centres. The problems here are bound up with those of other movements, such as commuting and freight haulage, and therefore need to be addressed through comprehensive transport policies; but in the matter of traffic control, some distinctively retail-related measures can be taken to improve circulation within the largest shopping centres, especially city centres. The second set of problems relates to the difficulties that are incurred by both suppliers and customers once they have reached their destinations. Their reception facilities, in terms of servicing bays, car parks, bus stations and the like, are frequently deficient in both quantity and quality. There is also a newer set of problems that will require increasing investigation in the future, that has less to do with physical transportation and pertains to the growth in telecommunication systems and other computerised informational transactions. These may have some impact on conventional forms of goods delivery and shopping behaviour over the longer term; but more immediately they are likely to have a greater effect on the usership of business services.

The Concept of Accessibility

An improvement in people's accessibility to shops and shopping centres

324

is one of the main goals of retail and commercial planning. Accessibility is a rather loose notion, however, that has several points to its meaning.[1] In one sense, it implies something about the locational relationships between consumers and shops and shopping centres; in another, it suggests something about the spatial environment through which consumers will have to travel; and in a further sense, it begs the question as to what opportunities are available to consumers to embark upon trips in the first place.

The locational aspects pertaining to accessibility were indirectly referred to in Chapter 1. There it was indicated that different types of accessibility surround different kinds of retail or business configurations. The so-called nucleated shopping centres command a general form of accessibility by virtue of their being central to surrounding populations. Higher levels of general accessibility are accorded the largest centres, namely town and city centres, simply because they are central to the urban population as a whole. Ribbon developments, on the other hand, command a special form of accessibility which, if mapped in terms of consumer usership, would seem to extend linearly along main roads, reflecting their greater degree of orientation to motorised travellers. Specialised functional areas also command special forms of accessibility but in this case due to the agglomeration of like kinds of activities in particular locations. Individual businesses are able to trade from a larger clientele than they would otherwise draw upon because of the collective attractions which are presented.

These theoretical distinctions in forms of accessibility, however, obviously become distorted in real-world situations. In the metropolitan county of Tyne and Wear, the general accessibility of Newcastle's city centre is very much greater to residents living to the north of the city than to the south because of the barrier effects of the river.[2] Many older ribbon developments emanating from the city centre have found their special accessibility reduced by the development of the inner ring road; and some of the traditional specialised functional areas have found their former attractiveness curtailed by redevelopment schemes. For the consumer, the variable standards of both the transport network and transport services may condition his or her perception of the ease of travelling to a particular centre. Access to the city centre of Newcastle by car drivers seems generally to be easier for those coming in from the east or west, on the northern side of the river; while for those using public transport, access from the north and parts of the east is better, in part because of the new Metro links from these areas.[3]

The ability to be able to choose between different travel modes is another factor that conditions the state of accessibility of particular centres to individual consumers. Generally speaking, higher-income consumers will be able to gain access to a wider variety of centres than lower-income consumers by having higher levels of independent mobility.[4] The use of a car, however, may be restricted to certain times of the day; and those stores which stay open later on selected week-days may become relatively more accessible for this reason than those that close for the evening. Various other groups in society are more seriously constrained in the time they have available for shopping. These include women who work, women with young children or other dependent relatives and some of the disabled and infirm. For people on very low incomes, the ability to use public transport services on a frequent basis may also be limited.[5]

There are essentially two ways in which people's accessibility to shops and shopping centres can be improved. The first is through the formulation of general transport policies, whereby the opportunities available for travelling to different shops and shopping centres are enhanced both for the population as a whole and for the specific groups in need of special assistance. The second is through the implementation of various types of traffic management schemes that deal with the efficiency of movement once people have embarked upon their trips.

Transport Policies

The chief element to be considered in the formulation of transport policies is the balance to be struck in the provision of new opportunities for those who travel by car, lorry, train, walking and by other means. In broad terms, this can be reduced to a choice in priorities as to how much money should be invested in public transport services as distinct from the infrastructure necessary to support private forms of travel. It is not the place here to debate this issue for it depends on a much wider range of travel purposes than those linked to shopping, but some reference to the influence which different types of transport policies can have on consumer interests is clearly desirable.

In the shopping context, transport policies revolve primarily around the question of how much support to give to bus users, car users or those who shop by walking. This is usually a political decision but is inexorably linked to those locational strategies pursued with respect to the development of retail and commercial activity. The level of demand for bus services, for example, will depend on how much retail and commercial activity is concentrated in various centres, particularly town and city centres, and how much has been dispersed to outlying, localised environments. Once this type of relationship has been clarified, the provision of an appropriate transport network can be worked out and what sorts of reception facilities will be required by different kinds of travellers at their destination points.

Clarifying the relationship between transport policies and retail locational strategies, however, is not as straightforward as may appear. Problems arise both from the nature of new retailing development that is concentrated within town and city centres and from the predilections of the population to use cars for shopping whenever they can. In the case of new retailing development, the bulk of this has been guided into purpose-built shopping centres which, being a transplant of North American concepts, are largely oriented to the younger, wealthier and more mobile sections of the community. Thus whilst most developers of these schemes, and their tenants, welcome good public transport connections, they are usually adamant in their demands for some minimal level of car parking. Amongst the population, shopping in the central area by car for those who have access to a car will ordinarily be their first choice in mode of travel unless there are constraints to deter them. Some of these constraints, such as congestion, may arise naturally; others might be imposed through deliberate restrictions on car parking or artificially high car parking prices. Establishing a suitable provision of bus services, therefore, becomes complicated by the need to protect the interests of the less well-off sections of society and to protect the physical environment of the central area from too much car-borne traffic.

Elsewhere in the city, these problems are less distinctive but nevertheless reflect on similar conflicting arguments. At the local level, ostensibly one would wish to encourage the continued provision of small local parades and neighbourhood centres in close proximity to those shoppers who would prefer to walk (and in some cases are dependent on walking) for their convenience goods needs. However, we know that the amount of spending that takes place in such centres has been diminishing rapidly and as a consequence new ventures of these sort are hardly viable to developers or retailers alike. In district-level centres, it may be easier to meet the demand for both bus services and car parking in new, planned centres, but those that are vestiges of a bygone era will generally suffer from a shortage of car parking provisions. Taking all these conditions into account, it would seem that the continued trend to greater independent mobility simply cannot be resisted; and therefore the formulation of transport policies for shopping (in residential areas) must first start with the question of how to meet the requirements of the car driver and then proceed to providing support services for those who shop by bus and foot.

There is much less to report in this section about existing policies towards the circulation of goods within the city. Most of the differences in transport modes that can be seen, as between the use of small vans operating from distribution centres or heavy goods vehicles travelling between supply points and warehouses, have been worked out by market forces through the actions of individual firms. The networks which these vehicles utilise and their penetration of different parts of the urban area are more properly a consideration of traffic management schemes.

Traffic Management Schemes

The chief function of traffic management schemes is to reduce the conflict that builds up in various parts of the city between different transport users. There are three main types of measures that have been adopted that have relevance to our concerns. Firstly, attempts have been made to separate 'through' traffic from localised traffic in important shopping and commercial areas. These include the building of inner motorway boxes and ring roads to carry 'through' traffic and the designation of distributary or feeder roads for those destined for a town or city centre. Secondly, inside the central area, steps have been taken to separate vehicles from pedestrians through pedestrianising streets, developing precincts and constructing underpasses or elevated walkways. Thirdly, a number of controls have been exerted on specific types of users, ranging from kerbside parking regulations to the allocation of special bus lanes and routes to be followed by heavy goods vehicles.

Considerable progress has been made in the last two decades to reduce the amount of lorry traffic passing through town and city centres. With the recent cutbacks in government expenditure, however, we are likely to see fewer new motorways or ring roads built in the future, although there appears to be a commitment to construct a number of new by-passes. We might expect, therefore, to see an increase in the severity of controls over the direction of lorry movements by local authorities, although there will be fierce resistance to this from the vehicle owners and operators. County councils were empowered by the Heavy Goods Vehicles Act of 1973 to implement stricter controls, particularly where environmental damage could be identified.

When the recent Armitage Report[6] recommendation for an increase in the permitted weight-size of lorries is enacted (in modified form), these powers are likely to be more widely used.

Much can be learned, however, from a variety of regulatory schemes that have already been tried in London.[7] For some years now, heavy goods vehicles have been prohibited from entering a 6 square mile area of the central city but attempts to extend this to 125 square miles have proved to be unsuccessful. Curbs have been put on overnight parking in inner residential areas instead and weight and width restrictions placed on those lorries which can penetrate small streets during the daytime. A number of small off-street public lorry parks have been established to ease the problems of parking for drivers and larger facilities are planned at strategic locations along the main approach roads for through traffic.[8] An attempt to designate specific lorry routes throughout London, nevertheless, has so far proved impractical because of the inadequacies of the major road network. Restrictions on the movements of heavy goods vehicles may be more easily applied perhaps in smaller towns and cities than within the conurbations. The Windsor Cordon Experiment appears to have been successful despite the radical nature of its effects.[9] Here lorries of over 5 tons unladen weight (with certain exceptions) have been barred from passing through the town as a whole by a series of checkpoints on all of the major approach roads. Following a trial period, the scheme has now been made permanent and is considered to be enforceable by the police. Increased distribution costs have been incurred by the vehicle owners, however, and although complaints have so far been somewhat muted one wonders what their reaction would be to the development of similar schemes in a large number of other towns and cities.

The cordon principle is one that has also been applied to the restriction of cars within the central area. The most notable example was the ill-fated Nottingham experiment that sought to compensate for a complete ban on cars in the city centre during the daytime hours by the provision of free bus services.[10] Public opposition to the scheme and difficulties over enforcing the controls led to its abandonment after only a few months in 1976. In other cities, smaller-scale attempts have been made to restrict entry to parts of the central area to disc-holders only; and this of course is a method widely employed to control the usership of many private car parks.

Pedestrianisation, however, has generally proved to be a much more effective way of curtailing car traffic within town and city centres and particularly in those shopping streets where congestion, pollution and safety hazards would otherwise be most acute. Curiously enough, and compared to several other countries in the EEC, nevertheless, the pedestrianisation of traditional shopping streets as distinct from the building of new precincts, has been advanced in Britain only during the last ten years or so.[11] Both the form and extent of pedestrianisation programmes have varied enormously. A few, such as those in Norwich and Leeds, comprise a relatively large network of converted streets that can be penetrated only by servicing vehicles. In other cases, such as in Birmingham and Oxford, converted streets are linked up with arcades and new shopping malls. The vast majority of schemes, however, comprise the pedestrianisation of just the main shopping street and one or two appendages to it. This may be fully pedestrianised, as in the case of Southampton, or be open to buses and taxis, as in the case of Newcastle upon Tyne.

Pedestrianisation, of course, has to be accompanied by a redistribution of vehicular traffic along other streets within the central area. Typically, the existing road network has not been capable of supporting additional traffic and an assortment of schemes have had to be introduced to improve the efficiency of circulation. The most widely employed method is the designation of one-way traffic flows. These have had the effect both of speeding up movement and acting as a deterrent to some car users because of the difficulties they impose on providing direct access to different parts of the central area. The emergence of many distributary or feeder roads as important traffic arteries, however, has caused considerable conflict to shoppers and other pedestrians outside the pedestrianised area; and the environment that surrounds people's approach to the main source of shops remains an unsatisfactory one in terms of comfort and convenience.

Specific Service Provisions

Although transport policies and traffic management schemes are of general importance to the relative health of retail and commercial activity, in the dialogue that has taken place between the business community and transport officials in recent years, two matters seem to have taken precedence over all others. The first concerns the provision of car parking, particularly within town and city centres; and the second, the provision of goods reception facilities. To these we might add the provision of bus stations, bus staging points and other localised services and amenities for consumers.

Car Parking

Discussions about car parking provisions have generally focused on the charges to be levied to customers, the types of car parking to be made available, and those standards to be adhered to in terms of numbers of spaces and the design of individual schemes. Generally speaking, there is now a broad consensus of opinion amongst the local authorities that car parking provisions within a town or city centre should pay for themselves. The revenue collected from car parking usage should pay not only for the maintenance of the facilities but also for their capital costs. The reasons for this are that

> by paying the 'real' cost of parking, the user of the private car will be more likely to assess the relative merits of making the same journeys by some other mode (public transport, cycle or foot); there is no reason why a service such as parking used by one section of the community should be subsidised by others, especially in a period of financial stringency; setting the objective of 'breaking even' creates a framework within which all local authorities are working to similar constraints, but while still having the opportunity to exercise a measure of local choice regarding the way in which the objective is achieved.[12]

Most retailers would go along with these arguments and the larger multiple firms have been disposed in the past to contribute to car parking support where schemes have been seen to be essential but have proved to be uneconomic.

There are considerable differences of opinion between the private and public sectors, however, over the types of car parking provisions to be made available. The main options that are open are shown in Figure 11.1. By and large, the local authorities prefer to develop a few, large car parks with distinctions being made between short- and long-term stays. They also favour park and ride schemes, particularly for Saturday shoppers, and some provision of on-street parking that is metred. Car parking within the main core area of shopping, nevertheless, should be limited and related to traffic controls of a broad zonal kind. In the example shown, provision is made for 8,000 private off-street and 2,750 public off-street parking spaces within the central area, for 1,000 on-street parking spaces and 1,115 spaces in the park and ride facilities. In the case of the park and ride facilities, parking is free but small charges are made for the use of buses which operate at 10 to 12 minute frequencies.[13]

Figure 11.1: Car Parking Policies in the City of Oxford

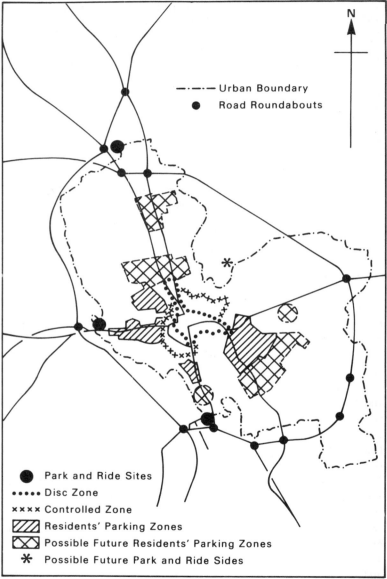

Source: Bullen, D.P., 'Parking Near Shopping Centres: Local Authority Responsibilities in Theory and Practice', in *Car Parking and Retailing — Report of an
URPI Workshop* (Unit for Retail Planning Information, Reading, 1979).

Such policies are clearly guided by a number of considerations, including the need to control the overall level of traffic entering a city centre and to accommodate an office workforce as well as shoppers and other visitors. The retailer's perception, however, is circumscribed to how best can his customer's requirements be served. Not unexpectedly, therefore, retailers tend to favour a greater number of small car parks, linked to individual shops; they prefer short-stay rather than long-stay car parks; they dislike park and ride schemes on the basis that these are essentially inconvenient; and, in the words of one observer, they regard 'meter parking as a bit of a joke'.[14] Most would also like to see more surface car park provisions as distinct from multi-storey car parks, although they recognise the problems of acquiring sufficient land within the central area to make this possible.[15] They have strong grounds, nevertheless, for being critical of the deficiencies found in many multi-storey schemes, particularly the inadequate turning spaces provided, the small sizes of lifts and the lack of clear signposting.

The British Multiple Retailers' Association has spoken for most of the industry in its prescription of what the ideal number of car parking spaces should be throughout the central area in relation to the amount of shopping floorspace to be found.[16] The latest recommended figures are for an average of 5.25 parking spaces per 100 square metres of gross retail area, but where these could be reduced to 4.00 in areas of low regional car ownership or increased to 6.50 in areas of high regional car ownership. Such ratios might be considered as rather optimistic, however, given that they slightly exceed those standards observed in American 'out-of-town' shopping centres. A recent survey of pre-Christmas weekend shopping in several regional shopping centres in the US showed a mean parking ratio of 4.4 vehicles per 1,000 square feet (92 m^2) of occupied gross leasable area.[17] This led to recommendations that in new shopping centres to be built, a norm of 5.0 spaces per 1,000 square feet of GLA should be adopted in schemes over 800,000 square feet (7,400 m^2) in size.

Car parking space standards, nevertheless, need to be looked at in more detail for individual shops and shopping centres, particularly in terms of their localised urban setting. Quite clearly, the provisions for large supermarkets, superstores and other specifically car-oriented shops should be much greater than those that relate to customers using a mixture of transport modes. Sainsbury works to a norm of 7.5 spaces per 1,000 square feet of GLA for its new developments; and a convention commonly adopted for new district shopping centres is 6.5 spaces per 1,000 square feet of GLA. Outlying superstores and hypermarkets may have as many as 10.

Goods Reception Facilities

Linked to the problems of car parking are the problems of how to accommodate those lorries and vans that require access to the central area and other shopping centres in order to deliver retail goods. In recent years, these problems have become more serious, partly because of an increase in the frequency of goods deliveries and partly because environmental improvement programmes such as redevelopment and pedestrianisation have reduced the effective road space over which the vehicles can operate. There is a combination of reasons why the frequency of goods deliveries has increased, including a reduction in the floorspace devoted by retailers to the holding of stocks, the use of smaller vehicles by suppliers operating from new distribution centres, and the diversification over time of the merchandise mix of stores. The reduction in effective road space has been accompanied in many cases by the provision of special-purpose reception facilities (either rear access, underground or rooftop servicing alleys and bays) but congestion still arises because of the compression of goods deliveries to certain times of the day, most notably the early morning.[18]

The problems the deliverer faces, however, are numerous and complex, as Table 11.1 indicates. No single one or group of these is adjudged by Rushton to be the most serious cause of inefficiencies or delays and hence no simple panacea exists for bringing about dramatic improvements.[19] Certain problems, nevertheless, may be more easily resolved than others and the following suggestions have been made. Firstly, the suppliers themselves can reduce much of the congestion that occurs, particularly over lorries queuing at reception points, by developing a vehicle appointments system. Secondly, the local authorities can adopt a number of more forceful measures to: increase the amount of on-street parking space to reduce the time taken to unload goods; ease the restrictions applying to on-street parking and unloading during various off-peak hours; provide more rear access reception facilities and accompanying lorry parking spaces; and provide guidelines on better standards to be adopted in new buildings for the delivery of goods.

These latter points are strongly endorsed by the British Multiple Retailers' Association which has complained that 'It seems that many authorities have, for varying reasons, dropped the provision of rear service access as a fundamental objective. The Association would urge that this can only be justified in extreme situations.'[20] Pickering has found that the special-purpose facilities provided in new planned

Table 11.1: Summary of Various Problems Related to Goods Reception in Shopping Areas

1.	The 'distance restriction' between the vehicle unloading point and the goods reception point, especially where on-street loading and front-door delivery is made.
2.	The lack of rear access reception points means frequent direct deliveries from the high street.
3.	Where rear access is provided, parked vehicles often block the areas.
4.	Related to lack of rear access is a lack of adequate on-street parking places.
5.	The variety of different building designs, many of which are historical legacies that lack attunement to modern delivery needs.
6.	The inadequacy and insufficiency of suitable materials handling equipment.
7.	The time taken physically to unload vehicles.
8.	The van-sales method of distribution causes delays because of the in-store selling functions that are incurred.
9.	The need to break down pre-selected loads causes further delays.
10.	Delays can also be incurred through the paper work procedures of delivery.
11.	Unit load palletisation can speed vehicle turn-round but there are often problems over manoeuvring wheeled pallets and obtaining returnable pallets.
12.	Drivers may need to move goods past the reception point and into the store.
13.	Queuing of vehicles can arise through lack of a vehicle appointments system and preferential reception given to certain vehicles.
14.	Delivery time restrictions tend to shorten the available delivery day.
15.	Problems arise with individual outlets, such as in attracting attention or drivers being refused loads.
16.	Certain basic infrastructure problems create physical constraints on vehicle size, e.g. narrow streets, low bridges, weight restrictions.
17.	The general traffic congestion of a town inhibits easy vehicle flow.

Source: Rushton, A., 'Restrictions on Retail Deliveries', in Unit for Retail Planning Information, *Restricting Retail Deliveries: The Lessons to be Learnt* (URPI Workshop Report 19, Reading, 1980).

shopping schemes are often not of a very high quality and that many of the problems that bedevil traditional shopping streets have still not been overcome.[21] This is in part due to the inflexibility of planned provisions which have not allowed for changes to the distribution system; but it reflects too on an imbalance in the conditions that surround the immediate store environment and those that are found outside. Rushton sees this state of affairs as having arisen because of a lack of communication between the various interested parties involved and has suggested the establishment of a three-way consultation procedure between the local authorities and the deliverers and receivers of goods.[22] This is an objective that could be fulfilled through the creation of a special-purpose consultative panel (or panels) for shopping and commercial concerns of the kind we have advocated in Chapter 4.

Bus Stations and Bus Staging Points

The retailing community, preoccupied perhaps by its perception of car parking deficiencies, has contributed little to a discussion about the siting and environmental standards of bus stations or bus staging points. These are of vital importance to the content of a town or city centre plan, however, by virtue of the fact that the use of buses often remains the predominant mode of travel for shopping, even in areas of high car ownership. Recent surveys in Coventry indicate that 57 per cent of consumers usually shop in the city centre by bus, as compared to 35 per cent by car and 8 per cent by other means.[23] The siting of bus stations and bus staging points will have a crucial influence on those parts of a town or city centre (and hence those shops) most likely to be visited by consumers; the environmental standards of these facilities will contribute to the overall image and general attractiveness of a town or city centre as a place in which to shop.

Studies of consumer movements within the city centre of Newcastle upon Tyne have provided some interesting insights into the spatial pattern of behaviour of people who go shopping by bus.[24] Admittedly, this is an area of low car ownership and where the use of public transport has been strongly encouraged by restrictive car parking policies. In 1977 (on a Saturday in February), some 58 per cent of shoppers in the city centre had come there by bus, as against 27 per cent by car and 15 per cent by other means. For users of the Eldon Square shopping centre, the figures were alternatively 47 per cent, 35 per cent and 18 per cent; with the differences here being accounted for by the greater appeal of the covered centre to car users as we have indicated before. In breaking the main sets of figures down into people shopping along particular streets, the surprising fact emerged that 63 per cent of shoppers in the main high street of Northumberland Street had travelled by bus as against only 23 per cent by car. This street alone captured approximately 38 per cent of total trade within the city centre (although prior to the opening of Eldon Square its share in 1976 was 54 per cent). Other major shopping streets likewise showed an above average proportion of bus-borne shoppers, except in those

Figure 11.2: Bus Station Influences on the Movements of Shoppers within the City Centre of Newcastle upon Tyne

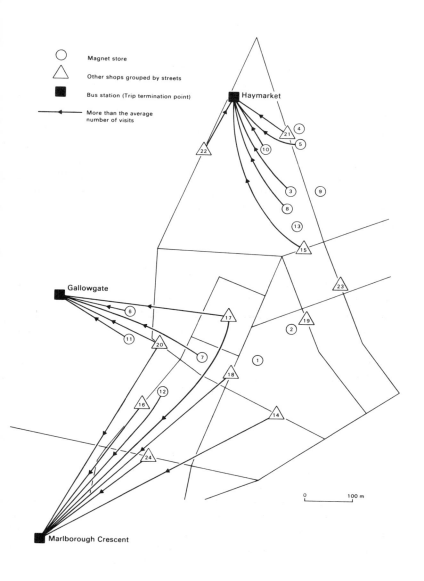

cases where there was a concentration of the highest quality shops.

Part of the explanation for this must be that car-borne shoppers tend to be more selective in the streets and shops they visit; but part has to do with the penetration of the high street by buses and a concentration of bus staging points within and around it. There are five bus stations within the city centre of Newcastle, however, four of which are located in rather peripheral positions (the exception being the Eldon Square bus station). The effects of three of these locations in channelling people's movements to particular quarters of the city centre is shown in Figure 11.2. Apart from their spending in Eldon Square and Northumberland Street, users of the Haymarket Bus Station shop predominantly in the north; those from Gallowgate predominantly in the west; and those from Marlborough Crescent predominantly in the south-west. The bus station not shown is that at Worwick Street, whose sphere of influence would extend over the east and south-east. The map is instructive in showing that if one or more of these bus stations were to be closed, the relative health of shops and streets within their vicinity would be seriously affected.

During the last two years, travel patterns within the city centre of Newcastle have been further influenced by the opening of three Metro stations.[25] These have reduced to some extent the spheres of influence of the bus stations; and since one of the Metro stations is located in the middle of the city centre there has been a greater concentration of public transport users entering and exiting from this point than existed before. There does not appear so far, nevertheless, to have been a major change in the overall proportion of people using public transport as compared to cars; rather, such shifts as have taken place have been between the use of the Metro instead of buses. This has been deliberately encouraged in fact by the re-routing of buses to connect with outlying Metro stations.

Developments in Communications

The Metro system in Newcastle upon Tyne is one of the few visionary ideas regarding new forms of transport to be realised in recent years. Back in the early 1970s there was much speculation about the introduction of other rapid transit systems in several of the major provincial centres; some soothsayers looked forward to the emergence of the electric car and the driverless bus; others talked about the provision of 'people-movers' along pedestrianised streets. With the cutbacks in local and central government expenditure, most of these ideas have now gone by the board, although some research and experimentation continues in the field of computer-guided public transport services.

Present interest focuses much more around the developments taking place in telecommunications. Here there has been considerable investment from the private as well as public sector and support from the former will greatly increase with the privatisation of British Telecom. There are four main areas of innovation that we have pointed to before. The first concerns the growing sophistication of the telephone system and the ability to transfer information in a conventional way more speedily and cheaply. Secondly, there is the use of the telephone network as the medium for a wide range of visual informational transactions. These include its use in transferring documents over large distances through facsimile processors; its use in providing teletext and viewdata services for business companies and consumers in the home, particularly via Prestel; and its use in creating conference-video facilities where the images of participants located in different places can be brought together at a single central point. The third dimension concerns the introduction of cable TV and the relaying of television programmes internationally via satellites. The fourth relates to the development of new computerised data capture systems both within the headquarter offices of firms and within their branch outlets. Of particular significance here is the experimentation taking place with electronic funds transfer systems (EFTS) in banks and the introduction of electronic point of sale equipment (EPOS) in stores.

It will be some years before these collective developments have a marked impact on existing patterns of movement and behaviour within towns and cities. Nevertheless, it is appropriate now to consider what the implications of such developments will be so that some advance planning can be undertaken. There are perhaps four likely scenarios that can be foreseen. Firstly, the net effect of the new technologies will be to strengthen the trading power of those multiple groups that currently dominate the retail and business service sectors. We can expect therefore to see a continued shift to increased consumer patronage of these companies. Secondly, the need for physical contact or personal visits will diminish considerably; hence there will likely be a greater centralisation of service provisions within the largest branch outlets with some functions relayed back through headquarter offices. In the short term this will probably be more pronounced in the case of business service activities; but in the longer term, as tele-shopping becomes more widely accepted, we might see a similar rationalisation within the retail trades. Thirdly, the innovations will initially be most widely adopted in the largest urban areas of Britain and within these we can expect to see the city centres of the provincial cities benefiting at the expense of smaller town and city centres. There will also be a marked social bias to the diffusion process such that the new technologies will have an impact on the more prosperous areas of the South in advance of poorer areas in the North. Finally, in the matter of goods circulation, applying particularly to the retail trades, there may be an increase in localised lorry traffic both within city centres and suburban areas. This may come about in the first instance through more frequent deliveries of goods to stores which have been able to reduce still further the quantity of stocks held; and in the second case, through the growth in home delivery services brought about by armchair shopping for grocery as well as other goods.

Conclusion

It is inevitable that many of the considerations in this chapter are bound up with issues of a broad transport kind. The topics that have been singled out for special discussion, however, are those which are integral to retail and commercial planning and deserve to be part of a special plan. The topics themselves are rather diverse and range from the general to the particular, and from clear-cut problems of the present to uncertainties over the future. This makes it difficult to specify the way in which a special plan should be prepared. There is a mixture of County and District level concerns, although the lead on transport policies writ large has always been taken by the upper-tier authority. To the extent that most of the problems identified are systemic in nature, then the upper-tier authority remains the most relevant body to take this role; but on such matters as car parking, goods reception facilities and bus staging provisions it can only provide guidelines on standards to be adhered to and ultimate responsibility for what is built on the ground will rest with the lower-tier authority. One hopes, however, that any specific attention which is given to the transport aspects of retail and commercial planning will not be hide-bound to the traditional concerns over the alleviation of congestion and improvements in accessibility, but that due regard will be given to the emerging developments in communications technology.

References

1. See, Jones, S.R., *Accessibility Measures – A Literature Review* (Transport and Road Research Laboratory, Report LR967, Crowthorne, Berkshire, 1981); Owen, W., *The Accessible City* (The Brookings Institution, Washington, DC, 1972); Starkie, D.N.M., 'Transportation, Planning and Public Policy', *Progress in Planning*, vol. 1, part 4 (1973).
2. Gleave, D., *Journey to Work in Newcastle, 1921-1966* (Department of Geography, University of Newcastle upon Tyne, Seminar Paper 13, March 1970).
3. Fullerton, J., *Shopping Travel Patterns in Tyne and Wear: A 'Before-Metro' Profile* (Transport and Road Research Laboratory, Report 1045, Crowthorne, Berkshire, 1982).
4. Thomas, C.J., 'Socio-Spatial Differentiation and the Use of Services', in Herbert, D.T. and Johnston, R.J. (eds), *Social Areas in Cities* (Wiley, London, 1976).
5. Bowlby, S.R., 'Accessibility, Mobility and Shopping Provisions', in Goodall, B. and Kirby, A. (eds), *Resources and Planning* (Pergamon, Oxford, 1979).
6. Department of Transport, *Report of the Inquiry into Lorries, People and the Environment*, presented by Sir Arthur Armitage (December 1980).
7. Dean, J.D., 'Controlling the Movement and Parking of Heavy Goods Vehicles – Experience in London', in *Restricting Retail Deliveries: the Lessons to be Learnt: Report of an URPI Workshop* (Unit for Retail Planning Information, Reading, 1980).
8. Greater London Council, *Freight Policy for London*, (London, 1977).
9. Wardle, J., 'Lorry Controls in the Windsor Area', in *Restricting Retail Deliveries: the Lessons to be Learnt.*
10. Jackson, N.W., 'Bus System Experiments and Developments', in Cresswell, R. (ed.), *Passenger Transport and the Environment* (Leonard Hill, Glasgow, 1977).
11. Stewart, J.R., *User Response to Pedestrianised Shopping Streets* (University of Birmingham, Centre for Urban and Regional Studies, Research Memorandum 73, 1979); See also, Roberts, J., *Pedestrian Precincts in Britain* (Transport and Environment Studies, London, 1981).
12. Gould, P., 'Measuring the Effects of Changes in Car Parking Policy', in *Car Parking and Retailing: Report of an URPI Workshop* (Unit for Retail Planning Information, Reading, 1979).
13. Bullen, D.P., 'Parking Near Shopping Centres: Local Authority Responsibilities in Theory and Practice', in *Car Parking and Retailing.*
14. Wade, B., 'Morning Discussion and Report-Back', in *Car Parking and Retailing*, p. 28.
15. Burdsey, C.W., 'A Retailer's View on the Provision of Car Parking', in *Car Parking and Retailing.*
16. British Multiple Retailers' Association, *Guidelines for Shopping* (BMRA, London, 1980).
17. 'Survey Finds Need for New Parking Ratio', *Shopping Center World*, February 1977, pp. 20-5.
18. National Materials Handling Centre, *Study of the Need for and Means of Improving Goods Reception* (Cranfield Institute of Technology, Cranfield, 1979).
19. Rushton, A., 'Restrictions on Retail Deliveries', in *Restricting Retail Deliveries.*

20. British Multiple Retailers' Association, *Guidelines for Shopping*, p. 4.
21. Pickering, R.C., 'Planned Shopping Centre Developments: The Problems of Goods Delivery and Reception', *Retail and Distribution Management*, vol. 9, no. 3 (1981), pp. 63-7.
22. Rushton, A., 'Restrictions on Retail Deliveries'.
23. Coventry City Council, unpublished surveys of shopping behaviour and consumer attitudes towards the city centre, 1983.
24. Davies, R.L. and Bennison, D.J., *The Eldon Square Regional Shopping Centre: The First Eighteen Months* (Retailing and Planning Associates, Corbridge, Northumberland, 1978).
25. Bennison, D.J., *The Initial Impact of Metro on Activities within Central Newcastle upon Tyne* (Transport and Road Research Laboratory, Supplementary Report 745, Crowthorne, Berkshire, 1981).

12 SPECIAL AREA-BASED CONSIDERATIONS

This final chapter of the book looks at the scope for retail and commercial planning within small, localised areas. In doing so, there may be some criticism that this reflects on a return to a rather traditional approach to planning, especially since many of the problems that can be pointed to are really the outcome of systemic processes and are better dealt with through the other avenues of planning that have already been reviewed. Our defence is twofold: firstly, that very often the concerns expressed by both businessmen and consumers stem from local incidences which, if treated in the areal context in which they have emerged, may be more quickly resolved than if referred back to some broader based programme of action; secondly, that there do exist within urban and rural environments particular places where a general problem becomes acute and needs special attention. The sorts of plans we have in mind, however, need not necessarily be confined to a single locality, as in the case of contemporary Action-Area Plans. It may well be preferable to direct such plans at several like kinds of areas, recognising that within these there may be differing degrees of severity to the problems that need to be addressed.

The types of areas identified in Chapter 4 as being most easily distinguished are: the inner, middle and outer residential tracts of the city; smaller town and city centres; and the remaining rural parts of a District. Of these, the problems of the inner city are perhaps the most pressing and warrant greater consideration than has so far been given to them at various stages throughout this book. The needs of the middle and outer city are relatively less significant at the present time but deserve some further discussion since they will become increasingly more important in the future. The problems experienced by smaller town and city centres have often been overlooked because of the glare of attention of much larger places; and rural areas can be fairly said to be the subject of benign neglect. This chapter, however, provides an opportunity to highlight the planning requirements of those areas that otherwise tend to be ignored and to pull together a variety of topics that collectively have much intrinsic interest.

343

Residential Area Requirements

The Inner City

There have been three previous occasions within this book when mention has been made of the problems of the inner city. The first concerns the high proportion of people who may be deemed to be disadvantaged as consumers by virtue of the lack of modern shopping facilities to be found within the inner city, especially large supermarkets and superstores. The second concerns the poor physical condition of many older inner city shopping centres and the conspicuous failure of a number of new redevelopment schemes that represented early attempts at environmental improvement. The third concerns the demise of numerous, small, independent shops that have been particularly densely concentrated within the inner city. Taken together, these three features represent the chief ailments of the inner city from a retailing and commercial point of view, but they are obviously bound up with a wider set of debilitating processes that require treatment of a more fundamental planning kind. A further issue in this context concerns the limited employment prospects of the inner city and the contribution which a declining retail and commercial stock makes to the burgeoning pool of the unemployed.

While the problems of the inner city are plain to see, however, resolving them is an extremely difficult proposition. The special study commissioned by the Distributive Trades Committee of the National Economic Development Office suggested that there still remains a basic ignorance of what sorts of efforts might be made.

> . . . existing knowledge fails to answer three significant questions:
> a) Whether particular types of retailing could provide the growth potential for helping to revitalise inner areas, and what their net economic benefits would be (taking into account their competitive effects upon other existing businesses);
> b) Whether there was a viable future for existing, and often declining, shopping centres and if so in what form. Little is known about the basis on which many businesses trade and about their profitability. This makes it difficult to evaluate either public or private investments which could affect shops in inner areas;
> c) What impact public policies generally could have on retail investment and viability. Retailers require positive policies on such matters as future population levels and road proposals before committing their own investment to an inner city area.[1]

The study itself produced only limited answers to these questions. An assessment was made of three different kinds of inner city shopping centres (Breck Road in Liverpool, Roman Road in East London and Lewisham High Street in south-east London) but this was largely descriptive of their form and functions and the changes that they had undergone in recent years. All three centres have been the recipients of new developments, respectively a superstore, supermarket and covered shopping mall, and comparisons were made of the different benefits derived from these. Although there were no detailed case analyses of centres without new developments, the conclusion was reached that 'old shopping areas in inner city districts are rarely capable of regenerating themselves without the introduction of a new dimension of modern retailing.'[2]

Pope[3] has provided an alternative view. He suggests that because many inner city shopping centres are basically unattractive to multiple retailers they offer more scope to enterprising independent traders, particularly amongst immigrants. Citing the evidence of Belgrave Road in Leicester and Saltley in Birmingham, he found that 'in both cases the multiple retailers have tended to move out. However, after a period of decay the influx of immigrant shopkeepers has distinctly improved the shopping environment. Fascias have been repainted, opening hours extended and merchandise changed so that in many ways the retail service to the community has been improved. Perhaps these are prototypes of the form of shopping groups particularly suited to inner cities.'[4]

These two different interpretations, however, need not be seen as contradictory. Quite clearly, the inner city comprises a variety of urban conditions and variable kinds of solutions to the revitalisation of retailing should be sought. Our own recommendations, frequently stated elsewhere in this book, are for more flexible development controls on both the building of facilities and their locations alongside main roads. One would like to see attracted into the inner city a wide range of those retail-related services that are growing so rapidly at the present time. A milder form of some of the American strip developments, with their purpose-built fast-food outlets, drive-in business services and repair activities might do wonders to enlivening some of our more depressed environments and enhancing job prospects for the young. If these could be supported by extensive car parking and positive traffic management schemes, they might prove a popular venue for consumers from other parts of the city.

The needs of the local consumers and businesses should come first, nevertheless, and many local authorities continue to put high on their list of priorities the improvement of neighbourhood shopping provisions. A clear commitment to this type of policy has been taken in Islington where the 'council considers that there should be local shops available to all residents within about 400 metres from home. This is about a ten minute walk, each way, for an elderly person or a parent with a toddler.'[5] On this basis, some 50 local centres have been identified within the Borough where the Planning Department will seek to protect existing shop frontages. All areas that fall outside a 400 metre radius from these have been designated as shopping deficiency areas where new investments or an upgrading of present resources will be required. Apart from stating that encouragement will be given to initiatives within these deficiency areas, however, there is no precise indication of how or from where the initiatives will be forthcoming.

Given the reservations that were expressed in Chapter 7 about the future viability of small localised shopping centres, there is an urgent need to think of alternative ways in which relatively housebound consumers such as the elderly and mothers with young children might be assisted with their shopping requirements. One possibility might be the use of telecommunications and micro-computer facilities to link individual homes or focal points within a community to a large store or group of stores some distance away. An experiment along these lines is currently being conducted in Gateshead in a joint venture between Tesco, the Borough Council and the University of Newcastle upon Tyne.[6] The specific objectives involved in this experiment are to improve the choice in shopping opportunities available to disadvantaged consumers and to give them access to those stores which offer goods at generally cheaper prices.

To date, three remote shopping outlets have been established which are linked via a micro-computer system to a Tesco superstore in the town centre. Two of the outlets are based in branch libraries and cater to the needs of people who, whilst not confined to their homes, nevertheless incur difficulties in travelling far to shop. Such people can go to their branch library and, by reference to catalogues that describe the sizes, weights and prices of goods, order their grocery shopping requirements from the superstore and then get these delivered to their homes free of charge later the same day or early the next morning. The third outlet has been established in the Social Services Department and caters for people who are virtually bedridden. These people can phone through to a switchboard and convey their orders to an operator who will then feed them into a micro-computer and have them despatched to the store. At the store end, another micro-computer in fact re-sorts the orders into picking lists to improve the efficiency of assembling goods from the shelves and to facilitate the different packaging requirements that may need to be met.

Prestel (British Telecom's viewdata system) is also being used to assist customers in the business of selecting goods. Through the help of an assistant, they can call up on a conventional television set such information as special offers that may be available for the week, the types of goods that may be particularly appropriate to people on restricted diets, the choice in kinds of meat, fish or cheese available, a recipe for the day and so on. In addition, a wide range of community information has been put at their disposal so that they might find out about local events, bus timetables, welfare entitlements and many other matters of a social kind. An assortment of visual aids, such as slide projections and poster displays, are also being used in the branch libraries to heighten the atmosphere of shopping and to encourage the consumers to use the outlets as meeting places, thereby engendering perhaps a role similar to that of the traditional corner store.

While the Gateshead Shopping and Information Service offers many pointers to how accessibility problems may be overcome in the future, however, it remains at present a scheme that is very labour-intensive and therefore needs to be heavily subsidised. It will be some years before there is an appropriate technology to automate the assembly of goods and the cost of their delivery will remain high. Meantime, the vast majority of inner city residents will continue to rely on an existing retail environment for their basic shopping needs. A more orthodox way of enhancing their opportunities will be to renew those shopping centres that remain relatively economically viable and these, as we have noted before, will generally be those of a district-level status. A recent District Plan that adopts this approach and points to what might be achieved is that for the Shields Road area of Newcastle upon Tyne.[7]

The Shields Road shopping centre lies in the midst of an inner city housing area that has been comprehensively redeveloped during the last eight years and which includes the controversial Byker Wall development. The new housing estates have proved to be popular locally, however, in part because the residents were widely consulted about their views and in part because the units, whilst densely built, have been designed imaginatively both internally and externally. Shields Road itself has been left untouched except with respect to the implementation of a number of small improvement schemes. The shopping centre therefore remains as a link to the past and a familiar corner stone to a community that has otherwise experienced considerable change. After extensive interviews had been held with the business occupants of the centre, the following policies were adopted by the Planning Department:

— to retain the old linear form of the centre, where the majority of shops would have frontage onto the main street;
— to provide grants to the local traders to enable them to upgrade their properties;
— to restrict the entry of business services in the main core of shopping and guide these to more peripheral positions;
— to permit new development on three existing derelict sites, two of which could accommodate large stores of up to 23,300 square feet (3,000 m^2) each (and for one of which preference would be given to the establishment of a DIY or other bulky-goods store);
— to introduce appropriate traffic management schemes (following the opening of a by-pass);
— to provide some 750 spaces of car parking, which is currently free;
— and to improve the pedestrian links to the centre from the surrounding housing estates.

The setting for these proposals is shown in Figure 12.1.

What seems to make this planning approach distinctive from others that have been pursued in the past is the emphasis given to redeveloping the surrounding infrastructure of the shopping centre whilst leaving the business composition intact. Certainly, there is a marked contrast between the changes wrought here and those effected on the west side of the city which was subject to considerable redevelopment in the late 1960s and early 1970s. There a former ribbon development serving the residents of Elswick was almost completely cleared away and the new shopping centre of Cruddas Park built in its place. This proved to be a disastrous failure in trading terms, as we have indicated before, in part because few traders could be enticed to enter the scheme and in part because its vast, concrete appearance simply lacked consumer appeal. Unfortunately, the centre continues to exist, an impediment to any new initiatives that might be taken in the area but so purposively designed that it will be difficult to convert to some other use.

The Middle City

Unlike the inner city, the middle city appears to be an area in need of

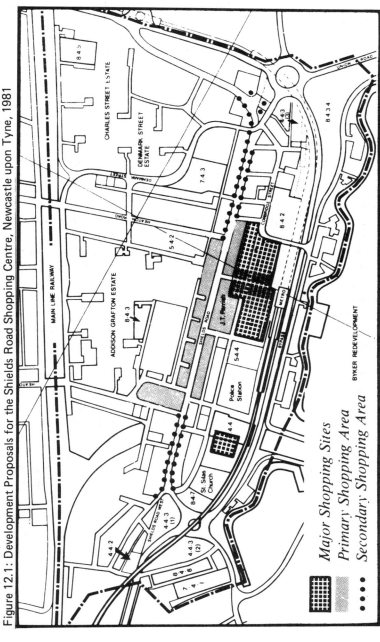

Figure 12.1: Development Proposals for the Shields Road Shopping Centre, Newcastle upon Tyne, 1981

Major Shopping Sites
Primary Shopping Area
Secondary Shopping Area

Source: City of Newcastle upon Tyne, *Shields Road District Plan – Written Statement* (Newcastle, 1981).

relatively little planning attention. It is an area characterised by large tracts of inter-war housing, intermittently spaced, nucleated shopping centres, schools with extensive playing fields, and not much else. It is the most stable part of the city in the sense that it has experienced the least amount of physical change and there has been comparatively little migration either into or out of the area during the last 30 years. Throughout this period of time, however, the population has been ageing, households have been shrinking and the physical conditions of buildings have begun to deteriorate. We can expect to see during the next decade, therefore, the emergence of a set of problems which, while small in comparison to those in other areas, will nevertheless need to be resolved.

In the shopping context, some of these problems are already well marked. The majority of the local centres are legacies of a pre-planning era and have grown up at crossroads locations without supporting car parking or goods servicing facilities. Most of the shops are owned by small independent traders but there is also a high proportion of first-generation supermarkets. With the increasing use of cars for shopping and the appearance of larger supermarkets in purpose-built distinct centres in the adjoining suburbs, more and more people have been by-passing their local centres and shopping outside of their local area. The local centres have therefore come to be dependent on the least mobile sections of the community amongst which there has also been a diminution of spending power because of the socio-economic changes noted above.

It is doubtful whether these trends can be reversed. This means that, as in the inner city, a high proportion of the smallest centres are doomed to decline; although some rationalisation of the number of occupants within a local parade might be to the advantage of those traders that do manage to survive. In certain circumstances, there might too be some scope for converting two or three vacant units into a single, modern convenience store. The main prospects for improvement, however, will again lie with the larger centres. Here, the provision of better car parking facilities will be the first priority, not only to try to entice consumers back to the centres, but also to seek investment in the development of new large stores or the enlargement of existing ones. How such car parking can be made available, however, is difficult to foresee because of the absence of open space. It might require some drastic action, involving the demolition of vacant shops or even unoccupied housing, but this would not be easy to achieve practically. Other problems present themselves in terms of the congestion that might build up on local residential roads should car parking be significantly improved and the conflicts that might arise from increased goods-delivery traffic should any centre become substantially revitalised.

The Outer City

The problems associated with local centres in the middle city are also manifest to some degree in the older suburbs of the outer city. By and large, however, the suburbs are distinctive for their under-provision rather than over-provision of shops and it is the absence of more essential shops, such as chemists and post offices, particularly in lower income outlying estates, that provides most cause for concern. A comparison of the numbers of shops per 1,000 population between outer suburban, inner suburban ('the middle city') and inner city areas in Newcastle upon Tyne is shown in Table 12.1. The shortage of shops

Table 12.1: Numbers of Retail Outlets in Localised Areas of Newcastle upon Tyne, 1975

Area	Population	Total outlets	Outlets per 1,000 population	% outlets vacant
Inner city				
Byker	10,700	291	27.2	16
Elswick/Benwell	40,235	378	9.4	23
Heaton	21,673	257	11.9	8
Newburn[a]	17,878	114	6.4	12
Inner suburban				
High Heaton/Benton	13,882	62	4.5	1
Jesmond	12,332	133	10.8	10
Walker	38,963	233	6.0	3
Scotswood/Fenham	42,111	317	7.5	8
Gosforth	27,967	186	6.7	4
Outer suburban				
Blakelaw/Kenton/Fawdon	35,072	136	3.9	3
Westerhope	31,367	99	3.2	6
Castle Ward	13,984	16	1.1	0

Note: a. Newburn is an older, outlying settlement that has been engulfed by suburban expansion, but which itself displays inner city characteristics.

Source: Butler, P., 'A Study of Local Shopping in Newcastle upon Tyne', in Jones, P. and Oliphant, R. (eds.), *Local Shops: Problems and Prospects* (Unit for Retail Planning Information, Reading, 1976).

derives in part from the need for modern shops to be supported by a higher threshold size of population and in part from the low densities of housing to be found in the suburbs, which means that centres will invariably be more widely spaced than elsewhere in the city.[8] Similar shortages can arise in various kinds of service facilities, such as health clinics, leisure centres and youth clubs. These again are precisely those sorts of facilities which are most intensively used by the least mobile sections of society.

The problems will obviously never be completely resolved to everyone's satisfaction. Nevertheless, a partial solution may again rest with the introduction of modern convenience stores or comparable types of developments. Some recent experience in Swindon is instructive in this respect.[9] There, considerable difficulty had been encountered by the Planning Department in finding a developer prepared to establish new local parades for two new communities known as Liden and Toothill. The 7-Eleven chain, however, offered to provide branches of its modern convenience stores in each area and these subsequently proved to be very successful. Buoyed by this, the local authority then went on to develop its own 'one-stop' shop in a further new housing area known as Freshbrook. In each of these cases, two additional small shops were built in association with the modern convenience store, although such an arrangement may not be the ideal to apply elsewhere. It could well be that in a different urban context a single mini-market based in a petrol station would be sufficient for an outlying community's needs.

A further possibility in the future relates once more to the use of telecommunication systems for shopping purposes. It is feasible that grocery shopping services of the kind being experimented with in Gateshead (together with links to a chemist and perhaps post office) could be offered on a commercial basis, with charges being made for deliveries and the packaging of goods. Orders would need to be placed from the home using either Prestel or a viewdata system based around cable TV. This would make such services a relatively expensive proposition and they would likely be oriented to a higher-income clientele. It will be some years hence, however, before such services could become commonplace for the operational problems that we have mentioned before will take time to overcome.

For the mobile population, the suburbs will generally provide a fairly satisfactory range of existing shopping opportunities. Depending on the size of a community, most of these consumers will have access to a purpose-built district centre or a free-standing superstore;

they will be within reach of a modern DIY or household goods store; there will be garden centres or nurseries to hand; and there will likely be a choice in garages or service stations. They may also be well placed with respect to a number of competing town and city centres for their more occasional shopping needs. Their ability to be able to move freely between different town and city centres, however, has become an increasingly significant factor to the relative health of these centres, primarily because of their higher levels of spending. With the further extension of urban sprawl, the competition that occurs between fringe belt centres can be expected to become more intense in the future.

Pressures on Smaller Town and City Centres

Generally speaking, town and city centres on the margins of a conurbation have tended to prosper at the expense of both their inner city equivalents and the major central areas. This is not only because of the enlargement of their catchment areas but also because they have been recipients of new investment in food retailing and the convenience trades as well as in specialist goods shopping. In more rural environments, however, there have been rather mixed experiences depending on the strength of the local economy and reflecting particularly on the rank of any individual centre within the local hierarchy. Two examples that illustrate this are the variable circumstances of Clacton and Chichester, each of which has been the subject of special study in recent years. The contrasting approaches adopted in these studies are also worth pointing to.

Clacton is a town which has for long been overshadowed in its retailing and commercial status by Ipswich and Colchester. It is a struggling seaside resort whose visiting population is predominantly composed of day-trippers rather than weekly or fortnightly vacationers and from whom spending is highly dependent on the vagaries of the weather. A large proportion of the residential population commutes to London; hence there is a considerable outflow of money as well as the seasonal inflow; and there is a substantial retirement community who, whilst dependent on a number of services, provide little input to the local economic base. All this means that trading conditions within the town centre are fragile, to say the least; but at the same time, the town centre needs to cater for a variety of needs, ranging from those of the very young to those of the very old. The planners have therefore been faced with a complex set of issues and perhaps not unexpectedly their new plan for the town centre is both ambitious and comprehensive in its approach.[10] It is ambitious in the sense that 54 policies have been identified as being necessary to put into effect, from which 51 specific proposals have been made for changes to ensue on the ground. These relate to employment, housing, shopping, community facilities, holiday-related activities, public utilities, transport and the built environment. The greatest number of policies and proposals revolve around the built environment and a sample of the policies advocated is reproduced in Table 12.2 to give some idea of the level of detail to which they go.

Chichester is a smaller but healthier town than Clacton, acting as the sub-regional centre for West Sussex and performing a much more important retail and commercial role than its population of 21,000 would suggest. It is essentially an administrative and service centre, typifying the strengths of the traditional market town, but one which also attracts some tourism. It is a town which, rather than facing gradual economic decline, has to come to terms with continuing growth and particularly the pressures surrounding its increased shopping use. Its problems are therefore less serious and fundamental in kind than those in Clacton but nevertheless require corrective action and a planned programme of change. The Unit for Retail Planning Information recently advised on what measures might be adopted to improve conditions in the future.[11] The study was oriented specifically to shopping needs and is distinctive because of the general methodology employed to arrive at the policies put forward. It resembles in its approach the reports of survey involved in plan preparation at much larger scales of inquiry. There were four main parts to its diagnosis and analyses of the problems to be resolved. Firstly, assessments were made of consumer movements to and within the town centre involving pedestrian counts and interviews with some 500 shoppers, who were also asked about their attitudes towards various servicing facilities and amenities. Secondly, the general accessibility of the town centre was examined and surveys taken of car parking and goods delivery provisions. Thirdly, an inventory was made of shops and the physical form of the town centre was looked at in relation to its composition. Fourthly, the retail composition of the town centre was compared with those in other places of a similar population size to see if it was deficient in any particular category of retail trade and whether in fact additional floorspace might be supported.

The policies that were then advocated read much like a multiple retailer's prescription for the ideal contents of a plan:

Table 12.2: Some of the Policies for the Environmental Improvement of Clacton's Town Centre

Policy 25

All development should conform to good standards of design and respect and enhance the individual scale and character of different parts of the town centre.

Policy 26

All development shall normally not exceed ambient noise levels within the town centre area.

Policy 27

The District Planning Authority will expect the choice of materials and colours to all development to be appropriate to the circumstances of the case. When proposing alterations or extensions, materials shall accord with those of the existing building.

Policy 28

Where appropriate, in granting planning permission for development, adequate provision will be made for the retention and planting of trees, provision of landscaping, paving and screening, and the making of tree preservation orders.

Policy 29

New shopfronts or alterations to existing shopfronts should be harmonious with the general street scene and respect the character of the existing building. The District Planning Authority will not normally permit:

1. The installation of fascias or canopies extending above the level of first floor window sills;
2. The construction of fascias of a common depth linking two or more buildings that have separate architectural identities;
3. The enlargement of existing windows above ground floor level e.g. for display purposes; and
4. The construction of permanent canopies of excessive bulk or that, by their height, would create a lack of visual unity between buildings.

Policy 30

Advertisements should be well designed in themselves and respect their surroundings. The District Planning Authority will:

1. Normally restrict signs and advertisements on shopfronts and commercial premises to the ground floor wall area;
2. Normally discourage large or strongly illuminated advertisements, excessively dominant lettering or additional signs which would create visual clutter; and
3. Take steps to remove existing unsightly or unsatisfactory signs.

Policy 31

Within the amusement area of Pier Avenue, as defined on the Proposals Map, the District Planning Authority will, in principle, encourage advertisement displays which would enhance the holiday atmosphere and character of the area.

Source: Tendring District Council, *Clacton Town Centre: District Plan — Report of Survey and Draft Written Statement* (Harwich, 1981).

(a) There is scope for the provision of further retail floorspace in Chichester, the scale of which should be determined jointly by the District and County Councils . . .

(b) There are two modern forms of retail trader that are not currently represented in Chichester, the superstore and the retail warehouse. The residents of Chichester and the surrounding area would benefit by the presence of both types of trader outside the central area.

(c) The attractive, compact layout of the central shopping area should be retained by locating new shopping facilities as near as practicable to the Market Cross, the 'centre of gravity' of shopping in Chichester.

(d) The object of the District Council's policies on parking in the centre should be to encourage short-stay parking by shoppers within the city walls at the expense of long-stay parkers.

(e) . . . the Council and Chamber of Commerce should jointly re-examine the problem of front servicing of shops and the restrictions on the lengths of delivery vehicles.

(f) The only cause for concern (in the growth of service outlets) is in the number of building societies and . . . the continued expansion of their branches should be resisted.[12]

Most of these palliatives have by now been reviewed in some detail within this book, but the above include reference to three broad sets of development that will have increasing significance in the future for the more vigorous, smaller town and city centres of Britain. The first concerns the potential impact of new large stores and purpose-built shopping centres; the second, the accommodation of quasi-warehousing activities; and the third, the growth of a wide range of services. These three considerations take us back to some of the basic issues involved in retail and commercial planning and which were sketched out in Chapter 1.

It was indicated in Chapter 1 that there has been something of a hierarchical diffusion to the introduction of both large stores and new shopping centres within the urban system of Britain as a whole. After nearly two decades of development within first, the largest places, and then more medium-sized cities, there is likely to be a greater concentration of development within the smaller settlements. This poses a greater threat to the well-being of established environments than has hitherto been seen simply because of the scale factors involved. New schemes could completely alter the character of a townscape; their trading repercussions might extend throughout an entire urban area rather than particular communities within it; the social fabric of a town might be totally disrupted by divided loyalties that emerged.

To date, however, most new shopping centres appear to have been absorbed with the minimum of disruption. A small, but illuminating, study by Schiller[13] has compared the experiences of four small market towns that have been the recipients of new schemes (King's Lynn, Salisbury, Andover and Yeovil) with four that, in 1978, had not (Bury St Edmunds, Taunton, Hereford and Banbury). In each of the former cases, the schemes were carefully designed to blend in with the surrounding environment and their external appearance is quite pleasing to the eye. In terms of their trading effects, most of the adverse competition fell on multiple retailers selling durable goods and few convenience or specialist goods shops, especially amongst the independents, were greatly harmed. 'The picture presented by the "scheme" towns is one of change, but scarcely one of devastation. There was indeed a reduction in shops in use, an increase in vacancies and a movement from retailing to services but the changes were small.' Less was revealed, however, about the social consequences of the schemes and the attitudes of different groups of consumers towards them.

Consumer considerations were a stronger feature of an alternative study, conducted by Development Analysts,[14] into the effects of an Asda superstore built in the town centre of Coatbridge. This had an enormous appeal to the bulk of the population, generating an estimated turnover of £10 million (at 1975 prices) in its first year of trading, almost twice the level that had been anticipated by the company. This was mainly the result of the lower food prices offered, which on average were 9 per cent below those of other stores in the town centre and 3 per cent below those of a large supermarket in the neighbouring town centre of Airdrie. The consumer benefits have been widespread in so far as virtually all sections of the community have had access to the superstore. Surveys undertaken in 1977 indicated that for Coatbridge residents (as distinct from the catchment area as a whole), one third of customers walked to the superstore, one third travelled by bus and one third by car. The trading impact of the superstore on other shops in the town centre, however, has been substantial, with food shops recording a total fall in their sales volume of 27 per cent and non-food shops registering a loss of 13 per cent.

The pressure that will be exerted on smaller town and city centres in the future from discount retail warehouses and similar commercial developments is more difficult to foresee than in the case of superstores and purpose-built shopping centres. This is because, although there will undoubtedly be growth in this sector of trade, there are mixed feelings amongst the operators as to the suitability of small town or city centre sites. The picture is somewhat confused by the variable range of activities involved and the ambivalent attitudes of many planning departments. Most growth can be expected to take place amongst the DIY and self-assembly furniture outlets which are relatively large space users and generate considerable lorry as well as car traffic.[15] One major spokesman for these has stated: 'I cannot find anything to say in favour of a town centre site for a DIY store. District centres are an option often quoted by planners. I can think of nothing to say in favour of those either.'[16] According to a recent Tyne and Wear Planning Department survey, however, the Wickes and Marley groups are well disposed to taking secondary sites in town centres and district centres and the former are keen to enter into redevelopment schemes.[17] Tyne and Wear's own policy towards DIY and related outlets is to restrict development to major shopping centres or within their fringe areas unless suitable sites are simply not available there. Large, new furniture stores, those geared to car maintenance products, electrical goods and camping and sports equipment are expected to locate within main shopping centres rather than within their surrounding areas. The rationale for these distinctions in policy, however, is not entirely convincing and our own preference would be for policies that revolve around broad areal designations rather than shopping centres as such for the accommodation of discount retail warehouses.

There are mixed views, too, about the future control of services, especially business services. An indication of the variable rates of growth of different service activities between 1965 and 1976 is given in Table 12.3. Wade,[18] of the Unit for Retail Planning Information, considers that the expansionary phase of building societies and other financial institutions may have peaked within the largest centres but that further growth will occur in the smaller town and city centres. He also perceives a new threat within such centres from amusement arcades and games outlets. The problems for the planner here are to mediate between the conflicting interests of established retailers and those promoting new service outlets. The retailer's case has been forcefully put by Seeley of the National Chamber of Trade.[19] He argues that services both dilute the retailing health of shopping centres, by creating dead frontages which have little appeal to consumers, and impede the business prospects of small shopkeepers by their ability to pay higher rents for property. But the question of dead

Table 12.3: Changes in Numbers of Service Outlets in 60 Surveyed
Town Centres, 1965-1976

| | Number of outlets | | Absolute | % |
	1965	1976	change	Change
Building societies	36	138	102	283
Cafés, restaurants	151	226	75	50
Travel and ticket agents	29	102	73	252
Estate agents	95	141	46	48
Take-away shops/fish and chips	6	48	42	700
Betting offices	25	66	41	164
Insurance and money agents	22	48	26	118
Employment agents	3	28	25	833
Banks	222	232	10	5
Hairdressers	107	117	10	9
Post offices	29	35	6	21
Opticians and surgeries	92	95	3	3
Launderettes	29	26	−3	−10
Shoe repairers	50	35	−15	−30
Dry cleaners	190	104	−86	−45

Source: Jones, P.M., 'The Expansion of Service Trades in Shopping Centres —
Results of an URPI Survey', in Unit for Retail Planning Information, *Service
Outlets in Shopping Centres — Report of an URPI Workshop* (URPI, Reading,
1979).

frontage and lack of consumer appeal has been refuted on the grounds
that many branches of building societies and other agencies generate
more customers than certain types of retailers, such as furnishers;[20]
and Jones[21] has indicated that there is little evidence to link the decline
in numbers of shops within traditional shopping centres with the
corollary growth in services. The service trades in any event embrace a
wide range of activities, some of which, like cafés and restaurants, are
highly compatible with most retailers and others of which, like solicitors
and accountants, are more distinctively offices.

The Use Classes Order is of little help to planners seeking to promote
an equitable set of policies. This permits certain services, such as travel
agents, post offices, undertakers and hairdressers, to start up from shop
premises without permission for a change of use. Faced with such
anomalies, several local authorities have sought to impose their own

land use distinctions. Typical of the efforts made are those by Trafford Borough Council in an experiment based on Altrincham.[22] There, the town centre shopping streets were classified into main shopping streets and other shopping streets, in the former of which further non-retail service penetration would be discouraged but freely permitted in the latter case. However, the policy allowed for certain exceptions to compete for main shopping street sites, provided they did not add to an existing service frontage and there were no objections to them. Such exemptions included those deemed to be complementary to retailing, namely cafés, restaurants and public houses, but also banks, building societies and estate agents. The policy smacks of being a compromise, but one that gives an advantage to the interests of the retailers. More worrisome is the fact that those retailers given some protection will generally be the multiple retailers occupying prime sites rather than independent retailers already relegated to locating along the secondary shopping streets.

Other policies that have been suggested as a means for controlling the expansion of services include: concentrating them within particular parts of a town or city centre, in addition to their location along secondary shopping streets; allowing their occupation of prime sites but only on a basis of limited tenancy; allocating them to specific sites in the way in which the developer or manager of a covered shopping centre might do; and permitting their penetration of main shopping streets according to some proportional representation, such as to a maximum of 30 per cent of the total frontage available. Delegates at a recent URPI workshop on this subject concluded that the last of these proposals might be the best solution.[23] The chief limitation of this and the other approaches, however, seems to be the assumption that a single blanket control will be appropriate to the entire range of services. Our own preference would be for a minimum of planning intervention, except perhaps in some of the larger centres. The exclusion of further services from main shopping streets in smaller centres will lead to both a consolidation of prime retail frontages in the hands of the multiples and the erosion of the mixed character of such streets that has hitherto made them so appealing. In larger centres, there may be some argument for encouraging special service quarters of the kind to be found in major central areas and which would then cater for specific client groups.

One feels, nevertheless, that the impact created by service growth is poorly understood and that much of the basic argument over whether controls should be imposed contains the same type of rhetoric and hyperbole that once characterised the hypermarket and superstore debate. There are two major issues that warrant detailed investigation. Firstly, there is the question as to what happens to the spatial evolution of a traditional shopping centre as more services occupy its prime sites. Does this in fact force more retailers, and especially independent traders, into more marginal positions of the centre and then weaken their trading capability? Or does it spread the inherent retail resources of a centre more widely and hence contribute to the lateral expansion and growth of the centre as a whole? Secondly, there is the question as to what happens to both the rental and rating surfaces within a centre. Is there an overall and in the long run a net rise in rents and rates or is there simply a redistribution of levels internally within the centre? Allied to this are perhaps two supporting considerations that need to be made: whether the potential implementation of service controls should have regard to the rent and rate generating income of a centre and also to additional forms of impact such as the changes in employment that might ensue.

A final thought within this section on the smaller town and city centres of Britain concerns their management in more prosaic and day-to-day terms. This is prompted by the frequent comments of retailers that the local authorities do not do enough to maintain high standards of cleanliness, traffic control and refuse disposal within these and other centres. Certainly in comparison to some other European countries British centres often look untidy and disordered but how much of this is due to a poor management function and the allocation of resources and how much blame can be apportioned to the habits of the population are difficult to say. The former ought to be continually reviewed, however, and there should be much scope when economic circumstances permit for considerable improvements to be made. One radical suggestion has been made that the various support services that relate to the upkeep of the physical environment should be brought under the control of a town centre manager, who would then be accountable for the standards to be found and who might also be responsible for initiating new programmes of environmental change, such as in pedestrianisation, car parking provisions, tree planting and the like.[24]

Rural Resource Impoverishment

A similar idea might be advanced for the establishment of rural area managers to be responsible for co-ordinating the provision of a wide range of services in designated rural tracts, perhaps on a parish basis. The scope of the responsibilities, however, might be more diverse reflecting on the differing needs both between town and country areas and between variable kinds of rural environments. There would also likely be a greater emphasis on the management services that related less to retailing and commercial matters than to housing, employment, public transport and the utilities. The prominence of problems in these latter fields helps to explain why so little has been written about the special difficulties faced by small shopkeepers and consumers in rural communities, especially those in more remote locations. Few of the Local Plans addressed to rural districts give special regard to shopping and related service needs and the textbooks on rural planning appear to be preoccupied with the broader concerns of depopulation, deprivation and the lack of people's accessibility to jobs, schools and health facilities. Even Dawson and Kirby's book on Small Scale Retailing in the UK contains but a single index citation to the retail and commercial problems of rural areas.[25]

The plight of the small country shopkeeper is perhaps the most obvious of several problems that need to be addressed in this section. Since the root causes of his demise are similar to those found in urban areas and these have been discussed in Chapter 10, we can restrict our remarks to a few special circumstances that apply in rural areas. Dawson,[26] in a separate publication to that referred to above, has highlighted four main factors. The first concerns the process of rural depopulation which, as in many inner city areas, has often left the village shop with a depleted and ageing clientele. Secondly, the village shop is frequently at a greater disadvantage than its counterparts elsewhere in joining voluntary trading groups, primarily because of its particularly small size and limited turnover. Thirdly, there is a serious distance constraint *vis-à-vis* the source of its supplies, meaning that many wholesalers are reluctant to provide delivery services and considerable costs have to be incurred by retailers in visits to cash and carry depots. Fourthly, the higher prices that the village shop has to charge puts it at a competitive disadvantage not only with large stores in market towns but also with other smaller outlets found in these more favourable locations.

A number of retail-related service establishments, not least chemists and sub-post offices, share these special difficulties but the business, leisure and auto-related activities raise a different set of issues. To a large extent, these activities constitute branch outlets of multiple chains which have deliberately sought to avoid entering into smaller rural settlements. Generally speaking, they will be clustered in the more prosperous market towns alongside other public service activities which may themselves have been encouraged to concentrate through rural planning policies. What then materialises is an imbalance in rural resources, with some communities extremely well-endowed with a service infrastructure and others completely lacking in any support facilities whatsoever. The imbalance has its greatest negative effect again on the least well-off sections of society which in this case would be the immobile consumers of isolated villages and hamlets.

These problems, if not widely considered in a retailing context, have at least received some attention from a public service point of view. The mobile library, travelling dentists and roaming social workers are all examples of where special efforts have been made to meet some of the needs of remote localities. Shropshire Community Council has also established a network of information agents, recruited from rural residents themselves, who act as informal advisers on how the public might best obtain a response when they have particular need of a service that may be available some distance away.[27] Further scope is offered, of course, from the development of telecommunication facilities of the kind we have referred to before. Two alternative possibilities are opened up in the rural context. One surrounds the use of a viewdata system linked to individual houses. Both community information services and shopping and related business opportunities could be communicated in this way, although there would be practical considerations over the costs involved and whether a commercial operation could be run in parallel with a subsidised social scheme. The other could revolve around a single community focal point, which might be a community hall or more preferably a village shop or sub-post office. A shop or sub-post office could be the source not only for information services but also the ordering point for goods not retailed by itself, with the owner making a small commission on any transactions made. Goods ordered from these points could also be delivered there for later collection using the regular postal service or possibly in conjunction with wholesaler delivery drops. Small charges would then have to be made to meet the delivery costs, but these might be well below the costs incurred by individuals using public transport or cars for their own shopping trips. A modern counterpart to the mobile shop might also be conceived, acting as an information and ordering outlet in hamlets and villages without any fixed commercial establishments, although the economics involved in the mobile shop being the means for the delivery of goods are not very sound.

A final set of problems that warrant consideration are the seasonal pressures to which many rural communities are subjected in more scenic and tourist areas. Examples that come readily to mind are the rural communities of the Lake District, Cotswolds, Derbyshire Peak District and parts of Devon and Cornwall. The problems here are essentially of two kinds. On the one hand, many small shops and service activities have to show an adaptability to wide fluctuations in demand that have major repercussions on the number of staff employed, the level of inventory carried, the size of premises occupied and pricing and cash flow considerations. Some businesses effectively become transient or ephemeral in operating only during certain times of the year but this can then erode the range of facilities available for the locally-based population. Special conditions, of course, apply to certain service provisions such as hotels, guest houses and restaurants. On the other hand, the build-up of traffic during holiday periods also puts a strain on the communities as a whole, through the requirements for additional car parking spaces, signposting, toilets and various kinds of amenities. Specific pressures arise through the demand for caravan and camping sites, and occasionally from the organisers of sporting and recreational events.[28] Then there are the more mundane needs of maintaining roads and pathways to a satisfactory standard and ensuring a clean and tidy environment.

Conclusion

The upkeep of the environment is obviously one of the main duties of retail and commercial planning at the local level, whatever the areal setting, but it is a responsibility that often gets forgotten in the zeal to get to grips with problems that seem to command greater priority. Among the bigger challenges presented is the question of whether the run down centres of the inner city can be revitalised and if so what are the chief instruments to be used in achieving this. Some observers have suggested that the attraction of large new developments into these areas will act as a catalyst for growth, but given the reticence of the potential investors themselves this seems to be too glib an answer. A variable set of initiatives would appear to hold more promise, ranging from the humble efforts of immigrant entrepreneurs to the establishment of new service activities in the automotive and fast-food trades. Perhaps what is most required within this theatre of events is a more expansive outlook on the part of the planners: that the basic objective should not necessarily be one of resurrecting or propagating a conventional set of resources but allowing freedom of change such that many existing retail centres effectively take on a stronger commercial role. Some shedding of the older principles governing what is acceptable in middle and outer parts of the city might be desirable, too, for the outlook for many smaller shopping parades in these areas is becoming decidedly bleak. The opposite may apply in many smaller town and city centres, however, especially where there appears to be an increase in demand for various goods and services. The traditional market centres of Britain in particular remain amongst the nation's most treasured environments, from a social as well as an aesthetic point of view, and a strict control over both retail and commercial investments should clearly be upheld. Finally, there is the challenge of the more remote rural localities where consumers, at the individual level, have perhaps already suffered over a longer period of time the shortfalls in opportunities that are now emerging within a variety of urban areas. The basic problem of inaccessibility is one that really commands no short-term solution. But if telecommunications do have a part to play in future years in overcoming existing transport constraints, then the rural communities might find themselves amongst the beneficiaries.

References

1. National Economic Development Office, Distributive Trades EDC, *Retailing in Inner Cities* (NEDO, London, 1981), p. 3.
2. Ibid., p. 5.
3. Pope, M.P.R., 'Problems and Opportunities of Inner Area Trading', in *Retailing in the Inner Cities: Report of an URPI Workshop* (Unit for Retail Planning Information, Reading, 1980).
4. Ibid., p. 28.
5. Islington Borough Council, *Islington Development Plan: Written Statement and Proposals Map* (Islington, London, 1980), p. 116.
6. Davies, R.L., 'The Experimental Shopping and Information Service for Disadvantaged Consumers in Gateshead: A Progress Report', *Proceedings of the PTRC Conference* (University of Warwick, 1982); Gateshead MBC, *Shopping and Information Service* (Gateshead, 1982).
7. City of Newcastle upon Tyne, *Shields Road Area Local Plan* (October 1982).
8. Guy, C.M., *Retail Location and Retail Planning in Britain* (Gower Press, Farnborough, 1980).
9. Blythe, G., 'Relationships Between the Local Authority and the Private Sector in the Provision of Retail Facilities, Using Swindon as a Case Study', *Proceedings of the PTRC Conference* (University of Warwick, 1982).

10. Tendring District Council, *Clacton Town Centre: District Plan – Report of Survey and Draft Written Statement* (Harwich, 1981).
11. Mackie, S., *Chichester: An Assessment of Shopping Facilities in the City Centre* (Unit for Retail Planning Information, Reading, 1979).
12. Ibid., pp. 49-51.
13. Schiller, R., 'The Impact of New Shopping Schemes on Shops in Historic Streets', *The Planner*, vol. 61 (1978), pp. 367-9.
14. Evely, R., 'The Impact of New Developments: The Coatbridge Study', *Proceedings of the PTRC Conference* (University of Warwick, 1980).
15. Gibbs, A., *An Analysis of Retail Warehouse Planning Inquiries* (Unit for Retail Planning Information, Reading, 1981).
16. Crofts, M., 'Site Finding: Practical and Planning Problems', in Unit for Retail Planning Information, *DIY Retail Warehouses: Report of an URPI Workshop* (URPI, Reading, 1981), p. 49.
17. Tyne and Wear County Council, *Bulky Goods Retailing in Tyne and Wear* (Newcastle upon Tyne, 1982).
18. Wade, B., 'Summing up and Conclusion', in *Service Outlets in Shopping Centres: Report of an URPI Workshop* (Unit for Retail Planning Information, Reading, 1979).
19. Seeley, L.E.S., 'The Retail Trade View', ibid.
20. Bradley, J.C., 'Building Society Branches in Shopping Centres', ibid.
21. Jones, P.M., 'Retail Planning: Recent Trends I – Expansion of Branch Offices in Shopping Centres', *Estates Gazette*, vol. 250 (1979), p. 953.
22. Stocks, N.R., 'A Local Authority's Experiences and Policies', in *Service Outlets in Shopping Centres*.
23. Unit for Retail Planning Information, *Service Outlets in Shopping Centres*, pp. 46-7.
24. Spriddell, P.H., 'Retailing: Town Centres in the Future', in *Town Centres of the Future: Report of an URPI Workshop* (Unit for Retail Planning Information, Reading, 1980).
25. Dawson, J.A. and Kirby, D.A., *Small-Scale Retailing in the UK* (Saxon House, Farnborough, 1979).
26. Dawson, J.A., 'The Country Shop in Britain: Objectives and Background to a Research Project', in Jones, P.M. and Oliphant, R. (eds), *Local Shops: Problems and Prospects* (Unit for Retail Planning Information, Reading, 1976).
27. Richardson, B., 'Some Innovations of a Rural Community Council', in Martin-Shaw, J. (ed.), *Rural Deprivation and Planning* (Geo. Abstracts Ltd., Norwich, 1979). See also, Clark, D. and Unwin, K., 'Community Information in Rural Areas: An Evaluation of Alternative Systems of Delivery', ibid.
28. See, for example, Goodall, B., 'Provision of Sites for Towing Caravans', in Goodall, B. and Kirby, D.A. (eds), *Resources and Planning* (Pergamon, Oxford, 1979).

POSTSCRIPT

Since the idea for this book was first conceived about four years ago, a number of changes have occurred in the background conditions to retail and commercial planning and in the way in which this field of activity has been pursued. What seemed towards the end of the last decade to be a temporary aberration to the general trend of economic growth has developed into a deep recession that still shows little sign of abating. Despite the sustained high levels of unemployment, the mood of the country has become more conservative and a Tory government has been re-elected on a programme which, amongst many other things, intends to abolish the metropolitan counties. The first generation of Structure Plans has been completed and District Plans are now being prepared that show a much greater degree of independence than that envisaged a decade ago. Trial experiments in tele-shopping have taken place pointing to the advent of technology into the community and a potential new source of power in the hands of the consumer. Small shops have borne the brunt of the depression whilst large supermarkets, superstores and discount retail warehouses appear to have proliferated at an unprecedented rate.

Each of these various aspects of change is indicative of a major obligation of retail and commercial planning:

1. 'Prices and Jobs' have long been the public's chief interests in the management of the economy but these have rarely been imbued in an explicit way into the formulation of retail and commercial planning policies. Policies in the past have been directed at providing a spatially balanced incidence of shopping and service facilities and at minimising the adverse consequences of new large competitive developments. A stronger socio-economic dimension must be brought into the underlying goals and objectives of retail and commercial planning in the future.

2. Whatever adjustments might be made to the administrative framework for local plan-making, or in the relative powers of the Districts and Counties, the course and direction of retail planning at the local level

must be set by guidelines laid down by central government. It is not enough to have a couple of Development Control Policy Notes that deal with quite narrow issues raised in specific categories of trade. A comprehensive statement on approaches to both old and new development is required together with a manual or handbook on ideal standards to be adhered to in the detailed changes made on the ground.

3. The new era of District Plan preparation offers much scope for some fresh ideas to be thought through and tested with respect to both old and new developments. The concept of the district centre was a major plank of plan-making in the 1970s but may need to be modified or even replaced in the years ahead. The central areas of the largest cities need to be looked at from a wider social and cultural perspective than in purely retailing and commercial terms. More generally, some new spatial design formats are required to govern the way that the retail and commercial system is integrated with other land use activities.

4. The introduction of new technologies into the home raises some profound questions as to how shopping and a wide range of service activities might be affected in the more distant future. There is considerable uncertainty about the time-scale involved but this should not detract from the need to anticipate events before they unfold. Certain local authorities might wish to grasp the nettle and to become active proponents of new forms of tele-shopping and tele-service provisions themselves. Others will inevitably be more cautious but hopefully concerned enough to examine the positive as well as the negative prospects in store.

5. A number of specific problems will continue to be prominent in retail and commercial planning in the years ahead, not least the decline of small shops, the concomitant growth of larger stores and a myriad of issues surrounding people's accessibility to and the relative health of traditional shopping centres. There is a strong case for the formulation of special plans on these themes so that a greater expertise can be developed nationally and more consistent measures applied. They need not be of a formal nature but represent a supplementary set of reports to those more general management plans prepared within the established legislative framework.

That there have been shortcomings in the practice of retail and commercial planning in the past, however, is not necessarily the fault of the planning profession itself. The limitations have arisen in part because of the low priority assigned this field of endeavour relative to other branches of planning and also through the lack of a clear exposition of what the aims and responsibilities of the field should be. These in turn are an expression perhaps of a scarcity of resources and the conflicting interests of various consumer and business groups who ostensibly should be those identifying what needs to be done. Some blame can be attributed to the educationalists as well who have tended to spend more time describing the process of change within the retail and commercial system rather than suggesting how it might be managed more efficiently and equitably.

This book has been written to help correct this latter imbalance. It would be presumptuous to think, however, that it provides a definitive account of how retail and commercial planning can or should be improved in the future. Much of the book has been backward-looking in reviewing examples of past plans; and often more questions have been raised than answers given when exploring the problems to be found on a particular subject. Retail matters have been given much more attention than those of a commercial kind but mainly because of the poor level of information and published insights about planning for the service and bulk transference activities. Most academic books, nevertheless, derive their sustenance from assessing what has been done to date; and the intention here has been to carry this a little further forward and indicate some of the more obvious areas where new planning initiatives or procedural changes might be made. Above all, an attempt has been made to show how retail and commercial planning might become a more coherent field of environmental management, with its own distinctive problems to be addressed and clear-cut programmes of action for dealing with them.

AUTHOR INDEX

SUBJECT INDEX

Washington 204-5, 277
Town Centre Shopping Schemes
   196-202, 277-88, 325
   blight and congestion 280-1, 287-8
   classification of schemes 201-2
   effects of schemes 277-88
   examples and characteristics
      197-201, 202, 280, 282-9, 291
   history of development 196-200
   type of developer 197-201
Trade Associations 83
Trade Centres 16, 213-15
   trade marts 114, 153, 188, 190,
      220-1, 254
Traffic Congestion 228, 320, 241, 243,
   270, 274
Traffic Management and Control
   228-30, 257, 324, 326-30, 361
   Cheshire 146, 150
   Newcastle 235, 238-41, 287, 325,
      338
Training in Retailing 306, 313, 319-21

Transport Policies 326-8
Transport Services Provision 330-38
Tyne and Wear Structure Plan 142-6,
   164

Unit for Retail Planning Information
   83
Urban Renewal 226-46
   see also Renewal and Redevelopment
Use Classes Order 11-13, 92
Voluntary Trading Groups 9-10, 55-6,
   311-12, 362

Wholesaling and Warehousing 7-8, 10,
   14-16, 25-6, 60, 62, 162, 213
   classification of 14-15
   distribution network 26
   hierarchy concept 25-6
   out-of-town warehouses 76, 78-9
   see also Bulk/Transference Activities
Windsor Cordon Experiment 329